# Making India Hindu

For the past few decades powerful political forces have sought to make the Indian state Hindu. Their rising influence since 1980 has occurred during a period of radical change in Indian society and politics, and has been accomplished by electoral means as well as by organized violence.

The 1996 elections have been a major test of their power and the influence of Hindu majoritarianism among the Indian electorate. Thirteen prominent scholars from India, Europe and the United States provide perspectives from the fields of political science, religious studies, history, art history, and anthropology, comparing trends in India with ethnic, religious, and cultural movements in other parts of the world.

The second edition has been brought up-to-date with a new preface in which Ludden provides an incisive analysis of the 2004 elections and highlights direct and indirect operations of Hindutva inside India's political mainstream. It also carries a revised bibliography.

**David Ludden** is Professor of History at the University of Pennsylvania.

# Making India Hindu

Religion, Community, and the Politics of
Democracy in India

*Second Edition*

*Edited by*
David Ludden

**OXFORD**
UNIVERSITY PRESS

# OXFORD
## UNIVERSITY PRESS

22 workspace, 2nd Floor, 1/22 Asaf Ali Road, New Delhi 110002

Oxford University Press is a department of the University of Oxford. It furthers the
University's objective of excellence in research, scholarship, and education
by publishing worldwide in

Oxford   New York
Auckland   Cape Town   Dar es Salaam   Hong Kong   Karachi
Kuala Lumpur   Madrid   Melbourne   Mexico City   Nairobi
New Delhi   Shanghai   Taipei   Toronto

With offices in
Argentina   Austria   Brazil   Chile   Czech Republic   France   Greece
Guatemala   Hungary   Italy   Japan   Poland   Portugal   Singapore
South Korea   Switzerland   Thailand   Turkey   Ukraine   Vietnam

Oxford is a registered trademark of Oxford University Press
in the UK and in certain other countries

Published in India
By Oxford University Press, New Delhi

© Oxford University Press, 2005

The moral rights of the author have been asserted
Database right Oxford University Press (maker)

First published 1996
By University of Pennsylvania Press, Philadelphia
First published in India by Oxford University Press 1996
Oxford India Paperbacks 1997
Second edition 2005
Oxford India Paperbacks 2006

ISBN-13: 978-0-19-568275-5
ISBN-10: 0-19-568275-0

Typeset by Eleven Arts, Keshav Puram, Delhi 110 035
Printed in India by Pauls Press, New Delhi 110 020
Published by Manzar Khan, Oxford University Press
22 workspace, 2nd Floor, 1/22 Asaf Ali Road, New Delhi 110002

# Contents

# *Preface to the Second Edition*

CONCEIVED IN THE AFTERMATH OF the Babri Masjid demolition, *Making India Hindu* compiles writing by thirteen scholars in various disciplines that elucidates genealogies, politics, and effects of Hindu majoritarianism. This edition reprints the original volume exactly as it appeared in 1996, but its context has changed dramatically since then. We had composed the volume to help explain how Hindutva rose to prominence after 1980, but now the book can also help to explain how Hindutva operates inside India's political mainstream.

In 1999, the Bharatiya Janata Party (BJP) became the leading party in a National Democratic Alliance (NDA) coalition government that held power until May 2004. Prime Minister Vajpayee and colleagues opened a new political era by leading India's first major non-Congress national government. The BJP outgrew its underdog identity and the Sangh Parivar took center-stage in national life. The NDA included as many as twenty-four parties, so though the BJP was not as dominant as the Congress had been for thirty years after 1947, it was, in fact, a new kind of dominant party as a pivot of national coalition building. Its Sangh brethren—the Rashtriya Swayamsevak Sangh (RSS) and Vishwa Hindu Parishad (VHP)—also moved from margins to mainstream by occupying the Prime Minister's office and all national ministries. Hindutva acquired official respectability as a national party ideology.

This volume indicates that Hindutva was here to stay in 1996, despite its precarious fortunes, small minority backing, and a long history on the sidelines. When we compiled the book, we could not have known how Hindutva would fare in the future. Now we have a better idea. Since 1996, our topics have become more complex and challenging. Themes, analyses, arguments, and information presented here have acquired new value amidst the national and international mainstreaming of Hindutva and the capture of institutions by its devotees and collaborators, thus making its academic study more difficult and more critical.

Our new context includes many old trends and patterns. The upward trend of BJP power continued into the new millennium, with one dip following violence in Ayodhya and another larger dip at the 2004 Lok Sabha elections. This may mark a shift in the trend, but only time will tell. Essays in this volume (by T. Sarkar, M. Hasan, R. Fox, and S. Sarkar) show how Hindutva's spreading and deepening influence has drawn sustenance from cultural trends that permeate modern Indian history and from multifarious media that propagate Hindutva (R. Davis, V. Farmer, W. Pinch, and P. Manuel). The Sangh Parivar has attended especially to cultivating a public culture of Hindutva. The Rath Yatra now seems but one episode in an, epic Sangh media blitz, where Ram, *kar sevaks*, rioters, police, judges, *sadhus*, journalists, movie stars, novelists, publishers, priests, scholars, politicians, and even the Archaeological Survey of India—which claimed to have found remnants of a temple under the Babri Masjid—all play parts. Hindutva is media-savvy and hi-tech: it floods the worldwide web.

With the BJP in power in New Delhi, the media's professional penchant for quoting people in high office propagated Hindutva ideas on every subject of public interest, while Sangh researchers and communicators worked the gamut of information venues from ministry briefings to broadsheets, bestsellers, and academic tomes. Public and private sponsors finance academic research, teaching, and publishing, to give Hindutva many voices, in many languages, in India and abroad. The Sangh took control of countless government agencies and offices, doling out public as well as private funds. In New Delhi, in all Indian states, and in districts, towns, and villages, RSS cadres educated, inspected, recommended, promoted, and assigned public servants. The Sangh captured the Indian Council of Historical Research and Ministry of Education to make government schoolbooks and examinations require students to learn that Hinduism is indigenously Indian and that Islam and Christianity are aliens. Government schools enforced the idea that Muslims and Christians conquered and exploited Hindu India. Official Hindutva gave communalism cultural validity that made Hindu violence against Muslims seem a natural manifestation of Hindu rage.

International trends have continued to inflect Hindu majoritarianism. Indian politics is increasingly sensitive to India's experience of globalization. WTO negotiations and world markets now affect Indian politics along with the US war on terrorism. Hindutva seems to have benefited particularly from the inflammation of Indian relations with Pakistan after Kargil and terrorist attacks on the Indian Parliament. US wars in Muslim countries enhanced US support for the NDA and BJP support in America, where Indian lobbyists found the BJP a natural ally as the NDA claimed that Kashmir was under attack by the same Muslim terrorists who threatened America. Ethno-religious chauvinism in other countries has made Hindutva seem more credible and

Hindu-Muslim conflict part of a global clash of civilizations. On the other hand, mounting desires in India for peace with Pakistan, for a peaceful world business climate, and for India to play a constructively independent leadership role—for example, in WTO alliances of poor countries—would seem to diminish the desirability of ethno-chauvinist Hindutva ideology among India's national leadership.

Inside India, Hindutva long ago settled into the bumpy roller coaster and dizzying vote calculus of the world's largest, most diverse democracy. Hindutva's political geography continues to distinguish the BJP northern heartland states—toured by the Rath Yatra in 1990 (R. Davis)—from southern and northeastern states, which remain BJP frontiers. Most media analysts of Indian politics continue to focus on the national opposition of BJP and Congress, but head-to-head battles between Congress and BJP typify elections only in eight states (Himachal Pradesh, Uttaranchal Pradesh, Goa, Gujarat, Rajasthan, Madhya Pradesh, Karnataka, and Chhattisgarh) plus Delhi, while other patterns of party competition typify twenty-one states holding three-fourths of India's population.

The 2004 elections established a Congress-led United Progressive Alliance (UPA) government in New Delhi. But six months ago, BJP had toppled Congress in the Legislative Assembly elections in Madhya Pradesh, Rajasthan, and Chhattisgarh. Thus in December 2003, the number of BJP-run states increased from four to seven; the percentage of India's population in BJP-run states increased by 47%; and the percentage of the population under BJP regimes in the states with head-to-head BJP-Congress battles jumped from 19% to 70%. In May 2004, the percentage of voters living in Indian states with BJP (25%) and Congress (27%) governments was about equal, while almost half (48%) of the Indian citizenry lived in states run by neither Congress nor BJP, in the northeast (Tripura, Nagaland, Mizoram, Sikkim), south (Andhra Pradesh, Tamil Nadu) and north (Bihar, West Bengal, Haryana, Uttar Pradesh).

In aggregate national voting statistics, BJP and Congress are evenly matched. Both depend on allies to win. In the 2004 Lok Sabha polls, each alliance received about 35% of the total vote, and total votes for NDA and UPA parties declined compared to 1999 (by 3.62% and 2.36%, respectively), while non-aligned parties increased their vote share, most notably the Bahujan Samaj Party (BSP) in UP. The 2004 change in national government came not from a voter shift away from the BJP but from a few key Congress victories and many good Congress alliances with victorious regional parties, which together with "outside support" gave the UPA over 320 Lok Sabha votes, more than the NDA ever had, and drove the NDA into Lok Sabha minorities in all but five Indian states.

The UPA is much bigger than the Congress is strong. Congress remains marginal in major states—Uttar Pradesh, Bihar, West Bengal, and Tamil Nadu—while its votes continue to dip in Karnataka. The only big Congress victories in 2004 were in Andhra Pradesh and Delhi. Shifty allies swell the UPA. Several partners had joined the non-BJP, non-Congress United Front government in the 1990s, and one, the Dravida Munnetra Kazhagam (DMK), had joined the NDA. Alliance shifting makes sense for regional parties that care more about regional rivals than about national leadership, as most emphatically in Tamil Nadu and Uttar Pradesh. Communist parties in West Bengal and Kerala disdain both BJP and Congress, but more so the BJP, and thus can live with Congress as outside supporters to bolster the UPA.

The UPA government, like its NDA predecessor, depends on decisions by voters and politicians who seem to respond most visibly to short-term assessments of practical self-interest. Expert analysts attribute electoral success increasingly to effective promises of good government and now typically argue that ideologies are of decreasing importance compared to perceptions of politicians' competence to serve voters. For example, when Sheila Dixit won in Delhi in 2003, experts attributed her success to her reputation for the efficient provision of public services, earned by keeping onion prices in line at election time and by launching the Delhi Metro (a project begun under the BJP). In 2003, successful BJP candidates in Madhya Pradesh, Rajasthan, and Chhattisgarh castigated Congress failures to deliver development, but the BJP also adorned voter self-interest with resplendent saffron. Holy men sermonized that the RSS guaranteed good government. Hindutva superstars Uma Bharti and Vasundhara Raje of the BJP rallied together voters and became Chief Ministers in Madhya Pradesh and Rajasthan respectively. Sangh Parivar cadres covered Chhattisgarh to convince Adivasis that tangible pay-offs would reward BJP votes. The BJP promise that good government serves the Hindu majority has acquired a viable niche in Indian politics. L.K. Advani duly proclaimed that 2003 election victories endorsed good governance by the BJP and NDA.

The BJP believed Advani, the media believed the BJP, and the BJP believed the media; so the BJP called early 2004 Lok Sabha elections, and lost. The NDA's "India Shining" advertising campaign flopped among voters left in the dark by liberalization, globalization, and hi-tech development policies. In Andhra Pradesh, high unemployment rates led educated young urban voters into the Congress camp. In Andhra Pradesh, Tamil Nadu, and Karnataka, shortages of drinking water and irrigation sent villagers to Congress and its allies. In Bihar, the Rashtriya Janata Dal (RJD) alliance, led by Laloo Yadav, rallied lower castes by promising dignity, not *"bijli, sadak, aur paani"* (electricity, roads, and water), but a victorious Laloo also demanded that the government restore farm subsidies and lower kerosene and diesel prices. In 2004, the voting majority apparently believed that the incumbent NDA had failed to provide adequate practical benefits, and so the UPA came to power as a collection of opposition candidates rallied around Congress.

Political economy wedged itself between Hindutva and voter interests. This poses a dilemma for those who would make India Hindu. Most poignantly, the BJP has lost more ground in UP, where the VHP dream of building a Ram temple in Ayodhya realistically requires a BJP government. In 1990, Chief Minister Mulayam Singh Yadav stopped assaults on Ayodhya with police shootings, and two years later, Kalyan Singh's BJP government let kar sevaks demolish the Babri Masjid, but then again, in 2003, Chief Minister Mulayam Singh Yadav arrested 30,000 kar sevaks *en route* to Ayodhya. In the early 1990s it seemed the BJP might win UP by making Ram an electoral force. But ever since, the BJP has lost ground to regional parties representing numerically predominant agrarian castes (Z. Hasan). In 2004, the BSP and Samajwadi Party (SP) together won 54 of UP's 80 Lok Sabha seats and BJP seats dropped from 25 to 10, one more than Congress retained from 1999, to maintain its minority status amidst BJP decline. In 2004, the BJP even lost Thakurs and Brahmans who had previously controlled the UP sector of the BJP heartland, and who defected to the SP and Congress, respectively.

Anti-incumbent victories tarnished the BJP's saffron glow in 2004, but the Hindutva synergy of practical self-interest and religious passion may again do effective political work when the Sangh Parivar finds suitable targets (A. Basu). Such targeting often entails violence. Indeed, saffron never looked more like political gold than in 2002 and 2003, when it colored communal violence, election campaigns, subsistence struggles, faction feuds, criminal gangs, and personal ambitions, all at once.

Once again, as in 1992, the targeting of Muslims in 2002 occurred in a BJP-run state, this time, Gujarat. On the morning of 27 February, a crowd of Muslim protesters surrounded the Sabarmati Express at the Godhra rail station. Two bogeys somehow caught fire, killing fifty-eight people, mostly *kar sevaks* returning from Ayodhya. Till date, the cause of the fire remains unproven, but on that very day, Gujarat Chief Minister Narendra Modi came to Godhra and declared it a Muslim conspiracy. The next day, well-armed, organized gangs began raping, plundering, and killing Muslims across Gujarat. Several thousand Muslims died; many thousands lost homes and livelihoods. BJP governments in Gujarat and Delhi did very little to stop the mayhem as local officials colluded in attacks on Muslims. Police, lawyers, judges, and thugs then stymied prosecution of rapists, arsonists, and murders. In the famous case of the Best Bakery murders, the Supreme Court observed on 12 April 2004 that, "When

xii       Preface to the Second Edition

a large number of witnesses have turned hostile it should have raised a reasonable suspicion that the witnesses were being threatened or coerced ... [and yet] ... public prosecutors did not take any steps to protect the star witness...." Thwarting prosecutions that implicated the government became easy as the BJP romped to victory in 2003 state assembly elections under Narendra Modi's campaign slogan, "Gujarat Unlimited", promising law and order and investment opportunities for jubilant business supporters.

The Gujarat killings represent a distinctively new cultural moment in the long history of Indian communal violence (S. Freitag, P. van der Veer.). Only the Sikh massacres in 1984 were similarly targeted. In 1992, the Ayodhya assault was planned but the widespread violence that followed was not, and Hindus and Muslims attacked one another haphazardly across many Indian states, Pakistan, and Bangladesh. By contrast, Gujarat mobs targeted Muslims across the state and mass killings acquired a definite appearance of deliberate strategy. Human Rights Watch researchers quickly concluded that "What happened in Gujarat was not a spontaneous uprising," but rather "a carefully orchestrated attack ... planned in advance and organized with extensive participation of the police and state government officials." Moreover, the Ayodhya violence had cost the BJP dearly in the 1993 polls in Uttar Pradesh, Madhya Pradesh, and Himachal Pradesh, but in 2002 and 2003, the BJP and allies won in Gujarat, Rajasthan, Madhya Pradesh, and Chhattisgarh, where voters seem at that moment to have accommodated state-assisted killings in positive assessments of the BJP's capacity to serve voter interests. Narendra Modi's protection of Hindus made him a model of good saffron governance. Investor-friendly BJP leaders won praise from big business, for instance, at a Bombay gala celebrating "Gujarat Unlimited" where one tycoon reportedly dismissed Gujarat killings as "a storm in a teacup".

Gujarat massacres again raise the question posed by Amrita Basu in this book as to whether we should look at Hindutva as a top-down "elite conspiracy" or bottom-up "mass movement". As she argues, some combination of the two is required. Today, the top-down approach now has higher heights to climb, deeper depths to plumb, and more intermediary linkages to explore than it did in 1996. Consider the career of one RSS man, L.K. Advani. In 1977–80, he served the Jana Sangh as Minister of Information and Broadcasting under India's first non-Congress national government, led by the Janata Party. In the 1980s, he became BJP strategist for the Ayodhya campaign. In 1990, he rode the Rath Yatra on a route planned by RSS comrade, Narendra Modi. In 1992, he rallied mobs to destroy the Babri Masjid. In 1999, he became Home Minister, and in 2002, Deputy Prime Minister. A man who rode a truck around India, posing as Ram, sparking riots and courting arrest to catch media attention—who could have faced criminal indictment for instigating communal violence—became the national minister responsible for law and order. Soon thereafter, violence against Christians escalated and provoked murders of missionaries. His response was not to condemn or prosecute but to call for a national dialogue on religious conversion. The RSS justification of religious minority killing as a defensive response by an aggrieved Hindu majority thus entered the highest ranks of Indian state authority. This mode of moral reasoning seeped down to the grassroots under the NDA regime, most thoroughly in Gujarat, the state ruled longest by the BJP, where in 2002, Advani's old RSS colleague, Chief Minister Modi, reportedly stopped police from suppressing what he called "the Hindu backlash," declaring, "there would be justice for Godhra."

Top-down analysis must investigate intermediate levels and linkages through which top-down mobilization activates the grassroots, as bottom-up approaches explore not only specific localities but also upward connections. Some pervasive cultural elements facilitate linkages from top to bottom. Nationalism is one. Ethnic and religious cultural identities are also active at all levels of politics. Globalization has spread the discourse of market freedom and consumerism during a worldwide replacement of state redistributive institutions by growth-centered, market-based economic policies. A new field of opportunity has thus opened up for competitive activists at all levels of politics. Who flourishes in this field of opportunity—when, where, why, how, and to what effect—is a pressing concern for scholars. Rather than imagining that obedient party funtionaries form links between India's national elite and local grassroots, it is more realistic to imagine a floating population of acquisitive actors seeking opportunity from various sources at all levels.

In India today, the top and bottom levels of politics are intricately connected. Local Hindutva shock troops swelled under BJP governments as elite Sangh Parivar leaders bought recruits among poor Dalits and Adivasis who played prominent roles in Gujarat. The BJP has used flexible top-down strategies to court local interests: it has tactically highlighted and downplayed Hindutva and deployed Sangh brethren who suit the task, according to local context. Its economic policy makers use Swadeshi to attract weak, defensive capitalists and farmers, and they use free-market globalization to attract aggressive capitalists and urban consumers. The contemporary development mantra of "growth above all" works at many levels: it suits most Indian parties, as well as the World Bank, IMF, major Indian capitalists, overseas investors, and India's expansive urban middle class, whose share of national wealth has steadily increased along with its support of Hindutva.

Voters, campaigners, and coalitions form flexible linkages between top and bottom levels of Indian politics, making any so-called ruling party in Delhi much less powerful than it seems. Congress and BJP alike bow to an economic policy framed by the World Bank. They both operate amidst trends of weakening state power, coalition dependency, regional party fracture, and votes floating free of party loyalty. Yet national power is an asset that BJP and Congress can use to move the tenor of Indian politics one way or another. The NDA did its best to use that power to make India Hindu. It remains to be seen what the UPA can do to alter that trend. Good indicators might be prosecution of criminal cases stemming from Gujarat massacres and effective amelioration of the victim's suffering. In any case, politicians at the pinnacle of national power remain hostage to shifting loyalties among voters and politicians who remain targets of opportunity for the opposition.

Research on Hindutva thus needs to focus attention not only on the Sangh Parivar but also on everyday environs that imbue Hindutva with diffuse meaning and substance. Scholars need to look closely at where Hindutva takes root, prospers, withers, dies, lives in surrogates, or never arrives. Places to study include foreign sites, which we barely touch upon here. In the US, Republican Hindutva is growing. Elsewhere too, ethno-religious bigotry dissolves, merges, and mutates into other idioms. The 2004 elections in India suggest that struggles against Hindutva may not be its undoing and that Sangh Parivar activism does not guarantee its own success. Hindutva may not be one singular thing at all, but rather disparate bits of ideology lumped together by specific groups in specific times and places. Hindutva has many histories, and maybe as many meanings as locations. We might usefully imagine Hindutva as being like the NDA, a pragmatic alliance of disparate forces, coming together in some settings, under its own media spotlight, only to fragment and dissipate elsewhere. Hindutva may find various sources of support under Congress-led government, as it has in the past.

We should think about Gujarat not only as an Indian state where the Sangh Parivar mobilized genocide and won elections, but also as a place where local, regional, national, and global influences converged to generate those outcomes. Here and elsewhere, BJP voters have had diverse motivations, options, and strategies, and by itself, Hindutva does not explain much. Various trends help to explain the Gujarat killings and their immediate election aftermath.

In the 1980s and 1990s, the Gujarat textile sector collapsed, and in Ahmedabad alone, over 100,000 unemployed industrial workers hit the streets. At least a million people found their family incomes and subsistence security dramatically reduced. This impoverishment came with retrenchment that also made workers more dispensable and insecure in villages and towns across

Gujarat. For decades, industrial unions had served a culturally diverse urban working class. Under the flexible production regime fostered by liberalization and globalization, the state abandoned its commitment to industrial workers, reduced the role of unions, and boosted business profits along with economic growth. Improving the business climate became the central government concern. At the same time, the organization directly serving Dalit interests, the Dalit Panthers, collapsed. Growing economic disparities among Dalits pulled potential leaders away to pursue enterprise in the entry ranks of the middle class. Meanwhile, thriving middle class and business families financed Hindu sectarian organizations that promoted Hindu unity with Sanskritization, which stressed patriarchal authority to raise the status of low caste families. Many Hindu organizations embraced the RSS, helped the BJP win elections, and won patronage in return. Also in the 1990s, far from the city, conflict arose between Adivasis and Muslim moneylenders. To repay usurious loans at 120% annual interest, many Adivasis fell into petty crime, including liquor smuggling in India's only prohibition state.

Free-market insecurity, fear, ambition, poverty, class anger, criminality, patriarchy, and communalism joined hands when Sangh Parivar recruiters used spiritual, political, and business connections to procure support from Dalits and Adivasis by giving jobs, loans, and other assistance. After the deadly spark at Godhra—a place with a local history of Hindu aggression—Adivasis killed Muslims in villages all around Godhra. Thus at one stroke killers eliminated the Adivasis' creditors and the Banias' Muslim competitors. In towns and cities across Gujarat, Dalits looted Muslim shops and homes, to reap the plunder of class war as they liberated real estate for Hindu investors. Well-heeled high caste women followed mobs into broken Muslim shops for riot season bargain hunting, while most of the middle class stayed home with doors locked. Fearing violence, even the Sabarmati Ashram founded by Mahatma Gandhi closed its gates to Muslims fleeing killer mobs. Mass rapes drove Muslim families from villages and neighborhoods in disgrace and fear. Muslims then stayed away from the polls. In 2002, the 55% BJP electoral majority in Gujarat included people who engaged in pogroms, people who feared them, and people who only valued economic stability they attributed to the BJP regime.

Gujarat may be unique. Its record of communal violence certainly is: the Justice Reddy Commission found almost 3,000 Gujarat incidents of communal violence in the 1960s alone. Events in Gujarat may indicate nothing about India. Each Indian state has a specific collection of local and regional issues, factions, and social forces. International influences arrive in each state differently. Law and order and economic development are primarily state subjects. Language, culture, and history inscribe state borders with potent meanings. At Lok Sabha election time, each state seems disconnected from others and connected only to New Delhi. Each Legislative Election operates in its own universe. As a result, national strategists must target each state separately. State politicians must look up to New Delhi and down at localities, but not across state lines. In this context, most Indian parties remain state-bound.

We can thus reasonably imagine two very different Indias. One is unitary. In this India, the line between top and bottom of the political system is variously complex, state-by-state, but all localities are influentially connected to the central government. In this unitary India, Congress and BJP contest the future. Another India, however, is composed of regions. State borders so heavily transect lines connecting Centre and localities that each state constitutes a separate polity. In this regional India, national trends are illusive, deceptive, or irrelevant; only state politics matter, even as each state is separately connected to the Centre.

A combination of top-down and bottom-up views of unitary and regional India forms a useful perspective for studying Hindutva. In a top-down view of unitary India, the BJP and Congress fight for national supremacy and for power to define Indian nationalism. A bottom-up view of unitary India reveals, however, that neither Congress nor BJP nationalism holds voters' loyalty. Voters easily defect. Hindu and secular loyalties bind a small proportion of voters. Most BJP voters ignore Hindutva and many Congress voters could embrace Hindutva. Combining top-down and bottom-up views of unitary India, we can conclude that national struggles for political power depend on combinations of ideology and performance, and that India now demands a national coalition government that appears to deliver benefits of economic development to the voting majority. BJP and Congress provide two different styles of national leadership, which lean Right and Left, respectively, but are both malleable in the face of bottom-up demands and obstacles.

By contrast, a top-down view of regional India pictures the BJP and Congress as regional parties vying for votes in regional languages from people in regionally specific local communities. The BJP thrived initially only in states where no other regional party emerged to oppose Congress. In UP, the BJP faded as soon as indigenous regional parties rose to challenge Congress. Only in Gujarat has the BJP become truly indigenous and dominant. Most states remain fertile for BJP and Congress alliances. In a bottom-up view of regional India, only local issues and people matter; BJP and Congress are abstract representations of a distant national administration. In localities, voters have more to think about than voting, and party strength comes from the toil and influence of local activists who address a range of local concerns. Internal diversity inside regions has led to an increasing fragmentation and localization of regional parties.

Combining top-down and bottom-up views of regional India, we can see that the Sangh Parivar promotes Hindu unity to attach Hindu identities to BJP votes. By targeting Muslim or Christian adversaries—even in such symbolic settings as cricket matches or beauty pageants—the Sangh Parivar generates a group feeling and public appearance of Hindu unity. When local conflicts of any kind become communal, they advertise the RSS idea that India is still wracked by Hindu failure to purify Bharat as a Hindu homeland. Metaphorically, communal conflict anywhere affirms that Hindu India lives forever at odds with its alien others.

This volume shows how social conflict attending social change has produced sites for communal mobilization since the days of the Cow Protection Movement. (S. Freitag, R. Fox, S. Sarkar) The salience of social change for communalism increased in the 1970s, when a Home Ministry study concluded that "the persistence of serious social and economic inequalities in the rural areas has given rise to tensions between different classes which may lead to a situation where the discontented elements are compelled to organise themselves and the extreme tensions building up with the 'complex molecule' that is the Indian village may end in an explosion." Potentially explosive localities provide the Sangh Parivar targets of opportunity for mobilizing communal antagonism. To understand such sites, we had best abandon the idea that each locality is a miniature of the Indian nation. For in addition to regional identities, localities inhabit spaces that open across international borders. Gujarat would not be Gujarat without Gujaratis overseas.

Under globalization, localities experience social, economic, and cultural trends that escape the nation. In this perspective, we can study places inside and outside India, side-by-side, and we find that violent discrimination against minorities typifies many countries, rich and poor alike, in Asia, Europe, Africa, and the Americas. We can also find opposition to ethnic chauvinism in other countries with lessons for India. For example, in nearby Bangladesh, Jyotrinda Bodhipriya has long struggled against Bengali domination as Chairman of the Chittagong Hill Tracts Regional Council, and on 22 December 2003, he called for securing minority rights by saying, "Only a secular, progressive and democratic system of government can ensure the equal rights of all citizens."

The future of Hindutva will unfold inside social change that no one controls. Activists who would design India's future navigate history with at best a precarious picture of their own location and with no means to escape events pushing this way and that. Scholars can help by providing perspective.

We can never rise above history's turbulence. We can never be non-partisan. We can merely work to identify people, forces, interventions, effects, and trajectories that help to explain where history is moving and why. We hope this new edition of *Making India Hindu* helps to establish a useful perspective for those who would improve our future.

I thank Shapan Adnan, Amrita Basu, Victoria Farmer, Bela Malik, Thomas Mathew, Dina Siddiqi, and Narendra Subramanian for insight and information that I have used liberally here. I thank all the authors in this volume and numerous other correspondents, including Ashok Chowgule, for improving the additional bibliography.

DAVID LUDDEN
Dhaka

# Preface and Acknowledgments

IN DECEMBER 1992, IT BECAME OBVIOUS that college teachers do not have good enough books at hand for teaching about the recent history of politics and communal conflict in India. Specialized studies do exist, but readers outside India cannot find sophisticated yet concise, accessible, and broadly interpretive books about recent events in India that center on a term that is obscure in the United States, "communalism." In the aftermath of events at Ayodhya that form the starting point for this volume, faculty and graduate students in the South Asia Regional Studies program at the University of Pennsylvania resolved to address this need. We received generous help in planning from three experts in the field: Amrita Basu (political science, Amherst College), Sandria B. Freitag (history, American Historical Association), and Peter van der Veer (anthropology, University of Amsterdam). We acquired funds from the Ford Foundation's International Predissertation Fellowship Program for an interdisciplinary social science seminar on "The Problematics of Identities and States," and we designed the 1993–94 South Asia Seminar, funded by a Title VI grant from the Department of Education, around the theme "Exploring Communalism in South Asia." We devoted the seminar in 1993–94 to producing a reasonably priced, accessible book, representing diverse disciplinary perspectives on communalism and written for a broadly defined audience of readers in the United States and worldwide. This volume is the result.

During the 1993–94 academic year, we discussed twenty-nine papers, which covered a broader range of issues than could be addressed in one volume. As we boiled down the subject matter of the seminar in discussions, Hindu nationalism emerged as the most critical theme. This volume seeks (1) to represent the current state of research on Hindu nationalism; (2) to combine methods, theories, and data from anthropology, history, political science, ethnomusicology, and religious studies to form an interdisciplinary framework for analysis and interpretation; (3) to stimulate new research and collaboration among disciplines; (4) to provide a multivocal, informative, and coherent book for college and university teaching and for the concerned public, presenting high quality scholarship to readers with minimal background knowledge about India; and (5) to organize a responsible intellectual intervention by a substantial group of scholars from India, Europe, and the United States into understandings of communalism among people who influence public policy and debate. The seminars that produced this volume involved wide-ranging discussions, during five hours of meetings each Wednesday for the whole academic year, among a group of about fifty faculty and graduate students, during a two-day workshop in February 1994 attended by six seminar authors and fifteen local faculty and students, and during intense communication among contributors at each stage of the volume's evolution. To keep the cost of the volume low and its coherence high, we reduced the number of chapters to twelve. Fortunately, many seminar papers not included here will be available to readers elsewhere, and many ideas from seminar papers and discussions have been included in the introduction and in the chapters below. The seminar papers not included here are the following:

Romila Thapar, "Communalism and the Interpretation of Early Indian History."
Dharma Kumar, "The Communalism Project." Published as "Left Secularists and Communalism." *Economic and Political Weekly*, July 28, 1994, pp. 1803–9.
Atul Kohli, "The Crisis of the Indian State: The Political Context of the 'New' Communalism."
Burton Stein, "Community Formation in Long Perspective."
Dorothy Stein, "Demographic Competition and Population Politics."
David Washbrook, "Caste, Community, and Communalism in South Indian History."
Dennis McGilvray, "Fieldwork under Military Occupation: Tamils and Muslims in Eastern Sri Lanka, 1993."
Rosane Rocher, "Inclusion, Segregation, and the Dharmic Management of Diversity."
Andrew Lightman, "Left- and Right-Hand Caste Disputes in Madras in the Early Colonial Period."
Sanjay Joshi, "Oppressive Present and Empowering Past: Hindu Assertiveness and the Middle Classes in Colonial Lucknow."
Valerie Stoker, "The Philosophy of Madhva."
Lise McKean, "The Transnational Context of Communalism: The 1993 Chicago Parliament of the World's Religions and Hindu Nationalism."
David Lelyveld, "The Colonial Construction of Muslim Identity."
Ayesha Jalal, "Exploding Communalism: The Politics of Muslim Identity."
Sumathi Ramaswamy, "We Are Not Hindu: We Are Tamil."
Ruchira Gupta, "The Story of the RSS."
Srirupa Roy, "The Politics of Hindutva and the BJP."

To make the volume more diverse and accessible, we have kept the essays relatively short and annotations minimal. Parenthetical references in the text are to items in the Bibliography. The Bibliography has been compiled to represent not only citations in the chapters but also the growing number of resources that are available for research and teaching on communalism and related themes discussed in this book. Acronyms in the text can be found in the List of Abbreviations. Non-English terms in this volume are rendered in italics (without diacritics) at their first appearances in the text; they appear with definitions in the Glossary at the back of the book. Plural forms for singular nouns in the Glossary have been formed by simply adding "s."

Sarah Diamond and Adam Zeff helped me administer the seminars. Supti Bhattacharya, Anjali Arondeka, Karen Vorkapich, Vivek Bhandari, Sandhya Purohit, Srirupa Roy, Sanjay Joshi, Richard Cohen, Victoria Farmer, Patricia Smith, Itty Abraham, Gyan Prakash, Greg Kozlowski, Dina Siddiqi, Christophe Jaffrelot, Thomas Blom Hansen, and Lavinia Braxton helped in many ways as the project unfolded. Sarah Diamond provided critical assistance at the final stages. All the authors, seminar speakers, and staff at the University of Pennsylvania Press have been generous, insightful, and cooperative. Ardeth Abrams produced the map and cover illustration. Thanks to one and all.

DAVID LUDDEN
Philadelphia

# *Abbreviations*

| | |
|---|---|
| *Bankim* | *Bankim Rachanabali* (Collected works of Bankim Chandra Chattopadhyay), ed. J. C. Bagal, 2 vols., Calcutta, 1965, 1969. |
| BJP | Bharatiya Janata Party |
| BKU | Bharatiya Kisan Union |
| BMS | Bharatiya Mazdoor Sangh |
| BSP | Bahujan Samajwadi Party |
| BSS | Bharat Sadhu Samaj |
| CPM | Communist Party of India (Marxist) |
| HP | Himachal Pradesh |
| IOL | India Office Library, London |
| IOR | India Office Records, London |
| MP | Madhya Pradesh |
| NWP | Northwestern Provinces (of British India) |
| OBCs | Other Backward Classes |
| PUDR | People's Union for Democratic Rights |
| RSS | Rashtriya Swayamsevak Sangh |
| SJM | Swadesh Jagram Manch |
| SVN | Selections from Vernacular Records (at IOL) |
| UP | Uttar Pradesh |
| VHP | Vishva Hindu Parishad |

# Introduction
## Ayodhya: A Window on the World

### DAVID LUDDEN

HOLY MEN DECLARED SUNDAY, DECEMBER 6, 1992, auspicious, and more than 300,000 people gathered that day in Ayodhya, a pilgrimage town north of Varanasi (Benares), in the state of Uttar Pradesh (UP). Most wore the saffron color of Hindu nationalism. At midday, a vanguard among them broke down police barricades around a mosque called the Babri Masjid, built in 1528 by Mir Baqi, under the authority of Babar, the first Mughal emperor of India. Cheering men swarmed the domes of the old mosque and in five hours they hammered and axed it to the ground. Video cameras hummed. Eyewitnesses took notes for news reports around the world. Hindu leaders, who had mobilized for this event since 1984, watched with satisfaction, for they and their followers believe that god Rama (or Ram) was born here and that the temple marking Rama's birthplace was destroyed to build this mosque (*masjid*). The construction of a new Rama temple (*mandir*) was begun that evening, amid the rubble of the Babri Masjid. Government officials looked on ineffectually. Violence triggered by the demolition killed 1,700 people and injured 5,500 across the subcontinent over the next four months.

Supporters justify the action at Ayodhya as the liberation of a Hindu sacred space to unify the Indian nation. Critics call it violence against Muslims; they decry such communalism — the antagonistic mobilization of one religious community against another — as an attack on Indian civil society. In this volume, we explore the mobilizations, genealogies, and interpretations of communal conflict that locate this one very emotional and symbolic day in the struggles that are underway to redefine India politically. We see Ayodhya as a window on a world of conflict that developed inside nationalism around the globe in the 1980s and as an instance of the global staging of national politics and cultures in the late twentieth century. Ayodhya symbolizes Hindu-Muslim conflict in South Asia but also conjures the nightmare of nuclear war between India and Pakistan; like other comparable conflicts, communalism in India is international (Midlarsky 1992). Not only in India, but also in France, the former Yugoslavia, Algeria, Turkey, Germany, the United States, Sri Lanka, Russia, Rwanda, Ethiopia, and Iran—anywhere that minorities face hostile majoritarianism—minority conditions worsened in the 1980s (Gurr 1994, 1993, 1986). Since the late 1970s, nationalist movements based on the assertion that one majority ethnic or religious group defines a nation have emerged with new force and creativity—with new rituals and spectacles, including televised violence—to revalorize old emotions and symbolic resources. The men who destroyed the Babri mosque marched to a cultural movement whose ideas, images, media, organizations, and resources are transnational in form, scope, and influence. Ayodhya is a refraction of "ethnic cleansing" in Serbia, the "moral majority" in the United States, and other movements that define nations by ethnicity and religion.

## Primordialism

In the early 1990s, when religious upheaval rocked India's stable, modern, secular, and multicultural democracy, economic crisis also upended India's treasury (Gordon and Oldenburg 1992); observers who assessed the condition of the country had to keep in mind that many states have crumbled since Iran's 1978 Islamic Revolution. In 1992, two large, multiethnic states much like India—the Soviet Union and Yugoslavia—were torn into conflicting parts. Many analysts concluded that Ayodhya reflected a wider alienation of cultures from states that was tearing the loyalties of peoples away from states in many parts of the world.

Loyalties more powerful than institutionalized nationalism seem to be breaking states apart in the last quarter of the century. In this context, scholarly interest in nationalism has increased along with skepticism about modern institutions (Anderson 1983; Chatterjee 1986, 1993; Connor 1994). Scholars discuss the invented, imagined nature of nationalism as popular movements deconstruct world politics. In the 1980s, United States politicians called for their government to "get off our backs," as governments collapsed in other countries under the force of popular assertions of their illegitimacy. In the 1990s, America's far right includes militia groups and others who see the federal government as the enemy of the people. Today, popular movements in many parts of the world (including ones that have not succeeded, as in China) pit people against government in new ways. Nationalism and national cultures are being redefined from many directions at once.

Religion plays an important part in this process. In the United States, India, Algeria, Poland, Iran, Israel, and elsewhere, religion entered politics with new force in the 1980s; and in the United States, it also permeated thinking about world politics, as militant Muslims appeared to pose a serious threat to the United States abroad. Apprehensions about Islam deepened during the Iran hostage crisis and Persian Gulf War, and in this context, in 1992, American journalists immediately interpreted events at Ayodhya as Hindu rage against Islam.[1] They were quickly joined by a prominent political scientist (Huntington 1993) and by scholars of religion (Juergensmeyer 1993) who consider Hindu nationalism to be a response in kind to Islamic nationalism (see also Kaplan 1994). In this perspective, Hinduism and Islam together form a single image of religious militancy, as they entangle one another, fighting like two armies at war, or boxers in a ring. *Newsweek* (December 21, 1992, 46) even used a phrase from media coverage of militant Islam to headline its story on Ayodhya: "Holy War in India."

Samuel Huntington formulated these ideas into a framework for analyzing global politics as "a clash of civilizations." In his post–Cold War world order, Islam is a civilization that expanded its power east and west, like an empire, so that today, nationalist Hindus fight Muslims on the east, while Jews and Christians fight Muslims in the west (Huntington 1993, 33–34 ff.). Communalism in India thus became symptomatic of a new world order emerging from the Cold War. Journalists Steve Coll and Edward Gargan explained how India entered this new world order. They

---

1. I refer to Steve Coll and Molly Moore (*Washington Post*), Edward Gargan (*New York Times*), Tom Masland (*Newsweek*, December 21, 1992), Scott Steele (*McLeans*, December 21, 1992), Jefferson Penberthy (*Time*, December 21, 1992). Gargan's report (*New York Times*, International Section, Friday, December 11, 1992, p. A10) set the tone for all the reports that appeared in the mainstream U.S. press during the months of rioting that followed December 6, 1992. For instance, *Newsweek* (December 21, 1992, p. 46) reported that the "battle over a mosque refuels the ancient conflict between Hindus and Muslims"; and the *Washington Post* (January 29, 1993, p. A20) attributed the violence to "centuries-old religious hatreds and modern-day economic deprivation." (By contrast, see Rudolph and Rudolph 1993.) My thanks to Adam Zeff, Anjali Arondeka, and Supti Bhattacharya for compiling and analyzing material for me on the coverage of India by the American media.

reported that the centralized Indian state, built on socialist lines by Jawaharlal Nehru, went bankrupt in the 1980s, releasing the powers of the free market and religious nationalism—both suppressed by "Nehruvian socialism." Indian business and the "Hindu People's Party," the Bharatiya Janata Party (BJP), thus represent populist forces, which together confront the weakening socialist state in India, in a conflict like that in Eastern Europe and the former Soviet Union (Coll 1994; *New York Times* July 24, 1992, December 11, 1992, September 17, 1993).

In this reading of recent history, religious nationalisms express primordial loyalties that were set free or unleashed by crumbling state control over political systems and societies in the 1980s. Religion seems to be a natural, populist political force, articulating people's cultural and national identity at a level of emotive meaning more basic and fundamental than other kinds of political affiliations. Religious identities naturally take over politics when constraints on their expression are weakened. So India is like Iran, Poland, and Russia. Evoking Yugoslavia, Gargan reported that "the hatreds of India" emerged in the 1980s from "Hindu memory scarred by centuries of sometimes despotic Islamic rule" (*New York Times* December 11, 1992, A10). Though Muslim sultans have not ruled India for two centuries, Hindus would seem to hold a lasting grudge, aggravated by traumas of the partition of British India into the independent states of India and Pakistan in 1947 and by continuous animosity between Pakistan and India since then. When Nehru's Congress Party declined—with the assassination of his prime minister daughter, Indira Gandhi (d. 1984) and then of her prime minister son, Rajiv Gandhi (d. 1991)—communal conflict erupted in electoral politics and in violent clashes that defied the Indian state and now threaten to overwhelm it.

## The Meaning of "India"

This interpretation gains support from firmly established ideas about the religious foundation of civilizations, nations, and cultures in Eurasia. When modern European research on India began, in the late eighteenth century, it focused primarily on classical languages and religion, and today the idea that religion defines India remains deeply rooted in modern scholarship. Histories of Indian civilization, art, society, politics, and culture routinely separate Hindu, Muslim, British, and national epochs. India and Hindu are often equated when defining Indian culture, whose core characteristics are most often taken to be Hindu. Anthropological research and museum exhibits often present Hindu ritual, texts, and art to depict Indian culture. Islamic artifacts are equally often used to describe a Muslim culture that originated in the Middle East and then expanded into India. Permanent galleries in the British Museum and the New York Metropolitan Museum of Art are organized on these lines, for example. Indian Islam is thus portrayed as being foreign and derivative, alien to India. The authority of these ideas and cultural practices increased understandably in 1947, when Hinduism and Islam became majority religions on opposite sides of borders separating hostile states in South Asia; and to the extent that Pakistan has been Islamicized, its heartland of cultural identity has been shifted away from South Asia toward the Middle East.

From this perspective, the Babri Masjid seems to be a foreign transplant. But in fact, Babar built his empire primarily in what is now India, where Islam is just as important for cultural history as it is in Pakistan and Bangladesh. Islam is as old in India as in Turkey. Indian Islam is older than American Christianity and European Protestantism. Indian Islam is no more derivative than Chinese, Tibetan, Thai, or Japanese Buddhism. In India's historical culture and civilization, Islam has very deep roots indeed, and the distinctiveness of Indian Islam represents the characteristic capacity of Islam everywhere to be adaptable to the environment—a feature that is equally important in diverse and changing regions of what is called its Middle East heartland (exemplified in the career of Pan-Islamism and the end of the caliphate) as it is in India, Indonesia, and Senegal (Eaton 1985, 1993, 1994; Al-Azmeh 1993). Yet the idea that Islam is foreign in India is axiomatic among the Hindu nationalists who destroyed the Babri Masjid; this idea is used to argue for second-class Muslim citizenship in India and even for the expulsion of Muslims from India. Making Islam appear foreign to India is part of the project of making India Hindu pursued by Hindu nationalist groups.

Thinking about communalism thus highlights the need to reconsider the basic terms that we use to talk about India, and to question common assumptions that have been built into modern knowledge (Breckenridge and van der Veer 1993; Ludden 1993, 1994). All of a sudden, in 1947, the word "India" came to denote simultaneously a civilization and an independent national state, but the two do not coincide. Indian history, culture, and civilization extend back to about 2000 B.C.E. and these were never bounded by the lines on the map that separate states today. Geographically, Indian history, in a long-term view, includes the territory of Pakistan and Bangladesh. The 1947 partition of India can thus be taken to mean the division of Indian civilization into separate independent states, only one of which is today called "India." But actually, the partition divided a territory that was formed by British imperialism without any reference to Indian civilization at all. (British India also included Burma, now the Union of Myanmar.) Ironically, therefore, the territory that we use to describe the landscape of Indian civilization was defined politically by the British Empire. India was never what it is today in a geographical, demographic, or cultural sense, before 1947.

Thus the conventional intellectual identification of "India" with the terms "Hindu" and "Hinduism" is deeply mistaken. In its demographic statistics, India today may be a majority Hindu country, and so was British India, in 1946; but this does not mean that India (even as defined by state boundaries today) was ever populated predominately by people whose identity was formed by their collective identification with a religion called "Hinduism" or with a "Hindu" religious persona. Moreover, the historical space of Indian civilization, which after 1300 included what is today Afghanistan, today contains as many Muslims as the Middle East (32 percent of the world Muslim population); and India today has the fourth largest Muslim population in the world, following Indonesia, Pakistan, and Bangladesh (Eaton 1993, 23). Like "Muslim," the term "Hindu" conjures an identity that is defined in many ways, and defined differently even by the same individual according to context. It is not known how many people in India would have identified themselves as Hindus, if asked, simply, "What is your religion?" in 1800, 1900, 1947, or 1993. But the vast religious tradition that we refer to as "Hinduism" has no single, unanimously agreed upon core set of institutions analogous to the Quran, *umma* (community of believers in Islam), the Bible, Catholic Church, or Talmud around which a Hindu religious identity could have been unified traditionally. Central philosophical tenets—*dharma* (religious duty), *karma* (fateful action), and *samsara* (the cycle of rebirth)—rationalize a division of Hindu believers into four ranked ritual status categories (*varnas*)—Brahman, Kshatriya, Vaishya, and Shudra—and it is the distinctions, not the similarities, among countless caste groups (*jatis*) that form the primary basis of Hindu social identity. Philosophically, each Hindu person's identity can be located ritually by religious duties appropriate for one's specific social status, ritual status, and age (one's *varnashramadharma*). Religious practices revolve around many different deities (*devas*), sectarian traditions (*sampradays*), and teachers (*gurus*) that form centers of personal devotion and affective religious affiliation. The ideas that define Hinduism as a religion, therefore, deeply discourage the formation of a collective Hindu religious identity among believers and practitioners. Hindu identity is multiple, by definition, and India consists of many other religious identities as well, including those among Muslims, Zoroastrians, Sikhs, Christians, and Jews.

The term "Hindu" came to have wide cultural meaning—and became a term that people use to identify themselves—primarily because it has been used by government in census statistics and elections. "Hindu" is an official term for counting people, and this gives the statistical impression that India is a majority Hindu country. But the terms "Hindu" and "India" also have the same derivation: both come from the name of the Indus River. From the days of Alexander the Great, people east of the Indus were called "Hindus" and their territory became "India." "Hindu" thus did not begin its career as a religious term, but rather as a term used by outsiders and by state officials to designate people who lived east of the Indus. Hindu India was first defined not internally, by the religious traditions of collective Hindu identity, but externally and by modern state institutions, in practices of religious identification. Under British rule, "Hindu" became a category for people in India who were not Muslims, Christians, Sikhs, Jains, Parsis, Buddhists, or others. This division of the population by religious categories was used to create descriptions of India that we inherit.

The practice of labeling things Indian with the term "Hindu" has caused endless confusion, obliterating lines between religious and census classifications. *Webster's New World Dictionary* (1984), for instance, describes Mohandas Gandhi as a "Hindu nationalist leader." True, Gandhi was a religious Hindu who was also an Indian nationalist leader, but he opposed Hindu nationalism; he was killed by a Hindu nationalist who blamed Gandhi's appeasement of Muslims for the partition of British India. *Webster's* reinforces the very political identification of India with Hindu that Gandhi opposed. A pattern of phrasing has also become common recently in news reporting that further confuses "Hindu" and "India." A recent article in the *Philadelphia Inquirer* (August 6, 1994, A10), for instance, reports that "predominantly Hindu India has long blamed Islamic Pakistan for financing and training the terrorists who planted the 13 bombs that exploded across central Bombay on March 12, 1993, after Hindu-Muslim riots swept India." This is like saying, "The predominantly Christian United States blames Islamic Iraq for human rights violations": it is not exactly untrue, but it implies an explanation of the government's action that is misleading. This phrasing reinforces in the mind of the reader the

idea that Hinduism constitutes India in a way that really is untrue, however, because the government of India is not Hindu, "predominantly" or
otherwise; it is less so, in fact, than the United States government is Christian, because most political parties in India explicitly oppose Hindu politics. The effect of this phrasing is to identify India, the Indian people, and
the Indian government as being Hindu by definition. Making this identification into a political reality is in fact the project of Hindu nationalism.
(As I write, the *New York Times*, July 10, 1995, describes India as "predominantly Hindu" in its report explaining India's conflict with Pakistan over
Kashmir, a usage that implicitly endorses Hindu nationalism.)

## Orientalism

Interpreting communalism in India as a struggle between Hinduism and
Islam fits a pattern of ideas about India that has dominated U.S. media and
public opinion since the 1950s (Isaacs 1959, 1972; Asia Society 1976; Cecil,
Jani, and Takacs 1994). The interpretations of events at Ayodhya by Gargan,
Coll, and Huntington are thus very accessible to their audience and easy
for most readers to accept; but this very fact makes their arguments susceptible to a form of criticism inaugurated by Edward Said's book *Orientalism*
in 1978. Many scholars have built upon Said's critique, imbuing the term
"orientalism" today with the connotation of ideological stereotyping, like
"racism" and "sexism," for Said argued effectively that by rendering non-
Western societies in religious stereotypes, European empires rationalized
their own world dominance, creating forms of knowledge about the world
that continue even today to support Western imperialism.

Modern European empires expanded into India and the Muslim world
simultaneously, in the late eighteenth century: British rule was formalized
in India in the 1790s, and Napoleon invaded Egypt in 1798 (see Adas 1993).
At the same time, European scholars, painters, novelists, museum cura-
tors, journalists, designers, policymakers, and politicians began systematically to create compelling images of Hindus and Muslims for Western
audiences. Alien, exotic, sensual, despotic, traditional, prone to violence,
backward, immoral, threatening, and irrational in their fervent religiosity:
such evocative images formed a repertoire of representations depicting
the non-European others that opposed the West. Producers of culture in
Europe created images of Europe as being the essence of modernity and

progress as they propagated stereotypes of tradition and backwardness elsewhere.

In Said's critical perspective, the otherness of the Orient for Europe became the founding principle and empirical substance of orientalism—the compilation of images that constructed Asiatic cultures in the Western mind. In this context, Indian civilization was defined by the texts that orientalists used to compile the laws and legacy of Hinduism. In the same vein, Muslim cultures were defined essentially by Islamic texts. Equating non-European cultures with non-European religions thus became a fixed cognitive routine in scholarship and colonial policy. This enabled Europeans to justify imperial expansion in both religious and secular terms: for Christians, European imperialism saved souls, and for modernists, it brought progress into a world of backwardness and tradition (Breckenridge and van der Veer 1993; Adas 1989).

Taking Said's point of view, we can look at U.S. media coverage in a new light. Images of fanatical Muslims (in Algeria, Lebanon, and Iran), Muslim terrorists (Libya, Palestine), and Muslim tyrants (Libya, Iraq, Iran) are common in the West. In the same vein, the word "frenzied" (usually in the phrase "frenzied mob") appeared in almost all U.S. newspaper accounts of the events at Ayodhya. "Hindu fanatics" and "Hindu zealots" appear almost as often (Zeff 1994). Such habits of phrasing are not ephemeral or unique to the U.S. press. They represent cultural patterns that are deeply ingrained. Western accounts of India have long stressed the exotic features that make India foreign to modern, Western, readers: mysticism, yoga, ritual, caste, untouchability, cremated widows (*sati*), female seclusion (*purdah*), "holy war" (*jihad*), and for that matter, communalism. The cultural connotations of these patterns of usage indicate the ideological legacy of orientalism, which created the religious stereotypes of Muslims, Hindus, and others that even today rationalize Western power in the world.

European imperialism thus invented the religious traditionalism that formed its ideological other in the orient, and this made imperialism appear ideologically as the equivalent of modernization and progress. As a result, we can read in history books that Europeans brought modernity to an East that was steeped in religious tradition. As a once-popular American textbook says, "India, like ancient Egypt, was a land saturated with religion; its people were obsessed with the destiny and status of man in the hereafter. Nearly every aspect of life, every thought and action, was con-

ditioned by faith and dogma, whether in business, in politics, or in social
behavior" (Wallbank 1965, 25). It is not uncommon to read that people
in the non-Western world are still living in the past, even in the Middle
Ages. Thus the master narrative of modern history as written by the West
for itself and for its worldwide power finds the progressive West—with its
secularism, science, rationality, economic development, and just institutions of law and politics—facing the mystical, irrational, stagnant, passive,
chaotic, mysterious East, which always seems to resist and fail in the process of modernization (Turner 1994).

So journalistic and social science renditions of Hindu-Muslim conflict in India in terms of India's primordial religious passions draw from
an old storehouse of imagery that identifies the religions we see in the
headlines with those that define Indian civilization and also implies that
the conflict at Ayodhya dramatizes the very religious traditionalism and
irrationality that describe and explain India's poverty and backwardness.
Ironically, however, European imperialism actually used its own political
power to fashion the Orient in the image of orientalism. Chains of real
historical causation connect orientalism and communalism because orientalism rationalized the institutionalization of oppositions and separations
between Hindu and Muslim, and these were built into colonial administration and law (Ludden 1993; Washbrook 1981). Colonial officials wrote
separate Hindu and Muslim law codes, which remain (with modification)
in effect today (Kozlowski 1990, 1993; Baird 1993); and in 1986, a Supreme
Court case concerning the rights of a Muslim widow, Shah Bano, became a
major event in the escalation of communalism, because Hindu nationalists
argued vehemently that the maintenance of a separate Muslim law violates
principles of Indian unity and social justice. Similarly, colonial officials
made it a policy to consult Hindu and Muslim leaders separately (Freitag
1989a)—a tradition that hardened in the form of separate electorates for
Hindus and Muslims, established in British India in 1911 and in force until
1947. The inability of the Indian National Congress to win officially designated Muslim seats, especially in Muslim majority provinces, laid the electoral basis of the partition of British India into the independent states of
India and Pakistan. When the British government rushed toward a pullout
from India, after World War II, the Indian National Congress and parties
that controlled the Muslim majority provinces of Punjab and Bengal—
most importantly, the Muslim League, led by Mohammad Ali Jinnah, the
founding father of Pakistan—could not reach a settlement on the division
of powers within a united India after independence. At that point, for the

first time, partition became inevitable (Brown 1985; Jalal and Seal 1981; Jalal 1985).

A supposed fact established by orientalism—that India was defined by its opposing religions—thus began its career as a colonial idea, an imperial theory, and became a modern institutional reality. This is a central argument in *The Construction of Communalism in Colonial North India* (1990b), where Gyanendra Pandey argues that the assumption of Hindu-Muslim antagonism became a guiding principle in colonial sociology and administrative practice. The modern colonial state produced mountains of authoritative data—in its ethnography, census statistics, law, and history—that appear to be the epitome of scientific objectivity. Upon this foundation, an edifice of inference and conjecture were built. The result is a massive colonial archive that documents the primordial qualities of religion in India, and of Hindu-Muslim conflict in particular. When writing about riots, for instance, colonial officers—usually police and local administrators, in the first instance—wrote what seem to be eyewitness accounts that were intended to appear as such. But many of these authors were absent from the scene and were far from being experts on local affairs. They often gave reports an air of expertise by using the phrase "communal riot." Because Hindu-Muslim conflict was assumed to be brewing all the time in India, the label could easily be made to stick, and it was very handy in describing conflicts for which local officials sought to deflect responsibility. "Communal conflict" became a catchall phrase for violent unrest; reports used it often, perhaps indiscriminately. Conflicts can be shown to have been about many things other than antagonism between religious communities: sometimes riots were antigovernment or antipolice uprisings; sometimes they were the product of state and especially police violence. One thing is certain: the political utility of the phrase for officials—further enhanced by the inherent explanation it implies for the origin of social conflict in religion—undermines the statistical reliability of data produced by its utilization. For the colonial period, it is often impossible to know what the category "communal riot" refers to in reality. These are also cautionary insights today for anyone considering communalism from afar and who thus depends on layers of intermediation for data about local events in India or elsewhere.

Most scholars of India today argue that communal conflict never was caused by the religions of Hinduism and Islam; many agree with Said and Pandey that as a historical and historiographic phenomenon, communalism is a product of orientalism and the colonial state. They argue that we should not imagine communalism as erupting from the "hatreds of India," as though from the unconscious of a civilization. Instead, we should explore how the state has been implicated in communalism since colonial times. From this point of view, explanations of Hindu-Muslim conflict that deflect attention away from the state toward religion are suspicious precisely because they are so persuasive. Such explanations became popular and convincing because of their incessant repetition; they have been repeated so often because they helped to sustain empire, because they still effectively exonerate the modern state and modern forms of power from responsibility for communalism, and because they make the institutions and personalities of the modern state into the arbiters in social conflicts in the world of social life under their jurisdiction (G. Prakash 1990).

## Communalism

This volume describes a framework for studying communalism that combines many academic perspectives to focus simultaneously on culture, society, history, and politics. We begin by recognizing that communalism can be defined differently for different purposes. For social science inquiry, however, it can be defined usefully as a particular formation of purposeful human activity: communalism is collective antagonism organized around religious, linguistic, and/or ethnic identities.

Ideas unite the organization, antagonism, collectivities, and identities that constitute communalism. These ideas do not form a closed system; they are dispersed throughout the heritage of modernity. In India, communalism is based on the fundamental idea that Hindus and Muslims constitute totally separate communities in essential opposition to one another. This idea precedes, facilitates, justifies, and provides an explanation for communalism. It has been used to construct every Hindu and Muslim as a member of one community and every communal leader as a community spokesman. It represents each collective identity as a community alive through all time; it enables past memories and emotions to fill the present and each Hindu and Muslim to become a sentient vehicle of communal experience. This basic communal idea creates religious community in the image of a family, a nation.

This communal idea cannot be proved or disproved. It cannot be effectively subjected to truth-testing, because, like other ideas about collective identity in the modern world, it is actually an argument that has become deeply rooted in modern systems of belief and understanding. This rootedness indicates how communalism participates in modern history and culture at many levels; its meanings are diverse and many-layered. Communalism is alive in everyday politics that invokes community identity—in the streets, courts, media, elections, religious and cultural institutions, schools, academic research, and intimate conversations—anywhere that people can be influenced to form their own identities and public opinion around oppositional ethnic or religious categories. Its most dramatic moments are massively organized public events—riots, demonstrations, processions, media spectacles, and elections—which in India engage society widely and directly and which animate competitions for power in India's constitutional democracy. Communalism is also a form of back room scheming. Today, some parties in India have elaborate communal platforms, most prominently, the Bharatiya Janata Party (BJP), "The Indian People's Party," which seeks to form a Hindu government, symbolized by images of Lord Rama's righteous, peaceful kingdom. Many candidates in other parties also use communal strategies and tactics, however. Indira and Rajiv Gandhi made alliances and mobilized campaigns on communal lines, though their own philosophy was secular, though their Congress Party is officially secular, and though India's constitution defines India as a secular republic.

Secularism and communalism arose together inside the institutions of modernity, and that fact is a major preoccupation of this volume. Though people whom we can identify as Hindus and Muslims did use religious ideas to mobilize religious identities politically in premodern times, the activity of organizing antagonistic Muslim and Hindu collective identities became widespread only in the 1890s, during the Cow Protection Movement, when Hindu groups attacked Muslims across northern India. By this time, the Indian National Congress had already been formed (1885) to embrace all religious, ethnic, and linguistic identities within one overarching Indian national identity. Defined in opposition to British identity, this Indian national identity carried an ethnic flavor, but its precise cultural characteristics were unspecified. Congress sought to represent all Indians as one nation of many languages, religions, and ethnicities. By contrast, the Muslim League was organized (1906) to represent Muslim identities in British India (Hardy 1972; Jalal 1985), a project that involved a logical opposition to Congress ideals but not necessarily political antagonism to Congress, because the League was founded to advance a particular minority collective interest within a multicultural polity. The Rashtriya Swayamsevak Sangh (RSS) was organized in 1925 to define and create India as a Hindu nation. This definition excluded all non-Hindus absolutely; so from the beginning, the RSS and allied organizations opposed not only the Muslim League but also the Congress conception of India as a nation of many religions (T. Basu et al. 1993).

Modernity in South Asia has entailed countless efforts to organize collective identities. Most of these have been regional, minority movements for political representation in the modern state system. In 1947, regional movements among Muslims in eastern Bengal and western Punjab culminated in the formation of Pakistan. In 1956, India's constituent states were reorganized on linguistic lines. In 1971, Bangladesh arose from a regional liberation movement. Tamils, Sikhs, and other groups have gained various degrees and types of regional power based on collective cultural identities. All these movements have mobilized identities that overlap and mix with others in everyday life—like most social identities—and they have sought to make them instead politically exclusive and competitive. At their boundaries, these movements often generate antagonism organized around religious, linguistic, and/or ethnic identities. Since 1984, terrible conflict has accompanied regional movements in Punjab and Kashmir, which bear comparison to Palestine, Ulster, and Jaffna in northern Sri Lanka.

The many regional conflicts in South Asia that could be embraced by our definition of communalism are not the subject of this book, however, though they do play a part in our discussion. We focus here on majoritarian Hindu nationalism in India, because it is such a prominent political force in India today, and because its adherents are so prominent in the representation of India abroad. As a majoritarian movement, Hindu nationalism defines the Indian nation as a whole and seeks to displace and remove alternative, pluralistic definitions. In efforts to unify India, Hindu nationalists give top priority to their opposition to Islam and Muslims, and the reasons why they do so preoccupies several essays in this volume. As we will see, one reason for the persistence of Hindu nationalism as a force in Indian political life lies in the fact that its basic tenets have been deployed many times to explain why Hindu-Muslim antagonism—and thus communalism—is morally correct, inevitable, necessary, and even progressive. These ideas circulate widely and freely in the public domain. They have acquired a common sense quality by their institutionalized repetition in textbooks, museum exhibitions, journalism, scholarship, and other media. Their discursive narration is a characteristic of modernity itself. Increasing the power and authority of these ideas and drowning out their intellectual competition are critical in the project of making India Hindu. Mainstreaming the idea that India is essentially Hindu in the United States—

through the patronage of academic activity, Indian cultural institutions, and policy analysis—is part of an international effort to make India Hindu in the world of nations (see McKean 1994, 1995).

Because India participates in a global history of modernity and nationalism, the ideas that underlie Hindu majoritarian communalism sound familiar in most of the world. They have the resonance of common sense. They can be summarized as follows.

Civilizations and individual human identities derive from cultures that are based in religion. India is Hindu. Hindus ruled their native land for millennia before Muslims invaded from Central Asia and, in 1206, founded the Delhi Sultanate. In 1757, British rule in India began with the English East India Company's victory at the Battle of Plassey. In the nineteenth century, under the British Raj, Indian nationalism arose to fight for independence. And in India, as in other countries, when foreigners threaten, conquer, or invade a country, the natives naturally assert their collective identity through their indigenous culture and mobilize on lines of allegiance that reflect their native cohesion as a people: thus they articulate their nationhood. Naturally enough, Muslims opposed Hindus in India. The Muslims' desire for their own independence forced the partition of India. Pakistan has fought three wars with India and still attacks India at every occasion, today, most visibly in Kashmir, where it arms Muslim secessionists. In India, where Muslims are the largest minority (12 percent in 1991) and Hindus are the great majority (82 percent), Hindu-Muslim antagonism continues, because the government has coddled the Muslim minority to maintain its power. Under the corrupt regime of the Congress Party, Hindus are still denied their own nation-state. The BJP (formerly the Jan Sangh) and its allied Hindu organizations—the Vishva Hindu Parishad (VHP), Bajrang Dal (the VHP youth organization), Hindu Mahasabha, and Rashtriya Swayamsevak Sangh (RSS)—together called the Sangh Parivar ("Sangh family") because of the parental role of the RSS—represent the effort by the Hindu nation to form a Hindu nation-state based on India's native culture.

## Communal Politics

The Sangh Parivar (or simply, the Sangh) represents the main protagonists in majoritarian Hindu communalism. Yet their Hindu nationalism (*Hindutva*) is a majoritarian idea that does not espouse communal conflict in principle. The Sangh promotes Hindu majoritarianism, cultural nationalism, and national "unity in diversity," based on its own definition of India's Hindu cultural heritage (Golwalkar 1966; Prakashana 1979; Elst 1991). From the Sangh perspective, communalism is alien to its own program, because Hindu nationalism does not represent one community

fighting others in India, but rather the real India struggling to become
itself. Communal conflict is an unintended by-product of Hindu national
self-assertion that results from adverse reactions from minority communities and from the Indian state. And indeed, it is true that the Sangh alone
did not cause the rioting and massacres that occurred during years of agitation leading up to the demolition of the Babri Masjid (Engineer 1984;
Akbar 1988; V. Das 1990). Even that demolition, which the Sangh did mobilize, took its meaning from a long history of communalism that many
sides have joined over the decades. The history of communalism cannot be
reduced to the activity or ideology of any one group or one set of social,
cultural, or political forces.

Today, one problem in the history of communalism stands out: Why
did communal conflict take center stage in India in the late 1980s? Thirty-
five years passed before communalism became a major force in independent India. Violence classified as "communal" in the official record did
occur in the interim; and the toll in lives and property—almost all Muslim—rose after 1969 amid turmoil caused by the split in the Congress
Party forced by Prime Minister Indira Gandhi. In the 1970s, some riots
were serious, prominently in Gujarat. But before 1980, the political impact
of communalism remained limited (Engineer 1989) and Hindu nationalist
parties won few votes (Graham 1990). After 1980, however, killing classified as "communal" increased rapidly and so did the Muslim body count.
The death toll in the 1980s quadrupled the 1970s figure and rose to more
than seven thousand. In this context, the BJP—the electoral party of the
Sangh—soared. In 1989, BJP candidates won eighty-five seats in the Lok
Sabha (the lower house of Parliament), with 11 percent of the popular vote.
In 1990, one hundred thousand Sangh Parivar activists assaulted the Babri
Masjid and thirty were killed in a police action to protect the mosque; and
the BJP effectively toppled the Janata Dal government of Prime Minister V. P. Singh, forcing new elections (Engineer 1993). Communal rhetoric fired election campaigns with rage over Muslim desecration of Rama's
birthplace (*Ram janmabhoomi*). Muslim politicians countered with rage
over Hindu plans to destroy the Babri Masjid.

In the 1991 elections, BJP candidates won 119 seats in the Lok Sabha,
with 20 percent of the popular vote; they also won control of four state
governments: Himachal Pradesh (HP), Madhya Pradesh (MP), Rajasthan,
and, most importantly, Uttar Pradesh (UP), where Ayodhya is located
(*Asian Survey* 1993). In 1992, the BJP state government in Uttar Pradesh
helped the Sangh to succeed in Ayodhya. The popular appeal of Sangh

leaders and orators—L. K. Advani, Sadhvi Rithambara, and Uma Bharati
—made them prominent public figures. Lord Rama and his epic, *Rama-yana*, had become political icons. Hindu nationalism (Hindutva) and com-munalism permeated Indian politics, media, and popular culture. After
December 6, rioting spread instantly into many regions of India and
also into Bangladesh, Pakistan, and the United Kingdom (London *Times*,
December 8–15, 1992). Bombs set Bombay afire and the Indian govern-ment immediately accused Pakistan (Padgaonkar 1993). Communalism en-gulfed South Asia, as it had in 1947, with violence and death. In April 1993,
the killing finally subsided. The Indian government banned the RSS, VHP,
Bajrang Dal, and two Islamic parties (the Islamic Sevak Sangh and the
Jamaat-e-Islami Hind), and though the VHP continued to operate widely
in India despite the ban (*India Today*, July 15, 1995, 15), in 1993 and 1994,
the BJP did not do as well at the polls as many people expected; it even
lost in UP to a coalition of non-Congress parties based on the support of
lower caste groups. But in 1995, the BJP won state elections in Gujarat
and formed a government in the state of Maharashtra in alliance with the
Shiv Sena. National elections must be held by mid-1996, and the Sangh
Parivar seeks to play a major role in forming the next Indian government.
Nor surprisingly, the VHP began to mobilize its forces in summer 1995 to
make Mathura and Benares the scenes of Hindu-Muslim conflict (Rama-krishnan 1995).

Why did communalism explode in the eighties? How did it take cen-ter stage in Indian politics so rapidly and, it seems, so decisively, in such
a short time? What is the relationship between the new communalism of
the 1980s and 1990s and its predecessors before 1947? How do its histori-cal continuities and antecedents help us to understand majoritarian Hindu
communalism today?

## Competitive Populism

Atul Kohli, in *Democracy and Discontent: India's Growing Crisis of Gov-ernability* (1990), explains how the Indian political system changed in the
1970s and 1980s, and his argument has been strengthened by other schol-ars (Frankel and Rao 1989, 1990; Kohli ed. 1988). Under Jawaharlal Nehru,
the Congress Party built a vast system of alliances with influential men in
villages, towns, and districts throughout India, based on the loyalties in-herited from the independence movement and on the ability of the ruling

party to provide patronage in return for votes. Local Congress men kept the party in power by providing votes in return for party support to maintain their influence over local voters. This Congress system limited the pace and extent of change that government could effect in India's local power structures; it required that state planning be conducted with the interests of local elites in mind; and it also encouraged forms of economic development consistent with the smooth operation of Congress organization. So India's economic development regime invoked the rhetoric of socialism and centralized power in the public sector, but also rested on a firm, socially conservative, local power base of Congress big men (Ludden 1992).

The Congress system depended on the reciprocal movement of votes and patronage from the national capital in New Delhi to the villages, and on the legitimacy of its power brokers in the eyes of voters. Intact in the 1960s (Kothari 1970; Weiner 1967) the pillars of the Congress system had crumbled by the mid-1980s. In the interim, Congress Party organization and public faith in the party had disappeared. In 1985, Prime Minister Rajiv Gandhi, soon after his election victory, following his mother's death, celebrated the party's one hundredth anniversary by blasting "cliques" that held "the living body of the Congress in their net of avarice" for their corruption, self-aggrandizement, "their linkages with vested interests—and their sanctimonious posturings" (Kohli 1990, 5). In effect, he announced that the Congress system was dead.

India's new communalism has arisen during a struggle to reconstruct India politically. The struggle is centrally concerned with the legitimacy of the state, the distribution of state resources, power in society, and justice. It involves ideological and organizational innovation, mass mobilization, reinterpretations of the national heritage, shifting loyalties, and competition for all the votes that have been let loose from the shredded net of Congress control. The struggle is thus actually many different kinds of struggles in localities, regions, and national politics; and it has a very dark side—political violence by the police, army, hitmen, *goondas* (thugs), gangs, rioters, and *kar sevaks* (Sangh volunteer workers). Whether we view political violence as a natural result of breakdown in the institutions of conflict mediation or as a public expression of coercion that was previously hidden in the private places where employers beat workers and men beat women, we can agree that collapsing political order has created disorderly politics. The death of Congress hegemony brought down an institutionalized system of rules and roles; and a new set of tactical options have entered the political game that are deemed illegitimate by public consensus. In this climate,

Hindutva has emerged as a solid competitor for popular loyalties and the RSS and BJP have increased their power, in significant measure because they have successfully used nonparliamentary means, including violence, to win elections.

Unlike the Congress Party—and unlike many other countries where communal conflicts rage—India's institutional structure is strong. The fundamental rule of Indian politics remains in force: only votes can make governments. As the national dominance of Congress waned, other parties replaced Congress in the states of Andhra Pradesh, Karnataka, Kerala, Tamil Nadu, Punjab, and West Bengal. The greatest turmoil attending the collapse of the Congress has occurred in states where Congress was strongest in 1980: Gujarat, Maharashtra, Rajasthan, Madhya Pradesh, Himachal Pradesh, Uttar Pradesh, Punjab, Bihar, and the Union Territory of Delhi. In these states, the struggle to reconstruct the Indian polity has been most intense, and thus we focus on them in this volume. Even as we write, rapid change is underway: it seems that the BJP has taken solid control of the newly created Delhi Legislative Assembly. In 1995, it took control of Gujarat and (in an alliance with the Shiv Sena), Maharashtra, which includes Bombay; and the collapse of the coalition that defeated the BJP in UP left the BJP more powerful in UP state politics.

In important ways, Gujarat set the pace. Congress had begun to lose its political base there by 1969, when it split nationally into two factions, one led by Indira Gandhi, which organized street agitations in Gujarat to topple its opposition in the state. This triggered fights between Hindus and Muslims that killed 1,500 people. Mrs. Gandhi's national strategy was to bypass party organization and go straight to the people for support. In 1971, her slogan was *garibi hatao* ("End poverty!"), which signaled her plan to mobilize the poor and marginal groups for a new Congress that was clearly to the left of the old party; it also signaled her commitment to use her personal power to conduct personalized, populist campaigns. In the struggles that ensued, Gujarat became the site of what Kohli calls "competitive populism." The state government established reservations for lower castes in educational institutions, and this policy was opposed by massive agitations. Competing populists created riotous street politics that led to deadly violence in 1971, 1974, 1981, and 1985. Using mass street mobilizations to topple governments became standard practice, and organized Hindu activists turned their violence against Muslims as part of their political strategy to dislodge the Congress (Kohli 1990, 238–66 ff.).

## Social Transformation

Atul Kohli's idea of competitive populism implies that complex connections need to be traced among state power, the institutions of government, electoral politics, popular mobilization, mass media, cultural production, consumer preferences, symbolic resources, collective emotionalism, economic liberalization, class formations, special interests, political violence, and social change. Tracing such connections is the project of this volume.

Majoritarian Hindu activism is only one facet of a deeply changing India. The new communalism of the 1980s is intricately woven into structural change in India that is driven by forces that circulate in the world economy and also hide in the private spaces of family life. One volume cannot do justice to all elements that implicate Hindu nationalism (Hindutva). This volume focuses on forces and conditions that account for the vitality and influence of Hindu majoritarian nationalism as it lives today in a sea of social transformation. We seek to understand Hindutva from the perspectives of history, anthropology, political science, media, art, literature, and religion. We consider iconography, dramaturgy, faith, electoral statistics, party politics, riots, media forms, music, literary imagination, caste inequality, gender issues, business interests, philosophy, and running through them all, territorial ambition.

Part 1 presents four studies of recent mobilizations that have contested established ideas about the Indian nation and sought to make India Hindu. Richard Davis describes a media spectacle that he witnessed and that led to Ayodhya, the *Rath Yatra* (chariot procession) staged like the procession of a deity around India to mobilize support for the demolition of the Babri Masjid and for building a temple at Rama's birthplace. Amrita Basu then asks a question that has been the subject of much debate: should we understand Hindu majoritarian communalism as a mass movement or as an elite conspiracy? She explains why it is both, and how the elite, high caste, predominantly Brahman leadership of the BJP, RSS, and VHP connects politically with poor, low caste people. Zoya Hasan then accounts for the rise of the BJP in the shifting political structure of Uttar Pradesh (UP), India's most electorally powerful state, where the crisis of the Congress makes sense of the BJP and its opposition. Victoria L. Farmer finds another set of connections between Congress Raj and BJP success in Mrs. Gandhi's utilization of state television (Doordarshan): her competitive, authoritarian populism, in India's state-centered development regime, soon implicated television in Hindutva.

Part 2 traces genealogies of communal divisions between Hindus and Muslims in the social and cultural history of northern India. Peter Manuel's study of Hindustani music explodes the idea that there was ever a deep, traditional division between Hindu and Muslim cultures. He then briefly describes the modern creation of separate domains of Hindu and Muslim music and the use of musical media in contemporary Hindu politics. Unified Hindu cultural tradition seems to be more a product of modernity than its predecessor; and Hindu-Muslim cultural opposition, more the outcome of communal politics than its basis. William R. Pinch considers history of *sadhu*s (holy men), who have been prominent in recent Hindu politics and who played a prominent role in Ayodhya. Pinch shows how the history of soldier sadhus has been written to make them appear as defenders of their faith, when their history by other lights does not support this idea; and how the sadhu's religious role and symbolic weight in modern society arose under colonial rule, to make the sadhu a purely religious figure and an activist symbol of tradition. Tanika Sarkar explores interactions between early Indian nationalist identities and ideas that sustain communalism, in the work of Bankim Chandra Chattopadhyay (often referred to as Bankim Chandra Chatterjee), the best known writer in nineteenth-century India. She shows the complex literary entanglement of nationalism and Hindu-Muslim opposition. Being Indian and being Hindu came together—amorphously and uncertainly—in the 1890s: the oppositional identity that defined an Indian became British, as the Other that defined the Hindu became Muslim. Mushirul Hasan expands the exploration of literary imagination to show how colonial and national discourse formed the Muslim as a counter-identity for Hindu India. Thus it became logical for persuasive assertions of political unity among Hindus to be achieved by opposition to Muslims.

In Part 3, four authors argue in favor of four different approaches to Hindu nationalism and majoritarian communalism. Each pair of chapters combines history and anthropology. The first pair, by Sandria B. Freitag and Richard G. Fox, looks at the problematic of modernity: the authors agree that modernity arose in India from colonialism, but they approach the implications of this fact differently. Freitag considers communalism today to be a feature of India's postcolonial public sphere—a domain of representation and contestation that lies between the modern state and civil society, connecting them for translations and articulations of the one to the other. Whereas in Europe, modern state and society share ideas about legitimate authority, Indian communalism arose in a colonial condition in which state and society were alienated from one another. Since the 1890s, therefore, struggles in the public sphere have been aimed at the state, but even today they remain culturally detached from institutions of government. There is thus much more at stake in communalism than winning elections: winning public opinion is paramount. Fox, on the other hand, stresses the formation of social identities and animosities that interact in public. He argues that modernity is a project that, instead of creating the world it describes, obscures its own failure and incompleteness, most glaringly in places like India. Fox attacks the idea of the public sphere as a stable realm for the staging state-society articulations and he argues that modernity not only failed to dislodge premodern identities but generated conditions for their hyperenchantment as a reactionary opposition. For Fox, communalism is the failure of modernity in the imperial periphery. For Freitag, communalism is a drama within modernity's distinctly colonial formation of the public sphere.

In the second pair of chapters in Part 3, Peter van der Veer and Sumit Sarkar focus on communal antagonism, which they both see as being deeply rooted in Indian society; but they differ as to its quality and sustenance. Van der Veer cuts to the heart of Hindutva's dark side—collective violence. He criticizes the standard narration of riots written for the public in India, which attributes violence to material motives and sees religious passion as being a mask for material conflict. This is mistaken and misguided, he argues, because violence is a total phenomenon that cannot be pulled apart merely to reify divisions between the categories of secular and religious. He shows that religious meanings and motives are built into the everyday reproduction of social power relations, and not only in India; Hindu nationalism is only one of many explicit representations of power politically, in deeply affective, religious terms. Sumit Sarkar, in contrast, takes the position that new social movements and the conflicts that come with them arise from changing social power relations, in which interests and passions emerge from historical experience and are expressed and organized politically. So in the same way that Indian nationalism arose from the experience of a particular population of Indians during the nineteenth century and was articulated in expressions of their emerging collective identity to direct political and social change, Hindu nationalism arose in the 1920s, from threats to upper caste dominance by lower caste social movements. Sarkar argues that Hindutva is an ideology of reaction and conservatism, thrown up today against the chaotic threats to dominant groups by women, tribals, peasants, and lower castes. Upward-aspiring social movements and social mobility in general have been facilitated by democratic, secular politics and by economic planning in India, so these are natural targets for Hindutva's hate. For van der Veer, Hindutva articulates religious meanings and emotions that live in everyday social power relations. For Sarkar, it is the populist ideology of India's religious right.

The effect of this volume is to unsettle assumptions that underlie discussions of majority cultures and majoritarian cultural politics in India and elsewhere, including the United States. Every chapter could have its analogue in other volumes exploring majoritarian religious, ethnic, and cultural movements in other parts of the world. Together, these chapters indicate how much remains to be done to understand adequately the contradictions that attend the majoritarian political mobilization of cultural identities within nationalism generally and within democracies in particular. The articulation of cultural diversity and minority rights within modern nations has always presented pressing political and intellectual problems, not least in democracies, which remain susceptible to domineering majoritarianism (Eco 1995). The problem remains for all to ponder: Who constitutes "The nation"?

# PART 1

# MOBILIZING HINDUTVA

# The Iconography of Rama's Chariot

RICHARD H. DAVIS

## The Rath Observed

ON OCTOBER 15, 1990, I WAS STAYING in upper middle-class South Delhi, awaiting a flight south to Madras, when Rama's chariot procession (Rath Yatra) came through town. That morning, large archways made of bamboo wrapped with leaves and festooned with marigold garlands were erected across the street, indicating that a noteworthy procession would soon pass. Posters had appeared on walls over the previous days, depicting a pristine sandstone-colored medieval north Indian temple below, while above, the light-blue complexioned god Rama, wearing a saffron dhoti and a red cummerbund, arose from the clouds. The posters portrayed Rama striding forward, his left hand holding his strung bow and his right bearing a sharp-tipped arrow, a look of divine confidence on his face. He seemed to be facing a storm, for his hair and dhoti fluttered behind him and the clouds were dark blue-gray.

The procession itself arrived a little after noon, and a crowd of onlookers three or four deep quickly gathered at the corner. First came gray-green unmarked flatbed trucks filled with policemen, then a bright orange truck decorated all over with the word *Rama*, the mystical syllable *Om*, and lotus designs. On the back of the truck one young man held a microphone, addressing those on the truck and the onlookers. Next a crowd of young men on motorscooters rolled by. Many of the men wore saffron-colored bandannas or caps, and most of the scooters carried orange banners with

* I am grateful to the American Institute of Indian Studies for a short-term research grant that brought me to Delhi in October 1990.

an upraised, half-opened lotus emblem affixed. After another small police vehicle passed, the main chariot (*rath*) appeared.

The chariot was an extended DCM-Toyota van redecorated as a strange-looking chariot. On the sides of the truck, sweeping cutout patterns rose up to provide a small roofed space above and behind the driver's cab, and the cutouts swung back to encompass a small air-conditioned cabin. On the raised platform behind the driver stood five men, with L. K. Advani, leader of the Bharatiya Janata Party (BJP), standing centermost and addressing the crowd through loudspeakers mounted on the roof of the driver's cab and atop the rear cabin. I was later told that the overall design of the BJP chariot was based on the design for Arjun's chariot in the "Mahabharat," a wildly popular series based on the vast Indian epic tale of mythic warfare, then running on national television. (See Farmer, below.)

The decorative scheme of Rama's chariot was complex and heterogeneous. Against a golden background, words indicating the procession's itinerary—from Somnath to Ayodhya—were printed above the van's front grill, partially obscured by a large wooden cutout of an upraised lotus. Rather fierce-looking lions in profile, seeming to strain forward, embellished the doors. Snaking their way around the two side cutouts were flowing lotus tendrils, ending in eight-petaled lotus designs. The rear tires had been covered with facsimiles of medieval chariot wheel designs. On each side of the rear cabin, large half-opened white lotuses rose against a circular blue background. On the rear of the cabin, underneath two large Om insignia, was a portrait of Mr. Advani, looking avuncular with spectacles and a light blue shawl. To Advani's left was a brief text exhorting him to go ahead and build the temple.

For most spectators, the intention of the procession was clear. The chariot was heading toward the pilgrimage city of Ayodhya, where a sixteenth-century mosque called the Babri Masjid stood on a site that Hindu activists were now claiming was the birthplace of the god Rama. The BJP and its confederate, the Vishwa Hindu Parishad (VHP), both offshoots of the Rashtriya Swayamsevak Sangh (RSS), planned to retake the so-called *Ram janmabhoomi* (birthplace of Rama), destroy the mosque if necessary, and build a magnificent new temple to Rama to consecrate the sacred site.

After the main chariot passed, several more buses and flatbed vans followed, mostly carrying young men. One was filled with older women, who were the most vigorous of all in their cheerleading. The women's truck had a large placard, embossed with a more-than-life-size Rama, announcing that this group was the "Lord Rama Birth Festival Assembly." Finally came another truck spilling over with policemen bringing up the rear of the procession.

By Indian ceremonial standards, the Rath Yatra did not make an impressive spectacle. In South Delhi, the well-heeled audience applauded politely, and a few pressed their palms together in the common gesture of respect. Many of those I spoke with in Delhi and later Madras, generally well educated and well-off, dismissed the whole show as "Toyota Hinduism." An amusing label, this seeming oxymoron drew an ironic chuckle from many, including myself, as if the use of modern technology would disqualify this particular cultural performance from any claim to Hindu authenticity.

Not everyone shared this mild and skeptical response to Rama's chariot procession, however. In other places, I learned, onlookers would rush from the crowd to touch the vehicle, throw flowers in its path, and present offerings to those on board. The processors themselves, though rather restrained in staid South Delhi, brandished swords, bows, and tridents elsewhere along their route. They dressed up as characters drawn from the Indian epics (*Ramayana* and *Mahabharata*): Rama, Lakshmana, Hanuman, and even Shiva with two live snakes around his body. These ardent displays, everyone was well aware, were not innocent, and I learned from the papers the next morning that when the procession had passed through the main street of old Delhi, the police had resorted to teargas and gunfire to quell disturbances that followed the chariot's wake.

As it made its way across north India toward Ayodhya, the procession drew large and enthusiastic crowds and provoked numerous civil disturbances. On October 23, anticipating more trouble, the chief minister of Bihar state had his police stop the procession and arrest Advani and other yatra leaders. On October 30, Hindu activists broke into the Babri Masjid in Ayodhya, placed saffron cloth around the spires of the mosque, and damaged it. Riots and mass arrests followed. Eighteen thousand troops were deployed in Ayodhya alone, and some two hundred thousand Indians were placed in detention. On November 7, the BJP withdrew its support from the coalition government in New Delhi, led by the National Front and headed by India's prime minister, V. P. Singh, which provoked the fall of the government. These events marked the first direct assaults on the Babri Masjid. Two years later, the complete destruction of the mosque set off a new wave of rioting throughout the subcontinent.

## The Problem

More than any other single event, the procession of Rama's chariot that I
glimpsed in New Delhi was responsible for making the dispute over the
site of the Babri Masjid in Ayodhya a central issue of public debate in
India. While I was in India in fall 1990, the newspapers and news maga-
zines were filled day after day with accounts of the yatra, reports of the
communal conflicts it instigated, and analyses of its significance. The Ayodhya issue, in turn, transformed the BJP from a peripheral party of the
right (winning just two seats in the lower house of India's parliament, the
Lok Sabha, in 1984) to a powerful electoral force (with 118 seats in 1991)
and the primary national opposition to the declining Congress Party. (See
Z. Hasan, below.)

By any reckoning, the Rath Yatra was a remarkable and unexpected
event. How is it that a visually unimpressive procession, led by a minor
electoral party, addressing a controversy about a modest sixteenth-century
mosque in an out of the way pilgrimage city, could generate so much
social turbulence, political upheaval, and public debate? That is the primary question of this essay.

Most journalistic and social scientific discussions of the Ayodhya controversy have answered this question by pointing to underlying economic,
social, and political changes in India during the 1980s. A lack of economic
growth led to widespread frustration with the brand of socialism built by
Jawaharlal Nehru that became the hallmark of the Congress Party. India's
educational system created a large pool of unemployed, resentful youth
congregated mostly in urban areas. The once widely accepted hierarchical
assumptions of Indian caste society had eroded, particularly in the cities,
which led to new struggles over status and access to scarce opportunities. New affirmative action policies on behalf of the lower classes triggered upper-class anger and resistance. The idealism of the independence
struggle, focused on democracy and secularism, which held sway in the
1950s and 1960s, and Indira Gandhi's personalized version of populism,
which dominated the 1970s, had been depleted as sources of government
authority and legitimacy by the 1980s. These analyses point to real conditions in Indian society that, in some combination, engendered a receptive
audience for criticisms of the existing order and for promises of radical
change. (Basu and Z. Hasan, below.) But how did the BJP and VHP mobilize diffuse popular sentiments toward their particular end?

Leaders of the Sangh Parivar—the "brotherhood" of interconnected

Hindu nationalist groups affiliated with the RSS, which includes the BJP, VHP, and others—played down their own role in this mobilization. As the BJP *White Paper* puts it, Hindus harbored a continuing grievance over the site of the Babri Masjid in Ayodhya, "waging unremitting struggle for centuries to repossess the birthplace of Sri Rama." The struggle culminated, according to this view of history, in a spontaneous popular movement: "the people of India, under the leadership of Sants and Sadhus, have launched the biggest mass movement in the history of India to regain the Ram janmabhoomi and to construct the Temple" (BJP 1993, 31). (On *sants* and *sadhus*, saints and ascetics, see Pinch, below.) At most, the VHP took credit only for playing a catalytic role in manifesting existing sentiments. In its own words:

The struggle for the liberation of Sri Ram Janmabhoomi and restoration of a magnificent Rama Temple at Ayodhya has been going on continuously, in one form or another, for several centuries. Many generations have participated in it and have paid a heavy price in martyrdom. Only the perverse and blind will say that the Vishva Hindu Parishad is the originator of this struggle. VHP represents only the latest reincarnation or organised manifestation of this centuries old Hindu aspiration. (VHP n.d., i)

In this essay, I take the "perverse and blind" position that the Sangh did play a constitutive role in the events leading up to the destruction of the Babri Masjid. I wish to examine the Sangh campaign as an enormously successful mobilization in which an aggressive, risky, and adept manipulation of cultural symbols through a variety of mass media provoked widespread popular response, transformed the marginal VHP into a major religious-cultural organization, and generated considerable electoral gains for the BJP. The organizers put forth a complex message calculated to appeal to differing audiences, found ways to pose difficult dilemmas for the ruling authorities, and advanced themselves as a viable alternative to the current political powers.

I will focus on the chariot procession of 1990 as the key initiative of the campaign, and examine the visual and verbal rhetoric of the mobilization. My primary sources for this essay, beyond my own brief personal sighting of the chariot in New Delhi, are the journalistic accounts of the yatra in India's English-language media, supplemented by public statements of the yatra leaders.[1] Admittedly, there are limitations to basing an essay

1. Specifically, I assembled a scrapbook drawn from four English-language newspapers (*The Hindu, Hindustan Times, Indian Express,* and *Times of India*) and four periodicals (*Front-*

on these sources. However, for a study of modern Indian media politics, print journalism offers a rich point of departure, particularly in an event that was covered and commented upon so extensively.

## Iconography and Iconology

Since the procession of Rama's chariot was an image-saturated cultural event, it makes sense to turn to a method of analysis centrally concerned with the interpretation of visual imagery. In his classic 1939 exposition of the iconographical method, the art historian Erwin Panofsky suggested that we separate our responses to works of visual art into three analytic levels: (1) the "primary or natural subject matter," the pre-iconographical reception and identification of forms; (2) the "secondary or conventional subject matter," the motifs and figures we recognize through conventional association as referring to culturally known themes, concepts, and narratives; and (3) the "intrinsic meaning or content," the underlying principles that "reveal the basic attitude of a nation, a period, a class, a religious or philosophical persuasion" (Panofsky 1955, 28–30). He proposed that the term "iconography" be restricted to discussions of the second stratum, while investigation aiming to explicate "intrinsic meaning" be known as "iconology"—a distinction that has never been strictly observed in art history.

I want to follow, more or less, Panofsky's suggested itinerary, from perceptual recognition through cultural explication to synthetic formulation, in discussing Rama's chariot and its excursion across north India. However, I will modify Panofsky's original formulation. Panofsky developed his approach for decoding visual artworks of the past, where only limited contemporary documentation may be available to modern art historians. Here instead we will be considering a cultural performance that evoked a great deal of easily available verbal commentary and debate. This allows a richer, but also less definitive, discussion of visual significances embodied in the event.

The Rath Yatra employed a large array of conventional Indian motifs

line, *India Today*, *Sunday*, and *The Week*), plus two American publications, *India Abroad* and the *New York Times*. I thank Jyothi Thottam and Mytheli Sreenivas for collecting and sharing Indian printed materials during summer 1992 and summer 1993, and the librarians of Sterling Memorial Library at Yale for allowing me to clip their 1990 runs of four Indian newspapers. I would also like to thank Linda Hess and James Lochtefeld for sharing their unpublished essays on the VHP-BJP campaign with me.

and figures to evoke religious themes and historical narratives. For Panofsky, iconography involved finding a correct match of icon (motif, figure) to referent (theme, narrative). Yet, as most contemporary art historians have come to recognize, icons may well be multivalent, historically mutable, and open to political disputation, which obviates any single correct or final interpretation. During the Rath Yatra certain images, such as the lotus emblem, weapons, and Rama himself, became points of interpretive contention, with very serious consequences. The lotus emblem featured so prominently on the rath, for instance, received a hearing before the Election Commission when a leader of the Congress-I Party charged that Yatra organizers were using the BJP's election symbol for religious purposes. The prime minister commented dryly, "When did Rama move around with the election symbol?" Accordingly, this essay will concern itself as much with the verbal discourse concerning visual images as with the images themselves. At the same time, I will argue that iconographic indeterminacy in fact offered strategic and rhetorical advantages to those who organized the yatra.

When ascending to the third level of iconology, we need to make another adjustment. Panofsky wished to place this level of synthetic interpretation "above the sphere of the conscious volition" of the actors involved, as a "symptom" of an existing personality, civilization, religious attitude, or the like. This implies a model of representation where certain essences (in this case they would be "Hinduism," "Hindu-Muslim antagonism," and so on) exist to be represented, and it locates the iconographer in a privileged position to ascertain the unthought-but-essential significance of the objects for analysis.

In discussing the Rath Yatra, by contrast, I will stress not only the conscious agency of those who organized the procession, but also the operative or performative character of their actions. Their iconographic choices were more often strategic than representational. The participants were not reflecting some preexisting state of affairs, but seeking to call into being something that did not exist previously. In selecting a heterogeneous assortment of conventional Hindu images, they were not iconologically expressing an existing "Hinduism," but rather, they were proposing and through their actions attempting to create a new formation, a reconstruction of Hinduism. The physical structure toward which the processors aimed—the Ram janmabhoomi—was an imagined construction; and the figurative goals they sought—Hindu unity and *Rama-rajya* (utopia)— were new religious and political configurations. Yet just as the new Ram janmabhoomi temple would be modeled on a 1950 recreation of a twelfth-century north Indian temple, so the moral state the mobilizers aimed to engender was also projected into the past, as an ancient configuration of moral order that had been temporarily displaced but now, by their efforts, would be restored.

## The Primary Terms

Let us begin this iconographical explication with the primary figures of the performance. In April 1984, the Vishva Hindu Parishad (World Hindu Congress) convened a large gathering of Hindu religious figures in Delhi, calling it a Dharma Sansad ("Assembly of the Faith"). This meeting issued a unanimous resolution for the "liberation" of three temple sites in north India, at Mathura, Varanasi, and Ayodhya, and chose to focus initial efforts on the Ram janmabhoomi in Ayodhya.

The call for the liberation of this site rested on three primary tenets: (1) the god Rama was actually and physically born on that exact place; (2) an ancient Hindu temple formerly stood at that place commemorating Rama's birthplace; and (3) the Mughal conqueror Babar through his henchman Mir Baqi had leveled the temple in the early sixteenth century and constructed a mosque atop the ruins. (The factuality of these claims has been the subject of serious historiographical debate: see Bakker 1986, Gopal 1991, Elst 1990.) The VHP proposed, by way of compensatory justice, to destroy or move the mosque so that a new temple could be constructed on the site to house an enlivened image of the god Rama. The posters announcing the Rath Yatra in Delhi referred in condensed imagery to this program with its two illustrations of the bow-wielding deity Rama and an architectural model of the proposed temple.

The choice of site, then, juxtaposes two figures well known to most people in north India, Rama and Babar. God and human, they are made to stand for two religions—Hinduism and Islam—in a highly imbalanced manner.

Rama is an incarnation (*avatar*) of Vishnu, "The Preserver" in the present-day Hindu trinity, who entered into the world to preserve moral order (dharma). The VHP most often depicts Rama in an aggressive posture, striding forward with bow ready for combat, a vigorous slayer of demons who defeats evil to stabilize the world order. Rama is the Hindu god most amenable to utopian projects, for in the epic *Ramayana* he created the state regime (*rajya*) that most completely instantiated dharma on earth, Rama-rajya. So it is noteworthy that the VHP selected Ayodhya for its agitations over many other sites of temple-destruction where historical evidence is much more certain, including the Krishna birth temple (*janmasthan*) at Mathura and the Kashi Vishwanath Shiva temple at Benares (Varanasi). As a morally transparent, interventionist, this-worldly, human deity, Rama serves the rhetorical purposes of the VHP better than any other deity of the Hindu pantheon, certainly better than the lovable-but-untrustworthy Krishna or the often-remote and nonhuman Shiva.

In the vision of the Sangh, Rama was singled out to represent much more than one deity among many. They advanced him as the primary metonym of Hindu India. As Advani wrote in the opening words of the 1993 BJP *White Paper*: "Sri Rama is the unique symbol, the unequalled symbol of our oneness, or our integration, as well as of our aspiration to live the higher values. As Maryada Purushottam Sri Rama has represented for thousands of years the ideal of conduct, just as Rama Rajya has always represented the ideal of governance" (BJP 1993, 1). The first person plural of Advani's statement denotes the Hindu community of India, following the Hindu nationalist definition first set forth by V. D. Savarkar, ideological progenitor of the RSS, in the 1920s. As Daniel Gold has pointed out, "a Hindu means a person who regards this land of Bharatvarsha from the Indus to the Seas, as his Fatherland as well as his Holyland"; this definition includes geographical, genealogical, and religious constituents—all of which, we will see, play an important role in Sangh iconography (Gold 1991, 549; see also S. Sarkar, below).

Of course, the Rama of Indian religious history is a more complex figure, who reappears in various guises at various moments in history. As the sixteenth-century poet Tulsidas put it in his *Ramcharitmanas*,

wise men who hear this marvelous story are not astonished, for they realize that there is no limit to the number of Rama's stories in the world. This is what they believe, that Rama has come down to earth in many forms and that there are a thousand million *Ramayanas* of measureless length. High sages have sung in different aeons and various ways the glorious acts of Hari. (W. D. P. Hill 1952, 22)

Rama's varied historical legacy has in fact allowed others who have opposed or questioned the Sangh project to contest the VHP's simplified depiction of Rama by bringing out other aspects that were obscured by the Sangh's characterization. For example, Madhu Kishwar argued in the feminist journal *Manushi* that "the Ram we imbibed as children bears no resemblance to the BJP-RSS incarnation. He continued to love and respect Kaikeyi as his own mother even though she got him banished. . . . We were taught that he triumphed over Ravan with moral force rather than through his superior skills as a warrior" (Kishwar 1990, 7, quoted in Hess 1994). Reciprocally, the Sangh sought to control the identity of Rama. So, when a touring cultural exhibition about Ayodhya featured a panel based on an early Buddhist version of the Rama story where Rama and Sita are brother and sister rather than husband and wife, BJP members raised strong objections in Parliament to this "anti-Hindu" representation.

Babar was the founder of the Mughal dynasty, the most powerful of all Islamic regimes in India. He was a Turko-Mongol conqueror who came from beyond the Hindu Kush and defeated the existing ruler of Delhi to establish a new polity. The Sangh never portrays Babar himself visually, but rather represents him iconically through "his" masjid, the residue of his alleged act of conquering iconoclasm. More significantly, this action is viewed not as a contingent personal or political act, but as an expression of principles inherent in Islam itself, repeatedly enacted by Muslim warriors. For Sangh purposes, therefore, Babar serves as a fitting synecdoche for the entire historical legacy of Muslim conquest and rule in India as a foreign occupation.

The alleged temple and mosque commemorate two very different events. The Ram janmabhoomi honors a birth, or more precisely an avatar, a "crossing down" of divinity into human form to institute a unifying dharma, a righteous social and cosmic order. According to Sangh history, the Babri Masjid celebrates a conquest, a forcible conversion of the site, an act of violence and disunity. All this points to a contrast between Rama's "Hindu" world order and a "Muslim" world order established by Babar, each projected as a distinct historical epoch. The Sangh portrays the first as peaceful, tolerant, autochthonous, and assimilative, and the second as violent, intolerant, heterogeneous, alien to India, and communally divisive. If the pre-Muslim order was fundamentally and harmoniously based on dharma, the advent of Islam in the subcontinent disrupted that ancient harmony. "It is the invasion by fanatic religious statecraft that intervened and introduced inter-religious disharmony and hatred towards all indigenous faiths" (BJP 1993, 15). The "fanatic intervention" is symbolized in physical terms by the Muslim practice of temple destruction and site appropriation, leaving behind mosques that still serve as "provocative ocular reminders of that violent and barbaric invasion."

Finally, Sangh rhetoric identifies these as distinct religious, ethnic, and even national moieties in contemporary India. As the BJP member of Parliament Pramod Mahajan put it when addressing the Rath Yatra procession crowd at Ajmer, "Are you children of Babar or Ram, Akbar or Rana Pratap, Aurangzeb or Shivaji? Those who do not answer this question properly have no right to be in this country" (Padmanabhan and Sidhva 1990, 60). By juxtaposing foreign Mughal conquerors with indigenous Hindu heroes, Mahajan is able to provide a clear-cut exclusionary definition of national citizenship that collapses genealogical descent into religious affiliation. Though well over 90 percent of Indian Muslims are in fact descendants of indigenous converts, Mahajan implicitly classifies all as "children of Babar," outside the Hindu, and therefore Indian, family.

The fundamental terms of the Sangh version of Indian history, then, are set forth in the clear dichotomy of two figures, made to represent two contrasted world orders and two national communities. Iconographically they evoke an uncompleted narrative of a golden age and a historical fall brought about through the activities of Babar and other Muslim invaders. This historical wrong remains embodied in the continuing physical presence of Babar's mosque. Evoking the well-known narrative of Rama's own life told in the epic *Ramayana*, where Rama slays the great demon Ravana in order to rescue his wife Sita and restore world order, the Sangh casts these Muslim invaders, and by extension all Indian Muslims, into the role of demons. And just as the story of Rama must not end with Ravana's dominion, so the Sangh places itself in the position of bringing its own narrative to a fitting conclusion. Through a compensatory act of destruction and reconstruction, the Sangh sets out to right the historical wrong by reappropriating Rama's birthplace for Rama, reconverting it to its "original" and therefore essential significance. Within this dramatic eschatology, the Sangh and its army of "voluntary workers" (*kar sevak*s) could look upon their activities not only as acts of devotion to Rama, but also as repetitions of Rama's own demon-destroying, dharma-creating paradigmatic activity.

## Nationalizing the Issue

The fact that a mosque stood in Rama's supposed birthplace may have held symbolic potency for Hindu fundamentalist groups like the VHP. Yet in 1984, when the VHP undertook its liberation campaign, it did not seem inevitable or even likely that the campaign would succeed. The VHP claimed that Hindus had vigorously sought to reclaim the janmabhoomi site for many centuries, but in fact it had seldom been more than a local or regional concern, and the issue had been dormant for over thirty years.

An inscription inside the Babri Masjid at Ayodhya records that one Mir Baqi, a member of Babar's court, built the mosque at Babar's command in 1528. However, there is no certain evidence to show that the Babri Masjid became a site of religious conflict until the mid–nineteenth century, nor is there any clear indication that anyone in Ayodhya before that time believed the masjid stood on the exact place of Rama's birth. In Ayodhya, a pilgrimage city closely identified with Rama, several places claimed to be Rama's birthplace. During the period of heightened tension and violence throughout north India surrounding the Revolt of 1857, a controversy between local Hindus and Muslims first brought the masjid into dispute.

Near the Babri Masjid stands the Hanuman Garhi temple, devoted to the monkey warrior Hanuman, one of Rama's most devoted followers. In 1855 a group of Sunni Muslims led by Gulam Hussain claimed that the Hanuman temple occupied the site where a mosque had formerly stood. Hussain and his followers advanced on the temple, but Hindu ascetic warriors (*bairagis*) who occupied the temple fought off the attack and pursued the Sunni assailants back to their refuge in Babar's mosque, the Babri Masjid. (See Pinch, below.) After punishing the attackers, the bairagis made no attempt to hold the masjid. Two years later, however, the *mahant* (abbot) of the Hanuman Garhi temple apparently decided that the best defense against Muslim claims on his temple might be an offensive against their neighboring holy spot. During the great revolt in north India against the British government in 1857, the mahant took over a part of the mosque compound and erected a raised platform there. This platform, he proclaimed, marked the site of Rama's birth. Local Muslims complained to the government repeatedly about the Hindu platform in their mosque courtyard, but there it remained.

The identification of the Babri Masjid site as the Ram janmabhoomi and the narrative of Babar's destruction of a Rama temple to build his mosque probably originated in this mid–nineteenth-century dispute. In 1866, H. M. Elliot wrote that Babar had demolished a famous Rama temple in Ayodhya, and from that point on, British accounts of Ayodhya accepted this as a fact (S. Srivastava 1991, 47). In the 1880s, the mahant of the Hanuman temple at Ayodhya sought to gain possession of the land where Babar's mosque stood by legal means. He wanted to build a temple over the platform, which he still identified as the janmabhoomi, and he needed the extra space. Seeking to avert unnecessary conflict between local religious communities, the British judge turned down the mahant's suit, and nothing much further happened at the site for almost fifty years. During communal riots in 1934, the dome of the mosque was damaged, but the government quickly repaired it.

In the aftermath of the partition and independence of India and Pakistan in 1947, another time of communal conflict in north India, a group called the All-India Ramayana Assembly (Akhil Bharatiya Ramayana Mahasabha) launched an agitation outside the Babri Masjid. The Mahasabha held a continuous nine-day recital of Tulsidas's *Ramcharitmanas* in front of the mosque in 1949, drawing thousands of people from the surrounding area. On the night of December 22, 1949, an image of Rama appeared surreptitiously inside Babar's mosque. The agitators immediately declared it a miraculous manifestation of the god and urged Hindus to enter the mosque to worship Rama. Civil order in Ayodhya turned precarious, and for a brief moment the fate of the Babri Masjid became an issue of national political concern. Prime Minister Jawaharlal Nehru and Deputy Prime Minister Vallabhai Patel advised local officials on different courses of action to resolve the problem. The issue entered the courts, and in 1950 the judges enforced an uneasy truce, which allowed the Rama image to remain inside the mosque. This effectively closed down the masjid as a site for Muslim worship, while also making it difficult for Hindus to worship Rama at the site they now considered to be his birthplace.

Unsatisfying as this legal solution may have been for both religious communities in Ayodhya, it held up for more than thirty years, until the VHP decided to resurrect the old dispute. Until then, the controversy over the Ayodhya site had been largely parochial and largely forgotten. The VHP's task was to advance the liberation of Rama's birthplace as a compelling issue of national significance. Their problem was that the VHP itself remained a small, peripheral religious organization with limited resources and cadres.

The Vishva Hindu Parishad was founded in 1964 by Swami Chinmayanand under the instigation of the RSS. His aim was to unite various Hindu religious figures and organizations around common goals and projects, and more ambitiously to create an umbrella organization that would unify Hinduism itself. Behind this aim was the assumption that Hindu "disunity"—its long tradition of religious pluralism, nonecclesiasticism, and tolerance for other views and practices—had contributed to the "weakness" of indigenous rulers, allowing a long succession of "foreign" invaders to gain and maintain political control in India over a subject Hindu majority.

For nearly two decades, however, the VHP remained on the peripheries, working in the northeast Indian states of Assam and Nagaland, proselytizing against Christian missionary activity. Only in 1983, with its "sacrifice for unanimity" (*ekatmata yajna*), did the VHP find ritual imagery with which they could reach a broad, national audience. In this "sacrifice," the VHP launched three processions throughout India, with trucks carrying large bronze water pots filled with water from the river Ganges. The Ganges water was distributed in villages and towns along the way, and the pots were then refilled from local sources of sacred water, such as temple tanks and river bathing places (*tirthas*), creating a pan-Indian reservoir of holy water. Employing a religious vocabulary drawn from Hindu pilgrimage and liturgical consecration, using the Ganges as a unifying metaphor for India as a sacred geographical entity, the VHP provided a compelling statement of the "Hindu unity" they aimed to engender (Seshadri 1988, 278–84).

In 1984, emboldened by the success of their "sacrifice for unanimity," the VHP decided to undertake a new and more sensitive project, the "liberation" of north Indian temple sites. The shift in imagery and strategy was clear: while the "sacrifice" stressed Hindu unity and only implicitly excluded Muslims by ignoring the sacred geography of Indian Islam, the temple liberation project indissolubly linked this Hindu unity with an active anti-Muslim rhetoric. To define and mobilize a Hindu community of faith, the VHP had decided, it would be important to identify an enemy. Far more widespread in their influence than the Christians of the northeast, Muslims would be cast as violators of the sacred homeland.

After a rather desultory opening move in the fall of 1984, suspended when Indira Gandhi was assassinated, the VHP developed a program that would involve a much larger part of Hindu India. The key image here would be the humble brick. VHP activists would ask Hindus all over India to make special bricks, inscribed with the words *Shri Rama*, for use in building the new Ram janmabhoomi temple. This was just the beginning. These bricks (*shila*) from throughout India would be consecrated locally in a ceremony (*puja*) called the *Ram shilan puja*, then collected and transported from their points of origin to Ayodhya in special chariots, like that of Rama. In Ayodhya, pilgrims and tourists could view the ever-increasing display of consecrated bricks, some in precious materials and some sent by Hindu organizations from abroad. Meanwhile activists would lay the foundations for the new Ram janmabhoomi temple with these consecrated bricks.

The brick program involved some of the same themes that had proven successful previously for the VHP. Here too a unified entity, now in a more solid medium, was to be created out of individual contributions from all over the country. Hindus of all regions and persuasions would engage in a common act of devotion to a single deity. As with many VHP actions, this program was simultaneously "traditional" in its vestments while highly innovative in form. As far as I am aware, no Hindu temple has ever been built with such a heterogeneous assortment of building materials, nor has the sponsor of a temple ever so explicitly involved the public at large in the building scheme. From the VHP perspective, the project allowed it to conduct a "mass contact" campaign as well as to keep up a continuous moral pressure, in the physical form of brick processions converging on Ayodhya, on the site and on government authorities. For local participants, the action did not require great personal commitment, since one could easily see the creating and consecrating of a brick as a small act of devotion to Rama, rather than an endorsement of the VHP.

Meanwhile, the VHP began producing and distributing other emblems that would spread the message of its campaign. Small stickers depicting Rama and the temple began to appear throughout north India. Hindu households were requested to fly banners of saffron, the color of renunciation, to signal their adherence to Hindu values. The syllable *Om*, taken as a unifying Hindu mantra, was painted on doors and worn in lockets. The VHP did not put its own signature on these ubiquitous visual products, but rather allowed them to appear as if they represented a spontaneous popular upsurge in Hindu devotional productivity (T. Basu et al. 1993, 60).

Perhaps the most resonant icon the VHP disseminated, however, was the depiction of baby Rama, the cherubic child held prisoner in a Muslim religious institution at the very site of his birth. The imagery again drew on the family as an overarching metaphor and enlisted another type of devotional sentiment on behalf of the mobilization. If the aggressive young warrior Rama of the posters served as a militant role model for Hindus taking control of their homeland, the infant Rama called upon maternal devotion from those who would nurture the young reincarnation of Hindu nationhood.

## The BJP and the Yatra Itinerary

As the "sacrifice for unanimity" led the VHP to undertake the more ambitious brick project, the success of that latter project induced them to plan a
much larger, more dramatic procession to Ayodhya in 1990. In September
1990, the Bharatiya Janata Party, responding to its own complex electoral
calculations, decided to join in the procession, fundamentally altering the
scope and complexion of the mobilization. Like the VHP, the BJP grew
out of the RSS and most of its leaders shared an RSS background and ideology, but its charge was different. The BJP was to operate primarily in the
sphere of electoral politics, and so it needed to pursue a more broad-based
and pragmatic rhetorical strategy.

With the much larger, respectable BJP participating, it was clear that
their leader, L. K. Advani, would ride on the podium of Rama's chariot,
and his auspicious, nonthreatening portrait would grace the rear of the
chariot. Yet the procession was planned jointly, with the VHP leadership
setting the stage and offering strategic advice behind the scenes. What is
most interesting from an iconographical point of view is the way in which
this double agency engendered a two-level message throughout the event.
"Hard-core" and "soft-core" imagery occurred side by side.

The hard-core imagery, for which the VHP and related groups were
primarily responsible, was religious, allusive, militant, masculine, and anti-
Muslim. Making much use of Rama as paradigm, it played out themes
inherent in the primary terms of the mobilization. The BJP and Advani
placed themselves often in the position of trying to reframe this imagery
or put a softer spin on it. They were successful in this, for as late as October 15, when the yatra had arrived in Delhi, the *Times of India* reported that
Prime Minister V. P. Singh believed the BJP had hijacked the procession
from the VHP and removed its threatening aspect. The soft-core message
the BJP sought to promulgate was, by contrast, political, realistic, and ostensibly inclusive, offering as an alternative opponent not Muslims as such,
but the "pseudo-secularists" who practice the "politics of appeasement" on
behalf of Muslims and other minorities.

This message-doubling held advantages for both parties. For the VHP
and kindred groups, the participation of the BJP ensured coverage of the
procession by major media, enabling them to project their message to a
much larger audience than had been previously possible. The BJP, on the
other hand, was able to disavow the more militant imagery as originating
from the VHP and so attempt to maintain its electoral respectability, while

at the same time profiting from the undoubted power and commitment that militant imagery evoked for some.

The procession of Rama's chariot was to leave from Somnath, on the Gujarat coast, in western India, on September 25, and cover some ten thousand kilometers in eight states over the next thirty-five days, until it reached Ayodhya on October 30 (see Map 1). Midway, the procession would pass through Delhi and take several days' rest in the capital. The itinerary showed every sign of careful planning for comprehensiveness, pacing, and symbolic value.

The choice of Somnath, in Gujarat State, as starting point for the procession was obviously significant. First, it was the site of the most famous episode of Muslim temple-destruction in India, by Mahmud of Ghazna in 1026. In the VHP's communalized history of Hindu-Muslim antipathy, therefore, Somnath occupied a preeminent position. Second, the ruined temple at Somnath had been rebuilt in 1950, as a symbol of Indian nationhood and Hindu dominance in Gujarat. From the BJP perspective, this event provided an important precedent for government compliance in the reconstruction of a disabled Hindu religious center. Advani portrayed the 1950 rebuilding of Somnath as the first chapter in a journey to "preserve the old symbols of unity, communal amity, and cultural oneness" (Vijapurkar 1990, 26). The liberation of the Ram janmabhoomi would be the second.

The route of the yatra was designed to pass through a maximum number of north Indian states. It would also pass through the centers of Sangh strength, while areas where the Sangh was weak, such as southern India, Bengal, and Kashmir, were conspicuously omitted from the itinerary. Geographically the journey would carve out a representation of the Hindi heartland, political center of the Indian nation-state and primary electoral target of BJP campaigning.

The choice to pass through Delhi en route to Ayodhya, too, was multiply determined. At the time, the English-language press portrayed it as an opportunity for midway negotiations between Advani and the government of V. P. Singh. Negotiations did take place. But the use of Delhi as a rest stop on the way elsewhere also implicitly disavowed the central government as the sole source of legitimating authority in the Indian polity. This also could be framed in either religious or political terms. For the VHP, Rama as the eponymous source for the utopian Rama-rajya enjoyed a higher authority than any state could. As the leader of a Rajasthani women's contingent put it as she was arrested, "Ram and not the govern-

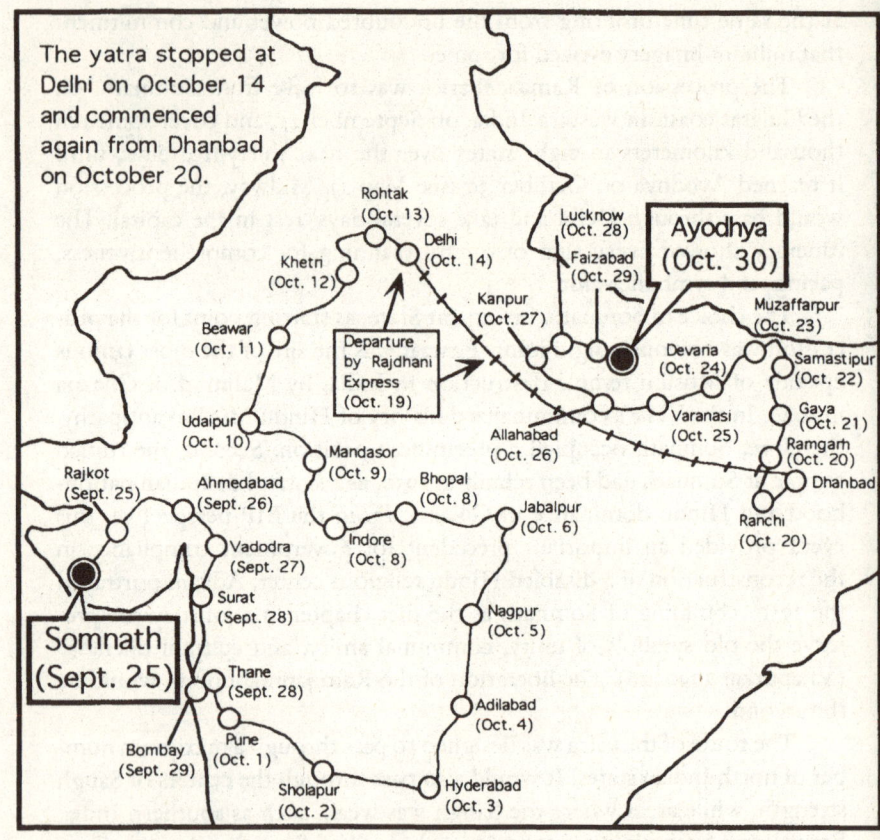

Map 1. The Rath Yatra route, September–October 1990.

ment is the keeper of our destiny" (Bedi 1990, 14). For the BJP, the message was political and populist; the democratic, grass-roots "people power" (*lok shakti*) focused on Ayodhya was positively contrasted with the elitist, inattentive ruling power (*raj shakti*) identified with Delhi (P. K. Roy 1990, 26).

According to the schedule, the procession was to depart from Somnath during the major Hindu festival of *Navaratri* ("Nine Nights") and arrive in Ayodhya on *Debothan Ekadashi*, another holy day (See Map 1). The ritual calendar was not used just to assure an auspicious journey, however, but also to serve certain tactical purposes. On Debothan Ekadashi, several hundred thousand pilgrims regularly come to Ayodhya for the annual ritual circumambulation of the city (*Panch Koshi Parikrama*). By having the Rath Yatra converge on Ayodhya the same day, the planners of the procession sought to swell their own numbers and at the same time pose a quandary for security forces guarding the Babri Masjid. The guards could not easily quarantine the area from Ram janmabhoomi activists without also excluding *Panch Koshi Parikrama* pilgrims, who viewed their circumambulation as the redemption of a pledge to the gods and would not take kindly to police preventing its fulfillment. (See Pinch and Freitag, below, on the political importance of festivals.)

## The Procession in Action

In a typical Hindu religious procession, a god embodied in a portable image is taken from the inner precincts of a temple, placed on a chariot, taken out to tour his or her domains, and finally returned to the temple sanctum. In comparison to liturgical practice inside the temple, such processions are relatively public and inclusive, inviting broader participation in worship than is possible or desirable inside. Processions are relatively open-ended and free-form ritually. They allow various participants to find modes of devotional expression suitable to their means and styles. Temple processions are explicitly concerned with ritual sovereignty, since the god is framed as a lord touring, displaying, and enforcing rule over his or her domain.

Some BJP politicians sought to deny the religious lineage of the Rath Yatra. The moderate A. B. Vajpayee, for example, compared the procession to Mohandas Gandhi's famous Salt March, with its moral and petitionary dimension. In 1930, Gandhi marched to the sea to pressure the British to rescind the salt tax; this was one of the key events in Gandhi's civil disobedience campaign and India's struggle for independence (Farmer, below). The rath did not carry a consecrated image, nor was Rama even depicted on the chariot. However, the procession quickly took on a ceremonial life of its own, often outside the control of the BJP leadership. Like a religious procession, the Rath Yatra evoked a range of degrees of participation, from the passive polite applause of the South Delhi cosmopolitans, to more devotional viewing and active offerings of worship, to such ardent vow-like actions as lip-piercing. Many along the route clearly took the chariot as a vehicle or mobile temple of Rama himself, even without the consecrated presence of an image, and honored it accordingly with coconuts, incense, sandalwood, and all the offerings of worship proper to a divine object.

Advani acknowledged and even celebrated the devotional character of the response to the procession. As he announced to his audience, "Many of the people that crowded the roadsides to welcome this rath hadn't even heard of me or the BJP. They came out of sentiment for Lord Ram" (Padmanabhan and Sidhva 1990, 60). Yet he also tried to play down the mythical statements that the rath engendered. When some began to ascribe irresistible ritual power to the rath, as Rama's own vehicle, Advani chastised them with crisp realism: "What is this rath but a mere DCM-Toyota? Anybody can stop it with the use of force" (Padmanabhan and Sidhva 1990, 32). In line with his softening role, he spoke of converting devotion to Rama (*Rama bhakti*) into national power (*rashtra shakti*), as if the purpose of the procession was to redirect the religious energies catalyzed by the procession into the political domain (N. K. Singh 1990, 57).

As Devi Lal, a prominent opponent of the yatra, suggested in Parliament, a better historical precedent for the Rath Yatra might lie in the sphere of royal ceremonial, such as the ancient horse sacrifice or the medieval royal military progress, where a king and his armed forces would venture out from the capital on a tour of subjugated territory, challenging all would-be rulers to battle. Geographical movement, military display, and provocation were all central features of the Rath Yatra too. Here too, religious ritual was employed to make political statements about authority. Yet the analogy requires a significant modification, for Advani and the BJP, though part of the ruling coalition, were not autonomous rulers. Once again, the imagery was more performative than representational. As Advani spoke of converting devotion into ruling power electorally, the procession itself sought to displace ruling authority symbolically away from elected officials onto the leaders of the yatra.

With Advani active in the driver's seat of Rama's chariot, V. P. Singh and his ruling National Front government found themselves in a dilemma. The procession posed a provocation that could not be ignored. Growing disorder, riots, and final destruction of the mosque loomed ahead. Yet there would be serious consequences to stopping it. Not only would Singh have to act against Rama, but he would also bring down his own ruling coalition and risk still greater disorder. The dramatic personal political confrontation between Advani and Singh became the primary narrative frame in press coverage of the Rath Yatra. The chariot kept moving toward its destination, with Advani maintaining the initiative. When Advani boldly took up Rama's bow, symbol of legitimate authority, Singh found himself cast in metaphoric position of Rama's opponent Ravana. Held passive by unpalatable choices, he dithered in Delhi. Civil disturbances grew apace.

## Weapons and Blood

The most heated split between the hard and soft lines within the procession occurred over the imagery of militant violence and blood sacrifice. Conspicuous in all coverage of the Rath Yatra were young men holding primitive weapons like bows and tridents. Here it was the young militants of the youth wing of the VHP, the Bajrang Dal, who challenged the BJP elders. Employing a Shaiva ritual vocabulary, Bajrang Dal activists were given an initiation prior to participating in the procession, during which they received a trident and took a vow "to protect women, temples, and religion from 'the irreligious.'" As Neeladri Bhattacharya (1991, 129) notes, the god Shiva here more suitably expresses "the new militant, aggressive spirit of Hindutva," willing to destroy in service of a subsequent recreation, where Rama is seen as too constrained by his duty as a ruler to maintain the existing order of things. Yet the Bajrang Dal militants also located themselves within the guiding narrative of the *Ramayana* by naming themselves "Hanuman's Troops," Rama's monkey army. To enforce the analogy, Hanuman himself—or one of the activists dressed up as the great monkey warrior—frequently accompanied the procession.

The young activists tried to incorporate Advani into their iconography of violence. At Ujjain, they presented him with weapons, and they often welcomed him by applying a ritual mark (*tilak*) of blood on his forehead. Sometimes Advani went along with the atmosphere of youthful enthusiasm and pageantry. Unlike the Bajrang Dal youth, however, Advani was aware of a larger audience he hoped to reach with a more moderate political message. Early on in the procession, the *Times of India* chastised him in an editorial for wielding a replica of Vishnu's irresistible discus weapon (*sudarshana chakra*), and so, most commonly, Advani maintained the posture of a respectable upper-class urban Hindu, in starched white traditional garb (*kurta* and dhoti), seeming to disdain the more fervid displays surrounding him. When a ritual potful of blood was presented to him, Advani asked his party functionaries to send out word that such offerings were not acceptable. In Delhi, he publicly scolded the Bajrang Dal for overzealousness and urged them to put away their weapons.

At the same time, Advani defended all the participants in the procession from outside critics. When asked about the profusion of tridents and bows around him, Advani could feign surprise: "What, are they weapons in the days of the AK-47?" (Vijapurkar 1990, 23). Surrounded by Indian police forces outfitted with modern weaponry, the youthful display of weapons more suited to ancient warfare embodied only a symbolic promise of aggression without constituting an actual threat—or so the BJP spokesmen could claim. Of course, the ambiguity of these symbolic armaments posed an interpretive as well as practical challenge for the civil authorities, since tridents could indeed serve as rather effective implements in the street battles that often surrounded the procession. When does an icon become a weapon?

The press could portray the procession as a civilized, Rama-like Advani leading his motley troops of Bajrang Dal activists, his monkey army, into battle. Like Rama, Advani was apparently willing to turn a blind eye to some of their militant activities, so long as they did not get close enough to tarnish his reputation for upright conduct. An aura of potential—and frequently actual—violence around the perimeters of the procession did not hurt at all, provided Advani could maintain his own position of blamelessness and mild disavowal for any disorders.

## Identifying the Enemy

The iconography of ancient warfare and Advani's soft-peddling of it corresponded to two different ways of situating the Rath Yatra and the Ayodhya campaign into overarching structures of historical meaning. These two narratives in turn identified two different enemies. The mythical war against demonized Muslims that the Bajrang Dal and the VHP were fighting was not quite the same as the political struggle that Advani and the BJP were waging against the Indian government. Yet in the end they were two parts of a single agenda.

The stronger narrative of the VHP, derived from the primary terms of the mobilization, placed the yatra within a strongly dualistic vision of history pitting indigenous Hindus against foreign Muslims. Here, as we have seen, Rama and the original temple represented a dehistoricized Hindu utopia; Babar and his mosque represented the Muslim invasions that brought the Rama-rajya to an end and began a series of oppressive foreign occupations. This great historical wrong required an act of redemptive violence directed at a Muslim holy object, and in a broader sense it required a forceful subordination of the present-day Muslim minority in India.

For an outside observer like myself, the most perplexing feature of the mobilization was the depth of anger engendered among VHP activists and sympathizers by its anti-Muslim polemic. Muslims constitute a minority of about 12 percent of the Indian population, and for the most part form a poor, dispersed, politically insignificant, and unthreatening religious minority. What could cause such a hysterical reaction toward these people? To answer this question properly, we need an ethnography of contemporary communal response as well as a cultural history of Muslim imagery in India. (See Basu, T. Sarkar, M. Hasan, and van der Veer, below.) Here, I offer a few observations on the way that Muslims were represented during the Ayodhya campaign.

Like many fundamentalist movements worldwide, the VHP required a worthy adversary to warrant its dichotomizing strategy of confrontation, and accordingly they aggrandized, reified, and mythologized their Islamic antagonist (Marty and Appleby 1991, 820). They did this first by referring primarily to past Muslims, as in Pramod Mahajan's dual genealogy where all Indian Muslims are cast as the children of Babar, Akbar, and Aurangzeb, formidable and aggressive conquerors all. Framing Muslim identity around a history of medieval conquest and iconoclasm embodied in the persons of Mughal rulers, rather than the social state of contemporary Muslims, rendered the Indian Muslim community much more of a threat.

The VHP portrays religious macrocommunities like Hinduism and Islam as homogeneous and continuous over time. Linking genealogy with religion, the VHP sees present-day Indian Muslims as morally responsible for the past deeds of Islamic warriors, as sons may be held liable for their fathers' debts. "Muslims should understand what kind of message they are sending by insisting on continuing the occupation of our sacred places, an occupation which was started by fanatics and mass-murderers like Babar and Aurangzeb" (VHP n.d., 32). The VHP suggests that the Muslim community freely return the Hindu sacred sites to their original proprietors "to make up voluntarily for the huge massacres, persecutions, slave-takings, abductions, temple-destructions and swordpoint conversions which its earlier generations inflicted upon Hindu society, as on other non-Muslim communities both in India and elsewhere" (VHP n.d., 31).

The BJP leadership tried to distance itself from the widespread demonizing of Muslims by publicly exhibiting a more inclusive policy. The driver of the rath was a Muslim. The yatra would stop at select Muslim

holy sites. The enemy is not Muslims, Advani would claim, but rather the
"politics of appeasement" pursued by "pseudo-secularists." The milder historical narrative promulgated by the BJP located the yatra within the story
of postindependence Indian politics.

According to the BJP, the relevant disjuncture in Indian history came
about not through medieval invasion, but through a mental "digression."

The nation in India always remained Hindu, whether the State was controlled
by Turks, Afghans, Mughals, Portuguese, French, English or Nehruvian Secularists. The Ayodhya movement became relevant and inevitable when the postindependence digression in the national mind seriously undermined the ethos and
traditions of the nation in India, and as a result, the state and the nation again got
virtually divorced by the rupture of national identity and the mindless adoption of
the Western as the modern. (BJP 1993, 15)

Who was responsible for the divorce? The BJP blamed not the "fanatics and mass murderers" of the VHP formulation, but rather Jawaharlal
Nehru for diverting Indian nationalism in the postindependence period.
He did not act alone. Rather he is held most responsible for introducing
the Western concept of "secularism" into Indian political culture, and this
foreign concept is the real demon. "The theory and practice of secularism (an intra-religious evolution in the West which had no application to
a multi-religious situation which always existed and existed peacefully till
the invaders arrived in this great nation) resulted in greater erosion of our
national identity and national consciousness than ever under the rule of
the invaders" (12–13). From here it is a small step to Hindu populism. The
Westernized political and cultural elite of the capital are transformed into
an occupying Other, who show a "callous unconcern . . . towards the sentiments of the overwhelming majority in this country—the Hindus" (BJP
1993, 13).

This history of ideas did not lend itself to dramatic visual presentation
evidently. In the half-page advertisements that the BJP placed in English-
language newspapers during the Rath Yatra, two small depictions of the
proposed temple and the BJP lotus emblem appear at the bottom, overwhelmed by the verbal contents above. The headline of the ad poses the
rhetorical question "What does Secularism mean?" and allows the reader
multiple choices. The first four possible answers involve "forfeiting the
rights of the majority," "appeasement of minorities at all costs," and the
like; the fifth, presumably correct response is "fair and reasonable treatment of people of all faiths." Of course this is the policy the BJP claims for

itself, while the "secular" policies of the Indian government since the time of Nehru are redesignated here as "pseudo-secular."

Different as they may initially appear, the two narratives converged on crucial points. Both viewed the Rath Yatra and the Ayodhya mobilization as a matter of "national identity." Both claimed this identity to be fundamentally grounded in the "Hindu ethos," portrayed as an ahistorical cultural essence of India and the fundamental basis for the Indian nation-state. Both identified moments of historical rupture, brought about through foreign penetrations—whether they be invading Central Asian warriors or insidious Western concepts. Both understood the liberation of Rama's birthplace as a symbolic instrument of restoration, of overcoming and resubordinating all foreign elements. Both therefore looked beyond this campaign to a more far-reaching aim: an autonomous national sovereignty, which they designated as a Hindu dominion (*Hindurashtra*) or the righteous regime of Rama (Rama-rajya), based on an "assimilative Hindu cultural nationhood." Religious vision and political agenda united.

## Sangh Hinduism

Prominent in all coverage of the Rath Yatra and of VHP conclaves were ranks of saffron-robed holy men. Seated on platforms or grouped around sacrificial altars, these venerable-looking sadhus with their necklaces of prayer beads, long beards, and ash-marked foreheads provided a strong visual counterpoint to the young militants of the Bajrang Dal. Evoking one of the most distinctive features of Indian religious history, here were present-day embodiments of the ancient lineages of Hindu sages and ascetics, suddenly returning to public life. (See Pinch, below.)

Despite BJP leadership, the Rath Yatra was dominated by religious imagery—from the primary terms of the procession, through the ritual idiom of pilgrimage, sacrifice, and initiation, to the devotional responses toward Rama's chariot. Even the displays of military zeal were dressed not in the vestments of modern armies or guerrilla warfare, but rather in costuming and weaponry appropriate to ancient religious texts. The ubiquitous saffron flags, the repetitive use of the Hindu mantra *Om*, and virtually all visual iconography were drawn from religious sources. Together, they promoted the claim that the movement to liberate Rama's supposed birthplace spoke for all Hindus, for Hinduism itself.

Many commentators and scholarly analysts have argued that this fabric of religious imagery was merely a cover, a cynical exploitation of the religious sentiments of Indian people for political ends. Even Advani seems to have shared this view some of the time, as when he spoke of turning Rama devotion into state power. And indeed, the BJP electoral calculations seem prescient, at least in the short run, for their promotion of the Ayodhya issue did earn them significant electoral gains.

These charges of exploitation rest upon the premise of a clear-cut distinction between religion and politics, and on the assumption that religion ought to be confined to the private domain while politics concern itself with organizing the public life of the community. These attitudes, of course, are the intellectual and moral products of a specific set of European historical events: the Reformation, the religious wars of early modern Europe, and the Enlightenment (van der Veer 1994a and below). Yet these Western premises, shared by many in the Indian political and intellectual establishment, are precisely what the VHP, and many in the BJP as well, would call into question. As with many fundamentalist movements worldwide, the VHP's central agenda is to relocate religious values as the defining principles of public life.

By way of summary, therefore, it will be most productive to reiterate the kind of religious worldview the VHP and other groups in the Sangh brotherhood promote. Ultimately the role of the BJP in the Indian electoral system will be decided more by program and leadership than mosque-destruction. What may well be more consequential are the long-term effects that the imagery of the Rath Yatra and the ideology of the VHP may have on Hinduism. Hinduism is a modern social construction that is constantly being redefined, renegotiated, and reenacted by those who now call themselves Hindu. If the Rath Yatra and the Ayodhya mobilization revealed, iconologically, underlying principles of Hinduism as the Sangh would define it—not as a symptom, but as a purposeful reformulation based on existing cultural resources—what does that new form of Hinduism look like?

The VHP, we recall, began with the recognition of Hindu diversity and pluralism, viewing it as a problem to be overcome. For the VHP, the Ayodhya campaign was not a matter of favoring one among many Hindu deities and leaving the choice of worship to the individual devotee in common Hindu fashion. Sangh Hinduism does not intend to be another new religious formation under the capacious umbrella of Hinduism, promoting one of many deities, one of several theological viewpoints, or one of various methods of religious attainment. Rather, the VHP asserts that Rama's historical and current claims to the devotional allegiance of all Hindus is singular and unique, and it proposes Sangh Hinduism as an encompassing synthesis of all Hinduism into a single organized entity. Although the VHP recognizes this hegemonizing project as a goal to be accomplished, it also projects it backward in time. So a favorite substitute term for Hinduism in the Sangh lexicon is *sanatana dharma*, "eternal religion."

The VHP effort surely has never gone uncontested. Commentators at the time, for instance, charged it with attempting to "semiticize" Hinduism, ironically turning Hinduism into exactly the kind of Western monotheism the VHP most disdains. Even the designation "Toyota Hinduism" was meant to subvert their claims to ancientness and autochthony by alluding to the prominent use of a foreign-made piece of modern technology. Historians of Indian religions, myself included, frequently point to the historical diversity and pluralism of Hindu traditions, and to the recent, nineteenth-century coinage of the term and category "Hindu" as a bounded religious grouping. All this may be beside the point. A significant number of modern-day Hindus, quite understandably, want to construct their religion as historically ancient, cohesive, and centered, as a viable "world religion" in the international parliament of religions (McKean 1994).

The project of consciously reconstructing Hinduism is not new, of course. However, the VHP reformulation of Hinduism differs from earlier nineteenth- and twentieth-century Hindu reform movements, such as the Brahmo Samaj and Arya Samaj, which sought to identify a fundamental textual basis for reforming and modernizing Hinduism based on its most ancient and supposedly pure sources. The VHP, so far as I am aware, has not engaged in the kind of critical rereading of Hindu texts that earlier Hindu reformers did. Its strategy is synthetic and accumulative rather than reformist and purifying. It assembles items drawn from many sources and traditions. Unlike many fundamentalist groups, adherents of Sangh Hinduism do not draw a sharp distinction within the parent religion between the "truly devout" and others. Rather, they accept all Hindus, and construct minimal signs of affiliation, such as brick contributions and saffron flags. Their claim to articulate the values and aims of all Hindus is put forth more effectively through repetitive, cumulative imagery than through verbal argument. (See Freitag, below.)

Minimal signs and visual symbols offer an appropriate means for articulating membership within a religious community that is grounded in culture rather than conversion. The Sangh, we have seen, defines "Hindu-ness" geographically and genealogically, rather than through shared text or creed, so its ritual often takes the form of pilgrimage and its rhetoric leans heavily on family. So too the demarcation and exclusion of specific religious "others" is of central concern to a religious community where identity is problematic and organic unity is a primary goal. It is less their beliefs or even current practices, but rather their allegiance to religious ideologies that are foreign in origin and which once ruled "Hindu society" that makes modern-day Indian Muslims and Christians the target of the VHP's wrath.

The preference for autochthony over foreignness carries over into the Sangh's critique of what it sees as the prevailing worldview of the Indian political and intellectual elite, namely secularism or, rather, "pseudo-secularism." It can be turned as well against the analyses offered by observers who charge the Sangh with manipulating religion toward political ends, since the removal of religion from the public sphere is a secular and Western project that does not find its locus within Indian tradition. Likewise, Sangh spokesmen can argue that academic historians who question the historicity of claims concerning the Ram janmabhoomi are using "foreign" methods to dispute matters of deeply held Hindu belief. "No judge can give a verdict on the birthplace of Lord Rama, which is a matter of faith for Hindus," Advani claimed (*Indian Express*, 10 October 1990). It is the authority to enunciate that faith that the VHP and its affiliates most seek (see McKean 1996).

Accordingly, the most effective critique of Sangh Hinduism must come from within the Hindu community. The enactment of religious opposition was also part of the larger cultural performance of the Rath Yatra, though less prominent in media coverage. By reappropriating and reclaiming the shared iconographic resources of Indian culture, Hindus who did not share the xenophobia and violence of Sangh ideology can create alternative formulations around icons whose meanings are never final. As Tulsidas reminds us, the glorious acts of Rama may always be sung in new ways. Rama himself might even reappear, as he evidently did at a counter-demonstration in Bombay, to admonish the new captors seeking to fix his identity once and for all, and to demand that they "leave me alone" (*India Abroad*, October 19, 1990, p. 4).

# 2

# Mass Movement or Elite Conspiracy?
# The Puzzle of Hindu Nationalism

AMRITA BASU

WHICH SOCIAL FORCES WERE ULTIMATELY responsible for the Hindu nationalist campaign that culminated in the destruction of the mosque in Ayodhya on December 6, 1992, and the massacres of Muslims that accompanied it? Scholarly accounts that have analyzed Hindu nationalism have devoted surprisingly little attention to this question.[1] However, in the weeks following the tragedy, speculation about the actors and their motivations filled the editorial pages of the major Indian dailies and formed a staple of drawing-room discussions in New Delhi and elsewhere in India. Those who are most politically engaged have articulated the clearest responses: on the one hand, sympathizers contend that the Hindu nationalist campaign emerges from a spontaneous outpouring of mass support at the grass-roots level. On the other hand, secular north Indian intellectuals— ironically accused of elitism (D. Kumar 1994)—consider the Hindu nationalist campaign to be a product of cynical manipulation by political leaders.

From the "mass movement" perspective, the Bharatiya Janata Party (BJP) and its affiliates gave voice to deep-rooted antagonisms within In-

* I am grateful for research and writing support from the Amherst College Research Award and the John D. and Catherine T. MacArthur Foundation. Christophe Jaffrelot, Mark Kesselman, Atul Kohli, and David Ludden made helpful comments on an earlier draft of this essay. This essay draws upon research in India mainly in 1990–91 and more briefly in the winter of 1992–93. I have used pseudonyms to refer to the people I interviewed unless they were public officials who did not request anonymity.

1. Accounts of recent developments include Chibber and Mishra 1993; Ganguly 1993; Gopal 1991; Jaffrelot 1993; Parikh 1993; Thakur 1993; Varshney 1993; Rudolph and Rudolph 1993. Although I very much disagree with the contentions of Ashis Nandy (1990) and T. N. Madan (1987) that the growth of Hindu communalism can be attributed in part to the bankruptcy of secularism, I value their recognition that Hindu nationalism has achieved mass support and their attempt to explain why this is the case.

dian society: positively, to the expression of faith, which the secular state had allegedly attempted to suppress, and negatively, to persistent Hindu-Muslim enmity. If Hindus remained aggrieved by the possible destruction of a temple in the sixteenth century, the argument runs, resentments from the partition era, reignited by the conflict in Kashmir, were fresh in their minds. Ayodhya thus provided a critical means of extending the BJP's base from north to south, urban to rural areas, and the middle classes to the poor.

Conversely, from the "elite conspiracy" perspective, the Rashtriya Swayamsevak Sangh (RSS), Vishva Hindu Parishad (VHP), and BJP orchestrated the Ram janmabhoomi campaign with initially fragile and fleeting mass support. This explanation focuses on the BJP combine's recruitment and training of volunteer workers (kar sevaks) to destroy the mosque. As irrational as the violence was, it succeeded for a time in polarizing the electorate and providing the BJP with a Hindu "vote bank."

The notion of an elite conspiracy is appealing because it exonerates "ordinary" Hindus from responsibility for the violence. However, while it may provide an apt description of the early phases of the campaign, it does not adequately explain later phases, when mass mobilization occurred. More disturbing is the question of why "ordinary" Hindu men and women participated in numerous riots that perpetrated unspeakable brutality between 1990 and 1993. Even if the BJP instigated these riots, they occurred under sufficiently diverse conditions and were far enough removed from Ayodhya that the BJP could only be held fully responsible for them in moral terms. (On riot violence, see van der Veer, below.)

At the other end of the spectrum, the "mass movement approach" mistakenly identifies what was primarily a political movement for a religious one. It does not even attempt to explain how the BJP combine could have overcome entrenched patterns of caste and class stratification to mobilize people on the basis of religious faith. The notion that Hindus were responding to long-standing grievances is ahistorical: Why did this movement occur in the early 1990s and not in prior decades and even centuries? Bruce Graham argues that the Jan Sangh failed to become a significant force in the 1960s because its intense convictions were not shared by a majority of Hindus (Graham 1990, 255). How less than thirty years later could the BJP have captured their imaginations?

As different as these two approaches are, they share certain questionable assumptions. The notion that elites shape and control popular belief in a largely uncontested fashion either disregards or demeans such beliefs and practices. Similarly, advocates of the "mass mobilization" approach impute to people untenable motivations. Furthermore, both approaches focus excessive attention on the principal actors—the BJP combine and its supporters—and neglect the political context. In particular, they neglect the many ways in which the actions of both the BJP and of ordinary men and women were informed by their antipathy toward the state.

One of the peculiarities of Hindu nationalism, which I will argue is key to its success, is that it shares attributes of both a social movement and a political party. Through close association with the RSS and VHP, which have intensively engaged in mass mobilization around issues that are conventionally deemed nonpolitical, the BJP in many ways resembles a social movement. For instance, one of the most important mass organizations affiliated with the BJP is the Bharatiya Mazdoor Sangh (BMS), which the 1980 report of the Ministry of Labor ranked as the second largest trade union in the country. The BMS experienced unprecedented growth during the period of Janata Party rule (1977–80). Since then, its growth has continued, and although it shares the BJP's positions on most issues and its top ranking leadership have RSS backgrounds, it has escaped government bans by deeming itself "non-political" (Saxena 1993). However, the BJP's motivations and achievements are principally electoral. For this reason, among others, the Hindu nationalist or Hindutva campaign with which the BJP has been so closely associated is in many ways the product of both an elite conspiracy and of a mass movement.

The BJP undoubtedly masterminded the Hindutva or Hindu nationalist movement to further its larger political ambitions. As a result of its increased representation in Parliament after the 1989 elections, it became a tacit coalition partner of the Janata Dal government. The political opening from which the BJP profited in 1989 had nothing to do with the heightened salience of religious identities and beliefs. Rather it had to do with certain political developments, the most important of which was the Congress Party's defeat in the national elections and the emergence of a multiparty system.

More specifically, the necessity for the Janata Dal to seek the BJP's support as an outside coalition partner in order to form a government in 1989 provided the BJP with an unprecedented opportunity to attain power at the center. At the same time, by remaining outside the ruling coalition, the BJP retained its autonomous objectives and character. The party's strength had dwindled in the years since the mid-1970s when it had adopted a Gandhian socialist platform; in the eighties and nineties the BJP was determined to maintain its distinctive character.

BJP resolve was further confirmed by the decision of the left-leaning Janata Dal government to implement the recommendations of the Backward Classes Commission headed by Bindeshwari Prasad Mandal (The Mandal Commission) for an expansion of the Indian government's affirmative action program by providing reservations in all institutions of public education and employment for so-called Other Backward Classes (OBCs). The government's decision heightened the salience of caste over religion and thus threatened to fragment the BJP's constituency. The BJP was faced with an acute dilemma. By openly opposing the government's implementation of Mandal recommendations, the BJP would expose its upper-caste character and risk alienating lower-caste supporters. But by supporting Mandal reforms it would alienate the upper castes and strengthen a reform that heightened caste divisions. The BJP opted to support formally Mandal recommendations at the national level while undermining them at the local level, particularly in places where it relied on upper-caste support. But its most effective response to Mandal was Hindu nationalism.

I will argue that the BJP has given voice to sources of frustration and aggression that have little to do with religious faith. It has effectively mobilized women by identifying an arena of politics that most political parties have ignored. Similarly, it has identified tensions pertaining to class and caste divisions that have been partially responsible for riots. By adopting different vantage points on what is broadly known as Hindu nationalism—from the national to state and local levels, elections to riots—I will show that a major reason for the BJP's sudden rise in popularity had little to do with its official program. The complicated logic of its actions cannot be reduced either to faith or to "communal" enmity.

One common element that helps explain the BJP's appeals at the state and local levels is that it has given voice to deeply held grievances against the state and the Congress Party. The BJP has generally fared poorly in states not dominated by Congress. Thus antistate and anti-Congress sentiment often go hand in hand. However, in Uttar Pradesh the BJP directed anti-state sentiment against the chief minister Mulayam Singh Yadav who was a living symbol of the growing power of the OBCs. Not only was he an OBC himself and a powerful proponent of Mandal, but he was also a close ally of V. P. Singh and bitter opponent of Hindu nationalism. Mulayam

Singh Yadav assiduously constructed an alliance between OBCs, dalits, and Muslims. In the 1991 elections the BJP profited from upper-caste backlash against Mandal, which it linked to its campaign around the temple in Ayodhya.

In explicating the logic that guides the actions of "ordinary" men and women in the Hindutva movement, my argument might mistakenly be construed as justifying their cruel actions. The mass movement and the elite conspiracy views are implicitly deterministic because they fail adequately to assess why people who eschewed Hindu nationalism in the past would embrace it today. Only by understanding the logic of people's beliefs and actions can we develop effective responses to Hindutva's seductive, deadly appeals.

In the pages that follow, I highlight the contradictory images that the BJP has projected since 1989 at the national, state, and local levels. At the national level, the BJP has emphatically proclaimed its commitment to Hindu interests and to the formation of a Hindu state to differentiate itself from other political parties. But this national image must be refracted to be meaningful to diverse constituencies. For example, in New Delhi, the national capital, the BJP must appeal both to the powerful middle classes and to slum dwellers, Hindu and Muslim alike.

In the four states in which it occupied office before 1995 — Rajasthan, Himachal Pradesh, Madhya Pradesh, and Uttar Pradesh — and in the Union Territory of New Delhi, the BJP has emphasized moderation over militancy. But here again, while the BJP must emphasize its commitment to stability, it has sought to deflect criticisms of its governments by periodically instigating riots that bolster its Hindu support. To the extent that riots are generally local affairs — whether they occur within small towns or large state capitals — the BJP has sought to translate its fiery rhetoric into grass-roots activism.

These distinctions between the national, state, and local levels are not merely of academic interest but help illuminate the BJP's strategic choices. The BJP must devise appropriate strategies for different arenas and constituencies. Conversely, people are likely to support the BJP for diverse reasons, which often have little to do with communal hostility. In New Delhi, for example, the middle classes may support the BJP because they favor a stronger, more authoritarian state with more ambitious foreign policy objectives, whereas slum dwellers may support the BJP because it promises to legalize their dwellings.

## The BJP's National Persona

I begin by describing the central elements that constitute the BJP as a party at the national level, emphasizing three dimensions: its conflation of a strong state with a Hindu state, its highly centralized party apparatus, and its links with the RSS and affiliated organizations. In all three domains, the BJP exhibits a high degree of flexibility: its commitment to Hindu nationalism does not preclude its abandoning these appeals if it considers other objectives more pressing; its centralized party organization does not preclude devolution of power to lower ranking party units; and its close relationship to the RSS has not prevented it from carving out a distinctive identity.

The BJP's long-term vision is best expressed in the concept of Hindu *rashtra* (nation-state), a term its leadership constantly uses. When asked to elaborate the traits of Hindu rashtra, BJP leaders express uncertainty, at best defining it negatively as the antithesis of the "pseudo-secularism" of the Congress Party. Interestingly, they never concede that the nation-state itself might be of Western inspiration, though they often level this charge at both secularism and democracy.

The BJP favors a strong, centralized state that puts a premium on defense to promote India's power in the region. It would redefine secularism to eliminate safeguards of minority rights—if not to eliminate minorities themselves—and to identify the state with the interests of the Hindu majority. The BJP frequently invokes the mantle of nationalism to legitimate its actions, implying that it has assumed the role that Congress abdicated after independence. This allusion to the nationalist movement implies another analogy: between Muslim rulers and British colonizers, thereby suggesting that Muslims must be expelled for the nationalist project to be completed. If there is no place for Muslims in this formulation of national identity, it also renders other minorities invisible.

If, as the discussion thus far suggests, the BJP's persona at the national level has been one of Hindu militancy, it must periodically refashion its image to suit the electoral climate. Recall that the BJP's most militant phase followed upon its gains in the 1989 national elections. As a result of reversals in the 1993 elections, the BJP moderated its stance. At its national council meeting in Bangalore in June 1993, for example, the BJP projected itself as a responsible alternative to the Congress Party. It downplayed religious issues and concentrated instead on such questions as economic liberalization and political corruption. Although Advani reiterated his opposition to the Congress Party's pseudo-secularism, he reaffirmed his commitment to a secular state.

Furthermore at every level at which it operates—the national capital, small towns, and remote villages—the BJP engages in what I term "doublespeak" in order to address the very different interests of its broad and diverse constituency. In New Delhi, the BJP propagates a "soft communalism" that is designed to appeal to the broadly defined urban middle classes, which include professionals, teachers, and retired civil servants. In this context, the BJP presents itself as favoring a stronger state that would be committed to more authoritarian means of maintaining stability. However, among the urban poor, its message is a populist one.

I observed this dual-pronged strategy at work during the BJP's 1991 election campaign. When I accompanied party members to affluent South Delhi constituencies, their appeals were both populist and nationalist. Its rallying cry at several demonstrations I attended was: "Power to the people, not to bureaucrats! Statehood for Delhi!" By contrast, in Delhi slums, BJP candidates were promising to legalize slum dwellers' occupation of municipal land, and provide them with electricity and clean drinking water. M. L. Khurana, a BJP member of Parliament from Delhi who was campaigning for reelection in 1991 and subsequently became the first chief minister of New Delhi, boasted in a public speech that the BJP was the only party that had fought for ration cards for slum dwellers. He also suggested that a BJP government might distribute vacant public land in Delhi to slum dwellers.

However, at the same moment, the BJP was evicting slum dwellers in Bhopal, Indore, and Jaipur, and reclaiming the land on which they lived for urban development. Underlying these apparently contradictory actions is a consistent electoral logic. When the dwellers were Hindu migrants from Kashmir, the BJP took up their demands without forfeiting appeals to the middle classes. Conversely, where slum dwellers tended to be Muslims from Bangladesh or elsewhere the BJP was more likely to favor slum eviction and to seek middle-class support for "city beautification," which rids cities of the poor and frees up urban land for real estate.

But as an electoral party, the BJP cannot afford to wholly antagonize the Muslim electorate. I accompanied B. D. Sharma as he campaigned for the BJP in the Chandni Chowk constituency of old Delhi during the BJP's 1991 election campaign. Here, the BJP appealed mainly to traders around such issues as the abolition of sales tax, the provision of better transportation facilities, and traffic management. I asked him why party workers had not mentioned the Ram janmabhoomi issue when it formed a staple of their electoral appeals elsewhere in the city. He responded that Muslims formed a large proportion of the population and their livelihoods were closely intertwined with those of Hindus. Thus at best he would seek to neutralize Muslim opposition to the BJP.

## Antipathy to the State

Both within the context of riots and of electoral politics, the BJP has skillfully exploited popular sentiments about the state. On the one hand, the BJP supports a stronger and more authoritarian state. On the other, it recognizes intense anti-state and anti-Congress sentiment. Perhaps to a greater extent than any other political party the BJP has decried the electoral opportunism of Congress. Indeed in New Delhi it gained the support of many Sikhs by criticizing the Congress Party for branding the Sikhs terrorists and instigating violence against the Sikhs after Mrs. Gandhi's assassination in 1984. Similarly, the BJP was more outspoken than any other political party in decrying V. P. Singh's electoral opportunism in implementing the Mandal recommendations in order to gain votes from the castes identified as Other Backward Classes.

That the BJP can credibly denounce other political parties for communal calculations in electoral politics constitutes an extraordinary irony. Perhaps it can feign a posture of moral superiority because it has not yet been tainted by the exercise of power at the center. Particularly around the 1991 elections, when the BJP's electoral gains were most significant, it depicted itself as passionately devoted to a cause that invited state repression. It thereby associated the martyrdom it imputed to the kar sevaks who were killed in Ayodhya with its own martyrdom.

Public anger at the Congress Party stems from its having escalated crises in the Punjab and Kashmir. The BJP has skillfully directed this anger at minority nationalism, particularly of Kashmiri Muslims. In fact, the meteoric rise of the BJP occurred precisely during the rapid escalation of secessionist militancy in Kashmir in the late 1980s, which became a full-scale war between separatists and the Indian Army. Majority nationalism then appears to be a defensive response to far more dangerous currents within the country. More broadly, high expectations of the role that the state should perform in economic, political, and even religious life has resulted in disillusionment with its actual performance. Such was the case with the outcry against the Mandal recommendations. For the lower middle classes, for whom employment prospects in the lucrative private sector are limited, public sector employment is key to upward social mobility. The government's adoption of Mandal provided an occasion for them to express accumulated resentment against the state for making special concessions to the lower castes.

Similarly, in the religious domain, as Donald Smith aptly notes, secularism has not implied the separation of church and state but rather the state's evenhanded intervention in the affairs of all religious communities (Smith 1963, 126). Recall that Rajiv Gandhi had intervened in the celebrated Shah Bano case, overturning a decision by the Supreme Court in favor of granting her alimony, and pushing through the Muslim Women's (Protection of Rights on Divorce) Bill, which retroactively applied Muslim law to her case and denied her alimony. The BJP attributes its increased militancy to the government's "appeasement" to Muslim fundamentalists. Advani described this case as "a watershed event" for the BJP (R. Thakur 1993, 649–50; Z. Hasan, below).

## Party Organization

One of the BJP's most important achievements is to have created a highly centralized party apparatus that allows considerable room for spontaneous mobilization among its local supporters. Two competing models with which the BJP compares favorably with respect to its organizational abilities are the Communist Party of India (Marxist) (CPM) on the one hand, and the Congress Party on the other. Committed as it is to democratic centralism, the CPM is more ideologically and organizationally cohesive than virtually any other political party in India today. However, as a result of its high level of centralization and electoral orientation, the CPM has become divorced from social movements. The Congress Party, on the other hand, is so loosely organized that, unlike the CPM, it has little autonomy from groups within civil society. As a result, Congress has been less effective than the CPM in spearheading social change.

The BJP's strong party organization is manifest in a variety of ways: coherent, distinctive ideology, solidarity among its national leadership, and cohesion among local, state, and national party units. Although factional divisions have grown with the passage of time and its exercise of power in several states, the BJP's strong party organization remains a major asset. One important explanation is that the BJP's top ranking leaders all have RSS backgrounds. The RSS quite appropriately uses the metaphor of family to depict relations among its members. Unlike members of political parties whose allegiances frequently shift, RSS members seem to feel a lifelong affinity to the organization.

The RSS, VHP, and BJP—at their many levels of organization—share a common fund of ideas and rhetoric. Traveling between Simla, Jaipur, and Bhopal, where, as we have seen, the BJP's local platforms differ significantly, party leaders mouth the same lines and party supporters shout the same slogans. The BJP's effective use of both the print media and audiovisual technology greatly contribute to this circulation of ideas. It suggests some of the ways in which the BJP combines a high level of party centralization with grass-roots populism. (See Davis, Farmer, Manuel in this volume.)

## Media Nationalism

The BJP's use of both print and audiovisual media is remarkably well suited to its project of creating an imagined Hindu community (Anderson 1983; T. Basu et al. 1993). Cassette tapes are readily amenable to such appropriation for they are cheaply produced and sold. Easily transported across vast distances, they bring the message of upper-caste Hindu nationalism to remote regions. But the messages contained within these cassettes do not express popular sentiments or regionally specific themes; rather, they are designed to nationalize anti-Muslim sentiment. In many towns in which riots occurred, people reported hearing terrifying screams from rooftops. These voices were in fact a cassette recording blasted over loudspeakers. The recording begins by invoking Allah (*Allah oh akbar!*) to indicate that a Muslim is crying out. It then invokes the Hindu god Rama (*Jai Shri Rama!*) presumably a Hindu cry. Cries follow: "Beat them! Beat them!" and, in the voices of women and children screaming, "Help, help!" This particular recording, played countless times, apparently had its desired effects (see also Manuel, below).

Similarly, the videos that the J. K. Jain Studios have produced for the BJP are distributed in the remotest regions of the country. During the 1991 election campaign, video raths (chariot-vans—often Toyotas) would travel to places that lacked electricity and play videos in which people would not only see images of deified politicians and people-like-deities but also throngs of ordinary men and women joining in the Ram janmabhoomi movement. J. K. Jain informed me in an interview (December 19, 1991) that onlookers often provided both the audience and the actors for these movies; the crew would film them and then replay the tapes, thereby identifying them visually with the Ram janmabhoomi movement.

The BJP appreciates popular interest in national politics. During the elections, when journalists were hungering for stories, the BJP would regularly organize meetings between reporters and its top ranking leaders. Unlike many political parties which feared negative press publicity, the BJP's main priority was simply to feature prominently in the news. Thus reporters who were sympathetic to the BJP would often publish stories about mundane events like Advani attending a ceremony commemorating the founding of a new school. In its attitudes toward the press, as with numerous other issues, the BJP has benefited both from skillful engineering from above as well as a spontaneous ground swell of support from below. On the one hand, editors and reporters who are closely associated with the RSS have infiltrated the major national dailies in order to promote Hindu nationalism. On the other hand, the aura of excitement that the Ram janmabhoomi campaign generated encouraged reporters to exercise creative license. The result was highly sensationalized, exaggerated accounts of the Ram janmabhoomi movement, particularly in the vernacular press (Charu and Mukul 1990; Farmer below).

Even when the BJP combine has orchestrated press initiatives, it has first sought to gauge popular sentiment. Arvind Agnihotri, the director of the VHP's media center in New Delhi, told me that the first thing he did every morning was to scan all the major daily papers to determine issues of public concern. Then he would formulate the VHP's stance on these questions so that "our name will be associated with whatsoever is on people's minds—and to make sure that we address these issues." Thus in keeping with its commitment to "electoral nationalism," the BJP has moderated its message through time and among social groups. Indeed the very electoral logic that has led the BJP to mobilize a Hindu constituency while in opposition, has forced it to broaden its appeals after coming to power. Not surprisingly, BJP state governments have shown little interest in creating a Hindu rashtra.

## The BJP at the State Level: Rajasthan, Himachal Pradesh, and Madhya Pradesh

In 1990, the BJP was elected to head the state assemblies of Rajasthan, Himachal Pradesh, and Madhya Pradesh. After the fall of the Janata Dal government and midterm elections in 1991, it was elected to power in Uttar Pradesh. Within India, Madhya Pradesh is the largest state and Uttar Pradesh the most populous; thus by 1991 the BJP was governing over 30 percent of India's population. These states account for almost two-thirds of the 119 BJP members of Parliament who were elected that same year. Although the BJP suffered serious reversals in the 1993 state assembly elections, one might still ask whether its earlier electoral victories did not herald the triumph of Hindu nationalist sentiment in these four states.

My general argument is that Hindu nationalism played a variable role at best in bringing the BJP to power in these four important northern states in 1991: it was of considerable importance in Madhya Pradesh and Uttar Pradesh, unimportant in Himachal Pradesh, and hardly significant in Rajasthan. But even in Madhya Pradesh and Uttar Pradesh, Hindu nationalist appeals were short-lived and proved much less important than economic and political issues. Here, I first assess the BJP's fortunes in the three states where it was elected in 1990 and then consider the somewhat distinctive situation in Uttar Pradesh.

In assessing the major reasons for the BJP's electoral victory in Rajasthan, Madhya Pradesh, and Himachal Pradesh in 1990, remember that these elections took place before the BJP had made the temple a major campaign issue (Davis, above). Rather, by 1990 a pattern was emerging in these states of BJP and Congress alternation in office, with the defeated party maintaining a sizable strength in the legislative assembly. The anti-Congress wave that swept the Janata Dal into office in the 1989 parliamentary elections continued to influence the legislative assembly elections the following year. In Rajasthan, the BJP allied with the Janata Dal and in Himachal Pradesh it ran numerous candidates who were not of RSS backgrounds.

It would be inaccurate to suggest that the BJP was divorced in the public mind from the Ram janmabhoomi campaign. In 1989 the VHP organized a highly successful *Ram shilan puja*, the collection of bricks and money to build a temple in Ayodhya. Many of the militants who participated in this campaign were elected to the legislative assembly in Madhya Pradesh (Jaffrelot 1993, 129). However, the BJP's gains from the Ram janmabhoomi issue should not overshadow other sources of its growing strength. The most important positive explanation had nothing to do with Hindu nationalism but rather with what would appear to be its antithesis, agrarian populism. This can be seen in a variety of ways: first, from the BJP's election platform, which reflected a good sense of popular priorities. Party officials in the three states emphasized the electoral dividends they had gained from supporting a scheme that promised to waive farmers' loans in excess of ten thousand rupees, a demand it adopted from the Janata Dal's election platform. In Himachal Pradesh, the BJP gained similar mileage from a scheme of economic assistance to the poorest rural families (*antyodhya*). In Madhya Pradesh, it promised tribals titles to forest land and opposed anti-forest-encroachment legislation. It also pursued a campaign it had started in 1986 of demanding a waiver of farmers' loans. In Rajasthan, its rallying cry was "A tap in every home!" Compared to such populist themes, Hindu rashtra played a small role in the BJP's election campaign.

Not surprisingly, the failure of BJP governments to keep their promises played a major role in their defeat in the 1993 legislative assembly elections. In Madhya Pradesh the BJP was widely seen as favoring the interests of moneyed upper-caste groups against those of the poor, the minorities, and the lower castes. The most unpopular government measures included the BJP's antiencroachment drive, which targeted poor, particularly Muslim families (A. Basu 1994a), its mishandling of the loan waiver scheme, which had been introduced by Arjun Singh's administration, and its open support for deforestation policies that would benefit powerful industrialists. Madhya Pradesh's large OBC and lower-caste population also resented upper-caste domination of the party and the administration.

The other critical reason for the BJP's growth in these states had to do with the steady decline of the Congress Party (Z. Hasan, below). Particularly under Indira Gandhi's reign, power had become extremely centralized in the prime minister's office in New Delhi. Thus for example, the central government in Delhi would frequently intervene to relocate chief ministers in Indian states when it felt they were becoming excessively independent or powerful. As a result, many chief ministers found themselves becoming alienated from their party workers and constituencies. Furthermore, while Congress was becoming increasingly fractionalized, the BJP was unusually centralized and cohesive. However, even aside from the particular deficiencies of Congress in the 1980s, the electorate wanted change and believed that the BJP had something new to offer.

Thus the BJP came to power in states in which the Congress Party's strength had eroded and other opposition parties were weak or absent. By contrast, in states like Kerala, Bihar, West Bengal, Tamil Nadu, and Andhra Pradesh, in which alternatives to Congress existed, the BJP failed to achieve major gains. Significantly, the major alternatives to Congress were leftist and ethnically based regional parties.

Why did the task of opposing Congress fall primarily to the BJP in Rajasthan, Madhya Pradesh, Uttar Pradesh, and Himachal Pradesh? The left did not provide a serious alternative to Congress in these states. The Communist Party had been weak historically and the Socialists, though powerful at one time, submerged their own identity when they formed coalitions with other parties, first in 1977–80 when the Janata Party was in office, and later in 1989–91 when the Janata Dal was in power. By contrast, one of the BJP's great skills, amply demonstrated in its relationship with the Janata Dal, was to combine the role of insider and outsider to the government. At the same time that it served as a coalition partner, the BJP was also its most scathing critic. Among all the parties that joined or supported the Janata Dal government, the BJP was most careful to maintain its distinctive character and remain faithful to its own ambitions. Yet from its association with the Janata Dal, the BJP acquired the populist aura that figured so prominently in its election campaigns.

Once in office, the BJP functioned in much the same way as previous Congress regimes and was judged by the same standards. This did not entail an abstract commitment to Hindu interests but rather the BJP's ability to manage the economy, maintain law and order, and provide capable administration. Between 1989 and 1991, when new elections were held, the BJP's parliamentary seats in all three states declined. But even more important were the results of the state assembly elections in 1993: the BJP was defeated in Madhya Pradesh, Himachal Pradesh, and Uttar Pradesh; it won narrowly in Rajasthan and by a good margin only in New Delhi, which it had never ruled before.

The 1993 election results are widely believed to have signified public disapproval of the BJP's involvement in the destruction of the mosque in Ayodhya and the riots in which thousands were killed. Significantly, the BJP's losses were greatest in Madhya Pradesh, followed by Uttar Pradesh, where its posture was most militant and where riots were numerous. By contrast, the BJP retained power in Rajasthan, where it benefited from the moderate, relatively secular leadership of chief minister Bhairon Singh Shekavat.

## The Uttar Pradesh Pattern

In 1991, while the BJP was registering electoral losses in Rajasthan, Madhya Pradesh, and Himachal Pradesh, it achieved a landslide victory in Uttar

Pradesh. Given Ayodhya's location and the magnitude of violence in this state, the BJP's election in 1991 would appear to demonstrate a highly communalized Hindu electorate. Yet even here, matters are more complex. (See Z. Hasan, below.) Although the BJP reaped electoral dividends from the Ram janmabhoomi issue in the 1991 elections, there had been a long-term decline of Congress in UP as in the three other states. Since 1967, there had emerged the Lok Dal opposition that gave birth to the Janata Party. Several BJP members in Uttar Pradesh admitted that the BJP owed its rural strength to its alliance in its Jan Sangh phase with the Janata Party. What differentiated Uttar Pradesh from the other states was the existence of an alternative to the BJP and Congress, the Janata Dal, led by Mulayam Singh Yadav.

However powerful the BJP's overt religious appeals may have been, the subtext was an appeal to the upper castes. If the state had been turning Hindus into second-class citizens by appeasing Muslims, the BJP logic ran, by implementing the Mandal Commission Report it was seeking to keep the sons of upper-caste families out of public employment, the main hope for upward mobility. Of all the states, the Mandal recommendations posed the most serious threat to the BJP in Uttar Pradesh, because Mulayam Singh Yadav had been forging a (Janata Dal) coalition of OBCs, Muslims, and scheduled castes. When Mulayam Singh attempted to prevent Advani's procession of Rama's chariot (Rath Yatra) from reaching Ayodhya in 1990, the BJP branded him anti-Hindu. From its own perspective, the BJP could channel onto Mulayam Singh Yadav upper-caste resentments at the growth of lower-caste influence in Uttar Pradesh politics. Furthermore, the BJP ingeniously combined antistate sentiment with anti-Mulayam Singh sentiment to defeat Congress in 1989 and again in 1991. However, the BJP's defeat in the 1993 elections by a multicaste, Hindu-Muslim alliance headed by Mulayam Singh Yadav signified that the OBC-Muslim-scheduled caste alliance remained a formidable political force in Uttar Pradesh. Indeed the BJP suffered the worst defeats in central and eastern UP, the heartland of the Ayodhya agitation. Although it made some gains in western UP, this probably had more to do with Jat support for its economic programs than with Hindu nationalism (P. Chopra 1993).

If the BJP's caste calculations were particularly critical in Uttar Pradesh because of the growth of OBC political influence, they were by no means unimportant in the three other states. In Madhya Pradesh, for example, the BJP leader Kusabau Thakre created special cells for scheduled castes and tribes by appealing to their economic interests. Whereas Muslims constitute less than 5 percent of Madhya Pradesh's population, scheduled castes and tribes together account for 34 percent and OBCs for 48 percent of the population. BSP and Congress gains in the 1993 elections came largely from these constituencies. The growing political assertiveness of the lower castes helped revive the Madhya Pradesh Congress Party; after coming to power, Congress appointed Yadav and members of scheduled-castes as deputy chief ministers and implemented the recommendations of an MP state commission (The Mahajan Commission) supporting reservations for OBCs at the state level.

One general conclusion that emerges from this state-level comparison is that the more the BJP could capture leadership of anti-Congress forces, the less it needed to appeal to Hindu interests. Conversely, the more opposition to both Congress and the BJP existed, the more apt the BJP was to issue nationalist appeals. Thus at one end of the spectrum is Himachal Pradesh, where there had been a gradual evolution of a two-party system in which the BJP formed the only viable opposition to Congress, thereby rendering Hindu nationalism unnecessary. At the other end of the spectrum, the BJP faced the greatest difficulties in establishing itself in Uttar Pradesh because its base was narrowly confined to urban traders. It was further weakened by the emergence of OBCs as a major political force in the state. Thus it was in Uttar Pradesh that the BJP most freely and militantly voiced Hindu nationalist appeals.

Another general conclusion is that in 1993 and then again in 1995, the electorate delivered an antiestablishment vote. This was a major determinant of the BJP's fortunes. As the incumbent party in 1993, the BJP suffered reversals in all of the states it ruled for it was judged by its performance in office. Significantly in 1995, the BJP only came to power in two states that it had not formerly ruled—Maharashtra and Gujarat—which were expressing their discontent with incumbent governments. This antiestablishment sentiment worked to the advantage of the Telugu Desam in Andhra Pradesh, the Janata Dal in Karnataka, and Congress in Orissa.

In both Maharashtra and Gujarat, the BJP's gains in 1995 were partly the results of the collapse of the Janata Dal. Thus the vote of dissatisfaction with Congress that had gone to the Janata Dal in the past, went to the BJP in 1995. Between 1990 and 1995, the Janata Dal vote fell from 11.21 to 5.73 percent in Maharashtra, and from 29.53 to 2.14 percent in Gujarat. The BJP-Shiv Sena alliance came to power with a slim majority—just 1 percent of the vote over Congress—in Maharashtra. In Gujarat, the BJP came to power with a comfortable two-thirds majority.

By 1995, the BJP had learned that religious appeals had ceased to pay off. This was evident from its defeat in the Uttar Pradesh election in 1991 and from the limited response to the VHP's attempts to mobilize support for the "liberation" of a mosque in Benares. On February 27, 1995, the festival of Shivratri, the VHP and its affiliates all converged on Benares to launch a program of "liberating" the Kashi Vishwanath temple and to rebuild a Shiva temple that they claimed the Mughal emperor Aurangzeb had destroyed. However, the program was so unpopular that the BJP ultimately maintained some distance from it. The BJP devoted only a paragraph to the Ayodhya issue in its 1995 election manifesto. Nor did communal themes figure prominently in its election campaigns in Maharashtra or Gujarat. Instead it emphasized its opposition to corruption, maladministration, criminalization of politics, and vote bank appeasement. It also attempted to broaden its economic appeals by sharply criticizing economic liberalization.

Ironically, the BJP took office in 1995 in the two wealthiest states in India. Pramod Mahajan, the general secretary of the party, captured the significance of this fact when he stated: "For the entire world and the foreign investor in particular, the seat of power in India is in Bombay and not in Delhi. Therefore they feel the power has shifted from Narasimha Rao to us. Give us six months more and we will remove all their apprehensions about our economic policies and show that there will be no turnaround" (*Pioneer*, March 19, 1995). Although Bal Thackeray, the Shiv Sena leader, rhetorically asked why "Mumbai" (as the Shiv Sena has renamed the state capital, Bombay) should need foreign investors, he has on other occasions changed his stance, and the BJP chief minister for Gujarat, Keshabhai Patel, has encouraged foreign corporations to invest in the state. Although BJP governments have supported some populist measures in both states—a cheap meal of millet *bajra* and *jowar* flour bread (*roti*) and lentils (*dal*) in Maharashtra and a cereal scheme for school children in Gujarat—it has assumed that in these affluent states, people are more concerned with amassing than with distributing wealth (*Hindusthan Times*, March 13, 1995).

## Riots at the Local Level

To what extent were the hundreds of riots that occurred during 1990–93 orchestrated by the BJP, or conversely, born of local circumstance? There is compelling evidence for both arguments. In support of the elite conspiracy view, many of the 1990 riots in Uttar Pradesh, where the worst violence occurred, took place in towns like Ghaziabad, Agra, Gorakhpur, Khurja, Bijnor, and Saharanpur, which had no history of communal violence. If these towns had escaped communal violence until 1990, they would probably have continued to do so had the BJP not intervened.

The question of timing is also relevant: most of these riots occurred around the BJP's processions to Ayodhya in October 1990 and December 1992. Others coincided with some event that the BJP turned into a pretext for violence, like the Ram shilan puja, which triggered riots in several states in September-October 1989, or Advani's arrest on October 24, 1990, which precipitated riots in Gujarat, Uttar Pradesh, and Rajasthan. The question of timing is also important in another respect: the BJP may well have planned the 1990 riots partly in anticipation of parliamentary elections. When it withdrew support from the Janata Dal government in 1990, it knew that the government would fall and elections would be held. In fact, Congress delayed the elections by creating an interim government in New Delhi headed by Chandra Shekhar. Still even in 1991, the BJP's electoral gains, and particularly its victory in Uttar Pradesh, were undoubtedly influenced by preceding riots.

The problem with the elite conspiracy view is that it does not explain why people respond to the BJP's exhortations to violence. Even if the costs of riots are borne unevenly, riots spare no one. Shopkeepers, for example, who form an important part of the BJP's constituency, must close their shops and often suffer serious losses from arson, looting, and vandalism (*Economic and Political Weekly* [*EPW*], August 27, 1994). Nor does it explain why people are receptive to BJP propaganda.

The role of rumors in the course of riots provides an excellent illustration both of how the BJP creates a climate of fear and of why it finds a receptive audience. In the course of my research I found that rumors had preceded and accompanied major riots. During the December 1992 riot in Bhopal, the prelude to the violence was rumors that Muslim mobs had attacked a women's college and raped eighty women (A. Basu 1994). On December 9, the city edition of the *Nav Bharat* newspaper (circulation 16,000) featured a major article entitled "Attack on Girls' Hostel." That evening, the *Jan Charcha* newspaper carried a lurid story of how the mobs had cut off these women's breasts. Shortly thereafter the Bajrang Dal, the VHP's youth group, organized murderous violence against Muslims. Although it is by now amply clear that the women's college was never attacked, interviews with residents in Bhopal a few weeks later revealed how widely these rumors had been disseminated and how much damage they had caused.

In the town of Khurja in western Uttar Pradesh, two successive riots occurred within a short period of time: the first began on December 14, 1990, and the second and more major one on January 31, 1991. Several rumors had circulated the day before the second riot: the BJP claimed that it had found corpses of fourteen cows outside its office. By midday hundreds of people had gathered at the police station to demand an investigation. The police could only find two corpses of cows in the town; an autopsy revealed that neither animal had been poisoned. This was followed by rumors that a Muslim had poisoned a water tank that he operated and, a few days later, that five hundred armed Muslim men were headed in the direction of a Hindu locality.

A political party can instigate a conflict without wholly designing it by spreading rumors that feed upon varied tensions within the society. In the situations I have described, members of Hindu organizations clearly spread these rumors in order to generate "communal" enmity. However, the power of these rumors ultimately rested upon people's willingness to believe them. A few people I interviewed dismissed the rumors outright and tried to convince others that they were unfounded. I interviewed a newspaper reporter in Khurja (May 10, 1991) who said he had confronted the BJP member who had spread the rumor about the water tank. The accused responded that he was taking "precautionary measures." The reporter addressed a gathering of frightened Hindus and asked them how five hundred armed Muslims could have crossed police pickets to come to their neighborhood. And how could Muslims have poisoned fourteen cows near a police station when the town was under strict curfew?

Most people said that they had always suspected that the stories had been fabricated. But like the BJP member in Khurja, they seemed to feel that caution dictated believing the rumors rather than repudiating them. Riots endanger all that people held most dear: their families, friends, homes, savings, and sources of livelihood. Thus it seemed safest for people to place faith in their communities in these times of danger. Furthermore, the power of these rumors rested upon their expressing the most pernicious and frightening stereotypes of the lustful, aggressive, beef-eating Muslim man (Pandey 1993a, 18–20). The rumor about abducted Hindu women forms a staple among riot-related rumors throughout the country; in Jaipur alone it recurred regularly between 1989 and 1992 (Mayaram 1993, 2530).

I will argue that riots provide an opportunity for people to address many grievances that are unrelated to either religious sentiment or communal enmity. However, unlike certain social psychological theories that associate collective violence with pathology, I would argue that in rioting people often address persistent social ills and affirm their class, caste, and gender identities (Gurr 1986). In making this argument I do not mean to deny the BJP's role in instigating riots but simply to suggest that even when they are externally instigated, riots come to embody local grievances.

## Riots as Caste Conflicts

The BJP's decision to organize the 1990 Rath Yatra to Ayodhya and its actions during subsequent riots were deeply informed by caste considerations. This is most apparent in Uttar Pradesh: the BJP had lost the OBC vote as a result of the backward caste movement, later compounded by the implementation of the Mandal recommendations, both of which ensured OBC support for the Janata Dal. The loss of the OBC vote made the support of the lowest caste groups (called scheduled castes because of their inclusion in schedules for government assistance) especially valuable for the BJP; the most fruitful opportunity to draw scheduled castes into the Hindu fold occurred during riots.

In the riots in Ghaziabad and in Khurja, scheduled castes (or *balmikis*, as they labeled themselves during my interviews) seemed to find an opportunity to address economic grievances. In both towns, many balmikis who expressed animosity toward Muslims lived in localities that adjoined the Muslim sections. The relegation of both groups to the periphery of the town resulted from discriminatory treatment by dominant groups. Crowded living conditions also precipitated conflicts between the two communities over land.

In Ghaziabad, where a riot occurred on January 25, 1991, fifteen people were killed, of whom twelve were Muslims. The catalyst to the riot came when a local politician organized Muslim schoolchildren to march in a procession opposing U.S. aggression against Iraq. When they marched past a balmiki locality, they were confronted by a group of balmikis observing Republic Day by singing patriotic songs. Each group demanded that the other turn down its music. A scuffle quickly ensued followed by more serious violence in the town a little later. Members of the BJP whom I interviewed claimed that balmikis had been incensed by the Muslims' disruption of their patriotic festivities. However, balmikis denied that this had been the major source of the conflict. Satya Chauhan, an elderly balmiki man, said that both Muslims and balmikis lived in congested surroundings and both groups wanted to take over a plot of land nearby (interview by the author, Ghaziabad, April 18, 1991). Rivalries over this land had been simmering for a while and finally boiled over.

The first riot that the town of Khurja experienced began on December 14, 1990, with a violent clash between some balmikis and Muslims. That day a Muslim boy was stabbed to death in the balmiki locality. Muslims whom I interviewed claimed that a balmiki woman named Mathuravali had murdered him at the BJP's behest; balmikis denied this and alleged that Muslims resented Mathuravali because she was a spokesperson for her community. When the police arrested Mathuravali and her son, the BJP organized hundreds of Hindus to demand her release. The following day, balmikis claimed that Muslims retaliated by looting twenty-four houses and killing eight of their pigs. It proved extremely difficult to establish why the balmikis had stabbed a Muslim boy. However, even if they had been bought off by the BJP, my interviews with balmiki men and women revealed that their grievances against Muslims were partly economic in nature. The balmikis claimed that Muslims were hoping to take over their land for a market. Furthermore, many balmiki women worked as maids in Muslim homes and complained of ill treatment by their employers.

In both Ghaziabad and Khurja, the BJP turned prior conflicts between balmikis and Muslims to its own advantage. After the riots, the BJP and VHP provided balmikis with food, clothing, and medical supplies to make them feel that their security lay with the Hindu community. Thus in the cases I have described, the conflict between Muslims and balmikis was engineered from above but also met with a favorable response for reasons that were not wholly determined or controlled by the BJP.

However, the solidarity that the BJP forged between scheduled castes and upper castes was relatively short lived. By 1993 scheduled castes had thrown their weight behind the alliance of Mulayam Singh Yadav's Janata Dal and Kanshi Ram's Bahujan Samaj and Samajwadi Party alliance, thereby defeating the BJP in the elections. In fact a 1993 survey of the Jaunpur district in Uttar Pradesh revealed that most scheduled castes and OBCs opposed the BJP and their opposition had deepened after the destruction of the mosque in Ayodhya (Lieten 1994, 779–80; Z. Hasan below).

Although it is clear that riots also enable the airing of class resentments, it is more difficult to determine the roles of particular classes than of particular castes in riots. Compared with class differences, caste boundaries are more sharply demarcated and more politicized by the state through reservation policies. At a very general level of analysis, many of the towns that have recently experienced riots are characterized by certain distinctive demographic and socioeconomic features. In Uttar Pradesh, for example, riots have been concentrated in newly formed towns inhabited by upwardly mobile rural migrants. In contrast to the dynamism of the western Uttar Pradesh countryside, the economies of these towns are stagnant. The Ram janmabhoomi movement coincided with a serious foreign exchange crisis, which was associated with inflation, unemployment, and an economic downturn (Bagchi 1991). In such a situation, the groups that participated in the riots may well have been mindful of possibilities for material betterment.

## Riots as Gendered Conflicts

Paradoxically, while Hindu nationalism is a deeply patriarchal project, it has created possibilities for women's expression of their subjectivities. Until 1989, those who spoke of women in the context of communal violence described them primarily as victims. With Hindu nationalist mobilization around the Ram janmabhoomi issue and in the accompanying riots, women have emerged as militant activists and instigators of violence (A. Basu 1993). First, in a manner that is only comparable to the anticolonial nationalist movement, Hindu nationalism has created new spaces for women's activism. It has done so partly by creating an aura of passionate commitment to a cause that demands tremendous sacrifices of its followers. Within such a context, urban middle- and lower-middle-class families—who tend more than others to practice female seclusion—have allowed women considerable freedom.

The BJP emphasized women's role in door-to-door campaigning in preparation for the 1991 elections. Many BJP members believed that women constituted their strongest supporters for they tended to be more devout than men. Perhaps, therefore, women's visibility in the election campaign would have affirmed the BJP's politically strategic commitment to Hinduism and communal appeals. The sight of women walking from house to house in the scorching summer months may also have been designed to signal the extraordinary sacrifices that the Ram janmabhoomi issue demanded.

Rohini Mehta (pseudonym), a lower-middle-class housewife from

Lucknow, told me in an interview (Lucknow, April 18, 1991) that in those heady days of the election campaign she would leave home early in the morning and only return late at night. Normally her in-laws would have worried about her reputation and safety but they knew that their sacrifice was justified in the name of the cause. They also knew she was safe in the midst of the Sangh Parivar (the RSS family, as it terms itself). This had been the first time that she had spent time away from her home and the experience had been an exhilarating one. Indeed her passionate commitment to the Ram janmabhoomi issue and to finding meaning within her own life seemed to be inextricably linked.

The riots also provided extraordinary opportunities for women's activism. If in the electoral context women's presence lent credence to the BJP's religious commitments, in the context of riots, it provided an injunction to violence. One of the most important means that the BJP has employed for justifying genocidal violence against Muslims is the notion that Hindus are being victimized. The BJP's characterization of Muslim men as aggressors elicits the most militant response from Hindu men when it is associated with notions of Hindu women's vulnerability. These supposed threats to Hindu women have formed a pretext for the activism of Hindu women and men in the recent period.

In the 1990 Bijnor riot, members of the BJP women's organization and the VHP-affiliated Durga Vahini (Durga's Army) led a procession of Hindu men through the Muslim quarters of town shouting ugly, provocative slogans that provoked violence (A. Basu 1995). In a major riot in Bhopal in December 1992, Hindu mobs congregated in an industrial center on the outskirts of the city and began to harass Muslim shanty dwellers. Shakuntala Devi, a woman who was a member of the municipal corporation, arrived at the spot and goaded the men into greater brutality against the Muslims in the area.

At first glance it seems puzzling that lower-middle-class women who would be reluctant to participate in demonstrations against "dowry deaths" (the murder of women in family disputes over dowry) would participate instead in communal riots. Why have women who turned their backs on violence against women become complicit in violence against a defenseless minority? But perhaps the paradox is not as great as it initially appears: the BJP has placed on the political agenda issues like rape that are of vital concern to women. If it has not encouraged women to confront sexual violence within their own community, it encourages them to vent anger at the supposed sexual violence of Muslim men.

That women have carved out a place from which to express their

subjectivities does not mean that Hindu nationalism has served their gender interests. Indeed by using women's participation to create the aura
of a mass movement, the BJP has avoided women's representation in the
party and state governments. Thus while women may participate in the
BJP's election campaign and in riots for reasons of their own, the top-
down, party-controlled quality of the movement greatly limits their gains
as women.

## Conclusion

Neither of the two opposing positions identified in the introduction to
this chapter can explain the phenomenal growth of Hindu nationalism in
the 1990s. On the one hand, the notion that the BJP could have undertaken
its actions in Ayodhya without significant support is implausible. At least
in the short run, both the Ram janmabhoomi campaign and the riots bore
dividends. The notion of an elite conspiracy fails to acknowledge that the
BJP raised questions of profound importance to the Indian electorate.

On the other hand, the notion that the BJP was radicalized by its supporters must be qualified. BJP spokespersons like Swapan DasGupta claim
that the BJP's positions on Ayodhya were forced upon it by the passions
of its Hindu constituency. Immediately after the destruction of the Babri
Masjid, many claimed that the party leadership had lost control over zeal-
ous militants. Although tensions between high ranking BJP officials and
militant rank and file members of Hindu organizations have been amply
documented, there is no persuasive evidence that the party high command
lost control of its militants either when the mosque was destroyed or at
other critical moments of the campaign (Jaffrelot 1993). Indeed tensions
between leaders and rank and file members have been most evident when
the BJP has been in power at the state level and has adopted a moderate
stance.

The strength of the Hindu nationalist campaign appears to have rested
upon the confluence of two forces: a party that was attuned to popular
hopes, fears, and aspirations, and a people that was for varied and diverse
reasons receptive to what the BJP had to offer. By way of illustration,
consider how the BJP projects itself as a deeply moralistic party that is
preoccupied with restoring ethical values to the conduct of political life.
Its position strikes a chord among an electorate that is deeply dissatisfied
with the existing political system. The BJP then conjoins its critique of im-

morality with a critique of secularism. More broadly, I have argued, the BJP's support rests in part upon the rage it expresses at the injustices of the present political order. Furthermore, the BJP has both encouraged and redirected hostilities that emerge from a class, caste, and gender stratified social context.

My analysis might seem to imply that riots are about everything but Hindu-Muslim animosity. It would be naive and irresponsible to ignore the communal hatred that riots unleash. However, to correct the common assumption that communalism is the principal if not the exclusive source of violence, I explore other animosities that people express through riots. I contend that far from having swept aside deep-seated conflicts within Indian society, Hindu nationalism has both encouraged and yet mystified their expression. I would also emphasize the divergence between people's motivations and the outcomes of their actions. Even when people address caste, class, and gender inequalities by rioting, their violence deepens distrust between Hindus and Muslims.

Nor would I suggest that relations between Hindus and Muslims historically are irrelevant to explaining the present crisis. If overall the BJP has played the Hindu card more often in opposition than in office, differences in Hindu-Muslim relations in the four states also help explain its strategy. In Himachal Pradesh where the Muslim population is very small and Hindu-Muslim tensions are absent, the BJP did not play the communal card. By contrast, among the four states, Uttar Pradesh has experienced the most acute Hindu-Muslim conflict historically and in the present. In short, the BJP does not find a *tabula rasa* on which to etch its own designs but accentuates existing patterns.

The attempt to synthesize a view from above and from below has some implications for public policy. Taken alone, the elite conspiracy view would imply that since a renegade political party has generated a furor, stability can be restored by curtailing its activities. To a large extent this has been the approach that the Indian state has adopted in the aftermath of the Babri Masjid's destruction, when it banned a number of Hindu organizations and imprisoned their major leaders. The problem with this approach is that the state usually becomes attentive to law and order only after it has been violated; when the state acts preemptively, it often violates civil liberties. In the short run, such strong-arm measures are only likely to increase support for Hindu nationalists by making them into martyrs; in the long run, such an approach will not alter the conditions that give rise to the BJP.

The notion that Hindu nationalism constitutes a grass-roots movement could foster resignation, because the state cannot do anything to influence deep-seated beliefs and prejudices; or by characterizing riots as being primordial, it could reinforce support for an authoritarian state. However, by synthesizing these two perspectives, we can see that Hindu nationalism is but a reflection of a more deep-rooted malaise within both civil society and the state. A restructuring of the state is central to tackling this malaise. But of equal urgency is the need to address questions of unemployment, caste discrimination, and women's subordination that generate the frustration, anguish, and despair expressed in Hindu nationalism.

# 3

# Communal Mobilization and Changing Majority in Uttar Pradesh

ZOYA HASAN

THE ELECTORAL TRIUMPH of the Bharatiya Janata Party (BJP) in the northern states in 1991 highlighted the latent possibilities of religious activism and communal mobilization in forging political majorities. This was an unlikely scenario only a few years before. As recently as the 1984 elections, the BJP could not win a single Lok Sabha seat from Uttar Pradesh. In 1991, BJP was elected to power in Uttar Pradesh. No political party has received such remarkable support in so short a time. What explains the sudden spurt in electoral support and political appeal of the BJP in Uttar Pradesh?

Recent analyses of these striking changes have attributed the achievement to the activities of the BJP and its affiliates, particularly Vishva Hindu Parishad (VHP) propaganda, its armory of symbols and modes of transmission in underpinning the support for the Hindutva movement (Chibber and Misra 1993; Jaffrelot 1993; Varshney 1993). While it is important to explore the ideological activities of the Sangh combine (the RSS, BJP, VHP, Bajrang Dal, and associated organizations) in spreading the influence of Hindu nationalism, it is equally necessary to consider the role played by caste and communal issues, and the tactics and strategies of political parties in the rise of Hindutva.

In this essay, these complex developments are unraveled through an examination of social and political processes in Uttar Pradesh and of how these factors might have contributed to making this key state politically Hindu in 1991. My argument emphasizes the crucial importance of politi-

* This is a revised version of a paper delivered at the South Asia Seminar at the University of Pennsylvania in December 1993. I am grateful to Mushirul Hasan, David Ludden, Ritu Menon, K. N. Panikkar, and Achin Vanaik for their comments and suggestions.

cal context, party strategies, and mobilization tactics in heightening the salience of community identities and in creating conditions conducive to the growth of the Sangh combine. This process was aided by the communal compromises and the decline of the Congress in the 1980s. But the electoral successes of the Sangh combine cannot be attributed to the political conditions and the vacuum created by Congress failures alone. Communal mobilization and the political violence engendered by the activities of the Sangh combine played a crucial part in buttressing Hindu support. This in turn altered political relationships and paved the way for an alliance of backward castes, scheduled castes, and Muslims creating problems faced by the BJP in retaining power in 1993.

# I

Until then a weak electoral force, political Hinduism acquired unprecedented strength in the late 1980s. While religious mobilization is not a new phenomenon in Uttar Pradesh, the electoral triumph of the BJP within a political movement of Hindu self-assertion represented a new trend. This was a surprising development. Unlike Rajasthan, Madhya Pradesh, and Himachal Pradesh, political competition in Uttar Pradesh centered after 1977 on the Congress and various Janata Party formations, and not on the Congress and the BJP. Seat adjustments with the Janata Dal, by which the two parties agreed on seats to contest, assisted the rise of the BJP in 1989, which allowed the BJP to make inroads quickly in nontraditional areas and among its nontraditional supporters. At no point before 1991 did the BJP win even a quarter of the votes or seats in the Uttar Pradesh State Assembly. The highest vote of 21 percent was achieved in 1967. But the party could not maintain this level in subsequent elections; the average vote (excluding 1967) was around 10 percent. It is noteworthy that BJP's area of strength even in the 1989 Lok Sabha was not Uttar Pradesh, where it won only eight seats against the fifty-two of the Janata Dal and Left Front, but rather Madhya Pradesh. Moreover, its victory in these eight UP assembly seats was due largely to the absence of the Janata Dal in the contest. The important point is that the 1989 election did not reveal strong evidence of a Hindu vote in Uttar Pradesh, despite attempts by the Congress and BJP to marshal support on those lines.

The Uttar Pradesh scene is in sharp contrast to Madhya Pradesh, for example, where the BJP has maintained a high vote percentage of

30 percent since 1967, rising to 40 percent in 1989–90. Christophe Jaffrelot's recent study highlights the specificity of the party building pattern in Madhya Pradesh, which relied heavily on the RSS party discipline and network from the early 1950s (Jaffrelot 1993). In Uttar Pradesh, the BJP's expansion is more recent—its impressive political presence in the 1990s is linked strongly to the Ram janmabhoomi movement and the erosion of the Congress base—though a long-term trend was clearly accelerated by it. The BJP's rise is so significant here because there were other alternatives, namely the Janata Dal and the Socialists. This was not the case in other north Indian states where the BJP was vying for power. Yet the BJP prevailed in Uttar Pradesh largely by harvesting gains from political mobilization around the Ram janmabhoomi issue.

The most important actor in the temple movement is the VHP and its assortment of priests and religious leaders. The party gained enormous strength from the ideological and religiocultural actions of the VHP and street power of the Bajrang Dal, formed in 1984. Political mobilization concentrated on ideological issues and a subjective articulation of historical grievances, memories, and cultural differences specially engineered for the purpose of mobilization. Three themes characterized this mobilization: the intrinsic tolerance of Hinduism, the destruction of Hindu temples, and state repression of *karsewa* (action by kar sevaks) in Ayodhya (P. K. Datta 1991, Nandy et al. 1993). Events surrounding the first attempt in October 1990 to demolish the Babri mosque were consecrated to highlight the "heroic" saga of Hindu warriors fighting against the state. Opposition to the state was dramatized by the police action ordered by the chief minister. But barring one single instance of opposition from Mulayam Singh Yadav, there is no evidence of opposition from the state. In fact, a great deal of the Ayodhya movement's strength derived from its ability to draw upon the cooperation of state machinery in Uttar Pradesh. The administration and security personnel were more than willing to oblige the kar sevaks whom they recognized as partners in forging the advancement of Hindu nationalism.

Forefronting the narrative of death and bloodshed against the Hindus supposedly perpetrated by the state had an extensive impact on middle-class Hindu audiences (P. K. Datta 1991). Their response however was not influenced by religious faith or religious opposition to the state, but by the cumulative failure of successive governments on material issues of everyday life. The antistate rhetoric allowed the Sangh combine to draw upon the festering dissatisfaction and discontent of the people. Popular reactions were linked more to antigovernment sentiment than to religious hurt or communalism (Basu above). Harping on the Ayodhya issue and on historical injustices done to Hindus could not have led to the consolidation of political Hinduism but for one very important factor: the steady deterioration of political authority and governance. The political appeal of Hindu nationalism was feeding on the crisis of the state and governance dominated by the Congress for four decades. Relentless violence and collapsing government and alienation and despair among the middle classes enabled the BJP to protect itself as the one party that was attentive to cultural identity and good governance. Political Hinduism was thus a symptom of the state's degeneration and weakening and more markedly of the long-term decline of the Congress. It was not the novelty of its project but the failure of political rule embodied by the Congress that explained the rise of the BJP.

## II

From the 1920s, Uttar Pradesh was a Congress stronghold. While its support was drawn from across the country, it was the party's influence in Uttar Pradesh that symbolized the essence of Congress politics. In 1991, for the first time in four decades, the Congress was voted out of power in the state in two successive elections. In 1993, its representation was reduced to twenty-eight seats in the state assembly.

The 1980s were a crucial phase in the transformation of Uttar Pradesh politics. Four factors dominated the process of change: the alienation of rural producers, discontent of marginal groups in rural society, growing assertion of the backward castes, and the challenge of communalism. Widespread social and economic disaffection was manifested in two different ways: by the decline of the Congress as the principal actor in Uttar Pradesh politics, and by its inept manipulation of social and political tensions. As is well known, the stability of the Congress Party had rested on the accommodation and co-optation of a wide range of classes, castes, and communities. In Uttar Pradesh, its capacity to accommodate groups and contain conflicts was restricted by the limited success of state intervention and opportunities for economic development. It was even less effective in the 1980s on account of the growth of a highly differentiated party system, dividing the electorate into clearly defined and separated social sectors. Poor governance, ineffective leadership, and severe infighting cost the Congress heavily in popular support. The consequences of such failures have been heightened sociopolitical tensions, conflicts, and cleavages, a climate of political violence, and a growing dislocation and alienation in civil society.

Social and political changes have been most marked in western Uttar Pradesh, which has experienced two interrelated developments (Z. Hasan 1994a). The first development was economic: the crystallization of an agricultural transformation that begin in the 1960s with the Green Revolution. A major breakthrough in agricultural production was achieved with new technology. The most significant improvements occurred in wheat, maize, and sugarcane. For example, average wheat yields increased from 15.5 quintals per hectare in 1979 to 18.9 quintals in 1985. The annual growth rate in food-grain production rose by 2.78 percent from 1969 to 1979. The second development was political: the growing assertiveness of surplus-producing farmers as a major political force. Significant opposition to government policies has come from the farmers movement, which came to the forefront from 1986 to 1990, demanding higher prices and cheaper inputs for agriculture. The growing influence of surplus-producing farmers is linked to increased food production in northwestern India, in Punjab and Haryana as well as UP (Patnaik 1991). From this region comes the great bulk of the food grains procured by the government to be sold in urban centers through the Public Distribution System at low, government-subsidized prices to a quarter of India's total population in urban centers; this has naturally boosted the importance of surplus-producing capitalist farmers vis-à-vis the central government and state governments. The alienation of the surplus producers from the Congress was more political than economic. The process began in 1977, with the formation of the Janata Party, which forefronted agrarian ideology and policy. Their alienation was accentuated by their perception that the price regime was tilted against them principally because of the urban domination of politics.

At the other end of the spectrum, the rural poor are clearly disillusioned with the failure of antipoverty programs. Available data indicate that rural inequalities remained virtually unaltered in the 1980s (Ahluwalia 1987). Unemployment and poverty are the distinct features of the state's political economy. According to the Seventh Five Year Plan, the physical quality of life index in UP was at the "abysmal lowest" level. In the 1980s, unemployment remained high, and moreover, opportunities for employment were confined to agriculture and government. Power, transport, irrigation, and industry that generate employment were underdeveloped. One of the reasons why the Congress regime was so singularly unsuccessful in tackling the specific problems of social and economic change lies in the low levels of economic development and the slow rates of growth in the state. Economic stagnation was responsible for the unemployment and underemployment of agricultural workers, which in turn are the major causes of the state's underdevelopment.

The transformative capacities of the Congress government were limited by the absence of an organized party capable of generating support for its policies. Gaining political power through appeals to the poor and disadvantaged worked well for some time; but in order to ensure that such support was not eroded, the much publicized socioeconomic policies had to be implemented. The pro-poor policies did not work in Uttar Pradesh as compared to the more developed states where social changes were much more visible. The public disillusionment that followed from slow economic growth was therefore charged to the Congress leadership. The government's failure to ensure social justice gave rise to social discontent and compounded cynicism among various groups regarding the efficacy of state intervention or, at any rate, about the political capacities of the Congress to effect social transformation.

At the heart of these changes was the failure of the Congress to rebuild the party after the 1969 split. The main challenge to the Congress domination was from the backward castes (Brass 1984, 1985). The Congress tried to mobilize the lower castes and classes through antipoverty programs, but made no attempt to include the backward castes in the new coalition forged in the 1970s (Z. Hasan 1989). Though a few symbolic gestures of accommodation were made, the leadership did not restructure the party to give it a different base, as it had in Karnataka in the 1970s or in Gujarat in the early 1980s. In Uttar Pradesh, on the other hand, upper-caste representation in the Congress ministries and also in the state and district leadership remained high in the 1970s and 1980s. Congress leadership was dominated by upper castes: 38 percent of the seventy-five presidents of district Congress committees and city Congress committees in 1973 were Brahmans, and forty of forty-five zillah parishad chiefs were either Brahman or Thakur. Backward castes were underrepresented in Congress, and in the early 1980s, Brahman representation in the leadership actually increased (*India Today*, December 30, 1983).

Why did the Uttar Pradesh Congress resist the political arrival of backward castes? One reason is that except during brief intervals, the Congress remained a crisis-ridden and vulnerable entity throughout Indira Gandhi's tenure. Election results in 1967, 1977, and 1989 brought no comfort to party managers. This left the Congress less room to maneuver change and also made party reorganization difficult in the 1970s and 1980s. Secondly, 40 percent of Brahmans in India live in Uttar Pradesh, the heartland of *Aryavarta*. They form 10 percent of the state's population as against Maharashtra and Tamil Nadu, where they constitute just 3 percent. No political formation could have ignored such a powerful group or disregarded the fact that it enjoyed a high ritual status, controlled land, and dominated the professions.

From the 1970s, however, the political domination of Brahmans was seriously contested by the backward castes, who have come into their own with ever more political influence. Individuals from Yadav and Kurmi backgrounds who have had access to education but have, at the same time, seen their prospects thwarted by upper-caste dominance, have asserted their position and staked their claims for adequate representation in the power structures. The backward castes have also used both their newly gained economic power and their numerical strength to challenge the stranglehold of the upper castes over the government (Frankel 1991).

Increasing power conflicts and endemic political instability led to social disorder and widespread violence. This was exacerbated by the criminalization of politics and the steady influx of the underworld into elected bodies, from the 1960s onward. It became pronounced in the 1970s and even more noticeable in the 1980s. Both the Congress and opposition parties accused each other of working with criminals. As one newspaper editorial put it:

In Uttar Pradesh no area is safe from dacoit gangs. Never before, not even in the turbulent days of the eighteenth century was the life and property as unsafe in Uttar Pradesh as it is today. Pride of place for a government that just cannot govern even its own citadel now goes not to Bihar, rated till the other day as the most mismanaged and inept state in the Indian Union, but to the stately state of Uttar Pradesh, allegedly the home state of the Prime Minister. (*Pioneer*, November 30, 1982, all *Pioneer* references to Lucknow edition)

The communal situation deteriorated sharply. Symptomatic of the growing intercommunity feuds was the extraordinary spurt in Hindu-Muslim rioting. The incidence of communal riots has increased over the last two decades, with a sixfold increase being registered between 1954 and 1985. A spate of communal rioting took place in UP from February 1981 to 1987, with a significant spread to rural areas. Nearly twenty-six conflagrations took place between February 1986 and June 1987. More than two hundred persons, mostly Muslims, were killed and a thousand injured. Damage to property was to the tune of fifteen million rupees. It is noteworthy that nearly all major riots during the 1980s occurred in towns with a spatial concentration of Muslims or in areas where Muslims have attained a measure of economic stability through their traditional artisan and entrepreneurial skills. This is a lesson drawn from Aligarh, Varanasi, Moradabad, and Meerut in the 1980s.

Communal politics and violence has played a decisive role in weakening the Congress base. Yet the secular agenda was accorded low priority with the Congress Party even contributing to its decline. Congress was not inclined to stem the rot set in the 1960s, because it comfortably held the reins of power. But as political pressures mounted from non-Congress coalitions, there was a decisive break from the previous decades in terms of party and government identification with patronage of religious symbols, traditions, and institutions.

In sum, political developments in Uttar Pradesh during the 1980s and early 1990s were the byproduct of two interrelated developments: an unlovely political struggle for the control of the state, pitting upper castes and classes against the backward and lower castes; and an intensification of intercommunity conflicts, which had the potential of displacing upper castes from positions of power. These structural underpinnings and social stirrings, combined with various political developments, resulted in a serious crisis of regime in the late 1980s. This crisis reshaped politics in new ways, especially conducive to Hindutva mobilization.

The underlying tensions of such sociopolitical conflicts could not be curbed or diffused by the Congress Party in the absence of extensive district and local networks. Indira Gandhi's 1975 declaration of a national state of emergency and the party's defeat in the 1977 elections seriously strained this capacity. By the 1980s there was very little left of the organization at the state or district levels. Ram Dhan, a former general secretary of the All India Congress Committee, denounced the Congress as an entirely "nominated structure headed by a bogus leadership." "In Uttar Pradesh the ruling party functions more on paper than in the field, the office bearer at various levels enjoying the spoils of office and shies away from the people. Office bearers appointed from above without any consideration to contact with grass roots or their capacity to organize and mobilize the people" (*Pioneer*, August 11, 1987). The growing frustration was partly because of the failure of state government to organize elections to fill positions in local government bodies and cooperative societies. These bodies were customarily ideal platforms to engage and involve party workers. The decline in Uttar Pradesh was striking because the Congress, though highly factionalized in the 1950s and 1960s, was nevertheless well organized. Rapid centralization of power in the 1980s speeded its decline thereafter.

The political importance of the state has played a pivotal role in the process of centralization and concomitant degeneration of the Congress organization. Delhi had the final say in the appointment of chief ministers and senior ministerial colleagues. Such an imposition produced the embarrassing and unedifying spectacle of a crop of chief ministers appearing or disappearing from the scene "like quick change artists" (*Pioneer*, August 4, 1981). In the case of Uttar Pradesh, the prime minister and inner coterie were disinclined to appoint state leaders who enjoyed a strong political base to the high office in Lucknow. Consequently, the mantle was invariably passed on to leaders with no popular backing. This is not all. State leaders were kept on a leash, their politics monitored and their activities kept under close vigil. It is not without significance that from 1980 to 1984, Uttar Pradesh had three chief ministers and the party unit had eight ministers. Not one chief minister completed the full five-year term; in fact the average tenure of a chief minister in Uttar Pradesh was less than thirty months.

Until the mid-1980s, Hindu nationalism had remained a weak electoral force, but there had always been a conceptual space for it in Uttar Pradesh society provided by the strong influence of Hindu revivalism and memories of interreligious conflict and the Muslim separatist movement culminating in the country's partition in 1947. The state had a poor record in providing the healing touch after the partition trauma. Even the state government was not immune to communal activity; despite repeated directives from Jawaharlal Nehru, it took little action to curb Hindu communalism. Many senior Congress men remained sympathetic to commonly perceived Hindu interests (Graham 1990). The first three chief ministers of Uttar Pradesh in the 1950s and early 1960s—G. B. Pant, Sampurnanand, and C. B. Gupta—were extremely conscious of "the northern origins of Hinduism" and were committed to a right of center consensus. Some of their major concerns, such as the Hindi-only language policy in government and education and the exclusion of Urdu, were incorporated in Congress politics. In the area of language and minority rights, the Congress offered few opportunities to right-wing parties to build a social base. Consequently political Hinduism could not produce any significant uprising of Hindu nationalist sentiment and was unable to replace the Congress in the affections of the Hindu majority. This was the main reason for the Jan Sangh's inability to achieve a decisive electoral breakthrough in Uttar Pradesh. But the political culture of conservatism nurtured by the Congress clearly shaped the growth of the BJP in later decades.

## III

Many new factors were responsible for reactivating communal sentiment in the 1980s. One catalyst was the alarm over the conversion to Islam of a group of low-caste Hindus in Meenakshipuram, far away in south India, in southernmost Tamil Nadu. This stimulated the revival of the VHP, which has specifically built upon the activities of Hindu organizations campaigning against conversions. The opposition to conversions was very strong in Uttar Pradesh; the VHP and the BJP organized numerous meetings and demonstrations in major cities to highlight the dangers of conversions to Islam. BJP members walked out of the assembly to protest what they alleged to be the indifference of the government to conversions to Islam in eastern Uttar Pradesh. During this period the Hindi-Urdu controversy was once again revived in response to the government's halfhearted proposal to make Urdu the second language of the state. Much of communal politics centered around these two issues. It is noteworthy that the Congress did not oppose the protest actions.

From 1983 onward, the VHP organized a series of elaborate processions to foster Hindu unity. Uttar Pradesh figured prominently in the ekatamata yajna programs (described by Richard Davis above). During these processions, VHP leaders repeated the theme of "save Hinduism" and condemned conversions, the concessions to Urdu, and politicians who pampered Muslim vote banks. In many districts yatras were accorded "a historic reception" (*Pioneer*, May 31, 1984). District Congress committees welcomed processions with arches and *pandals* (covered stages). Support for the yatra was fairly strong at the *tahsil* (sub-district) levels (*Pioneer*, May 17, 1984).

During this period, the Uttar Pradesh Congress had clearly begun to experiment with different methods of gaining legitimacy. The Congress first changed its strategy in the early eighties, especially when it faced the prospect of losing power. The new design for regaining support was clearly majoritarian—best understood as a political idiom that seeks to build electoral majorities on the basis of a majority defined by ascriptive factors such as religion and language. Uttar Pradesh provided an active field for the trial of this project as a long period of plural and communal/segmented existence was leading to a sense of unease with mainstream politics. The growth of revivalism was a reaction to the coalition built by Indira Gandhi consisting of the religious minorities and the large majority of India's deprived and marginalized peoples in the 1970s. Following the party's virtual rout in the south and the growing evidence that it was losing support among Muslims, Indira Gandhi in an astute move completely reversed the strategy in the north, especially in Uttar Pradesh, building upon the confrontations in Punjab and Jammu and Kashmir, and indirectly against Pakistan and the foreign hand, "to give to the Hindus a big boost and a firm stake in the Congress," commented the *Pioneer* (November 12, 1984). The strategy formed the centerpiece of the Congress election campaign in 1984 held in the aftermath of Indira Gandhi's assassination, which had created a "wave of unprecedented gloom" in Kanpur, Lucknow, Varanasi, Allahabad, Ghaziabad, and Shahjahanpur (*Pioneer*, November 1, 1984).

The 1984 election played upon two themes: national unity and the need to save the country from internal and external enemies. Assassination and opposition betrayal were the leitmotif of the Congress crusade. The message of national unity explicitly appealed to Hindu voters; for the first time, the Congress tried to distance itself from Muslims, and consequently no effort was made to solicit their support. This catalyzed communal sentiments and provided the Congress an opportunity to emerge as the chief advocate of majoritarian interests, the only party capable of protecting India from the dangers of communal strife and disunity. Rajiv Gandhi's slogan "Not Kashmir Desham, not Assam Desham, not Telugu Desam, but Bharat Desham" elicited a fervent response and reached a climax in the 1984 Lok Sabha elections, creating a "tidal wave" of support for the Congress (*Pioneer*, December 18, 1984). Transcending caste calculations and local considerations, the Congress routed the BJP, which had espoused the same line of national unity.

It is significant that much before the Babri mosque imbroglio led to a serious communal polarization, the Congress government was already devising an "Ayodhya strategy." The "Ayodhya strategy" was not specifically designed for Uttar Pradesh, but it dramatically changed the agenda of this state, perhaps more than anywhere else. Designed to reverse the weakening and waning of the Congress, it contributed profoundly to the party's downfall. Given the Congress Party's hegemonic position in the state, its decline opened the space for communal and caste assertions. The popular appeal of the Ram jammabhoomi issue and the BJP success derived from it serve to spotlight the importance of the Ayodhya movement in catapulting the BJP to the center stage.

During Congress rule, the "Ayodhya strategy" unfolded in several different ways. For example, places mentioned in the *Ramayana* were developed, the Ayodhya *ghat*s (banks) and the *parikrama* procession route around the town of Ayodhya were beautified, and a *Ramayana* study center was established. The government announced that the Hindi Language Trust (*Hindi Bhasha Nidhi*), a government organization, would publish low-priced editions of Tulsidas's *Ramcaritmanas*. The state government was instrumental in facilitating the unlocking of the Babri Masjid in 1986. The "Ayodhya strategy" was crafted by the government to appease and conciliate the VHP-BJP combine that had mounted an emotive movement to pressure the prime minister to accommodate Hindu sentiments. But the hallmark of Congress strategy was not just the appeasement of the VHP, but equally the accommodation of Muslim fundamentalism. A former associate and minister in the government of Rajiv Gandhi stated that he had unimpeachable evidence that a deal had been struck between the prime minister and Maulana Ali Mian, a noted and influential theologian of Lucknow. Rajiv Gandhi agreed to concede to his demand on revoking the Shah Bano verdict on the express assurance that he and the All India Muslim Personal Law Board would not involve themselves with the Babri Masjid dispute (M. Hasan 1993a). The deal was that Muslims would get the revocation of the court verdict through Parliament while the Hindus would be granted *darshan* (viewing) at Ram janmabhoomi by unlocking the gate. So in May 1986, Rajiv Gandhi's government introduced the retrograde Muslim Women's (Protection of Rights on Divorce) Bill. In retrospect, the bill accorded considerable legitimacy to the communalization of Indian polity, on the one hand, and gave the Sangh combine a unique opportunity to press its claims on the disputed site in Ayodhya, on the other.

As the 1989 elections approached, the Congress government in Uttar Pradesh capitulated to the rising Hindu sentiment by allowing the VHP to lay the foundation stone of the proposed Rama temple at the disputed site. The Uttar Pradesh government put pressure on the VHP to go ahead with its Ram shilan puja on November 9 despite continuing Hindu-Muslim violence in different parts of the county. The agreement worked out at a meeting in Lucknow, convened by the chief minister of Uttar Pradesh with the representatives of the VHP in the presence of the union home minister, allowed the VHP to carry the "sanctified bricks" to Ayodhya for laying the foundation stone of the Rama temple on November 9, 1989. The agreement enabled the BJP vice president, S. S. Bhandari, to claim that whatever is happening at Ayodhya is with the full knowledge and approval — both legal and administrative — of the state government (*Statesman*, October 16, 1989).

The Congress government clearly underestimated the intensity of communal feeling aroused by the Ayodhya movement. An important consequence of the strategy was the escalation of communal violence and the polarization of communities, contributing to a ground swell of support for Hindu nationalism. However, this upsurge was not a spontaneous phenomenon; it crested during a period of crisis caused by the decline of the Congress. The opening of the locks on gates protecting the Babri Masjid sparked violence in Barabanki, Varanasi, Lakhimpur Sheri, Meerut, Rampur, Moradabad, Kanpur, and Allahabad. Indeed the Meerut riots in April 1987 signified a sharp escalation of communal conflict. Government action provoked strong protests from Muslim leaders who vitiated the communal atmosphere by launching a strident campaign for the restoration of the status quo in the Ayodhya dispute. Janata Dal leader and editor of *Muslim India*, Shahabuddin warned the Muslim community in Lucknow that "if they do not raise themselves from slumber the day is not far off when each and every masjid will be snatched away from us" (*Pioneer*, March 25, 1986). The VHP quickly stepped up its campaign emphasizing that Muslims were insensitive to Hindu sentiments. Clearly the Congress had ignored the fact that the communal energy released by divisive symbols would create the most widespread friction and strife in Uttar Pradesh because of the growing social segregation that fostered distrust and because these disputed shrines were located there.

For several years, the Congress frittered away opportunities to prevent the spread of communalism in the state, for it believed that its "Ayodhya strategy" could be a winning political gamble. This assumption hinged on an escalating series of compromises. In the end it was a process that the Congress could not control. The encroachment into Hindu political territory intensified communal politics and threatened the structural stability of the political system. Attempts to occupy both the secular and communal spaces left an imprint of ambiguity on Congress politics. Indeed the 1989 election strategy was a summation of this even as the Congress claimed to have successfully accommodated the interests of the majority and minority communities. Nevertheless, the way this was accomplished caused a decisive shift in the Muslim vote, while the party's attempt to garner a Hindu vote shifted the balance of power decisively in favor of political Hinduism.

# IV

From this point on, politics was marked by increasing pressures from the Sangh combine on the political structures of the state. A concerted bid was made by the Sangh combine to change the political discourse by making disputed shrines an emotive focus for mobilization. It was concentrated on a single symbolic issue—the continued existence of a mosque on the site in Ayodhya venerated by the Hindus as Ram janmabhoomi (Nandy et al. 1993). The BJP made masterly use of religious symbolism to mount the most ambitious program of socioreligious mobilization.

The upheaval created by the Ram janmabhoomi movement in Uttar Pradesh was strongest there because all three disputed shrines—Ayodhya, Mathura, and Varanasi—are located in that state. The Sangh combine also gained enormously from its ties with the VHP and the numerous social, cultural, and religious organizations associated with the RSS, which appear to link the party with the traditional values and concerns of popular Hindu culture in Uttar Pradesh. It used these ties to amplify the friction between the state and a public increasingly dominated by the RSS-VHP through its congregational politics linking the home, the street, and the temple (Chakravarthi et al. 1992). This new style of politics is specifically built around religious festivities requiring public participation and culminating in processions winding through major streets and towns. Insistence on taking processions through communally charged towns intensified pressure on the state as any denial of public space was interpreted as anti-Hindu (Freitag, below).

At the heart of the Sangh combine's project was the goal of creating a Hindu political majority with a distinctive cultural dimension. But this was not all. In Uttar Pradesh the effort was by no means confined to an internal consolidation of the Hindu community alone. The cohesion of the community was based on a rejection of cultural pluralism and the exclusion of Muslims who had formed an important part of Uttar Pradesh's social and cultural milieu for centuries and who have contributed significantly to the high culture of Awadh. This is why the Hindutva project is divisive: it privileges exclusiveness. This polarization along religious lines was bolstered by the high concentration of Muslims in Meerut, Moradabad, Bulandshahr, Ghaziabad, Rampur, and Aligarh, some of whom have been eager to defend the symbols of their religious identity. The last few decades have also seen the economic advancement of some sections of Muslim weavers, artisans, and craftsmen who have benefited from the

rising demand for handicrafts and the expansion of exports. Muslim economic prosperity in the 1970s and 1980s threatened Hindu domination of
trade and industry and bred resentment and anger among those Hindus
accustomed to the Muslims' invisibility and deference. This infuriated the
VHP, which has castigated the new markers of Muslim affluence, especially
when it finds expression in the mushrooming of mosques and *madrassah*s
(Islamic schools).

As a social phenomenon, political Hinduism derived strength mainly
from the ranks of the upper-caste, middle- and lower-middle-class population in smaller cities and semiurban areas of the state (Chibber and Misra
1993). The majority of volunteer workers (kar sevaks) who assembled in
Ayodhya for the demolition of the Babri Masjid in December 1992 were
urban, partly modernized, and educated men (*Times of India*, February 2,
1993). The growth area of the Sangh combine is western and central Uttar
Pradesh, where Muslims are either economically prosperous or culturally
visible. In both it has made significant inroads into rural areas.

The Hindutva movement ran into difficulties on the issue of caste,
especially the policy of reservation, which was the centerpiece of the Janata
Dal's strategy to counter the politics of Hindu communalism. Formed in
1989, the Janata Dal government in New Delhi decided to reserve 27 percent of the posts in the central government for the members of the backward castes, in accordance with the recommendations of the Backward
Classes Commission, headed by Bindeshwari Prasad Mandal, which identified 3,743 castes as "backward" and needing affirmative action measures
by government. In addition to this, the Uttar Pradesh government passed
an ordinance to raise the reserved quota for backward castes in the state
government by 12 percent. The reservation policy provided significant new
opportunities for social mobility to the backward castes, who were underrepresented in the central and Uttar Pradesh government. Precisely for this
reason, the reservation policy was rejected by the upper castes who dominated the bureaucracy and public institutions. Accordingly, the issue of
reservation polarized the backward and upper castes in towns and villages
throughout the state, which broke into an orgy of violence. The most vehe-
ment opposition to the reservation policy came from the universities of
Allahabad and Lucknow, the Indian Institute of Technology, Kanpur, and
Benares Hindu University, the leading universities for recruitment into the
civil services.

As long as the Congress Party remained dominant in Uttar Pradesh
and was the main vehicle for social mobility and political self-expression

for the upper castes, they were secure. Its defeat in 1989 heightened their anxieties as they sensed a political and economic threat to their domination. Mandal created the impression of an imminent transfer of power from upper to backward castes. Mandal made visible all the preexisting social divisions and tensions of Hindu society, which could not be wished away by the Ayodhya movement. For the BJP, the political fallout of Mandal was damaging to its project of Hindu nationalism and its unifying symbol. The problem was compounded as the party made significant inroads among the backward castes in major parts of the state and thus could not afford to alienate them by openly opposing Mandal. But for the BJP—as a party that has tried to project the notion of an undifferentiated Hindu society—the legitimation of caste as a basis for political organization can be highly problematic because it undermines Hindu consolidation by reinforcing alternative social allegiances.

At this time, the VHP decided to send kar sevaks to Ayodhya for the construction of the Ram temple. This diverted attention from the radical possibilities implicit in Mandal at the moment when UP was set to join the backward caste axis and instead focused attention on the urgent need for unity and cohesion. The unifying content of the symbol of Rama provided a rallying counterideology against both the supposed divisiveness of Mandal and the pseudo-secular state's policy of minority appeasement. Community conflict was at this juncture significant because it took the heat off the Mandal issue; it shifted attention away from intra-Hindu divisions into communal discourse. Very soon, caste conflict was turned into Hindu-Muslim polarization and rioting in which Muslims were the main victims.

The escalation of community conflicts sparked off an upsurge of violence and frenzy. It is important to note that high communal frenzy was most evident in 1990, and not before or after that. Inflammatory pamphlets and provocative slogans raised during VHP marches were instrumental in unleashing violence geared toward achieving political ends. There was a spate of rioting for two months preceding the 1989 elections, a pattern repeated in 1990 and 1991. Most of these riots took place during or after major chariot processions (rath yatras) that created a tense atmosphere in the towns they traversed. From November 1990 onward, the greater proportion of violence was concentrated in UP: thirty-four towns were under curfew in November. The proposal to bring a second round of kar sevaks to Ayodhya in December after the fall of the Janata Dal government saw another round of widespread violence. (See also Basu, above, and van der Veer, below.)

The disorder in Uttar Pradesh from August 1990 to June 1991 contributed to the fall of the Janata Dal government in New Delhi as well as in Uttar Pradesh. Championed and nurtured by the BJP, the UP farmers' movement and the Congress, the anti-Mandal agitation played a crucial part in dislodging the Janata Dal government in New Delhi. From October 1990 onward, as anti-Mandal agitation slid into violence between Hindus and Muslims, intensifying social conflicts and confrontations between various groups and identities, hitherto peaceful towns and surrounding rural areas were incorporated into the ambit of communal violence.

On the face of it, the 1991 election seemed to turn overwhelmingly on the Ayodhya controversy. The crucial issue is whether the voters supported the BJP simply on emotive-religious appeal or were favorably disposed to the BJP because of the unprecedented political mobilization mounted by the Sangh combine to highlight the state repression of the kar sevaks in Ayodhya. Most accounts of elections clearly show that the Hindutva propaganda and its demonization of the state—and not merely the innate religiosity of people—played a vital part in turning the tide in favor of the BJP (Basu, above). The BJP exploited the prevailing opinion against Chief Minister Mulayam Singh Yadav, turning it into a broad-based sentiment against the state. Because the Janata Dal led by Mulayam Singh Yadav provided a viable alternative to the Congress in Uttar Pradesh, unlike in Rajasthan and Madhya Pradesh, where political contestation alternated between the Congress and BJP, the BJP discredited and decried Mulayam Singh Yadav's leadership.

The Ramjanmabhoomi issue provided the charge for the BJP's battle to control Uttar Pradesh. The BJP successfully used nonparliamentary means to win elections in 1991. The party's high success was clearly based on the appropriation of public space that it transformed into communal space (see Basu, above). Violence played an important part in the enlargement of the political base of the BJP (see van der Veer, below). Overall, the Sangh combine seized the opportunity provided by the unlocking of the gates around the Babri mosque to rework the balance of advantage in its favor. The important point is that the situation out of which these conflicts and opportunities arose was not inherently communal: its transformation into communal conflict depended upon the activities of state authorities, political parties, and politicians.

# 4

# Mass Media: Images,
# Mobilization, and Communalism

VICTORIA L. FARMER

THIS CHAPTER EXPLORES WAYS in which mass media have been implicated in communalism, focusing on media imagery surrounding the destruction of the Babri Masjid. It is meant to be heuristic rather than comprehensive, providing basic information about Indian media and research materials. It is also far from conclusive: totalizing explanations of media effects are impossible to construct because of the complex ways in which media both shape and are shaped by larger social, political, and cultural structures. Though various methodologies can provide useful insights, any research on media and social outcomes is necessarily partial and tentative.

Of many possible approaches, this chapter privileges an institutional, historical approach: How did various media genres develop in India? How did legislative, administrative, technological, and market forces combine to shape both message and audience? And what are the connections between the evolution of these genres and expressions of communal violence? Through this approach, and using the destruction of the Babri Masjid and resultant riot-related deaths as a focal point, we will see that various genres lent themselves to very differing roles in expressions of communal sentiment. Some—such as cinema—largely avoided communalization, while others—particularly the Hindi press—were easily appropriated for communal ends.

One media genre in particular—television—emerges as most crucial in this analysis. Briefly, a confluence of technological, legal, and administra-

* I thank participants in the seminar that led to this volume for their helpful suggestions, though I alone am responsible for interpretations in this chapter. An American Institute for Indian Studies Dissertation Fellowship funded part of my initial research.

tive developments created a window in the late 1980s—after unprecedented infrastructural investments in the mid-eighties and before the advent of transnational satellite television in the early nineties—during which the government of India held a monopoly over a vast television broadcasting system. Because of this novel, hegemonic position, Doordarshan (Indian state television) programming decisions took on extraordinary salience. Since the late eighties, many, often well-founded, charges have been made that other forms of media were politically biased or promoted communal tension. However, these charges implicated a limited number of media professionals who stood accused of perpetrating communal violence. Such charges against Doordarshan, however, precisely because it was under centralized national control, have highlighted questions about the very legitimacy of the government's secular and democratic credentials.

## Specificity, Language, and Causality

Before I present more details, I must take three brief methodological detours—on specificity, language, and causality—to help situate this discussion for those who are new to the study of media in India.

First, examples in this chapter were chosen specifically for their communal content and do not comprise a representative sample of all Indian media messages. Every day in India, thousands of newspapers, hours of television programming, a thriving cinema industry, video and magazine production, and a host of other media forms generate entertainment, advertising, education, and political persuasion. In the vast majority of these productions, communal issues simply do not arise or are studiously avoided. Furthermore, the focus of this chapter on communalism in Indian media in no way implies either that Indian media messages are subject to some natural gravitational pull toward communal uses, or that there is something peculiarly Indian about the use of media for divisive ethnic, religious, or racial purposes. As David Ludden (1994) points out, cultural chauvinists are mobilizing their troops not only in South Asia, but also in Russia, Eastern Europe, and elsewhere. Particularly after the 1995 bombing of a federal office building in Oklahoma City, it is crucial to note that the United States is no more immune than other areas to the harnessing of mass communications technologies for violent parochial messages (Justice 1995).

Second, language in India is not simply a neutral means of conveying political messages, but is itself a contentious political issue. While this issue is much too complex to be detailed in this chapter, two basic issues must be understood: Hindi is not universally used throughout India; and there is an important difference between commonly spoken Hindi, or Hindustani, and what has come to be known as "Doordarshan Hindi," a stylistically Sanskritized form of the language.

While Hindi in the Devanagari script is constitutionally the official language of India (according to Article 343), some dialect of Hindi is the mother tongue of at most a third of the Indian population. Furthermore, Article 351 directs the union government to promote the spread of Hindi, drawing for its vocabulary "primarily on Sanskrit and secondarily on other languages." Efforts to spread Hindi to non-Hindi-speaking areas, particularly through primary education, have caused considerable political unrest (Krishna Kumar 1991; Rudolph and Rudolph 1972; *Seminar* 1992). Similarly, the use of Hindi on national television programming has rendered Doordarshan a focal point for regional linguistic discontent. Also, because television is controlled by the Centre (the national government based in New Delhi), charges that Doordarshan's use of Hindi constitutes cultural imperialism radiating from Delhi bring into question the legitimacy of federal rule in a way that is not seen, for instance, with respect to more market-driven Hindi cinema production.

The heavily Sanskritized Hindi used by Doordarshan, particularly for news broadcasts, renders television liable to charges of communalism as well. The communalization of Hindustani—by at least the minimal definition of a differentiation of linguistic and cultural markers that divide Hindu and Muslim Indians hierarchically—predates the advent of electronic media (see, for example, Bhandari 1994). It was institutionalized in radio shortly after independence. Under Sardar Vallabhai Patel, India's first Minister of Information and Broadcasting, and his successor B. V. Keskar, All India Radio promoted Sanskritized vocabulary over Urdu forms in spoken language (Lelyveld 1990) and devalued Muslim musical contributions as well (Lelyveld forthcoming). The use of Sanskritized Hindi—a type of language easily perceived as not only Hindi, but also as Hindu—further institutionalized this division.

Clearly, then, language can be used as a method for lending communal interpretations to messages that otherwise carry no communal content. In other words, analyzing Indian media requires examining not only what is said, but also the language used to say it. While this may seem obvious, it has profound implications for media research. One of the most highly developed methodologies in communications research is content analysis. Content analyses that consider only content, however, without taking into account the language used to convey that content and the implications of that language in the social context of its deployment, miss by design the media messages—including communal messages—that are carried by the choice of language used. And because the codified data created by content analysts are readily quantified, it is easy for researchers who study content alone to generate seemingly scientific statistical data that can be claimed to prove media messages are free of communal implications.

This raises the third methodological issue, concerning causality. It is virtually impossible to prove causality in media studies. From a positivist social science perspective, adequate data simply do not exist. From more nuanced theoretical perspectives that are skeptical about empiricism, no amount of data would be conclusive. Because of this, wildly differing interpretations of the connections between media and communalism have been presented by a variety of analysts, ranging from those who posit (but cannot prove) that media images promote communal violence to those who argue that there is no connection whatsoever between media and communal antagonism. The very insolubility of the causality puzzle connecting mass media images and political mobilization has rendered mass media a resilient scapegoat. In the vicious communal polarizations of the last decade, concerned writers have sought to pinpoint causes and isolate feasible solutions, and the media have come to be counted as culpable in many accounts of the recent conflicts. On the other hand, the absence of correlative data supporting cause-effect hypotheses about the media's role in communalism has also opened terrain for arguments that mass communications do not have measurable social effects, but simply reflect a traditional ethos or national identity (in the cultural variant) or consumer taste (in the market variant). From this perspective, for example, it can be argued that Rama is a cultural and not religious figure (see, for example, Varshney 1993), and that Doordarshan's serialization of the *Ramayana* is therefore devoid of religious—and thus communal—connotations. Such perspectives are at best naive, however, particularly given that the state-run communications systems are predicated on inculcation of a national identity; and often, on closer examination, such arguments prove to be self-serving normative assertions regarding society, culture, and nation. As Richard Fox notes below, one popular but misguided way to discuss communalism is to see it as "an excrescence of Indian tradition, an atavism or primitivism." With respect to mass media, though, we must ask what these arguments teach us, what is hidden? These smoke screens mask agency, funding, and the content of media imagery by neglecting the mobilization of both communications hardware and media imagery. Overly deterministic cause-effect models, rigid content analyses, and broad assertions differentiating realms called "culture" and "religion" all neglect what is coming to be called the study of "media ecology," which concentrates on the way media imagery shapes viewers' values and conceptions of society (Stonehill 1995).

## Television and Communalism

The relationship between media and communalism with the most far-reaching political implications is the connection between television programming and communal mobilization. This is because, even though no explicit cause-effect linkage between television imagery and violence can be clearly demonstrated, the broadcast of programming widely perceived as having communal undertones has highlighted and focused criticism on the legitimacy of the government's secular stance. The core of these accusations concerns the serialization on state-controlled television of two Hindu epics, the *Mahabharata* and *Ramayana*. Though communal violence and civic unrest were certainly not an intended goal of these programming decisions, the broadcast of the *Ramayana*, in particular, inadvertently promoted Rama-related imagery that was easily appropriated by Hindu nationalist leaders of the Sangh Parivar, especially by L. K. Advani.

Rama existed in India long before television was invented, and Doordarshan was not the first to attempt a hegemonic *Ramayana* narrative (Lutgendorf 1990; Pollock 1993; Thapar 1989; Babb and Wadley 1994). Nonetheless, many scholars have come to the conclusion that the serialization of the *Ramayana* on Doordarshan was fundamental to the project of fundamentalism, creating a shared symbolic lexicon around which political forces could mobilize communal praxis (van der Veer 1994b, 177–78). Perhaps the greatest evidence of the effects of the serialization of the epics has come from scholars in the humanities. One scholar, for example, noted that when people were asked about Ayodhya in studies done before the *Ramayana* broadcast, they would answer that Ayodhya is the birthplace of Rama, but they would leave its location vague. Maybe Ayodhya is a mythological place, maybe it exists wherever God exists; Ayodhya could be in one's own backyard, or at the local temple. After Doordarshan's *Ramayana* and contemporary BJP mobilizations, however, people responded to questions about Ayodhya by defining it precisely as a town in Uttar Pradesh (V. Narayana Rao, personal communication). In 1991, Anuradha Kapur analyzed the "new," post-Doordarshan, iconography of Rama in popular posters, in which Rama as a militant warrior, poised to use his bow, is depicted more often than other iconographic possibilities. She wrote:

The transformation of the Ram image from that of a serene, omnipresent, eternally forgiving God to that of an angry, punishing one, armed with numerous weapons, wearing armour and even shoes, is truly remarkable. Where does this new Ram, laden with all manner of martial gear, come from?
He appears to come from television epics—Ramanand Sagar's "Ramayana" and B. R. Chopra's "Mahabharata." The "Mahabharata," especially, feeds upon the escalating notions of a militaristic and virile Hinduism. (*Times of India*, October 1, 1991)

Barbara Stoler Miller devoted much of her 1991 presidential address to the Association for Asian Studies to a discussion of the serialization of the epics, noting that "it is the religious intensity, linked with politicized communal feelings, that has made the Ayodhya situation so compelling. The way militant Hindus have structured the narrative of Ayodhya's sacred history and bent the epic universe to their definition of Indian national identity is a striking example of how vulnerable the past is to the passions of the moment" (Miller 1991, 790).

How did this state-sponsored depiction of Rama come to be? An answer requires an examination of the history of Doordarshan. Television in India began, as had radio, through the urging of Western companies seeking markets in India. It took many years from the first broadcast in 1959, however, for television to develop into a mass market media. Stations outside India's capital city were not set up until the early 1970s, and significant expansion of television did not occur until the 1980s. This hesitancy to expand, based on the high cost of television as compared to radio, was overcome by linking television and national development. The 1966 Chanda Committee report on radio and television argued that difficulties in implementation of India's five-year plans could be ameliorated by using electronic media to promote understanding of and compliance with planning. Simultaneously, Vikram Sarabhai, in one of his initiatives to promote India's space program, argued that television could be used to "leapfrog" India into sustained economic development (Sarabhai 1974, 41–42). This argument, combined with a commitment to rural development, culminated in the Satellite Instructional Television Experiment (SITE) of 1975–76. This experiment in rural development, however, did not prove to be the basis for the subsequent evolution of television.

The major impetus for the growth of Doordarshan was a political decision made after the phenomenally popular telecast of the Ninth Asian Games in 1982, during which color television was introduced in India. Realizing the enormous potential influence of television, Prime Minister Indira Gandhi's government decided to embark on a major expansion of television in time for the 1985 elections. S. S. Gill, who had overseen the creation of stadia and other infrastructure for the Asian Games, was appointed Secretary of the Ministry of Information and Broadcasting. Under his guidance, the number of transmitters rose from 39 to 140, increasing potential coverage from 23 percent to 70 percent of the population. Transmitters were produced with indigenous technology, massive schemes were launched to train engineers, and import laws were liberalized to allow the production of more television sets. Commercially sponsored serials were introduced, partially because Doordarshan was simply unable to produce the amount of programming that would be required as broadcast time increased, and also because it was felt that sponsored programming would be more lively and popular, building the audience necessary for effective political communication. This new programming included commissioned serialization of the epics.

These initiatives led to a spectacular increase in the percentage of the population that could receive Doordarshan signals. The rapid pace of expansion from 1983 to 1985 slowed thereafter, mainly because further increases became more difficult, requiring low power transmitters to be installed in geographically remote areas. Current estimates are that Doordarshan signals are available to 83 percent of the population; the percentage is this low only because of difficulties in reaching very remote and mountainous regions. In 1983, the comparable figure was 26 percent. In 1983, there were less than three million television sets in the country; in 1992, there were nearly thirty-five million.

Mrs. Gandhi did not live to reap the benefits of her investment in television, and the sympathy vote for Rajiv Gandhi after her assassination overwhelmed the salience of television in the election process. Nonetheless, she had opened the door to a nexus linking state control of television for electoral ends with commercial pursuit of profit through advertising. This decision was no doubt facilitated by her knowledge that eroding support for Congress in the early 1980s would require increasingly persuasive

forms of electioneering, since more forceful measures—particularly blatant press censorship—had been largely delegitimated by her imposition
of emergency rule (1975–77).

Furthermore, legislative precedent had rendered television a tool
easily appropriated by the incumbent party. Technological innovations are
seldom anticipated through the creation of new administrative and legal
infrastructures to govern them. Instead Indian television evolved within a
legal structure whose genealogy can be traced to the 1885 Telegraph Act
under British colonial rule. The act stated that "the Central Government
shall have the exclusive privilege of establishing, maintaining and working
telegraphs." "Telegraph" was defined to include virtually any communications technology, and so in the 1920s, radio also came under direct governmental control. An initial attempt to create an independent broadcasting
corporation failed, in part because licensing fees allowable within colonial legal structures were inadequate. Although initially reluctant, the state
agreed to protect radio-related capital by settling radio under the protective wing of the British Raj.

This hegemonic role of the state in broadcasting was embedded in the
1935 Government of India Act, which reserved broadcasting for the Centre. It also stated that the Centre should not unreasonably prevent provincial governments from creating transmitters. After independence, the 1953
constitution incorporated many features of the 1935 act, including the reserving of broadcasting for the Centre. The constitution did not, however,
include even the minimal provision for decentralized, provincial control of
broadcasting found in the 1935 act. The legal basis for centralized control
of broadcasting thus continued, and in fact was strengthened, across the
1947 watershed of Indian independence.

At independence, Prime Minister Jawaharlal Nehru did argue that
broadcasting should be made autonomous from direct governmental control, but he also maintained that this was secondary to more pressing issues
of political stability and sovereignty. Calls for media autonomy accompanied by the political inability to implement change have since become a defining feature of the administration of mass media in India. The two most
coherent policy initiatives toward media autonomy from central government control—the 1978 Akash Bharati report (by the Janata government)
and the 1990 Prasar Bharati Bill (by the National Front government)—
both succumbed to political paralysis. To this day, no political initiative
has successfully altered the administrative and legal infrastructure governing Indian electronic media that was created under colonial rule. Further-

more, in the late 1980s, state-controlled television faced no competition. Before transnational satellite television became available in India in the 1990s, Congress was free to televise its conception of the Indian nation.

The crosscutting tensions of state centralization, development policies, and commercial sponsorship resulted in an array of programming that conflated national development goals and popular cultural traditions. Increasingly through the 1980s, television was used as a tool for cultural engineering and electoral gains through creation of an "Indian" national character closely identified with the ruling party. Commercial interests had no reason to counter the attempt to create an Indian market—defined by the state and nationalized cultural forms—provided that laborious historical and political documentaries did not supplant more popular programming on TV. The Doordarshan epics are examples of an array of programs that arose from the triadic nexus of a growing middle-class, increasing commercial advertising, and the use of television as an election strategy.

What was depicted inside the public sphere created by Doordarshan, therefore, included a fuzzy conflation of state authority, Hindu legitimacy, Hindi supremacy, cinema tunes (*filmi geet*), and commercial promotions. Identifying what is absent from or marginal to this television public sphere is more difficult, but protests against specific Doordarshan presentations do indicate some boundaries. For example, *Tipu Sultan*—a story about an eighteenth-century Indian Muslim ruler who tormented British armies for decades before being conquered—did not fit easily into Doordarshan's nationalist paradigm, because it depicted the Muslim, Tipu, as being modern and progressive, and it was broadcast on Doordarshan only after lengthy arbitration. The result of the court battle was that a disclaimer was aired before each episode to say that the story was fiction, not history, thus marginalizing Tipu Sultan as a historical figure and contributing to a nationalist history in which Muslims somehow become non-Indian. Other struggles over the electronic media have spilled beyond institutional confines into violent confrontations by some anti–Centre groups, in which Doordarshan and All India Radio personnel and infrastructure have been the target of terrorist actions. This has occurred when antisecessionist programming—typically dramatic presentations in Hindi, set in a timeless Punjabi or Kashmiri village, depicting primordial communal harmony—has been unaccompanied by actual decentralization of control over programming policies. Broadcasting language policies have become a focal point for regional demands; and violent assaults on and assassination of

Doordarshan personnel continue today. (For more information on media in Kashmir and Punjab, see Press Council of India 1991.)

Serialization of the *Ramayana* was not the only Doordarshan attempt to create a centerpiece for national culture that would be comforting to the Indian, mainly Hindu, middle classes. As Romila Thapar (1993) notes, one of the functions of nationalist depictions is to locate cultures, usually by defining a national culture that selects some aspects of history and symbolism, but sidelines others. The television serial *Chanakya*, set in the Mauryan empire and aired on Doordarshan in 1991, is a good case in point. This empire, during the fourth to second centuries B.C., consolidated its control over more of the subcontinent than any other force until the British Raj. Chandragupta Maurya, who became emperor in 321 B.C., first gained control of the Ganges River basin, then moved northwest into a power vacuum created by the departure of Alexander the Great, and finally accepted the trans-Indus territories of the Greek Seleucid dynasty after a battle in 303 B.C. The empire reached its greatest extent when Chandragupta's grandson, Ashoka, conquered Kalinga, in present-day Orissa, in 260 B.C. Ashoka erected numerous stone edicts throughout the extent of his empire (Thapar 1966, 70–74). The existence of Ashokan edicts as landmarks in many Indian cities renders Ashoka a commonly evoked name in many contemporary and popular histories. But Doordarshan's serialized drama about the Mauryas did not focus on Ashoka, who converted to Buddhism, but instead depicted his Brahman adviser Chanakya as hero of the Mauryan empire.

Numerous additional examples could be presented of the ways in which mass media have constructed images that have been or could have been appropriated for communal ends, but I do not mean to imply that these images were consciously constructed to promote communal strife. S. S. Gill felt it necessary to defend his decision to promote serialization of the epics as examples of Indian culture, rather than Hindu religion, through an editorial in the *Indian Express*. In an interview in 1990, he also expressed his view that the decision to serialize the epics was based on their encapsulation of pan-Indian, and indeed universal, values. With chagrin, he noted that "these idiots gave it a religious gloss! If I'd been there, I'd never have let them do this! *Ramayana* and *Mahabharata* are not *religious* epics!" (interview with author, New Delhi, 1990).

No doubt L. K. Advani, probably the most media-savvy figure in Indian politics, would also argue for the universal cultural significance of the *Ramayana*. It is certainly clear that he was able to capitalize on the availability of Rama imagery as a tool for communal mobilization. What is less clear is what would happen if the BJP were to gain control of Indian television. While Advani argued vociferously for media autonomy from government control during the 1989 elections (Farmer forthcoming), similar arguments made during that campaign have gone by the wayside. For example, in a 1989 interview with me, he downplayed the Sangh Parivar's emphasis on Hindi as the national language, emphasizing the need for linguistic flexibility for effective communication (personal interview, 1989). Nonetheless, in early 1995, after winning control of the government of Delhi in local elections, one of the BJP's first actions was to declare Hindi to be Delhi's official language. Similar discrepancies can be found between the BJP's 1989 free-market sloganeering and current Sangh Parivar efforts to undermine an agreement for the Enron Corporation to invest in a power plant in Maharashtra. This economic nationalist stance has now been institutionalized through the formation of the Swadesh Jagram Manch (SJM), The Forum for National Awakening, a wing of the RSS that is devoted to driving multinationals out of India (Ramachandran 1995).

## The Print Media and Cinema

Connections between communal mobilization and the print media do not carry the same ominous political implications as do connections between television and communal violence, mainly because communalist messages in the press do not automatically call into question the state's secularism. While it is not difficult to uncover instances of political interference with the press, the roots of the robust and multilingual print media are found in the struggle against colonialism, providing the press with the lingering aura of an oppositional, civil, and fundamentally legitimate media. Direct state intervention in the print media is not easily sustained and is hotly contested in political discourse. Nonetheless, the communalization of print media during and after the Ayodhya conflict had severe effects on India's social fabric, civic discourse, and individual lives.

When Mohandas Gandhi mobilized nationalist opposition to British rule by leading the Salt March in 1930 to protest the colonial salt tax, the effectiveness of this symbolic statement was enhanced because "the press reported the daily progress" of the march (Kulke and Rothermund 1990, 290). The press served a similar role in Hindu fundamentalist mobilizations of the last five years—it is perhaps not coincidental that Advani likens his rath yatras to the Salt March. And, at a rally organized by the SJM in Delhi in August 1995, former BJP president M. M. Joshi launched an economic nationalist campaign by addressing demonstrators arrayed around a statue of Gandhi on the Salt March (Graves 1995). It is now widely accepted that the Hindi press in particular was crucial in propelling the transition from Hindu symbolism to communal violence. The Press Council of India conducted an investigation of the role of the Hindi press during the late 1990 communal crisis. Its resolution states:

There is little doubt that some influential sections of the Hindi Press in U.P. and Bihar were guilty of gross irresponsibility and impropriety, offending the canons of journalistic ethics in promoting mass hysteria on the basis of rumours and speculation, through exaggeration and distortion, all of this proclaimed under screaming, banner headlines. They were guilty, in a few instances, of doctoring pictures (such as drawing prison bars on the photograph of an arrested Mahant), fabricating casualty figures (for example, adding "1" before "15" to make "115" deaths), and incitement of violence and spreading disaffection among members of the armed forces and police, engendering communal hatred. (quoted in Ram 1992)

Journalist N. Ram wrote that, "through its coverage of the October–November 1990 events in Ayodhya, a considerable part of the press—indeed the overwhelming part of the mass-circulated Hindi press—turned *kar sevak* in response to the crisis. The problem has clearly recurred during the much graver crisis of 1992" (*Sunday Observer*, December 15, 1992). N. Ram does not let the English press off the hook entirely; the first half of his article focuses on the way in which journalists reported communal incidents as they occurred, without adequately theorizing them as part of a unified process. This "episodic framing," as Shanto Iyengar (1991) terms this journalistic style, tends to isolate readers from broader understandings of political structures and processes. Ram implies that English-language journalists similarly succumbed to a myopic view of major transformations. Zoya Hasan and others at Jawaharlal Nehru University in New Delhi have also analyzed the role of the English press in communal mobilizations (Mediawatch n.d.).

Nonetheless, it is clear that the Hindi press was most directly culpable media genre in fomenting communal rioting. In her study of the press, Radhika Ramaseshan wrote,

The [Hindi] press was directly responsible for causing most of the communal riots that erupted in UP after the masjid was attacked, resulting in a death toll of over a hundred. By carrying out a sustained, feverish campaign highlighting the alleged 'bloodbath' in Ayodhya, caused by police firings on November 2, against the "police repression" of *kar sevaks* lodged in different jails, especially the one in Unnao, and against the pro-Muslim bias of chief minister Mulayam Singh Yadav, this press has achieved three objectives: it has whipped up emotional fervour for the "cause" of the Ram temple even among a large section of disinterested and apolitical Hindus, and as a corollary, completely polarised the Hindus and the Muslims, since the shrine ultimately symbolises Hindu animosity against Muslims. Lastly, it has seriously undermined the moral authority of Mulayam Singh Yadav, who by steadfastly maintaining that he adhered to the letter of law in this dispute, came to represent the voice of moderation and sanity. Although Yadav has reiterated that he will not allow the temple to be constructed on the disputed site, the critical dependence of his government on the support of the Congress (I), which has not only loudly condemned the alleged "atrocities" committed on the *kar sevaks* but has also demanded that the temple be constructed on the contentious site, the passage of the Vishwa Hindu Parishad (VHP) and its allies towards their ultimate goal—that of breaching the shrine and erecting a temple—has been rendered that much easier. (Ramaseshan 1990, 2701)

Charu and Mukul (1991) offer similar assessments in *Print Media and Communalism*, while providing examples of media distortion in the original Hindi, and broadening their scope to important issues outside of Ayodhya, including protests of the Mandal Commission report. In a seminar discussion of her paper in this volume, Zoya Hasan offered one extremely interesting explanation for the communal propensities of the Hindi press. She found that Hindu priests and mahants will pay sometimes up to twelve thousand rupees for the clout that comes with being a stringer for Hindi newspapers, thus gaining access to their audiences.

While space does not permit a full discussion of other resources that are available for the analysis of the print media, interested scholars may want to consult Dhawan (1987) for the history of laws pertaining to the press; JPRS Report (1993) for a compilation of press clippings related to secularism and Hindu nationalism; and Olsen (1994) for an analysis of *Economic and Political Weekly* articles about communal riots.

The cinema, while not devoid of political content, appears to be less implicated in recent communal mobilizations than do television and the print media. This is remarkable in itself, and may be related to the paucity of research on recent Indian cinema. Additional research may uncover complex linkages between cinematic imagery and popular conceptions of the state (Ganti 1993) that could have implications for the study of communalism. The avoidance of explicitly communal themes in the commercial cinema may also result from a form of self-censorship on the part of film producers, who must face inspection by the Indian government's Film Censor Board. As K. Hariharan (1994) argues, while producers engage in numerous battles over specific pronouncements by the Film Censor Board, there is little mobilization to fight the concept of the board, since the board obviates the need to create industrywide mechanisms for self-regulation. More importantly, though, it may be that the market-driven and capital-intensive nature of film production has steered cinema away from communal divisiveness. If so, further research is called for on the driving forces behind both television and the vernacular print media, to ask why these media more than others generated communally incendiary messages. Future researchers will have to examine whether or not cinema continues to be an industry relatively free of communal violence. A fore-boding omen of possible future trends occurred in July 1995, when Mani Ratnam, director of the controversial film *Bombay*, was injured in a bomb blast in Madras. *Bombay* explored the love of a Muslim girl and a Hindu boy, and was briefly banned to placate Islamic fundamentalist protestors.

## New Media Forms

Technomarket trends, in the context of state-run communication infra-structures that controlled television and radio, stimulated a boom in alter-native media, especially audio- and videocassettes, but also including ver-nacular media. These forms facilitated the expression of two additional and more fundamental trends, which are less easily disentangled: increasing opposition to the Congress Party and Congress Party governments, first at the state levels but increasingly at the Centre; and the rise of the middle classes, in an increasingly consumerist milieu.

Burgeoning new media outside state control allowed the BJP's prag-matic emphasis on communication to thrive; the BJP's dramatic use of public spectacles was disseminated and enhanced as a multimedia ex-travaganza, including audio- and videocassette tapes promoting Hindutva (Davis, above, and Manuel, below). One video, for example, depicted Rama's "miraculous" 1949 appearance in the Babri Masjid; an excellent discussion of this video and use of clips from it is available in Anand Pat-wardhan's documentary film *Ram ke Nam* (In the Name of God).

Ironically, the importance of videocassettes to communal mobiliza-tion arose in part from government policies. Strict governmental control over television resulted in lackluster entertainment shows and the manipulation of news reports, which became particularly severe before the 1989 elections (Farmer 1996); this fueled markets for videocassette entertainment, for independent video news programs, like *Newstrack*, and for the VCRs on which to play them. A 1990 *Economic Times-Pathfinder* poll found that 36 percent of metropolitan families with monthly incomes of twenty-five hundred rupees or more possessed a videocassette recorder or player (*Times of India*, March 20, 1990) and a 1991 National Council of Applied Economic Research poll found that low-income households with up to twenty-five thousand rupees in annual income purchased 33 percent of all VCRs sold in India (*India Today*, August 15, 1991). Viewing videocassettes had become a common practice in India and the BJP disseminated its messages by distributing cassettes and providing mobile video viewings from video raths.

The BJP, and especially former Information and Broadcasting Minister L. K. Advani, make sophisticated use of new media technologies. The Sangh Parivar has far surpassed other political groups in media manipulation (T. Basu et al. 1993). The setback suffered by the BJP in the 1993 legislative assembly elections shows that its one-issue message may not be adequate for electoral success, but the mobilization it fostered for the destruction of the Babri Masjid was clearly assisted by calculated use of various media forms, particularly those that are outside of state control.

The proliferation of new communications technologies may allow the forces of Hindutva new ways to broadcast their messages. For example, cable television systems have been created throughout urban India in the last few years. Cable operators can transmit programming throughout a neighborhood using either a VCR or air signals. For the 1993 elections, the BJP created a publicity committee to use cable systems as part of a media-based election strategy. Videocassettes of party leaders' speeches were provided to cable operators. The Delhi Pradesh BJP president, O. P. Kohli, noted, "We know our operators. On an average we have one out of every two cable operators operating from a colony who has party leanings and they would be ever obliging to play the tapes for us" (*Times of India*, September 30, 1993). It should be noted that the BJP did win the legislative assembly elections in Delhi, although there is no way to calculate the contribution of their media strategy to their success. The BJP also plans to distribute videos to rural homes that have VCRs and to facilitate public viewings in other areas. In the party's assessment, the most important feature of the cable network is that it reaches sections of society that neither attend public meetings nor read newspapers, particularly women voters and senior citizens (*Times of India*, September 3, 1993). As Amrita Basu (above) notes, the BJP seems to have been particularly successful in mobilizing women; this media strategy may help communal parties build on these gains in the future. (For an eloquent exploration of gender issues and communalism, see Anand Patwardhan's documentary, *Father, Son, and Holy War: A Film on Men, Religion and Violence*.)

Additional media developments bear examination, though it is again too early to understand their implications. There is a rapid proliferation of new satellite television channels, also to be broadcast through these cable systems. One, for example, was the idea of J. K. Jain, BJP member of the Rajya Sabha, the upper house of Parliament. The project is being launched by Joint American Indian Network (JAIN) Satellite Television, and promoted by Jain Studios. It will broadcast religious, moral, and spiritual programming (*Times of India*, September 6, 1993). Also difficult to measure is the impact of new communications systems on grass-roots sympathizers rather than official BJP leaders. For example, in mid-1993, a colleague told me of asking the cable operator in a posh Delhi neighborhood to provide a few hours of Pakistani television as one of many offerings. The operator said this was impossible; he had received threats when he had briefly aired Pakistani television in the past. This operator indicated that it is apparently common knowledge that an operator broadcasting Pakistani television would have his cable lines cut by BJP activists.

Technological innovations have allowed electronic communication to be tailored for specific target audiences, and state control of television has provided the fillip to create a market for these technologies. One outcome is that electronic media outside state control, like the print media and notably unlike television, have been able to develop the ability to tailor communication for India's diverse linguistic areas. Activists devoted to using new communications technologies for social empowerment of traditionally disempowered groups herald this capability, and many exciting projects are underway to create development programming. While these schemes generate much enthusiasm, however, it is also important to note that these new technologies are not inherently liberating; small is not always beautiful. Hierarchies of oppression are at least as easily replicated as they are overcome at more local levels of social organization. Localized programming can be used for myriad ends, and, as with all media forms, political organization and funding skew the outcomes.

## Conclusion

Two questions arise from this examination of Indian television. First, if we
limit our examination solely to the serialization of the epics, it is relatively
easy to jump to conclusions about a media-communalism nexus. Putting
the television *Ramayana* in the context of broader programming decisions, however, reduces the sense that the *Ramayana* was an overwhelming
presence on the airwaves. It instead becomes the center of a sphere that
extends into many peripheries. In the context of Indian federalism, this
center-periphery imagery is translated into center-state relations; secessionist movements in Punjab and Kashmir loom very large. We may want
to ask if our emphasis on Hindu-Muslim relations, propelled by the brutality of their consequences, have blinded us to broader issues. To what degree was the communalism of the last decade a symptom or by-product of
increasing centralization and state control of cultural production and economic distribution? In other words, if an explanation for recent communal
outbreaks could be devised, could this be done without simultaneously explaining secessionist movements? Are these phenomena unrelated, or are
they both outcomes of political institutions created in independent India?

Second, it does seem clear now that serialization of the *Ramayana*
created a symbolic lexicon that aided Hindutva mobilization of communal
praxis. However, an examination of the history of Doordarshan also shows
that this serial was televised because of an explicitly political decision, and
that both this decision and its salience for communal politics rested on the
identification of Hindus as a majority target for both electioneering and
advertising. This emphasizes the need for studies of communalism to examine closely both the class basis of political mobilization and the effects
of India's current rapid economic transformations on these class formations. Will liberalization increase the sense of economic insecurity—what
Barbara Ehrenreich (1990) calls the "fear of falling"—among the middle
classes? And could this insecurity be politically manipulated into increased
communal tensions? Or will a more competitive economic climate foster
a rejection of communal politics that will be deemed too costly not only
in human lives, but also in business profits? For example, Mushirul Hasan,
in a seminar discussion on this volume, noted that when the BJP recently
turned its attention to mobilizations around the Kashi Vishwanath temple
in Benares, the head of the Benares VHP publicly denounced the BJP, because he feared harm to his business interests from local BJP mobilization
(see also Basu, above). To rephrase the question, might Rama as politi-

cal symbol be surmounted by an even more effective Indian symbol: the newly convertible rupee?

In a final note of guarded optimism, it should also be emphasized that the promulgation of the Rama imagery so easily appropriated for communal ends by the Sangh Parivar occurred during a unique political moment. As noted above, the serialization of the epics resulted from a political decision made by leaders of an insecure Congress Party, during a moment in which it held uncontested control over a powerful new medium. Such media imagery is unlikely to prove as potent in a fundamentally altered media and political landscape. Or so we may hope, given that, as of the writing of this chapter, the Sangh Parivar has announced plans for more rath yatras during the 1996 Lok Sabha election campaigns.

# PART 2

# GENEALOGIES OF HINDU AND MUSLIM

# 5

# Music, the Media, and Communal Relations in North India, Past and Present

PETER MANUEL

MUCH OF THE DISCUSSION of communalism has attempted to ascertain the depth of the evident communal sentiment reflected in recent disturbances and the rise of Hindu militancy. Amrita Basu's essay above echoes a similar question about cultural history: do current developments reflect profound, long-standing, grass-roots animosity, or, alternately, are they merely the products of contemporary elite manipulation, ultimately conditioned by factors other than religious ones? While sociopolitical history is a natural focus for such inquiries, the study of expressive culture may reveal much about social practices and attitudes, both elite and grass-roots, past and present. This chapter focuses on musical culture in north India, outlining relevant aspects of the social history of classical music, and presenting some observations on twentieth-century folk and popular musics. My discussion of the contemporary scene will also refer to related forms of expressive culture, notably Hindi cinema and the sociopolitical uses of cassettes.

Given the extraordinary diversity of South Asian musical genres and practices, any attempt to generalize about music's relation to communalism is destined to a degree of superficiality. However, a few themes recurrent in north Indian musical culture do stand out in historical perspective. First among these is the inherent syncretism of the most characteristic forms of north Indian music, whose style, patronage patterns, and associated social practices reflect their evolution as the common heritage of a society more profoundly divided by class than religion. Secondly, north Indian musical culture can be seen as a site of interaction of two opposing tendencies: one, the tendency for music to transcend sectarian differences,

and, conversely, its often inherent association with particular religions and
the associated desires of individual communities to claim music in their
bid for cultural hegemony. An exploration of these themes may provide a
significant perspective on communal relations, while helping us situate recent socioreligious uses of the mass media in the context of issues of class
and technology.

## Syncretism in the Evolution of Hindustani Music

Since the spread of Muslim patronage in the twelfth century, north Indian
classical music (Hindustani music) has served as a site for the intense
and direct interaction—both amicable and competitive—of musicians and
patrons from both Hindu and Muslim communities. It has also been a
site for the confluence of distinct, yet in many ways compatible streams of
Hindu and Muslim aesthetics, ideologies, and social practices. Hindustani
music has thus evolved as an inherently syncretic and collaborative product of Hindu and Muslim artists and patrons. As such, while music has in
some respects been a site of contention, it has often been praised as a symbol of the fundamental pluralism of north Indian culture.

   In accordance with Muslim political domination of north India from
the thirteenth to nineteenth centuries, and the concurrent disbanding of
large temple establishments and their retinues of *devadasi* (temple courtesan) performers, art music in the north—much more than in south India—
was patronized and sustained for some six hundred years primarily by Muslim potentates. Indeed, Muslim patronage remained crucial to the art even
until 1947, as the several predominantly Muslim princely states recognized
by the British continued to be important centers of musical activity.

   While music has often been censured in orthodox Islamic ideology,
such proscriptions have generally had little direct impact in north India,
due to the more tolerant forms of Hanafi Sunni ideology that prevailed
from the Mughal period on. Moreover, in India, as elsewhere in the Islamic
world, music has always been embraced by particular Sufi orders, and by
a more general Sufi-derived attitude that regards song as a means of expressing devotion and, ideally, attaining mystical ecstasy. Thus, *qawwali*
has flourished since the fourteenth century as a devotional song genre,
while Sufi tradition allowed virtually any amatory verse to be interpreted
as expressing divine love as well as or instead of worldly love. Accordingly,

Muslim dynasts and nobles in South Asia were, with a few exceptions, ardent patrons of music, and insofar as they felt obliged or inclined to find religious justification for their love of music, they could always turn to Chishti Sufism for legitimation. In the absence of orthodox Islamic institutional music patronage, the Sufi orientation of performers and patrons further served to predispose music toward syncretism and tolerance rather than toward notions of sectarian or aesthetic purity.

The inherent pluralism of Hindustani musical culture was to a large extent a product of the combination of Muslim patronage with an inherited musical system that was to some degree imbued with Hindu extramusical associations. While at one level Indian classical music could be apprehended as an abstract system of modes and meters, at another level it was (and in south India, remains) linked in various ways to Hinduism, with its Krishnaite song texts, quasi-religious Sanskrit theoretical treatises, and its traditional associations with Hindu cosmology, mythology, and epistemology. The fact that Persian-speaking, ethnically Turkish dynasts so ardently patronized such music reflects how effectively South Asian such rulers had become in culture and self-identity. As has often been noted, what transpired was a process of Indian reconquest of the Muslim invaders through assimilation and acculturation.

Of course, the tenuous nature of Muslim rule itself necessitated accommodation with the overwhelmingly Hindu population, both by means of cultural pluralism as well as by the widespread reliance on Hindu revenue officers, soldiers, and indigenous feudal infrastructure in general. However, from the Mughal period on, the Muslim aristocrats' patronage of Indian music was clearly motivated less by a sense of strategic expediency than by a genuine enthusiasm for an art they came to regard as their own. Such attitudes were epitomized by poet, musician, and Sufi devotee Amir Khusrau (1253–1325), who, while synthesizing Middle Eastern and local musics, composed songs in Hindvi and praised Indian music as superior to that of any other country. By the time of Akbar's rule as Mughal emperor (1556–1605), nobles, Sufi literati, and the emperor himself were taking pride in penning Hindi (*Braj-bhasha*) lyrics and singing Krishnaite classical *dhrupad* songs. Occasional bigots—like Mughal emperor Aurangzeb (r. 1658–1707)—notwithstanding, throughout subsequent centuries Muslim rulers and nobles avidly patronized Indian music, wrote vernacular Hindi poetry, commissioned translations of Sanskrit treatises, and cultivated interest in indigenous culture in general. One can generalize that among the dominant class, traditional elite values of cultural patronage, connoisseurship, and personal cultivation of the fine arts were more significant than sectarian ideologies.

The structural and cultural ties uniting Hindu and Muslim nobility became particularly strong in nineteenth-century Awadh (Oudh), where, as Dwarka Prasad Mukherji argues (1948, 66–67), both groups came to form a single socioeconomic class, ultimately answerable to a third party, the British (Manuel 1990, 55–56). As a result, Hindu-Muslim amity and cultural interaction reached a sort of zenith, as elite Hindus mastered Persian, wore Mughal *sherwanis*, and worshiped at Shia shrines, while Muslim nobles celebrated the vernal Hindu festival of *holi*, and the Awadh *nawab* (ruler) Wajid Ali Shah staged dance-dramas in which he himself played the role of Krishna.

Particularly influential on musical culture was the spread of syncretic devotional forms of worship, especially as associated with Sufism and Vaishnava *bhakti* (devotion). The two traditions had much in common; Sufism's pluralistic saint worship could conflate with folk Hinduism, and both traditions stressed the utility of vernacular-language music as a form of devotion and a vehicle to mystical ecstasy. Both traditions emerged primarily from the lower classes, offering alternatives to male Brahmanic and Muslim priestly orthodoxy; at the same time, both sects were influential in elite circles as well. Thus, for the Muslim gentry, patronage of music and poetry cohered with venerable poetic and Sufi traditions of mocking Islamic orthodoxy and celebrating madness, inebriation, and antinomianism in general; at the same time, bhakti's implicit monotheism and inherent syncretism made it palatable to Muslim patrons. Hence, Muslim rulers at once cultivated ties to Sufi shrines and enthusiastically patronized Krishnaite poetic and musical traditions.

While north Indian music retained its Krishnaite texts, from the Mughal period on, its actual performance, like its patronage, came to be dominated by Muslims—specifically, hereditary professionals—unlike in south India, where Brahmans continued to dominate the field. In the subsequent centuries, Muslim preeminence became absolute, such that by the early twentieth century, there were very few prominent Hindu performers. Given the orthodox Islamic disapproval of music, the dominance of Muslim musicians might seem paradoxical, but it was largely conditioned by other factors. It appears that the ranks of low-caste Hindu converts to Islam included many professional rural musicians (for example, Mirasis) seeking to improve their status in the more egalitarian Islam. Other Hindu performers may have converted in order to adapt better to Muslim patronage. Although we can only surmise as to the precise motivations of converts like Tan Sen (the foremost musician of Akbar's court), one can generalize that Muslim patronage has tended, however benignly, to promote the Islamicization of performers, and vice versa. Thus, for example, it may not be coincidental that in the century before Indian independence, Hindu performers were most prominent at the Hindu court of Gwalior, and in Benares, with its Hindu maharaja and substantial religious institutions (Qureshi 1991, 161). As we shall mention below, Hindu performers are becoming increasingly numerous and prominent under the modern patronage of India's predominantly Hindu bourgeoisie.

Nevertheless, what is more striking than such coherences is the way that the social and patronage patterns of Indian music have tended to transcend sectarianism. Thus, for example, it has long been common for Muslim musicians—from south Indian *nagaswaram* (oboe) players to north Indian dhrupad singers—to provide music in Hindu temples. *Shahnai* (oboe) artist Bismillah Khan for years initiated Hindu prayer sessions in Benares, while in Rajasthan's Nathdwar temple, dhrupad singer Ziauddin Dagar performed in a sacred ritual space inaccessible even to officiating Brahmans. (Equally remarkable is that drums with leather straps were allowed in such temples.) Similarly, leading performers of light-classical devotional music have belonged to distinct religions; Muslim vocalists like Bade Ghulam Ali Khan and Abdul Karim Khan were famous for their Krishnaite devotional *bhajans* and light-classical *thumris*, while conversely, the Hindu duo of Shankar-Shambhu were among the most prominent qawwali performers of the last generation, specializing in explicitly Sufistic songs.

Given the character of its patronage and performers, it was natural for Hindustani music to evolve as a fundamentally syncretic art form that cannot be characterized as Hindu or Muslim. Thus, dhrupad, the predominant genre of the Mughal period, evolved as the product of a triangle of the Agra Mughal court, the Hindu court of Gwalior, and the temples of the Mathura region. Instruments like the sitar and sarod combined Near Eastern features with local ones, and Persian modes (*maqam*) like Huseni were transformed into Indian *rag*s. In the eighteenth and nineteenth centuries, the semiclassical thumri, with its Krishnaite Braj-bhasha text, and the Urdu *ghazal*-song developed as complementary sister genres, sung side by side by the same performers; the light idiom *dadra* epitomized the syncretism by combining Braj-bhasha and Urdu verses.

In general, the Muslim rulers did not introduce any revolutionary changes in the music system they inherited. Whatever imported elements that Muslim performers incorporated into Hindustani music were on the whole woven seamlessly into its fabric. Such admixture was facilitated by the essential compatibility between Indian and Middle Eastern (and Central Asian) musics, all of which were based on monophonic, linear modal systems; on a more general level, the syncretism was also aided by the fundamental compatibility of Central Asian Muslim and Hindu feudalisms.

As Daniel Neuman (1985) has shown, the most significant effect of Muslim rule on Hindustani music was a subtle process of secularization, rather than any form of Islamicization per se. While this trend may be true of the arts in general, the change was particularly evident in the realm of song texts. The Muslims do not appear to have made any attempt to discourage the use of Krishnaite Braj-bhasha texts, which continued under their patronage to pervade dhrupad, *khyal*, and thumri. Similarly, Muslim patrons made no significant attempt to Islamicize song texts either in language or content (aside from also cultivating ghazal and qawwali). Instead, as Neuman argues, the song texts in classical dhrupad and khyal were simply deemphasized, becoming insignificant and often unintelligibly rendered concatenations of syllables, while emphasis shifted entirely to abstract exposition of melody and rhythm. The very few khyals composed in honor of Muslim saints are sung in Braj-bhasha rather than Persian or Urdu, even at the expense of mangling the saints' names with Hindi phonetic equivalents (for example, Nazakat and Salamat Ali's recording of the khyal "Hazrat Turkomen," in which the holy man's name is unintelligibly sung as "Ha-ja-ra-ta To-" (on EMI CLP 1308). In this sense, Hindustani music contrasts markedly with south Indian classical (Karnatak) music, whose devotional texts are intrinsic to the art form, and are correspondingly expected to be rendered clearly. Similarly, the Hindu ideal of the Brahmanic singer-saint—epitomized in the north by Swami Haridas and in the south by Tyagaraja—was largely replaced under Muslim patronage by that of the secular craftsman (Neuman 1985). Accordingly, Hindustani music came to be regarded less as a form of prayer and devotion than as one of the secular "fine arts" (*funun-e-latifah*). One may again note the contrast with Karnatak music, which retains its devotional character even in the modern concert hall. Secular-humanist tendencies in Akbar's rule were particularly pronounced, as evident, for example, in the ordinary scenes depicted in representational painting, the trend toward rational and practical rather than mystical music theory, and the entire orientation of Abul Fazl's writing (Greig 1987).

The secularization of Hindustani music has in some ways rendered its underlying aesthetics more compatible with that of Western music and has perhaps facilitated the genre's remarkably successful adaptation to modern bourgeois Indian patronage as well as to reception by international audiences. At the same time, however, it has opened Hindustani music, as cultivated by Muslims, to the accusation of being sensuous and decadent. In Hindu ideology, explicitly erotic artworks can be sanctioned if they admit mystical or devotional interpretation, but the quasi-secularized Hindustani music, as patronized by Muslims, could be seen as ineligible for such legitimation. Thus one reads in numerous modern books and articles on Hindustani music how the art became fleshly and vulgar under the patronage of the sybaritic nawabs. In this perspective, the Muslim impact is thus seen to cohere with that of the British, in that both were foreign, secularizing conquerors. Such a view also contributes to the present Hindutva ideology, which sees the Muslims as being pampered and appeased by the Westernized and similarly anti-Hindu Indian elite.

In the twentieth century, Hindustani music successfully underwent the transition from Muslim feudal patronage to predominantly Hindu bourgeois patronage (H. S. Powers 1986, Meer 1980). The concurrent renaissance of Hindustani music has derived largely from its becoming allied, whether overtly or implicitly, with modern Indian cultural nationalism. Inspired by the early twentieth-century proselytizing efforts of V. D. Paluskar and V. N. Bhatkhande, the emergent middle class came to regard traditional art music as an important cultural heritage worthy of support from the state, private sources, and a network of institutions. In the process, it has been inevitable that Hindustani music has become to some extent a contested entity in the redefinition of national culture. Regula Qureshi (1991) has perceptively outlined some of the aspects in which the Hindustani music world, in the process of serving the new nationalist agenda, has in some ways become subtly re-Hinduized. In the hands of its new patrons—the Westernized, mainly Hindu elite—music, she argues, has become part of "the assertion of Hindu ideals and traditions, but in a frame of reference that [is] Western, or at least Westernized" (Qureshi 1991, 159). Thus, for example, pioneering musicologist V. N. Bhatkhande (writing in 1932) explicitly envisioned the cultivation of a modernized music theory by Hindu scholars as one means of rescuing the art from the hands of the Muslim musicians and patrons (Purohit 1988, 873). And indeed, as Qureshi notes, Muslims have played a negligible role in modern Indian music scholarship, hampered as they have been by their traditional reliance on oral transmission and by the absence of Islamic institutional support (especially in Pakistan).

Accordingly, just as most Muslims now constitute a poor, backward, relatively un-Westernized minority, so has their contribution to music often been devalued by modern Hindu writers, some of whom have pointedly criticized Muslim performers for their illiteracy, ignorance of written theory, alleged lack of spirituality, and historical ties to archaic court and courtesan culture. In accordance with the bourgeois nature of modern patronage, Muslim musicians have in many cases been hard-pressed or unwilling to affect the Westernized, middle-class manners now deemed appropriate for artists. With every generation, more and more prominent Hindu musicians—often from bourgeois families—are emerging and may soon outnumber Muslim hereditary professionals. Similarly, as Qureshi observes (1991, 165), one now encounters Muslim musicians speaking openly about their supposed Hindu ancestry, and occasionally adopting secular surnames (for example, sitarist Jamaluddin Bharatiya). Nevertheless, it is important to note that music itself has not been significantly marked by the Hinduization process, aside from such phenomena as the eccentric form of *tabla* (drum) pedagogy used in music schools (Kippen 1988, 138).

Ideologies surrounding the now-archaic dhrupad are particularly illustrative of the current tendency to identify musical traditions with one religion or the other. The leading dhrupad family in India, the Dagars, are remarkably explicit about the Hindu orientation of their art, perhaps in accordance with their hereditary associations with Rajasthani temples, and with the current Hindu domination of art music patronage in general. Hence, as Richard Widdess (1994, 70–71, and personal communication) notes, vocalist Aminuddin Dagar, although a Muslim, describes his art as "an offering to the feet of *bhagwan* [God]" and likens the genre's reverential, serious, opening *alap* section to the ritual decoration (*sringar*) of a Hindu deity's image. Dagar further claims that the nonlexical syllables used in *alap* (that is, *a, na, ri, ta, nom, tom*) derive from the Hindu invocation *ananta narayan hari om*. Conversely, vocalist Amir Khan claimed that these syllables (as used in the related genre *tarana*) derived from Persian, while Pakistani dhrupad singers of the Talwandi *gharana* (family tradition) claim that the word *alap* derives from *Allah ap* ("Allah, you"). In the current polarization of traditions, some Pakistanis have gone to further lengths to de-Hinduize Hindustani music, referring to it, for example, as *ahang-e-Khusravi* ("Khusrau's sound").

It is of course inevitable and natural that both Hindu and Muslim musicians may interpret Hindustani music as expressive of their own religious and cultural heritages. Muslim musicians take natural pride in their preeminence: *accha khana, accha gana* ("good food, good music"), as one Muslim singer told me when I expressed my fondness for Mughlai cuisine. Similarly, for a devout Hindu singer like Pandit Jasraj, Hindustani music has a strong religious component, and he commences his recitals with Sanskrit devotional verses. Yet despite the attempts by some Hindus and Muslims to claim Hindustani music for their own communities, it remains a fundamentally and indissolubly syncretic art form, and its network of practices, institutions, and related aesthetic ideologies still constitute a powerful symbol of communal harmony. While sectarian conflicts tear at the nation's social fabric, classical music remains an arena where Ravi Shankar and Alla Rakha formed an inseparable duo, where Hindu music conferences routinely book Muslim artists, and where a Pandit Jasraj does not hesitate to sing at a 1992 arts marathon devoted to communal reconciliation.

## Folk and Popular Musics

While generalizations about north Indian folk music are inherently even more hazardous than those about classical music, one can posit that many of the tendencies we note in classical music—syncretism, transcendence of sectarianism, and prominence of Muslim professionals—also obtain in folk music. Naturally, while classical music is to a large extent a secular, abstract art form, much folk music is specifically associated with particular religions, especially given its generally greater emphasis on song texts and, often, life-cycle events. In Hinduism, such music would include the vast and diverse body of explicitly devotional songs, as well as all manner of less overtly sacred genres that nevertheless acquire devotional status by being incorporated into religious functions. Since there is no orthodox Islamic music per se, Muslim devotional music constitutes a smaller category, consisting primarily of traditional qawwali, the ambiguously Sufistic ghazal, and lesser Shia devotional genres like *na't* and *marsiya*.

Like Hindustani music itself, many of the most popular and widespread folk music genres are the shared heritages of their regions, and are enjoyed, patronized, and often performed by members of all religions. Such is the case, for example, with Punjabi *Hir-Ranjha*, Bhojpuri *birha*, Braj *rasiya*, and other genres. Even explicitly devotional genres are often interpreted in a mystical, pluralist fashion in order to apply to all religions. Thus, for example, qawwali has traditionally been performed not only in Muslim shrines, but for Hindu ceremonies in Benares and elsewhere, while Bengali Baul music is widely sung by both Hindu and Muslim musicians, who freely interpret the lyrics' Tantric Hindu content in mystical fashion. Whether due to the heritage of devotional Bhakti and Sufi movements, or to the nature of music in general, it is much more common for devotional folk music to celebrate pluralism, syncretism, and mysticism rather than orthodoxy and bigotry. The poems of Kabir, synthesizing Hindu and Muslim devotion, remain paradigmatic and still-cherished symbols of this pluralism. And while contemporary Hindu militants may promote an exclusivist and chauvinistic image of Rama-rajya, still more familiar to most north Indians is the conception of Rama articulated in the familiar bhajan text:

Raghupati raghava raja Ram patita pabana Sitaram
Ishvar Allah tero nam, sab ko sammati de bhagwan . . .

[King Rama of the house of Raghu, savior of the fallen.
Whether your name is Ishvar or Allah, let everyone give respect . . .]

As with classical music, one finds among folk musicians a disproportionate number of Muslim hereditary professionals, most presumably descendants of former lower-caste Hindu converts. Many such musicians perform primarily or exclusively for Hindu patrons, such as the Rajasthani Manganhars, who even provide ritual music at Jaisalmer's Bhattianji temple, while claiming to be of Hindu Rajput descent (Jairazbhoy 1977, 54). As with art music, again and again in the realm of folk culture, one sees that music, in terms of its meanings and associated social practices, enjoys a special status that transcends communal boundaries. In that sense, folk music's ethos of pluralism and syncretism reflects the shared village life and class affinities of its primarily subaltern patrons and performers.

## Film Music and Film Culture

Although commercial Hindi film music represents quite a distinct idiom from folk and classical music, one can generalize that it has exhibited a similar tendency toward pluralism and syncretism. Muslims have figured prominently in the ranks of music directors (Naushad, Ghulam Haider), lyricists (Kaifi Azmi), singers (Mohammad Rafi), and actors (Amjad Khan, Nasiruddin Khan, Shobana Azmi, Zeenat Aman, Waheeda Rehman, and others) (Jain 1994). Accordingly, however varied and eclectic film songs may be in terms of style, they cannot be marked as either stylistically Muslim or Hindu, and their appeal crosses sectarian boundaries. As with classical and most kinds of folk music, there are no distinct "Hindu" or "Muslim" ways of singing or playing. Similarly, while some film songs use Braj-bhasha and invoke Krishnaite themes, most have been in Urdu. Indeed, both the dialogue and song lyrics of most so-called "Hindi films" have generally been in a simplified form of Urdu, which, communal tensions notwithstanding, has continued to enjoy a privileged status as a proverbially sweet and romantic language. Accordingly, pop versions of the Urdu ghazal have attained mass popularity since the late 1970s, sung and enjoyed by Hindus, Muslims, and Sikhs alike.

An allied and more problematic issue is the relation of Indian film culture in general to communal sectarianism. On perhaps the most overt level, film culture's influence on communal relations can be seen as relatively benign. Commercial films have generally avoided being communally provocative; for example, the religions of villains and heroes are generally the same, so as not to inflame sectarian sentiments. Many films, from classic costume dramas like *Mughal-e-Azam* to more recent blockbusters like *Koolie*, are steeped in Muslim culture and present its protagonists and their religion in a sympathetic and moving manner. Other films, like *Baiju Bawra*, juxtapose Hindu and Muslim cultures without glorifying or demonizing one or the other. In this respect, most commercial films, with the obvious exception of Hindu mythological dramas, have adhered roughly to the avowedly secularist and balanced orientation of the state broadcast media. Indeed, if films and their music have been criticized for weakening rich and diverse folk arts and homogenizing Indian culture in general, such effects may not be entirely unwelcome in the realm of communal relations, insofar as Muslim and Hindu audiences unite in appreciation of such a genuinely syncretic and ostensibly pluralistic idiom.

In other respects, however, the superficial pluralism of Indian film culture may mask a more subtle and perhaps more influential form of fundamentalist chauvinism. In his insightful book *The Painted Face: Studies in India's Popular Cinema*, Chidananda Das Gupta argues persuasively that Hindi cinema promotes, however obliquely, the "macabre marriage of consumerism and fundamentalism" that now threatens the unity and integrity of Indian society (1991, 253). The 1980s revenge films of Amitabh Bachchan and others glorify nihilistic violence and pander to the asocial values of an alienated lumpen proletariat easily manipulated toward fascism and bigotry (Das Gupta 1991, 240–41, 267). Far from promoting multiculturalism and tolerance, Hindi cinema largely excludes or marginalizes minorities, reducing India's plural society to "the one dimension of Hindi-speaking North India," as represented by fair, well-built, upper-caste stars (Das Gupta 1991, 271); regional cinema merely perpetuates these exclusivist stereotypes in different languages. The compatibilities with resurgent Hindu fundamentalism are even more marked in the phenomenally popular television version of the *Ramayana*, which transformed what was originally a rich, complex, profound, and secular epic into a simplistic good-versus-evil cartoon pitting the militant and virtuous Rama against the alien Other (Das Gupta 1991, 176ff.). Das Gupta's indictment of popular cinema and its relation to communalism is trenchant; at the same time, he pointedly argues that its faults derive less from hoary Indian traditions or grass-roots attitudes than from the insular and culturally shallow world of the Bombay film producers and their targeting of a lowest-common-denominator consumer (1991, 268–69).

## Music, Cassettes, and Contemporary Communal Conflicts

Like commercial cinema and its music, the state-run broadcast media in independent India have maintained a generally neutral stance in the field of sectarian relations. Influential All India Radio (AIR) director B. V. Keskar has been criticized as a moderate Hindu chauvinist, and, given the nation's demography, a certain predominance of Hindu-oriented music, reporting, and language has been inevitable. On the whole, however, radio and television have reflected the Congress Party's traditional official policy of secularism and communal harmony, and its practical goals of maintaining a coalition, however fragile, of power blocs, which included the Muslim vote. In the 1980s this status quo was altered, first, by the decline of the Congress Party and the subsequent power vacuum, and second, by the emergence of new mass media, specifically, video- and audiocassettes (Farmer, above).

The propaganda potential of audiocassettes—with their accessibility and relative immunity to censorship—was first exploited on a mass scale to disseminate Ayatollah Khomeini's speeches in 1978 during the Iranian revolution. In India, promotional videocassettes were first used for Indian political campaigns in the 1983 Andhra Pradesh state elections and, subsequently, by Rajiv Gandhi's Congress-I Party in 1985. Separatist movements in Punjab and Kashmir subsequently used audiotapes to considerable effect, as have competing Pakistani political parties. In the 1989 Indian national elections, both video- and audiocassettes were widely used by the three major parties (Congress, Janata Dal, and BJP). The BJP has made the most extensive and sophisticated usage of videos, touring the north with specially constructed video raths (chariots) bearing three-hundred-inch screens. Promotional video- and audiocassettes are widely disseminated by the nation's vast informal duplication infrastructure (otherwise used for commercial piracy). Activists play audiocassettes at rallies, from speakers mounted on trucks, and from party centers, be they formal offices or enthusiasts' tea-stalls. Most tapes contain various mixtures of speeches and songs, the latter often consisting of new lyrics set to familiar film-music tunes.

Of particular relevance here are the audiocassettes associated with the Hindutva campaign, as led by the VHP-BJP-RSS combine. Aspects of the Hindutva use of the media have been discussed elsewhere (T. Basu et al. 1993, Manuel 1993). In the following pages I offer some further perspectives on the usage and roles of audiocassettes and music in the contemporary communal disturbances, and conclude by relating these phenomena to the themes discussed above.

In 1989–90, audiocassettes produced by Hindutva militants played a crucial role in raising the Ram janmabhoomi campaign to fever pitch. The three most influential cassettes contained vitriolic speeches, recorded at rallies, by VHP-BJP leaders Uma Bharati, Ashok Singhal, Sadhvi Rithambara, and others. The speeches reiterate the now-familiar Hindutva themes: the marauding, barbaric Muslims came as foreign invaders, looting, pillaging, and enslaving the peace-loving and tolerant Hindus; not content with dividing the country and taking Pakistan, they now have seized Kashmir and still seek to rule the country; but the time has come for Hindus to follow the tradition of Maharana Pratap and Prithvi Raj Chauhan; not only will the Babri Masjid be destroyed, but three thousand other mosques as well; India is a Hindu nation in which only devotees of Rama may remain. And so on.

On the cassette entitled *Jai Shri Ram*, the unidentified speaker (evidently Rithambara), rants in a hysterical tone of voice:

Today's Muslims shun the tradition of Rahim and [Krishna devotee] Ras Khan, and think of themselves as Babar's progeny, tying themselves to Aurangzeb. . . . You Muslims link yourselves to Aurangzeb, not to India. Mahatma Gandhi sang songs of "Hindu-Muslim *bhai-bhai*" [brotherhood], but it didn't happen. We were ready, but you tried to rule us. Your Quran says to destroy all idols, while our tradition says we should be tolerant even if we're being ground underfoot. The two religions are as different as the earth and sky. But we tried, we sang, "*Bande Mataram*" [Hail to the Motherland], but now we need our Ram Janmabhoomi. . . . Hindus, wake up! They've looted you and you stayed silent; they sacked your temples and you stayed silent. What reward did you get for your forbearance? Your mothers and daughers went on being raped, your temples destroyed.

The speaker recites a Hindi poem also printed on the inlay card:

> May our race not be blamed
> And may our mothers not say
> That when we were needed, we weren't ready
> If there must be a bloodbath
> Then let's get it over with
> Because of our fear of a bloodbath before
> Our country was divided [at partition]
> Since their arrival until today
> They have killed so many Hindus
> We tried to appease them
> But there was bloodshed after all
> Instead of having it simmer slowly
> It's better to have it burst with a big flame
> If they don't understand our words
> Then we'll make them understand with kicks
> If there must be a bloodbath, then let it happen.

Another tape, entitled *Mandir ka nirman karo* ("Build the temple"), mixes speeches with snappy songs, most rendered by film singer Narender Chanchal. These contain lyrics such as the following:

The time has come, wake up, young men, and go to Lucknow
You must vow to build Ram's temple
The conches sound, Ram's forces are standing ready for battle
Gandiv [Arjuna's bow] is twanging, his conch calls
Whoever joins with the wicked, smash their dreams
Turn the political dice and blast their policies
Advance in the battlefield of politics and hit hard
To compare Ram with the wicked is beyond disrespect
Destroying his temple is the limit of madness
Don't play their farcical game of acting in a courtroom
Liberate the janmabhoomi of the jewel of the house of Raghukul
If they don't heed with words, whip out your swords . . .
Face our enemies with courage
Now isn't the time for contemplation.

The Hindutva tapes are regarded as playing direct roles in insti-gating the wave of anti-Muslim riots and pogroms that subsequently swept north India, in which thousands of lives (mostly Muslim) have been lost. Other tapes containing bloodcurdling screams, gunfire, and inflammatory slogans were blared from speakers on cars that drove at night through tense neighborhoods of Agra, Ghaziabad, and elsewhere, bringing armed men into the streets and directly igniting riots (Davis, Basu, and Hasan, above).

Despite being officially banned, the Hindutva cassettes continued to circulate freely, albeit clandestinely, and were still deployed in the late 1993 regional elections. By this period cassette stores were also openly market-ing more "moderate" tapes by Chanchal and others (for example, *Le Ram ka Nam*), with bhajans hailing Ram-rajya: "We'll bring back Ram-rajya, let the *nagara* and *dhol* [drums] ring, Jai Shri Ram!"

It is interesting that the Muslim community does not appear to have retaliated by circulating similarly inflammatory cassettes. Of course, in Pakistan, political parties like the Jamaat-e-Islami have produced their own promotional tapes, using catchy film tunes. But my own investigations in India turned up no tapes of speeches by militant leaders like Imam Bu-khari and Syed Shahabuddin; in winter 1993–94, the only relevant Urdu tapes I encountered were speeches by Maulana Obed Ullah Khan Azmi, whose tenor was overtly moderate, albeit indignant in its denunciation of the VHP for "spreading the poison of hatred in India's atmosphere." For example, Azmi denies the Hindutva depiction of Indo-Muslims as descendants of Babar, noting that Islam was spread in India more by Sufi saints than by conquerors, and that Babar himself instructed his son Humayun to ban cow slaughter in respect for Hindus. As suggested by the results of the 1993 elections, the explanation for the evident absence of inflammatory Muslim cassettes would seem to be that on the whole, the Indo-Muslim community is rejecting the militancy and fundamentalism of Bukhari and Shahabuddin, recognizing that its best hope for security lies not in confrontation, but in joining the secular mainstream.

In my volume, *Cassette Culture: Popular Music and Technology in North India* (1993), I explored some of the ramifications of the advent of cassettes, stressing how they constitute a democratic-participant "people's medium," resistant to centralized control and conducive to grass-roots expression. Cassettes and tape players are cheap, portable, durable, and easily mass-produced. As such, their spread has revolutionized the formerly monopolistic Indian music industry, making possible the emergence of several hundred production companies of various sizes, which have revitalized regional folk traditions formerly threatened by homogenizing film music, and spawned the growth of dynamic, syncretic folk-pop genres. At the same time, the negative potential of such a democratization of the media is painfully evident in the uses of cassettes by the Hindutva movement to foment bigotry and violence.

Musical genres, like individual mass media, are not entirely neutral entities, but are linked to certain forms of usage, control, and associated social practices. Like religion, music deals in sentiments rather than engaging reason or empirical logic, and thus lends itself well to devotional uses. Similarly, the social meaning of a given musical genre or work, like that of a religious doctrine, is often largely dependent upon the context and forms of its reception, usage, and subsequent interpretations. As we have seen, the polysemic ambiguity of musical meaning has allowed the most characteristic forms of north Indian music to transcend sectarian boundaries, such that, for example, devout Muslims have been able to sing explicitly Hindu texts without sense of contradiction. The variability of musical meaning is similarly evident in some of the uses of Hindu devotional music in the contemporary situation. On the one hand, when a Muslim classical vocalist sings a Rama bhajan, he may be interpreting it as a form of mystical devotion; when such a song is performed in a Sai Baba worship session, its significance may be tied to a self-conscious ideology of religious pluralism. On the other hand, the meaning of a Rama bhajan is quite different when it is sung in an RSS rally, or when—as sometimes happens nowadays—it is noisily rendered by a militant Hindu procession that has paused in front of a mosque at prayer time.

The potential contradictions in music's uses are similarly evident in texts like that cited above, "We'll bring back Ram-rajya, let the *nagara* and *dhol* ring." The nagara (*naq qara*) is a drum-pair of Middle Eastern origin, introduced to India by the Muslims; the common dhol (Persian *duhul*) may be of similar ancestry. From one perspective, we have seen that Hindu devotional music has often been performed by Muslims, on Muslim-derived instruments, such that a song text like this could be taken as another illustration of the ability of music to transcend religious differences. However, the inclusion of such a verse in a cassette associated with the Hindutva campaign is fundamentally contradictory; how could the Muslim-derived nagara be used to praise Rama-rajya? There is no place for Muslims in Rama-rajya; they must either emigrate, worship Rama, or die. (As the slogan says, *"Hindi Hindu Hindustan, Muslim jao Pakistan"* ["India is for Hindi and Hindus, Muslims go to Pakistan!"]) But the nagara is also part of north Indian culture as a whole.

Such contradictions are in fact inherent in the very language used by militants like Rithambara, whose Hindi, like that of most north Indians, is full of Urdu-derived words, which she (again, like most Hindus) pronounces by substituting Hindi phonemes for Urdu equivalents (for example, *j* for *z*). One may contrast her usage of such substitutions with that of Nazakat and Salamat Ali in the aforementioned example. When these classical singers (who are said to be devout Muslims and ardent Pakistani nationalists) deliberately Hindi-ize *Hazrat* as *Hajarata*, they do so out of knowledge and respect for the conventions of a Hindi-language tradition. Rithambara's distortions, by contrast, are based on ignorance and linguistic chauvinism, in the tradition of *"Hindi men bindi kyon?"* (loosely, "Why should there be Urdu diacriticals in Hindi script?"). Ultimately, however, while Urdu is clearly declining in India, its vocabulary continues to pervade common Hindustani speech, and the VHP orators, if they wish to be understood, can no more excise it from their diction than can Muslims and their contributions to local culture be surgically removed from India.

Given the collapse of extant forms of socialism, it may seem anachronistic to look to the left for solutions to fratricidal conflicts like that besetting India. One need not, however, be an orthodox Marxist to detect that a sense of lower-class solidarity, grounded in materialist consciousness rather than obscurantist mythology, is precisely what could arrest the cycle of religious persecution, in which the upper castes manipulate lower-

class Hindus against Muslim scapegoats. It is hardly coincidental that the
northern state least beset by communal violence has been Bengal, where
a resilient left movement, however imperfectly represented by the CPM
government, has created an atmosphere of proletarian solidarity where
communal sentiments have been unable to flourish. Such an orientation
also helps explain the resounding victory of the Bahujan Samajwadi Party
(BSP)—with its dalit-lower-caste-Muslim alliance—over the BJP in the
1993 UP elections. Ultimately, however, such campaigns will have to use
the new media—including audiocassettes and popular music—in as skillful and sophisticated manner as has the VHP. If cassettes have proven to
be an ideal medium for the instigation of communal riots and the propagation of religious bigotry, they could be used with equal effectiveness to
promote a progressive platform.

    Although such uses of cassettes remain marginal in north India, there
have been significant and innovative attempts, however tentative. Particularly noteworthy in this regard are the cassettes produced by Jagori, a
Delhi-based organization devoted primarily to women's rights. Jagori's
cassettes feature songs that are intended to be listened to, sung, and freely
altered by women in informal song sessions. The songs, set to familiar folk
and film tunes, are recorded by women singing to dhol accompaniment,
without elaborate instrumental backing. They thus lack the market appeal
of commercial film music, but they can be cheaply produced and may also
serve as performance models to women who are not trained musicians but
who retain strong traditions of informal collective singing. In their use of
borrowed film melodies they encourage disenfranchised people to resignify
and appropriate entities taken from the mainstream media. The songs deal
with a wide variety of topics, including religious bigotry. Some are of particular relevance to the contemporary situation, including the following:

> God has become divided in temples, mosques, and churches . . .
> The Hindu says the temple is his abode
> The Muslim says Allah is his faith
> Both fight, and in fighting die
> What oppression and violence they wreak upon one another!
> Whose goal is this, whose scheme?

    In such songs, Jagori activists are reclaiming and revamping the hoary
Indian tradition of using music to transcend sectarian difference. More importantly, they are exploiting the liberating and democratic potential of the

new medium of cassettes. Such tapes represent precisely the kind of oppositional, grassroots use of the new media that some progressives have envisioned (Enzensberger 1970). Free from state and corporate patronage and guidelines, resistant to official or market censorship, and oriented toward amateur consumption and reproduction rather than commercial success, the Jagori tapes could ideally be duplicated throughout north India, inspiring other low-budget cassettes and strengthening the foundation for a national movement to oppose class, gender, and religious oppression. Cassettes thus provide an ideal technological infrastructure for the mass dissemination of a progressive discourse; it is only the subjective social conditions that inhibit the spread of such a message and that have allowed cassettes to be used more extensively by elites to manipulate grass-roots anxieties.

## Conclusions

This essay has emphasized the ways that north Indian music and its associated social practices—past and present, elite and popular—have tended to transcend sectarian differences, embodying syncretism and pluralism rather than exclusivity and chauvinism. Of course, the concept of "syncretism" is itself inherently ambiguous, and when interpreting it as a favorable historical phenomenon, one must be careful to specify what sort of syncretism is involved; does it relate, for example, to the conditions of production and consumption, or to the nature of the artwork itself? For example, if a Muslim ruler builds a mosque from the rubble of a Hindu temple he destroys (or a Hindu prince builds a temple from a Jain shrine he smashes), we might naturally be mistaken to celebrate the product as a syncretic, collaborative creation. Similarly, if a Muslim ruler sacks a Hindu palace and brings its musicians to adorn his own court, we should not necessarily hail the subsequent coexistence of Hindu and Muslim musicians as evidence of communal harmony and collaboration. The nature of Hindu-Muslim creative collaboration under an imperial Muslim authority is not the same as that represented, for example, by the amicable and voluntary interaction of Hindu and Muslim folk musicians of relatively equal social standing. Similarly, as Sumit Sarkar suggests below, it would be a mistake to overromanticize premodern India as a multicultural paradise ruined only by colonialism and modernity.

However, as this essay has tried to illustrate, the exclusivist and chauvinist aspects of north Indian musical culture are far less striking than the genuinely pluralist features—in particular, the transcendence of sectarianism not only in style, but in sociomusical practices and attitudes, whether in the realm of classical, folk, or film music culture. From this perspective, the attempts by certain zealots to claim Hindustani music for one community or the other, or to link Hindu bhajans to provocative cassettes, seem to stand out as exceptions in a musical culture otherwise distinguished by tolerance and cooperation.

In view of the recent communal disturbances, there are two possible ways of interpreting the evident pluralism of north Indian musical culture. One would be to regard the music world as representative of north Indian culture as a whole, suggesting that the present communal tensions do not reflect deep-seated, pervasive prejudices, but are rather the product of recent sociopolitical and economic developments. The second and contrasting approach would be to interpret north Indian musical culture as merely an island of harmony and transcendence in a vast sea of communal mistrust and hostility—an island conditioned by special and unusual circumstances (for example, the preponderance of Muslim patrons and artists, and perhaps the natural inclination of music itself toward sentiments of bonhomie rather than bigotry). In other words, is the syncretic and pluralistic spirit of Indian musical culture representative and typical, or is it a sort of felicitous aberration?

Answering this question fully is beyond the scope of a short essay and, indeed, beyond the scope of this author. However, a few initial points can be made. First of all, even if one were to conclude that Indian musical culture represented merely an atypical island of communal harmony, it would constitute not a tiny atoll, but rather quite a large island (perhaps, indeed, as big as a subcontinent). Musical culture, with its associated ideologies and social practices, is a substantial and significant part of South Asian culture as a whole. Furthermore, similar sorts of Hindu-Muslim creative syncretism and collaboration can be seen in the other arts as well. Without digressing too far beyond the scope of this essay, we may point out that Indian miniature painting from the Mughal period on evolved as a truly syncretic form, typically, for example, incorporating Persian influence in the realm of composition, architecture, ornamentation, and color scheme on the one hand, and Hindu Rajput-style depiction of figures and landscape on the other. It was routine in the Mughal courts for an individual picture to be the work of two or three artists, who, judging from the rosters of court painters, were often of different religions. Similarly, the mutual influences between Hindu and Indo-Muslim architecture styles have been well documented, from the temple-derived layouts and decoration forms of innumerable Indian mosques, to the many small Hindu temples, which, with their Mughal-style onion domes, are virtually indistinguishable from Muslim shrines when viewed from the exterior (Brown 1956, 1–2, 48ff.). Finally, as we have noted, in the realm of poetry, many Muslim rulers and nobles patronized and personally cultivated Krishnaite Hindi poetry, just as Hindu literati avidly mastered Persian until the twentieth century. Thus, one can see a prodigious degree of pluralism and syncretism in north Indian artistic culture as a whole.

Secondly, regardless of our verdict on the depth, age, and extensiveness of grass-roots communalism, the study of musical culture would seem to corroborate the conclusions of other essays in this volume—that communal attitudes and relations are conditioned primarily by nonreligious forces. In musical culture, the amount of stylistic syncretism and collaborative social practices within each horizontal stratum of society suggests that class divisions may be more important than religious ones. Such a perspective coheres with the interpretation of recent communal tensions as being the product of sociopolitical and economic factors, including the elite exploitation of grass-roots anxieties. Finally, such an approach also suggests that a successful campaign to overcome communalism must combine a materialist social theory, a skillful use of the new mass media, and, lastly, an invocation of the profound traditions of tolerance and multiculturalism in Indian society.

# 6

## Soldier Monks and Militant Sadhus

WILLIAM R. PINCH

THE STRATEGY OF MILITANT Hindu political organizations in recent years, particularly with respect to the Ayodhya issue, has been to attract the support and participation of sadhus (monks, ascetics, and holy men) throughout India. This strategy is based on two premises. The first is historically plausible: namely, that the monastic orders represent important, indeed crucial, access to popular sentiment. The second is a fanciful portrayal of long standing: namely, that sadhus, and particularly soldier sadhus, have for many centuries played a patriotic role in defending Hindu India from foreign, and particularly Muslim, depredation. Given the current political context, this chapter poses the following question: How are the militant Hinduism of the late twentieth century and the image of the precolonial sadhu patriot upon which it draws related to the very real military monasticism that flourished in pre-1800 north India?

I begin to answer this question by examining and comparing various portrayals of and assumptions about the sadhu as defender of faith and country over the past century. These include the recent political maneuvering by what is generally referred to as "the Hindu right" over Ayodhya; an imagined history of conflict over the Ram janmabhoomi in Ayodhya; the nationalist imagination of one of Bengal's greatest authors; and the political strategies of Mahatma Gandhi during the noncooperation movement. At some remove, but revealing in their assumptions about the nature of Hindu-Muslim conflict and historical causation, are academic inquiries into the origins of soldier monasticism from the perspectives of religious and social history. The second part of the chapter seeks to shed some light on the history of soldier monasticism in the late Mughal and early colonial periods. The unprecedented numbers of soldier monks in the service of regional states in the eighteenth century suggests that the discipline, hierarchy, and institutional loyalties implicit to monastic life were easily adapted to successful military organization. Much of the religious politics of soldier monasticism occurred during an important pilgrimage festival — the *kumbh mela* — which during much of the eighteenth century existed beyond the purview of the state. The kumbh had, as such, gained prominence as the main arena for resolving monastic rivalries, and often was the scene of considerable sectarian violence. The rise of the modernizing state, embodied in the English East India Company but evident as well in Maratha rule, served to undermine the military viability of soldier monasticism; as part of that process, colonial officials deemed sectarian violence at the kumbh socially and politically undesirable, and took measures to prohibit it. In any case, as the nineteenth century drew to a close, political conflicts articulated in terms of religious identity would be resolved through collective mass violence in public arenas no longer constrained by ritual boundaries.

Understandably, the image of the soldier monk in the Indian past, both real and imagined, flies in the face of the pacifism and relativist tolerance often presented as key components of Hindu philosophy. This point is central to Lochtefeld (1994), who focuses particularly on sectarian violence between sadhus at Hardwar over the past four centuries, and on the implications of such intra-Hindu conflict for VHP attempts to craft a religiopolitical Hindu unity in the present. Let there be no mistake: the evolution of a powerful martial tradition within Indian monasticism was very real, the battles fought between monastic orders at the kumbh were ferocious and deadly, and the mercenary service undertaken by soldier monks in the eighteenth century was extremely dangerous and lucrative. Tolerance and pacifism were ancillary to the world of the soldier monk. And indeed, as recent scholarship in intellectual and cultural history has demonstrated, neither pacifism nor tolerance was a given in Indian religious traditions prior to the eighteenth century. Both were brought to the fore to respond to ideological needs in the colonial, nationalist era. Tolerance reconciled the variant religious traditions of the colonized subcontinent into a serviceable theological whole by the late eighteenth century, while pacifism was Gandhi's way of turning a Jain and bhakti-driven aversion to sacrificial violence into a weapon with which to mount a civilizational attack on the West in the early twentieth century (van der Veer 1994b, 43–44, 67, 70–71; Chatterjee 1984). This should not be taken to mean, however, that the precolonial period was rife with religious violence and intolerance. When soldier monks signed on as mercenaries for the state, as often as not the state for which they fought was ruled by Muslims. Hence the wars they waged were not religious wars. Religious conflict involving soldier monks was usually enacted in a circumscribed setting—the kumbh festival—where the status of and boundaries between religious orders were negotiated continually.

## The Sadhu as Patriot

The kumbh mela (or simply, kumbh)—which every three years alternates between Hardwar, Allahabad (Prayag), Nasik, and Ujjain—is India's pre-eminent pilgrimage festival, and the Allahabad kumbh is the largest and best known. In attendance at the 1989 Allahabad kumbh (January 14 to March 6) were two important organizations expressly devoted to religion in the service of the nation, the Vishva Hindu Parishad (VHP) and the Bharat Sadhu Samaj (BSS). Both the VHP and the BSS held conferences during the festival—the former to be convened on January 28, the latter on January 31.[1] The participation of these religiopolitical organizations in the 1989 kumbh was of particular significance because the proceedings of the VHP conference were marked by increasingly aggressive statements culminating in a resolution to "capture" the birthplace of Rama, allegedly located in Ayodhya's Babri Masjid, and to construct a temple to mark the spot. The events at Ayodhya of November 9, 1989, and December 6, 1992, would make clear that these were no idle promises. Perhaps more important, however, was the fact that several "hard-line" BSS leaders felt upstaged by the aggressive VHP stance and chose consequently to invite the VHP to the BSS convention. There followed a series of statements in the BSS meeting supporting the "reclamation" of Ayodhya. One speaker is said to have observed that "there are six lakh villages, and 80 crore Hindus.

1. The BSS was founded in 1956, ostensibly "for the purpose of bringing together the sadhus of India in the field of constructive and social service activities for an allround [sic] development of the country and for the betterment of the world on the basis of Truth, Non-violence (Ahimsa), Fearlessness, Equality and Unity" (Harinarayanand 1986, 2). A major behind-the-scenes player in the BSS is Swami Harinarayanand, who is generally regarded as a mainstay of the Congress Party and is the head of the Bihar Sanskritik Vidyapith (Bihar Cultural College). The BSS, consequently, is thought to represent the Congress's attempt to draw the large population of Hindu religious figures into the work of post-1947 nation building. This impression is reinforced by the BSS's claim on such figures as Jawaharlal Nehru and Rajendra Prasad, who are reported (in BSS literature) to have welcomed the formation of the organization. Both the VHP and the BSS have been conspicuously present at kumbh assemblages over the past three decades.

If every village donates one brick and every Hindu donates just one rupee, the battle for the Ram Janam Bhoomi will be half over. This program has to be taken from village to village" (Chakraborty 1989, 6). Observers from the press corps considered the VHP coup an ominous development in Indian politics precisely because of the massive membership of locally prominent religious figures from all over India in the BSS. With the gravitation of the BSS to the aggressive Hindu line of the VHP and, by extension, the BJP, the Congress government (it was argued) effectively lost control of its only means to influence religious opinion.[2]

The historic significance of this political maneuvering, however, is that it took place at the six-week kumbh, which has long been the occasion for the gathering of large bands, or *akharas*, of warrior monks. Indeed, lay pilgrims flock to the Allahabad kumbh in such large numbers for two reasons: namely, to bathe in the confluence of the Ganga (Ganges) and Ya-muna (Jumna) rivers at preordained auspicious moments, and to witness the impressive processions of the akharas as they make their own way to the sacred waters. The series of events that led to the VHP takeover of the BSS agenda culminated just days before February 6, which was the most important bathing day (*mauni amavasaya*) of the festival and for which ap-proximately five million pilgrims had been arriving from all parts of the subcontinent (*Hindustan Times*, February 6, 1989, 10; *Hindustan Times*, January 13, 1989, 9). Hence the very public events of the VHP and BSS not only occurred under symbolically auspicious circumstances but had the potential to attract a massive national audience. The VHP-BSS announce-ments were timed so as to just precede these events and thereby align in the public mind the Ram janmabhoomi movement and Hindu national-ism with Indian soldier monasticism.

The 1989 kumbh was not the first instance in which soldier monks were linked in the public eye to the Ram janmabhoomi struggle. A pam-phlet published in 1976 by Baba Ramlakhansharan, who at the time de-scribed himself as the "non-stop *kirtan* [singing] conductor" just outside the perimeter of the Babri mosque in Ayodhya, tells of a series of sixty-five battles during Mughal rule between Muslims and Hindu soldier monks over the site—beginning with five in Babar's reign, ten in Humayun's,

2. The fact that Congress had cultivated that link in the first place, and over the course of three decades, is of great significance in the history of politics and religion in the twenti-eth century, particularly with regard to the Mahatma's broad appeal to a variety of religious discourses prior to 1947. Unfortunately, given the scope of this essay, this question cannot be pursued here.

twenty in Akbar's, and peaking with thirty in Aurangzeb's.[3] This prolonged warfare is said to have climaxed with a confrontation between Aurangzeb's forces and Hindu soldier monks, wielding *chimtas*, large, iron
pincers with sharpened ends.

> When Aurangzeb became the emperor of India after Shah Jahan, his attention fell
> first and foremost on the janmabhumi and he immediately dispatched a formidable
> army there under the generalship of Jambaj Khan. At this time there resided at *Jan
> ki Ghat* in Ayodhya one Mahatma Shishya Vaishnava Das, a disciple of Shivaji's
> venerable and capable Guru Shri Ram Das. With him was allied a powerful group
> of 10,000 *chimta*-wielding sadhus, fully versed in the martial sciences. When this
> group of sadhus learned that Aurangzeb's army was rapidly approaching Ayodhya
> to destroy the janambhumi, they immediately took it as a question of honor and
> spread the news like electricity throughout the surrounding countryside. Conse-
> quently, thousands of Hindus prepared to take up arms to defend their integrity
> and formed a fierce force comprised of sadhus and *grihasta*s [householders] and
> faced the Mughal army at Urvashi pond. In a vicious, seven-day battle, the Mughals
> were forced to retreat in desperation from the deadly chimtas. (Ramlakhansharan
> 1976, 11–12)

According to the account in this pamphlet, Aurangzeb learned of this defeat and amassed a much larger force of fifty thousand troops under Saiy-
yid Hasan Ali Khan to raze the Ram janmabhoomi. Hearing this, Vaishnava Das is said to have approached Guru Govind Singh, the tenth guru
of the Sikhs, for assistance in opposing the Mughal army. Together, the
pamphlet concludes, "Sikhs, Hindus, and sadhus completely routed the
Mughal force in a dreadful battle that left no Muslim survivors."

   From the strictly topographical perspective, it is not at all surprising
that the Ram janmabhoomi should be linked with armed sadhus in the
minds of Vaishnavas familiar with Ayodhya as a pilgrimage center. The site
is located very near to north India's main headquarters of Vaishnava soldier monks, the Hanuman Garhi, and any pilgrim visiting Ayodhya would
encounter and perform *puja* (ritual offerings) at or near both in quick succession (Lal 1869, 19–22). And, indeed, there is even a historical record
of conflict between armed sadhus and Muslims involving the Babri Masjid, though it comes to us not from the Mughal period but the middle
of the nineteenth century (Nevill 1905, 174; K. N. Panikkar 1991b, 30–33;

---

3. Baba Ramlakhansharan 1976, 13. Peace is said to have reigned between 1605 and 1658,
the dates for Jahangir and Shah Jahan (p. 9). I am grateful to Professor Philip Lutgendorf,
Department of Asian Languages and Literature, University of Iowa, for providing me a copy
of this pamphlet.

S. Srivastava 1991, 22–24). (I have come across no record of the conflicts described by Baba Ramlakhansharan, and so far as I know most observers complain of the relative silence of Persian sources on this aspect of Awadhi history.) In 1855, a large assembly of armed Muslims attacked the Hanuman Garhi, ostensibly to liberate a small mosque said to be housed inside. The Muslims were quickly repulsed by the armed monks from the fort, who then counterattacked, killing seventy-five of their opponents on the steps of the Babri Masjid itself, which spot has since come to be known as Ganj Shahidan (the martyrs' ground). Interestingly, the armed sadhus chose not to occupy the mosque following their one-sided victory; instead they returned to their fort—an action that, K. N. Pannikar (1991b) has suggested, indicates the relative insignificance of the Ram janmabhoomi issue prior to the twentieth century. (See Davis, above.)

Leaving aside for the moment the question of historicity, the idea that the Ayodhya pamphleteer Baba Ramlakhansharan invokes—soldier sadhus rallying in defense of a utopian Hindu social and political order—has its own history embedded in the Indian nationalism of the nineteenth and twentieth centuries. The earliest representation of Hindu monks as defenders of an idealized Indian homeland is the well-known portrayal of the so-called Sannyasi Rebellion of the late eighteenth century by Bankim Chandra Chattopadhyay (1838–94), the acclaimed Bengali writer generally regarded as the originator of the Indian novel. (See T. Sarkar, below.) Bankim wrote *Anandamath* (later translated into English as *Abbey of Bliss*) in 1882 as a work of political fiction, in which he cast the protracted skirmishes between wandering bands of armed sadhus and the English East India Company Army as a proto-nationalist defense of India by a brotherhood of monks organically sprung from the soil of the peasant countryside. In fact, the resistance to company rule on the part of the various bands of soldier monks in Bengal—both Hindu and Muslim—in the last three decades of the eighteenth century was not grounded in a patriotic vision of India, but, rather, in a monastic desire to retain a right to carry arms, levy contributions from the countryside while on pilgrimage, and serve as mercenaries for local notables in the province (Lorenzen 1978, 72–75). Bankim, however, ascribed to these monks a patriotic vision of India that combined territorial nationalism and Hindu religious symbolism—embodied in the conversion of Mahendra, the central character, to the cause of India's liberation from foreign rule. Mahendra is guided by the spiritual leader of the *sannyasi* (renouncer) army, referred to as "Mahatma," through a series of subterranean rooms containing successive images of

India: first a resplendent India of past glory (prior to foreign conquest), then an India of present-day "famine, disease, death, humiliation and destruction," above which hung a sword (symbolizing subjection to foreign rule), and, finally, a golden India of future greatness—"bright, beautiful, full of glory and dignity" (Chattopadhyay 1992, 42–43). The second part of an early installment of the novel, published in *Bangadarshan*, Bankim's monthly journal, depicted sannyasis battling against the (often drunken and lecherous) British. Since Bankim was faced with the threat of official censorship, Muslims were made the enemies of the piece, and the British were depicted as the benevolent (if, at times, careless) caretakers of ancient Indian glory. (Even so, Bankim's career suffered from official censure: he was passed over for promotion and remained a deputy magistrate until his retirement. See Raychaudhuri 1988, 117.)

Bankim's work of fiction would become an important source for the structure and emotive content of Bengali terrorism and Indian nationalism. Bengali revolutionaries of the turn of the century would pattern their organizational cells on Bankim's fictional akhara model, would engage in strength training and martial arts techniques in partial emulation of Bankim's sannyasi soldiers, and would worship the country itself personified as a mother goddess, replete with the shakti—power incarnate—evoked in Bankim's hymn, "Bande Mataram" (Hail to Thee, Mother), sung by the rebellious monks. (On this hymn see T. Sarkar, below.) Less radically committed Indian nationalists would adopt this hymn as the unofficial anthem of the freedom movement, particularly after the partition of Bengal in 1905 and, again, following the rise of Gandhi in 1920. As Tapan Raychaudhuri opines (1988, 134), "one has the feeling that [Bankim] had almost expected such a result." Bankim may not have expected, however, his work to become the centerpiece of Hindu nationalist indoctrination after 1947, but that is precisely what has happened. Following partition, the RSS training of Indian youths concluded daily sessions with a singing of "Bande Mataram." According to a recent critical study of the RSS, "the entirety [of 'Bande Mataram'] is given special emphasis [in RSS cadre training] since the hymn supposedly encompasses the authentic shape of undivided prepartition *Bharatmata* [Mother India]: an abbreviation of the hymn, consequently, implies a symbolic surrender of her symbolic integrity" (T. Basu et al. 1993, 39).

Gandhi himself was taken not so much with the rhetoric as the reality of soldier monasticism, particularly its potential for spreading nationalist dissent into the peasant countryside. According to colonial intelligence reports, hundreds of *naga* (warrior) sadhus attended the Nagpur Congress in 1920 and pledged to carry out Gandhian noncooperation propaganda. Gandhi personally thanked the sadhus for their support and urged them to "visit the vicinities of cantonments and military stations and explain to the native soldiers the advisability of giving up their employments." Krishna Ram Bhatt, the intelligence agent deployed to report on these proceedings, reacted with an alarm not unlike that of present-day journalists describing the proceedings of the 1989 kumbh at Allahabad: "Sadhus visited most of the villages and towns and the masses had a high regard for them, and thought a great deal of their instructions and preachings. When these nagas took up non-cooperation, the scheme would spread like wild fire among the masses of India and eventually Government would be unable to control 33 *crores* [330 million] of people and would have to give Swaraj." As it happened, most naga sadhus were unwilling to subordinate their institutional religious loyalties to the nationalist code of Gandhian *satyagraha* (strategy of nonviolent protest), and would consequently walk away from the nationalist movement (Bihar and Orissa 1921, 2:3).

Though highly divergent in their intent and in their conception of the sadhu as patriot, these vignettes share in common the notion that the sadhu resides at the heart of the Indian body politic. For those depicting him as a foot soldier in the fight against foreign tyranny, whether Muslim or British, the sadhu represented a homegrown, organic patriotism, free of the sophistication of urbane nationalism, and allied with the common man. Bankim's sannyasi rebels began as peasants and landowners before uniting to take up arms under the leadership of a mysterious mahatma against foreign rule; Baba Ramlakhansharan's sadhus were said to have been assisted in their confrontation with Mughal troops by thousands of householder-peasants from the surrounding countryside. By contrast, Gandhi in 1920 and the VHP in 1989 sought the involvement of sadhus in their political campaigns because they perceived those sadhus to be an influential link to an untapped countryside, not because they presumed sadhus to occupy a hallowed moral ground as quintessential Indians or Hindus. Indeed, as with Gandhi, the VHP articulates its own particular vision of what is meant by the term Indian, and the successful participation of sadhus in its political strategies depends in large part on the extent to which sadhus share that political definition. As we shall see, such a shared political ideology is not a given in the post-Ayodhya climate.

## Historiographies of Fighting Ascetics

An interest in naga sadhus was not confined to the worlds of literature and politics, but extended as well into academic circles. The existence of tens of thousands of naga sadhus, ranged in various orders and organized according to military akharas has sparked the interest of numerous historians, scholars of religion, and Indologists. The question that has dominated the scholarly inquiry into precolonial soldier monasticism is not one of nationalist patriotism, but of origins: When and why did soldier monks first appear in Hindu religious orders? The answer arrived at invariably posited Hindu-Muslim antagonism as the causative factor in the institutionalization of monastic arms.

J. N. Farquhar is generally regarded as the pioneer in the study of soldier monks; because his work established a pattern of understanding, not to mention a set of a priori assumptions, that would not be broken for many decades, I focus on his argument and argumentation in some detail here. Farquhar wrote in the 1910s and 1920s and was particularly interested in the history of "fighting ascetics" from the standpoint of Indian religion generally. Hence his questions were directed mainly to the chronology of soldier monasticism, and how that chronology corresponded to the history of monasticism "proper" in India. Farquhar's understanding of the history of the major Shaiva and Vaishnava orders relied in large part on the oral traditions of monks themselves, with whom he had extensive and prolonged contact between 1890 and 1920. Farquhar spent sixteen years (1891–1907) in Calcutta, where he "was constantly in touch with Chaitanyas, Brahmans, Aryas, Theosophists, followers of Ramakrishna and young men interested in other north India movements" and five years (1907–12) traveling all over India, during which he was "brought into personal contact with men of almost every type of religious belief" (Farquhar 1914, viii–ix). He would continue to visit important religious centers and conduct interviews with representatives of the major and minor sects during the next several years. In February of 1918 Farquhar visited the kumbh mela at Allahabad (Farquhar 1920, 185) and had numerous conversations with Dasnamis and Ramanandis—respectively, the largest Shaiva and Vaishnava monastic orders in India. There is little doubt that his interviews and observations on this occasion were a major factor in shaping his opinion of the history of soldier monasticism.

Farquhar contended that, despite the early references to armed ascetics in quasi-historical and literary texts of the first millennium A.D., the origins of full-blown soldier monasticism proper were dated to the sixteenth century, during the reign of the Mughal emperor Akbar (1556–1602), and that the catalyst was Muslim persecution of Brahman monks. The institutionalization process, as described by Farquhar, began with the formation in the mid-sixteenth century of soldiering groups of Shaiva monks in several Dasnami suborders. As evidence, Farquhar cited oral tradition. He had it "from the lips of sannyasis" in both Benares and Allahabad that soldiering orders were mobilized in the mid-sixteenth century to repel the brutal and random attacks by armed *faqirs* (Muslim ascetics) inflicted on unarmed Brahman sannyasis. Dasnami lore, according to this account, tells of an interview between a prominent scholar-monk named Madhusudan Saraswati, the emperor Akbar, and the latter's folkloric courtier and adviser, Raja Birbal:

Madhusudana stated the grave danger in which sannyasis stood, since they were themselves defenceless, while there was no possibility of getting their enemies punished by law. Raja Birbal then suggested that Madhusudana should initiate large numbers of men of non-Brahman caste as sannyasis and arm them, so that they might be ready at all times to defend Brahman sannyasis from attack. The Emperor agreed to the proposal and promised that fighting sannyasis should be immune from prosecution, precisely like the faqirs. I am inclined to date the interview about 1565 A.D. (Farquhar 1925a, 442; also 1925b, 482–83)

Farquhar allowed that no textual confirmation of this agreement can be found in any historical work. But he insisted nevertheless that "though it has come down to us only by tradition, there can be no doubt about its truth. All sannyasis in North India hold the tradition; and we may also be certain that the Emperor who had given the Hindu an equal place with the Muslim in his empire would at once recognise the justice of Madhusudana's appeal and would respond to it" (Farquhar 1925a, 443). Nevertheless, Farquhar felt the need for some form of confirmation from textual sources. He turned to the Mughal chronicle, where he found "an incident recorded in the Emperor's life, which fits so well into the [oral] tradition that *I am sure every historical mind* will at once acknowledge that it ought to be accepted as full corroboration of the story" (Farquhar 1925a, 443; emphasis added). Farquhar paraphrased Akbar's early twentieth-century biographer, Vincent Smith, as follows:

Akbar was in camp at Thaneswar, north of Delhi, early in 1567 A.D. News was brought to him that two companies of armed sannyasis, *Giris* and *Puris* [Dasnami subgroupings], who had quarrelled about the possession of the gifts in the shrine

150 William R. Pinch

of Thaneswar, were about to have a fight. Like the keen soldier he was, he at once went to witness the encounter. When he arrived, he found that the Puris were out-numbered by the Giris, and he therefore ordered some of his own men to join the weaker side and redress the balance. The battle was fought, and the Puris were vic-torious. In this fight some twenty men were killed. We are told that the emperor greatly enjoyed the spectacle. *Since* [in reference to the oral tradition] *he had agreed to their organization, in order that they might fight Muslim foes, he must have chuckled inwardly to see them turn their swords against each other*. (V. Smith 1917, 78–79, cited in Farquhar 1925a, 443; emphasis added) [4]

I emphasize the last sentence to draw attention to Farquhar's rhe-torical technique: As he himself noted, the oral tradition wherein Akbar agreed to the forming of military ranks among the Dasnamis is not men-tioned at all in any textual account, and certainly not in Abul Fazl's. Yet Farquhar consciously appended mention of this alleged agreement here, and conjectured furthermore the wry pleasure of the emperor in witness-ing the internecine strife of Hindus, so as to prod the reader toward his desired conclusion—namely, that the military orders resulted from Hindu-Muslim conflict. Thus Farquhar was able to bring to bear evidence that, in fact, can in no way be taken as corroborative. Quite to the contrary, the evidence clearly depicts conflicts of Shaiva against Shaiva, and it can be used to undermine the communal element of Farquhar's oral tradition. In any event, the written record from the sixteenth century should be given greater weight than oral tradition dating from the early twentieth century. And if we leave aside its communal aspect, oral tradition can be inter-preted, to the contrary, as confirming the Mughal chronicle, which de-scribes Akbar as endeavoring to enhance the institutionalization of Shaiva armies. Why the Mughal emperor should wish to do this remains an en-tirely separate and important question, which cannot be answered without further research.

By 1925, when his work on soldier monks was being published, most of Farquhar's readership was only too willing to accept that Hindu-Muslim conflict was fundamental in medieval and early modern Indian history. Farquhar's rhetorical skills continue unabated in the next passage, when he slowly begins to shift the discussion by commenting on the willingness of

4. Smith relies on *The Akbar Nama of Abu-l-Fazl* (Abu al-Fazl 1939), *Tarikh-i Badauni* (Badauni 1898), and *Tabakat-i Akbari* (Ahmad 1975). It should be noted that Abul Fazl de-scribes the combatants as Gurs and Puris, which Farquhar (following Smith) takes to mean Giris and Puris; Badauni and Nizamuddin Ahmad, however, speak of "Jogis" and "Sann-yasis." In any case, they all refer to internecine conflict among Shaiva monks.

Akbar to "tolerate such things in his empire instead of strengthening the law to deal vigorously with all breakers of the peace!" He continues by saying that Akbar "acted in harmony with the ideas of the times. It would not seem strange to sixteenth-century India that the Emperor should stand by and see a fight in which twenty men were done to death. It did not shock India of the sixteenth century, any more than duelling shocked England in the eighteenth century" (Farquhar 1925a, 443–44). Having turned the discussion to what is on the face of it eminently reasonable talk of English dueling, Farquhar in the next sentence is able to "conclude that, around 1565, large numbers of non-Brahmans were initiated as sannyasis and armed to fight Muslim faqirs" (1925a, 444).

Farquhar argued, then, that Muslim aggression produced, by the sixteenth century, the arming of Hindu ascetics in defense of religion. Following that moment of creation, which is said to have occurred among Shaivas, the spread of military monasticism to other orders and sects was merely a matter of imitation. Hence, though Farquhar was less certain in dating the spread of soldiering among Vaishnava monks, he settled on 1600 and located the process squarely in the Ramanandi order (1925a, 444–45). Later, other Vaishnava orders would take up arms, including Vishnuswamis, Nimbarkis, and Vallabhacharis; the spread of militarism would even extend to such peace-loving sects as the Satnamis, Dadupanthis, and, lastly, by 1699, to the Nanakpanthis (better known as Sikhs).

Remarkably, the first serious challenge to Farquhar's depiction of the origins of soldier monasticism did not come until 1978, and even then the idea of Hindu-Muslim conflict remained central to the analysis. The author of that challenge, David Lorenzen (1978, 64–68), argues that Indian religious communities evinced an ad hoc willingness to engage in violent behavior as early as the eighth century A.D. in order to protect temple and monastery endowments from plunder, primarily by Hindu, Buddhist, Jain, or (after 1000) Muslim rulers strapped for treasure. But, Lorenzen (1978, 69) argues, institutionalized soldier monasticism proper, though still predicated upon the protection of economic holdings, seemed to develop as a feature of religious conflict only after the fifteenth century, the earliest evidence for which is Akbar's having witnessed the pitched battle between two Shaiva suborders in the late 1560s. Indeed, notwithstanding his observations regarding the long-standing (pre-Sultanate) need to protect monastic wealth, Lorenzen proposes that the coming of Muslim rule in India—and with it broad legal, political, and cultural sanctions in Islam for the persecution of non-Muslims—acted as the catalyst that resulted in the formal militarization of ascetic orders. He speculates that

if we grant that the basic purpose of the resort to military organization by religious institutions was the protection of these institutions from robbery and/or state persecution, a supposition which is probable *a priori*, then we may in part attribute the appearance of such ascetics in the medieval period to the new religious sanction which Islam gave to such persecutions. Although [ancient] Hindu kings of Kashmir . . . oppressed Brahmans and temples, they did so against public opinion and against their own religious tenets. Muslim rulers who did the same had the support both of their co-religionist subjects and of Muslim law and tradition. Whether or not state persecution of Brahmans and confiscation of the wealth of Hindu religious institutions actually became more frequent—a point which is uncertain but probable—the coming of Islam did make it possible to openly advocate or threaten such actions. It also tended to foster local conflicts between Muslim fakirs and Hindu monks and these conflicts may have been as much responsible for the militarization of the fakirs and monks as any "official" persecution. Whatever the exact case, the new situation was evidently sufficient to provoke the creation of the military orders. (Lorenzen 1978, 68)

Hence, though Lorenzen corrects Farquhar on the antiquity of monastic recourse to arms in Indian history, he reinforces the idea that Muslim tyranny was crucial to the rise of formal soldiering bands in Indian monasticism.

To summarize, the portrayal of Hindu monks as precolonial patriots has a long history, an important part of which is Bankim's ingenious description of sannyasi rebels arrayed against British and Muslim tyranny, and the avowedly secular-nationalist and, later, RSS, VHP, and BJP appropriation of that fictional portrayal for propagandistic, consciousness-raising purposes. (See T. Sarkar, below.) Obliquely related to this was the scholarly argument, first proposed by Farquhar and based largely on oral traditions of the early twentieth century, that armed asceticism was predicated on the victimization of Hindus by Muslims in the medieval period. Given the rising communal tensions among the middle classes in the 1920s, which included the foundation of the RSS (S. Sarkar, below), it is not difficult to imagine how such oral traditions evolved; and given the impulse felt both in administration and scholarship to represent all medieval and early modern history as a function of Hindu-Muslim antagonism (Pandey 1992), it is easy to imagine the enthusiasm with which such oral traditions would have been seized by scholars such as Farquhar, not to mention his readers.

## Monastic Soldiering to 1796

Whatever the origins of armed monasticism, by the eighteenth century, soldier monks had evolved into major players in north Indian political and economic affairs, and were involved in activities that extended well beyond the defense of religious property. The major soldiering orders were, as financiers and traders, central to the expanding economic integration of the subcontinent, making up for the decay of Mughal political unity. Soldier monks, according to Bernard S. Cohn (1964) and D. H. A. Kolff (1971), combined their command of subcontinental pilgrimage routes and privileged status in society with a formidable martial tradition to extend and diversify their institutional (monasterial) savings into urban landowner-ship, money lending, and luxury goods in a variety of urban centers. C. A. Bayly (1983, 125–44), building on this argument, emphasized the impor-tance of ascetic orders in facilitating trade and investment links between increasingly regional political economies in the dynamic eighteenth cen-tury. For Bayly, the purchasing power of the states that were inheriting the mantle of Mughal authority relied increasingly on the flow of capital between regions, a flow that was often secured with the "neutral" (that is, nonaligned) armed force that accompanied the trading caravans of as-cetics. Indeed, Bayly argues that of all the groups engaged in the process of social and economic change in the eighteenth and nineteenth centuries, the soldier monks "came the nearest of any Indian business community to the emerging bourgeoisie that European theorists from Sleeman to Marx wished to see" (C. Bayly 1983, 242).

In addition to their financial and commercial talents, by the mid-eighteenth century, some of the Vaishnava and Shaiva naga akharas had evolved into highly effective—and highly sought after—military forces, and they attracted employment with a wide range of north Indian rulers. Without question, the most celebrated army of soldier monks in the eigh-teenth century was the Dasnami force under Rajendragiri and his disciples, Anupgiri (alias Himmat Bahadur) and Umraogiri. In crafting military alli-ances with numerous regional power-holders, these three *gosains* (Shaiva nagas)—and particularly Anupgiri, who would by 1761 command about twelve thousand mobile and highly disciplined troops—earned consider-able military reputations (not to mention fortunes) in the central and western Gangetic plain (Bhalla 1944; Sarkar and Roy 1958, 123–261; R. B. Barnett 1980, 56–57, 80–81). In eastern Rajasthan, an army of Ramanandi bairagis (Vaishnava nagas) was rising to prominence at the same time, under the command of Swami Balanand, in the service of the Jaipur state. In contrast to the constantly shifting alliances of Anupgiri and Umraongiri (who served, at various stages of their careers, the nawabs of Awadh, the Mughal emperor, the Jats, the Marathas, and finally, in the case of Anupgiri, the British), Balanand and his troops maintained a strong loyalty to the ruling lineage of Jaipur. This loyalty was mutually felt: Maharaja Madho Singh, who reigned from 1751 to 1768, considered Balanand his personal religious guru and elevated him thus above the many respected "rajgurus" or officially sanctioned spiritual figures in the Jaipur region (A. K. Roy 1978, 172, 193). Balanand's akhara headquarters was (and remains) at the base of the massive wall that connects the Nahargarh fort overlooking Jaipur from the north with the northwestern sector of the city. And though the Balanand *pith* (center) today retains only a hint of its former military glory, Balanand himself is recognized by most Vaishnavas as the individual responsible for organizing the itinerant bands of armed Ramanandis (known as the Ram Dal) into a disciplined and structured armed force (Sinha 1957, 119–20).

When armed bairagis and gosains were not fighting on behalf of the principalities with which they were aligned, they were often found to be fighting against each other. This is clear from stray references throughout the sixteenth to nineteenth centuries, describing clashes at the periodic kumbh festival and elsewhere. The first major recorded conflict in which armed ascetics were involved, it appears, was the protracted skirmish at Thaneshwar among Shaiva yogis and sannyasis in 1567 referred to earlier, in which the Mughal emperor Akbar was decisively complicit. Conflicts during the seventeenth and eighteenth centuries, mainly between bairagis and gosains, seemed to be decided mostly in favor of the Shaivas. Major victories occurred in particular at the Hardwar kumbh—which had become by the mid-eighteenth century a major commercial event in northwest India—in 1640 and 1760, and at the Nasik kumbh in 1789 (Lochtefeld 1994, 594–95). Indeed, according to Vaishnava tradition, incessant attacks by Shaiva gosains on bairagis in the seventeenth century, including the Dasnami capture of Ayodhya in 1699, inspired Vaishnavas to arm themselves soon thereafter (Burghart 1978, 126–30; Sinha 1957, 119–20). Gosain dominance in this period, particularly in the northwestern Gangetic region around Hardwar, may have been sustained in part by the military and political successes of Rajendragiri and his disciples, Anupgiri and Umraogiri. Rajendragiri was appointed *faujdar* (commanding officer) of Saharanpur in 1752 by the Mughal emperor Ahmad Shah (A. L. Srivastava 1933, 204–5), an office that would have given allied Shaiva akharas the upper hand in Hardwar at the peak of its commercial success. Rajendragiri would die in battle soon thereafter, and Umraogiri would be appointed commander in his place by Safdar Jang; both he and Anupgiri would thrive in the tumultuous political intrigue of the period and their influence would increase exponentially in the Agra-Delhi region in the following three decades.

## Soldier Monks after 1796

Gosains would retain complete control of the Hardwar festival, including the right to tax pilgrims, police the gathering, and dispense justice, until 1796. However, in that year, they would experience a humiliating defeat at the Hardwar kumbh; ironically, the instigators and victors in the 1796 conflict were not Vaishnavas but the armed *khalsa* (or "army of the pure") of the Nanakpanthis, better known today as Sikhs, who were on the verge of consolidating a powerful state in the Punjab under Ranjit Singh (Hardwicke 1801, 312–19). Perhaps it is not coincidental that the late 1780s saw the declining influence of the gosain commanders Anupgiri and Umraogiri in this region, in part as a result of a falling out with Mahadji Sindia and their greater attention to affairs in Bundelkhand (Bhalla 1944, 133–34). Meanwhile, as a result of the Vaishnava blood spilled by Shaiva swords in 1789 at Nasik, a complaint would be registered on behalf of the bairagis in the court of the Peshwa in Pune, which would decide in 1813 to assign separate bathing areas to each order.[5]

Similar arrangements would be made by the British in Hardwar and Allahabad, so as to prevent bloodshed during the massive periodic gatherings (Prior 1993, 31–32). Finally, in what can be considered a low point for Shaiva soldiering, a conflict said to have been instigated by gosains at the 1826 kumbh in Ujjain resulted in their utter defeat and the plunder of their monasteries and temples in the vicinity of that city at the hands of the Vaishnava bairagis, who were said to be assisted by local Marathas (*Delhi Gazette* 1850). By 1850, Vaishnava bairagis would be the dominant presence at the Ujjain kumbh. Part and parcel with this process of gosain decline was

5. The evidence usually cited for this is a copperplate inscription, a copy of which was shown to one of Ghurye's associates by one Mahant Radhamohandas of Nasik. For reasons that are unclear, Ghurye (1964, 177–78) reports the date of the Nasik battle as 1690, and the Peshwa court decision as 1702, which is clearly impossible. Burghart (1978, 137 n. 4) cites a reproduction of this inscription published in the Indian periodical *Jagriti* 10, 4 (1945): 896–97, which gives the 1789 and 1813 dates, respectively.

the gradual usurpation by Vaishnavas of Shaiva shrines through the eighteenth century, the classic case in point being the town of Ayodhya itself (van der Veer 1988, 142–51). Even in Kashi, the city of Shiva, numerous Ramanandi monasteries would begin to challenge Dasnami dominance after 1700, but more so after 1800 (Saraswati and Sinha 1978, 49–52, 118).

In retrospect, the military decline of the Shaiva akharas and the concomitant rise of their Vaishnava counterparts were gradually eclipsed (and rendered militarily irrelevant) by the emergence in India of the modern state, which demands uncompromising loyalty, absolute sovereignty, and monopolistic control of armed force. In this context, the kumbh, which by the eighteenth century had become a popular occasion for audacious display of monastic military prowess, became a religious theater verging on caricature, wholly removed from subcontinental politics, and closely supervised by colonial officials. An article on "The Great Fair at Oojein [Ujjain]" in the *Delhi Gazette* (June 12 and 15, 1850), provides a telling glimpse of this new scenario. Responding to the threat of violence between gosains and the much more powerful bairagis during the main bathing day of the festival, local rulers solicited the armed assistance of two companies of the Gwalior infantry under the command of Captain Macpherson. Prior to the onset of the monastic processions, Macpherson deployed his troops throughout the city, on the bathing ghats, and in temple balconies overlooking the river. He then endeavored to arbitrate the conflicting claims of the various orders for ceremonial precedence and eventually convinced the Shaivas to conclude their military procession and ritual bathing in the morning, well before the arrival of the much larger and more powerful Vaishnava armies. In case either party would later renege on the timing of the processions, heavy guns were "posted to command the whole breadth of the stream," and a fenced barrier was constructed in the middle of the shallow river "so as to form two separate pools" where the bairagis and gosains could bathe independent of each other. As a final precaution, one hundred Brahmans were positioned between the two pools to assist the sadhus in their ablutions, thereby providing a buffer of sorts between the two armies. Save for a potentially serious dispute over protocol between two Vaishnava battalions, which was quickly ironed over by Macpherson himself, the entire day passed without incident. Gone were the days of unbridled monastic warfare at the kumbh; the contrast with the eighteenth century could not be more pronounced.

## Sadhus, Sectarianism, and Religious Politics

Though soldier sadhus were rendered militarily obsolete after 1800, the kumbh remained an important venue for monastic politics and nagas remained central to the kumbh. Subject to colonial supervision, the control of the pilgrimage site and the wealth that flowed from it—which usually resulted in armed conflict between Shaivas and Vaishnavas—were no longer the main issues of contention; rather more important was the question of supremacy within the sectarian group itself. Such conflict would be resolved not through the use of arms but through faction building, debate, and (after 1850) the dissemination of published religious tracts. Of particular importance in the articulation of intrasectarian conflict after 1800 was the emergence of populist strands among Ramanandi and Dasnami sectarian groups (Saraswati and Sinha 1978, 96–97; Pinch 1996). This new populism would result, by the early twentieth century, in the alienation of high-caste elements that were seen to espouse orthodox, exclusivist views and to have exercised a disproportionate leadership influence in each community. Among Dasnamis, high-caste orthodoxy was generally associated with *dandi* sannyasis; among Ramanandis, with Ramanuji *acharyas* (religious leaders). Before the 1920s, the accepted custom was for the rank and file ascetics within each order to pay great respect to these orthodox elements, particularly during the kumbh processions when dandis and acharyas would be carried on ornate thrones on the shoulders of warrior gosains and bairagis, respectively. By the 1930s, however, such deference would no longer be forthcoming, reflecting the fact that nagas no longer felt obliged to endure the haughtiness of the dandis and acharyas associated with their orders.

The rise of an anti-Ramanuji sentiment in the Ramanandi sampraday (sectarian community) would have major transformative implications for the structure and content of Vaishnava monasticism in north India, inasmuch as the Ramanandi faction that prevailed did so on the basis of the claim that the Ramanujis in their midst were at best indifferent to—and at worst disdainful of—the worship of Rama. That claim won the day at a debate at the Ujjain kumbh of 1921, and Ramanandi radicalism was increasingly successful in the following decades; this should be seen as an assertion of independent naga influence in Vaishnava monastic politics and also as a reflection of the increasing religious importance of Rama worship in the north. Naga mahants (abbots) not only dominated the jury deliberations at the Ujjain kumbh debate that was decided in favor of the anti-Ramanuji faction (van der Veer 1988, 104; Prapann 1992, 15), but they were by definition instrumental in prohibiting Ramanujis from participating in the 1932 kumbh in the same city (Ghurye 1964, 152). At the forefront of the anti-Ramanuji faction was a young sadhu by the name of Swami Bhagavadacharya, who would go on to publish numerous works of revisionist scholarship centered on revealing the true egalitarian teachings of the fourteenth-century Swami Ramanand—regarded by Ramanandis as the founder of their monastic community. At the Allahabad kumbh in 1977, Bhagavadacharya, over one hundred years of age, would be declared the first *Jagadguru Ramanandacharya* (supreme pontiff of the Ramanandi sampraday) since Ramanand himself. Such a declaration could not have been sustained at the kumbh without the consent of the Ramanandi naga akharas, particularly given Bhagavadacharya's role in the 1921 debate.

The banning of sectarian violence at the kumbh by colonial officials and the disarming of soldier monks by the colonial state did not, of course, result in the elimination of religious conflict in Indian society. To the contrary, as nationalist sentiments began to spread among the urban middle classes in the late nineteenth century, religion became for many the basis of political identity and, consequently, communalist violence. Sadhus were at times involved in articulating Hindu communal issues—such as cow protection and Hindi language debates—but they did not take the lead in communal movements. That role fell to educated town and city-based politicians, local notables who saw religion as a way of shoring up their own political base (Freitag 1989b). The assertive confidence of the middle classes in religious nationalism was part of a larger process of discursive displacement in the nineteenth century, whereby socioreligious reform was propelled by public men whose claim to moral authority was derived not from membership in a respected religious order but from their proficiency as speakers, conference organizers, and pamphleteers. Most often their audience was the putative caste group (Pinch forthcoming [1996], chap. 3), but it could just as well have been lovers of Hindi, protectors of the cow, or devotees of the country. Religion thereby entered a public sphere, and with it came religious violence. As Peter van der Veer notes,

At the most general level, the great shift in the nineteenth century is the laicization of institutionalized religion. A lay Hindu and Muslim public had come to occupy a sphere that was previously the domain of sacred specialists. To put it very crudely, warfare between religious specialists was replaced by civil warfare between lay communities. (See van der Veer, below p. 260.)

Viewed in these terms, sadhus and the sampraday they represent were not implicit to or complicit in the rise of Hindu religious nationalism and, more importantly, the militant (and quasi-military) organizations that promoted it, such as the RSS. All indications are that the two worlds held each other at arm's length, until, that is, the creation of the VHP in the 1960s and the drive to engage India's holy men (not to mention the considerable monastic wealth they controlled) in the politics of religion and nation. The real push, however, only came in the 1980s, with the decision on the part of political leaders in the BJP to look to the Ram janmabhoomi issue in Ayodhya as a way of catapulting the party into national or, at least, north Indian prominence. The strategy clearly worked, though it is not without a variety of risks, prominent among them being one of control. Though Vaishnava sadhus are united in their broad sectarian stance, they are divided according to sampraday; their thousands of *math*s (monasteries), akharas, and *sthan*s (regions) are functionally and legally autonomous and are the personal property of individual mahants to do with as they please. Historically, sadhus have been fiercely independent and resentful of state control, even while benefiting from the land grants of emperors and regional rulers, even more so when confronted with the intractability of the modern bureaucratic machine. How they will respond to the desire of party politicians to dictate behavior over the long term remains to be seen. Another risk is the possibility that Vaishnava mahants will resent the participation of their Shaiva counterparts in deciding the fate of Ayodhya, particularly given the institutional memory of conflict between the two sects in centuries past.

Indeed, the reluctance of mahants to be beholden to any one political party explains in large part the initiative taken by several prominent monastic figures in the summer of 1994 to create an independent *Ramalaya* (Rama's abode) trust. The proclaimed mandate of the self-described "apolitical" trust is to design and construct a temple marking the birthplace of Rama in Ayodhya, pending the release of the sixty-seven-acre site by the government. The Ramalaya trust has been the target of attack from the Hindu right, particularly from Ashok Singhal, the VHP leader, as a Congress government attempt to wrest the initiative in the Ayodhya dispute from its rightful political owners; conversely, it has been vilified by critics from the left as yet another step toward legitimizing (not to mention glorifying) an act of communal barbarity for which Hindus, they feel, collectively should hang their heads in shame. However, the creation and survival of the trust, and the fact that some prominent VHP mahants defected to it between September 1994 and February 1995, drives home the point that the VHP (with the BJP and RSS in the background) does not exercise control over the minds and actions of India's monks. Many sadhus, with hindsight, felt used by the Sangh Parivar during the height of the Ayodhya movement in 1992, and they have chosen not to be pawns any longer in a game of chess between political giants. These points are made ever more forcefully by the fact that one of the main players in the Ramalaya trust is Baba Gyan Das, an influential, charismatic, highly articulate mahant of the formidable Hanuman Garhi (fort) — north India's Ramanandi naga head- quarters and home to hundreds of bairagis, a mere stone's throw from the contested Ram janmabhoomi. Furthermore, it is clear from a perusal of press clippings between August 1994 and February 1995 that a broad spec- trum of prominent Ramanandis from Benares, Patna, Chitrakut, and, most especially, Ayodhya itself, not to mention a host of other major Vaishnava and Shaiva leaders, have gravitated toward the independent trust and away from the more aggressive stance of the VHP. As the mauni amavasaya of the 1995 *ardh-kumbh* (half kumbh) in Allahabad drew to a close on Janu- ary 30, and the eighteen million pilgrims who had thronged the *triveni* (sacred confluence of rivers) turned their faces toward home, this was the new political reality that confronted the VHP.

There remains, however, an as yet unbridged gulf between, on the one hand, those supporters of the Hindu right who see themselves as politi- cal moderates and feel that an independent monastic trust in charge of the construction of a Ram janmabhoomi temple is a step in the right di- rection, and, on the other hand, committed secularists who feel that the destruction of the Babri Masjid and the violence that surrounded it did ir- reparable damage to the national fabric, so that the creation of a trust only adds insult to injury. The latter blame mostly the VHP-RSS-BJP combine, the Sangh Parivar; but a strong measure of their resentment (mixed with fear) is also directed to the thousands of anonymous, saffron-clad sadhus who took part in the movement, who were featured prominently in the many video images of mobs attacking and razing the mosque, and who symbolize for the left the irrational forces of religion run rampant. What anger is left over is pointed at the Congress Party, first, for having let itself be led down the road toward Ayodhya in the 1980s and, second, for trying to beat the BJP at its own game, namely, that of mixing religion with poli- tics. For committed secularists, the construction of a temple on or near the place where the mosque stood would only cement a great national mis- deed (though that construction is today nowhere near a certainty); and yet they can take some solace from the fact that serious thought and debate is now taking place among reasonable people in the akharas over the appropriateness and tenor of sadhu participation in the public life of the nation. They may also find some comfort in the knowledge that, notwithstanding popular portrayals to the contrary, the naga sadhu was not a precolonial patriot sprung from the soil and bent on defending Hindu India from foreign (primarily Muslim) invasions. And while there is no cause to doubt the genuineness of patriotic feeling among postcolonial naga sadhus, there is plenty of reason to believe that it differs in important ways from BJP-VHP-RSS definitions of Hindutva.

# 7

## Imagining Hindurashtra: The Hindu and the Muslim in Bankim Chandra's Writings

TANIKA SARKAR

BANKIM CHANDRA CHATTOPADHYAY (1838–94) was the real founder of the Bengali novel as well as of serious Bengali discursive literature on political theory. He was also a brilliant humorist and satirist who laughed at most traditions, agendas, and social types. Generally regarded as the most powerful formative influence on nineteenth-century political thinking in Bengal, he is a difficult author to read with certainty, because he seems to straddle very different positions with felicity at different times (Raychaudhuri 1988) and seems to mock convictions and resolutions that he himself had constructed (T. Sarkar 1994a).

Scholars generally regard Bankim as a crucial force in the making of both a nationalist imagination and a Hindu revivalist polemic (Tripathi 1967). A particularly striking instance of this dual impact is his celebrated hymn to the motherland—"Bande Mataram" (salutation to the mother), which became the most potent patriotic slogan at peak points in twentieth-century mass nationalist struggles (S. Sarkar 1973), as well as the Hindu rallying cry at moments of Hindu-Muslim violence after 1926 (P. K. Datta, personal communication). For the Sangh Parivar, "Bande Mataram" is the authentic national anthem, not Rabindranath Tagore's "Jana gana mana," the official national anthem for the Republic of India. The hymn is apparently sung in its entirety (including Bengali passages) daily at RSS training meetings (*shakhas*). Any change or abbreviation is strictly forbidden, since the song symbolizes the undivided, inviolate body of the pre-partition motherland; hence, an abridgment amounts to a symbolic mutilation of the sacred body, a repetition of the partition of India in 1947 (Asha Sharma, interview with the author, Delhi, December 1990). When the BJP came into power in Delhi during the 1993 state elections, it made singing "Bande Mataram" compulsory in Delhi state schools.

The use of "Bande Madaram" by both Indian nationalism and Hindu communalism can lead scholars who see nationalism as a nonhistorical, undifferentiated phenomenon to read the meanings of one usage into the other in their understanding of Bankim's work (Pandey 1990b). Bankim's work has also been split up into different, isolated components and his concept of Hindu nationhood is read on its own as an exercise in nationalist imagination, without any reference to the Muslim in his discourse (Kaviraj n.d.a). Bankim's polemical references to the Muslim are also sometimes detached from his novels. They can then be seen as a seamless whole, without internal shifts. The communal impulse is then related to his nationalism as its displaced and disfigured form.[1]

I would like to explore the location of the Muslim and of the Hindu nation in Bankim's work as an interlinked formation that has to be situated simultaneously within his novelistic and his discursive prose. The two set up an internal dialogue and self-interrogation that move across his earlier, relatively open-ended and often radical phase (T. Sarkar 1994a) and his later, more dogmatic and recognizably revivalist work. I am centrally concerned with the profound breaks in thinking and expression across these two phases, as well as with continuities preserved with narrative tropes and devices, by which Bankim continued to destabilize his seemingly unambiguous agenda of a triumphalist Hindu people. My focus will be on his last five years, when he composed three historical novels on Hindu-Muslim antagonism—*Anandamath* (first published 1882; fifth and final version, 1892), *Debi Choudhurani* (1884), and *Sitaram* (1887)—and on two polemical essays on an authentic and reinvigorated Hinduism that needs to be attained through a disciplinary regimen that Bankim spelled out in some detail—*Dharmatattva* (1888) and *Krishnacharitra* (1892).[2]

1. Partha Chatterjee (1988) has completely ignored Bankim's novels as important ways of negotiating with political themes. Even the reading of the discursive prose is severely limited by a literal reading of texts in complete disregard of his literary strategies and devices that were significantly deployed here. Sudipta Kaviraj, in a series of unpublished monographs on various texts of Bankim, has also chosen to read each text as a fairly isolated, autonomous unit, although he is extremely sensitive in his reading strategy.

2. Two incomplete manuscripts were posthumously published: his commentary on "Shrimad Bhagavat Gita" (1902) and "Devatattva O Hindudharma" (1938). Since both were incomplete and since Bankim extensively revised his writings before the final publication, I have not made any use of them here. All references to Bankim Chandra Chattopadhyay's

In sharp contrast to his prolific earlier production, Bankim wrote far less in this later period. There is much less satire, caricature, or humor. For the first time, his prose remains uncompromisingly solemn, weighty, and ponderous, all of which, at least overtly, seems to embody a single and authoritarian polemical thrust rather than an argument that continuously poses new questions and issues to itself. *Dharmatattva*, in fact, is written in the form of a guru preaching to his disciple. The authorial voice is intrusive and cast as a self-proclaimed proselytizer-cum-pedagogue. One is reminded of RSS training classes; though, whereas in *Dharmatattva*, master and disciple proceed through arguments and counterarguments, in RSS training sessions, small boys are told stories with correct messages and listeners practice silent acceptance.

This phase of Bankim's work is considered to be a decisive component of Hindu revivalism, and indeed it provided vital resources for late-twentieth-century Hindutva and its RSS leadership. I prefer to treat this phase more as constituting the link between nineteenth-century Hindu revivalism in Bengal—whose Hindu supremacist agenda was not primarily turned against Muslims or Islam—and the hard, aggressive Hindutva politics that started organizing itself in the 1920s on an exclusively and explicitly anti-Muslim platform (T. Basu et al. 1993; see S. Sarkar, below). I am also concerned, however, with what has not been appropriated from Bankim's thinking on the Muslim and the Hindu nation, and with how Bankim negotiated these themes differently from those who later used his work for their own purposes.

## I

Until the end of the 1870s, Bankim had very boldly and thoroughly probed the specific forms of caste, class, and gender oppression in precolonial Indian traditions. He had occasionally questioned the need for self-rule and nationhood for Hindus, given these internal and structured power relations, which might even be loosened up somewhat under foreign rule.[3] In *Samya* (Equality), published in 1879, he moved well beyond the notion of companionate marriage that liberal reformers advocated for the new,

---

writings are to *Bankim Rachanabali*, ed. J. C. Bagal, 2 vols., Calcutta, 1965, 1969. Citations to these works are abbreviated henceforth in the text as *Bankim*, with the volume and page number of the citation (where it is important). All translations are mine.

3. "Bharatbarshe swadhinata ebong paradhinata," in *Vividha prabandha*, *Bankim* 2:244.

educated woman; he made startling suggestions about her future economic independence and about men sharing housework. He questioned the supreme emphasis that reformers, revivalists, and the colonial state equally placed on the absolute chastity of the Hindu wife, who was situated within a framework of male polygamy. He saw caste, class, and gender hierarchies as interlinked facets of a system that embodied the most absolute form of inequality anywhere in the world: "Our country is the land par excellence of inequalities, any kind of discrimination springs into life and flourishes as soon as the seed is sown" (*Bankim* 2:399).

Even in *Samya*, however, certain kinds of freedom and oppression are dealt with in a rather cursory manner. He questioned British rule and its ideas about progress in relation to persistent peasant poverty (*Bangadesher krishak*, 1875) but he rendered foreign rule and political freedom a lesser priority than internal stratification and oppression inside Indian society. The peasant, moreover, is the object of enlightened social engineering, but political initiative is obviously beyond him. In his historical novels, too, political change is invariably initiated by kings and ascetics; when the ordinary folk initiate direct action, it degenerates into mob rioting (*Anandamath* and *Sitaram*). Demands for freedom and welfare for victims of social oppression are powerfully articulated but the agenda is left without an agent. It is the colonial state that, after all, is asked to assume a corrective role (*Bangadesher krishak*).

In the 1870s, when Bankim was writing his socially aware and courageous prose, the absolute vulnerability of all categories of agricultural tenants on issues of rent increase, illegal cesses, and the arbitrary powers of eviction by landlords had hardly been breached (B. B. Chaudhuri 1967). In the 1880s, however, plans for substantive amendments in tenancy laws had been set forth (Bose 1993), and the state was systematically compiling and classifying information about low castes with a view to improving their conditions. In 1881, Bankim was, in fact, selected by H. H. Risley to assist in preparing an ethnographic glossary, with detailed research on castes and tribes, for Howrah district, where he was then posted (Bandyopadhya 1990, 33). It also became increasingly difficult to regard peasants as passive victims. Powerful forms of peasant self-organization and movements against arbitrary landlord exactions had become a central feature of the agrarian scene. The spread of commercial jute cultivation, moreover, had benefited Muslim and low-caste peasants more than the *rentier* groups, who constituted the base of the new middle class (Bandopadhyay 1990, chap. 2). In addition, the failure of Bengali entrepreneurship to find space for itself in the higher rungs of trade, business, and industry was definitively established by the 1870s (S. Bhattacharya 1991). There was a keen sense of exclusion from the commanding heights of the civil society for people in Bankim's own middle class. His earlier critique of the oppressive privileges of a parasitic upper-caste middle class now seemed to require a further deepening of these processes of exclusion, leading conceivably to a partial reversal of power relations rather than the benevolent and responsible paternalism of upper-caste landowners that Bankim had prescribed in the 1870s. There was now a real problem of choice.

After the late 1870s, Bankim would never return to the themes of peasant poverty and caste oppression. He would repudiate *Samya* and refuse to bring out a new edition (Bagal 1969). Even without necessarily imputing narrow motives to this choice, we have to reckon with this absence and the implications this holds out for a possible radical social agenda at a time of limited but real social change. We have to recognize that the choice was made and exercised through a silence, through certain excisions from his earlier concerns. It is also a fact of considerable significance that the definitive transition from a predominantly liberal to a markedly Hindu revivalist discourse was made within Bengal around the same time, and against this context, Sumit Sarkar has pointed out a somewhat similar predicament in the 1920s that partly enabled a turn toward organized communalism (S. Sarkar, below). The posing of the problem of power and exploitation was, therefore, unambiguously radical, but Bankim's radical imagining failed or refused to construct a resolution that could be adequate to itself.

If the peasant or the dispossessed low caste was not to be the subject of his own history, then the immediately realizable and convincing agency for self-improvement within Indian society—an agency that, moreover, already seemed activated—could be the middle class, with its Western education, liberal values, and reformist agenda. If reform of Hindu patriarchy was the major concern for this group, Bankim, too, had his own critique of Hindu domestic norms, which, if anything, was far sharper than that of the reformists. Bankim, however, was relentlessly critical of reformist aspirations and methods of work. He saw reformist dependence on colonial legislation for initiating improved family laws as a basic moral flaw, since this neither generated a will for change within wider society, without which reform would be doomed, nor did it make "men" of modern Hindus by vesting them with independence of effort and hegemonistic capabilities. Any dependence on foreign rulers perpetuated and exemplified for him the lack of a will to freedom and nationhood that had kept

Hindus subjected for centuries. Bankim spared no effort at mocking this dependence on alien legislation as well as the emasculation it produced. He also mocked the surrender of the new middle class to orientalist forms of knowledge on India, although he retained great respect for strands within mainstream Western social and political philosophies.[4]

Since he saw it as a class that was born retarded, Bankim refused the middle class its demands for political freedom and rights. He made himself extremely unpopular by supporting British moves to muzzle the vernacular press to suggest that it was behaving irresponsibly and that it needed controls (Bagal 1965). He used the entire and formidable resources of his satire and caricature to make fun of the politics of associations and organizations, of the mimicry of imported political models that was involved in such exercises and the ridiculous misadventures in handling them ("Byaghracharya Brihallangul," in *Lokrahasya*). He, therefore, undercut precisely the struggle for democratic and public spaces where Indians could grow through debates and experiences of organization and protest. Neither a radical nor a liberal form of democracy was compatible with the heroic agenda that held his imagination. In fact, if Bankim prefigures the trajectory of some features of Hindutva, he also powerfully embodies some aspects of a far softer and pluralistic form of liberal indigenism. The latter, out of its commitment to a non-"alienated" authentic politics and its suspicion of liberal rights or radical social protest that derive some of their terms from the post-Enlightenment political radicalism and democratic traditions, finds itself in the same space as aggressive, intolerant Hindutva in its critique of secular democratic politics. This, in the final analysis, emerges as a far more consistent and powerful strain than its critique of Hindutva, which is sporadic and milder.[5]

The thrust toward a pure and authentically Hindu site for generating the social will for change complicated his social concern, his sharp criticism of the traditional, precolonial form of Hindu domesticity, and his daring imagining of the nondomesticated, strong, passionate woman that had earlier created a marked distance between him and the contemporary

4. See his argument against the strategy of Vidyasagar in "Bahuvivaha," in *Vividha prabandha*. Satirical pieces in *Lokrahasya* (1874) make fun of the English educated Babu quite mercilessly. He criticized Indologists like Max Müller in "Bangalir Bahubol Prabandha Pustak" (1879). He was extremely sarcastic about dependence on Western reflections on Indian history and religion in *Dharmatattva*. At the same time, his affiliation with Western political theories, especially that of radical utilitarian and French revolutionary and socialist thinkers was openly asserted, not just in *Samya* but even in *Dharmatattva*.

5. This interpretive thrust has been well developed by Ashis Nandy (1983) and extended by Gyanendra Pandey (1990b) and P. Chatterjee (1993).

Hindu revivalist-nationalists (T. Sarkar 1993a). While he grew intellectually through a simultaneous and interanimated imbibing of Enlightenment universalism and Hindu philosophical resources and used the resources of both to interrogate both—and here lies the ineptness of the notion of hybridity that misses out on the criticality and the mutually transformative nature of this intellectual encounter—the compulsion to opt for a pure site of exclusively Hindu knowledge triumphed after his exchanges with the Reverend Hastie (Raychaudhuri 1988).

In 1882, Hastie of the General Assembly wrote a tract that was brutally critical of Hinduism. Bankim, who had always ridiculed orientalist pretensions about scientific knowledge on India, prepared a long, careful, and angry reply. It was after this that he repudiated *Samya* and, in his discursive prose, became exclusively preoccupied with the theme of a reconstructed Hindu form of knowledge and leadership. The anger was probably fueled by the changing political environment since the mid- and late-1870s. The post-1857 Mutiny repression, clearly racist in nature, had initiated serious self-doubt among the Bengali middle class, which had been entirely loyal in 1857. The escalation in discriminatory colonial policies during Lytton's era (Gopal 1966; Seal 1968) was followed by the violent racist backlash at the time of the Ilbert Bill agitation. Apart from the exposure to the most extreme and naked form of white racism in a concentrated dose, the middle class was also troubled by a reversal of trends that had promised a milder climate under the viceregal policies of Lord Northbrook, and later the liberal Ripon (Gopal 1953), which were on the point of opening up a few minor but real opportunities of incorporation within the colonial decision-making process (Gopal 1965; Seal 1968). This led to an intensification of both liberal and Hindu revivalist forms of anticolonial critiques and organization. Liberal nationalists formed secular, open organizations for self-strengthening and formulated economic critiques of the colonial drain of wealth, Indian poverty, and deindustrialization that remained the foundational concepts for all nationalist economic thinking down to Gandhi (B. Chandra 1966). Hindu revivalists, on the other hand, used their anti-Western rhetoric to close off all interrogation and transformation of power relations within the Hindu community as false knowledge contaminated by alien forms of power knowledge (T. Sarkar 1993a).[6] Revivalism thus assumed a markedly fundamentalist kind of defensiveness.

6. Dipesh Chakrabarty (1993) has recently reiterated the logic and politics of this revivalism in the same terms in his critique of contemporary "secular feminists."

Faced with this crisis of conscience, Bankim reacted by repudiating *Samya* and by excising the frontal contestation of Hindu caste, class, and gender hierarchies from his prose. The excision, despite his best efforts, remained somewhat incomplete, and Bankim reinserted some of his earlier critiques insidiously in his later novels (T. Sarkar 1994a).

Historical developments as well as certain earlier political choices, then, blocked off, for Bankim, any inclination to consider the liberal reformers as a vehicle for Hindu self-improvement. As class, caste, and gender as central concerns abruptly disappear from his work, their absence is filled up in the eighties by a new and coherent problematic: What constitutes authentic Hinduism? What possibilities existed within the Hinduism of the past and in the reauthenticated Hinduism of the future for nation building? What precisely was the culpability of the Muslim in Indian history and how and why had Hindu power capitulated to it? It is not that these problems were not reflected on in his earlier prose, but there they had locked horns with an equally powerful set of social concerns.[7] Their centrality now becomes absolute and uncontested. Bankim looks for an ethicoreligious site for a Hindu people whose dominant priority is not social justice but rather what is truly indigenous—that is, Hindu. This is explicit in *Krishnacharitra* and *Dharmatattva*. The latter, in fact, begins with the theme of poverty and hunger—a deliberate invocation of Bankim's earlier concerns. Then the guru persuades the disciple that both can be overcome by the cultivation of the right Hindu disposition and knowledge. He thus relocates the roots of these problems within the individual disposition and mind-set—away from social structures (*Bankim* 2:585–86).

With the reoriented problematic, the obvious agency could now be restored to the Brahmanic forms of knowledge and upper-caste social leadership. This, however, presents equally powerful problems. Bankim continues to believe that past traditions of Hinduism had not generated any impulse for freedom and nationhood. If these new changes need to be improvised, then old forms of knowledge or rule will not automatically yield them. Even in his later discursive phase, he continued to polemicize against certain forms of Hindu knowledge and devotion, as earlier he had critically reviewed the Sankhya traditions ("Sankhyadarshan," in *Vividha pra-*

---

7. Themes of Hindu history and nationhood were taken up in "Prabandha pustak." Many of the concerns of *Dharmatattva* and the form of its presentation had been anticipated in "Gaurdas babajir bhikshar jhuli," in *Vividha prabandha* (1874). *Krishnacharitra* was originally written to form a part of *Vividha prabandha*, but was later much altered and extended. See Bagal (1969, 21).

*bandha*). At no phase had he shown much sympathy for Vedic or Vedantist philosophies, perhaps because their quietist, reflective modes were inappropriate for a politically militant, even violent heroic agenda, and also because these were resources that Brahmo reformers had celebrated. In *Dharmatattva*, he says, "Vaidic religion lacks the concept of devotion . . . there are only propitiatory sacrifices to attain one's earthly desires" (*Bankim* 2:623), and he polemicizes against all major Hindu religious philosophies to assert the correctness of a reoriented bhakti (devotion). Bankim conducted a relentless polemic against dominant Bengali forms of devotion, especially its Vaishnava form, which worshiped Krishna as a figure of erotic excess (*Krishnacharitra*); he was also critical of the quietism of Kali-devotion preached by his contemporary, Ramakrishna (S. Sarkar 1992). He chose the Puranic tradition and pulled together from it the figure of a heroic, vindictive, wily, and violent savior figure. He used as his model the mythical-epic dimensions of the later life of Krishna, when he was no longer the shepherd boy or the great lover, but when he had grown up into the king, the politician, the warrior (*Krishnacharitra*). Throughout his life, he held lively arguments with the orthodox repositories of Brahmanic knowledge—the pandits of Bhatpara (Shyamali 1988). He cast doubt on the learning of the doyen of Hindu orthodoxy of his times—Pandit Sasadhar Tarkachuramani (T. Sarkar 1994a). The criticality and intellectual and polemical energies that continued to shape his writings even of the later period would be something that Hindutva today entirely eschews. Even in *Dharmatattva*, the guru preached to a well-read, argumentative disciple. RSS pedagogic principles, on the other hand, are entirely exhortative and rhetorical, and internal debates and productive differences find no space there. It is not for nothing that they select recruits from very young children who lack the capacity to argue (T. Basu et al. 1993).

Existing representatives of old Hindu ruling groups—upper-caste landowners and *rentiers* who opposed the new Western learning, and leaders of Hindu religious establishments, the pandits—failed to convince Bankim that they were in any way deserving of their privilege or that they could offer the potential for active leadership. In his later novels, he returned to his sharp satirical bite in portraying the classic figure of the traditional Hindu patriarch—the upper-caste parasitic landlord paterfamilias—as embodied in *Debi Choudhurani*, in Haraballabh's inhuman, patriarchal orthodoxy and lack of honor and dignity. The virtuous founder of a Hindu power that he imagined in *Sitaram* could sustain neither his virtue nor his power. Contemporary sexual and financial scandals about the mahant of the celebrated Shaiva pilgrimage center at Tarakeswar that rocked Bengal in 1873, reported in the *Bengalee* and the *Statesman*, and the earlier scandal about the maharaja of the Vallabhachari sect in Gujarat probably made Bankim unable to imagine the present representatives of organized religion as saviors. Even the ascetics of *Anandamath*, the quintessentially militant patriotic novel, astonish the ordinary devout Hindu who keeps on asking them what kinds of Vaishnavas or sannyasis they are (*Bankim* 1:724–37).

It is notable that in this phase, as earlier, virtue, activism, and heroism are more effortlessly embodied by the woman as almost a characterological trait. This is true of all three novels: in the characters of Shanti and Kalyani (*Anandamath*); Prafulla, Diba, and Nishi (*Debi Choudhurani*); and Shree, the *sannyasini* (female sannyasi), and Nanda in *Sitaram*. Bankim had stopped polemicizing against the subordination of women and the bold feminist of *Samya* had buried himself. In *Krishnacharitra*, in fact, he devoted much space to justify an act of force committed by Arjuna in abducting the sister of Krishna on his advice. Krishna convinces Arjuna—and Bankim tries to convince us—that male guardians can and should override the question of the woman's consent in the interests of her own larger welfare, which they necessarily comprehend better (*Bankim* 2:498–504). The disproportionately large space that he devotes to justify this rather minor incident in the life of Krishna, however, tells us how difficult he found it to persuade himself. In *Dharmatattva*, he overturns his earlier images of conjugality as the equal and mature mutual passion between two adults, which had deconstructed the revivalist nationalist celebration of nonconsensual infant marriage between a polygamous male and an utterly monogamous child wife (*Bankim* 1:620). At the same time, even in the later phase, the woman remained the locus of the nation in a far more activist way than the passive, iconic role ascribed to her by revivalist nationalists, who saw in her submission to Shastric prescriptions and in her total insulation from new alien norms a measure of her symbolic capacity to embody and sustain the nation (T. Sarkar 1993a). In Bankim, however, the only approximation of the figure of Savior Krishna is the figure of the dacoit queen Prafulla who earns this capacity not by being faithful to Hindu domestic prescriptions but by surviving outside her household and by fighting against British forces. Even though the pedagogic training for the new Hindu that Bankim filled out in *Dharmatattva* is imparted to a male disciple, in the novel *Debi Choudhurani*, the dacoit queen Prafulla actually undergoes the training. In *Sitaram*, too, the woman causes virtuous action, tries to save Hindu power, and suffers a wrongful trial and humiliation, which constitutes a striking parallel with and an implicit critique of Rama's trial of Sita (*Bankim* 1:944–48).

The woman's activism, however, is occasional and exceptional even when it sustains some of the critical energies of the earlier Bankim. It is certainly not a sign of an investiture of the woman with leadership of the patriotic agenda. It is also something that happens entirely within his fiction. In the directly polemical prose, on the other hand, the critical energy is well contained, and even the feminine figuration of the motherland that Bankim achieved in *Anandamath* is absent. The new Hindu is emphatically a Hindu man with a difference. He is the embodiment of a rigorous, disciplinary schedule that will eventually transpose discipline from an external ethicoreligious authority to the self-monitoring ethical agent who has internalized reinterpreted concepts of Hindu knowledge and devotional practices: these are Bankim's explanations of *anushilandharma* and *bhakti*, respectively. The process of training that incorporates knowledge, dispositions, physical capabilities, and devotion and replaces the privileges of birth and ritual expertise distinguishes the new Brahman—the ideal patriot and nation builder—from the old, unreformed Hindu authorities. Inherited and normative control are replaced with hard-earned leadership; Brahmanic authority is revived as intensively cultivated hegemonistic aspirations. This represents a return on a higher plane, perhaps, but a return, nonetheless. The imagined Hindu nation cannot, even in the imagination, be made and ruled by agents who are not male and upper caste. (Note that the RSS has very real Maharashtra Brahman origins; T. Basu et al. 1993).

## II

Let us now turn to some specific dimensions within the construction of the new Hindu. We shall begin with a theme that we touched on in the first section: the "Bande Mataram" hymn. We shall use it as an illustration of the imaginative and rhetorical devices with which a militant Hindu form of patriotism is constructed. Bankim had originally composed this as a song in 1875. Later, when he had finished the highly influential novel *Anandamath*, he inserted it within the story and vested it with highly significant narrative functions (Bagal 1965, 23). The song, on its own, would have made an original move toward a deification and fetishization of the country. That sense was further heightened by other resonances within the novel, which spent much effort in constructing a sequentialized imagery of the deified motherland (*Bankim* 1:728–29). Apart from that, the narrative framing, acquired from the novel's plot, endowed it with additional and very new properties. The hymn, subsequently, was detached from the novel and achieved a life of its own as a slogan in mass nationalist rallies and, later, in communal violence. The novel, however, remained contained within the slogan as implied resonances, associations, and emotions and provided a reference point for larger messages.

The song begins in Sanskrit, then turns into Bengali and ends with Sanskrit passages again. It begins with an evocation of the bounteous, lovely land that generously nurtures its children. Then bounty and physical richness turn into an image of a motherland with latent strength derived from the image of Durga, the demon-slaying goddess, from the numerical strength of her population, compiled in census statistics, and from the supreme sacred significance that Bankim ascribes to the motherland within the Hindu pantheon: "It is your image that we worship in all temples" (*Bankim* 1:726). The land, for a while, is at one with the icon of Durga. The image of Durga then quickly and insidiously transforms itself into that of Kali, another manifestation of the Mother Goddess, but a destructive, angry force. The hymn ends with a reiteration of the original sense of bounty and nurture, and the goddess exhorts her children to enrich her strength with their own. In between, there is just a suggestion of her present weakness—"with such strength, why are you helpless?"—but the overwhelming sense is one of power. The power is undifferentiated and flows back and forth from the mother to the sons, though it certainly originates with the mother. The song encapsulates, in an unbroken musical flow, the three distinct images of the nurturing mother of the past, the dispossessed mother of the present, and the triumphant mother of the future that are developed at much greater length within the novel (*Bankim* 1:728). Later nationalists clearly saw the demon slayer as pitted against the colonial power and used the song as an abbreviated history of the growth of colonial exploitation and the patriotic struggle for liberation. The RSS, on the other hand, certainly took it to imply a "historical" struggle against the Muslim, since from its inception, the RSS stayed away from the anticolonial movements and devoted itself to an exclusively communal agenda. As a matter of fact, in the song itself, the demon is nonspecified and is eclipsed by the image of the armed mother. What is of importance is the reiteration that the patriotic son is quintessentially a soldier at war.

The novel itself is ambiguous about whom the mother is fighting. It is set in the transitional historical moment of the late eighteenth century,

against the backdrop of the famine of 1770, armed combat by marauding
ascetics of Naga Dasnami orders against the puppet Muslim nawab, and
the indirect control of the British in Bengal (*Bankim* 1:726). Bankim makes
no mention of the role of Muslim faqirs who also led plundering bands of
starving people. Even though historically, the sannyasis were from Shaiva
orders, here they are worshipers of Vishnu, with a brand of militant, war-
like bhakti of their own. Leaders are recruited from Bengali, upper-caste,
landed origins, and they have transformed themselves with devotional and
rigorous physical and martial training, with the vocation of ascetic celibacy
for the duration of the struggle, which is meant to restore Hindu rule.
Even though they do accomplish the ouster of the puppet nawab, they
also are instrumental in ushering in direct and complete British dominion. A divine voice tells the supreme leader that this is providential, since
Hindus need apprenticeship in modern forms of power. The leader, however, remains disconsolate and unreconciled and considers the historical
mission of *santans*—the ascetic leaders—to be aborted, since one foreign
ruler is exchanged for another. Nationalists took this bitterness as a call
for struggle against the colonial power, whereas to the RSS brigade, the
divine command would indicate sanction for staying away from the anticolonial struggle, since the divine purpose is stated to be the elimination
of Muslim power.

Within the novel, the song initiates a number of political breaks and
innovations. It is meant to be a sacred chant or "mantra." Yet, chants
are compulsorily composed in *debbhasha* (Sanskrit)—"the language of the
gods"—to which women and low castes do not have access. Mantras are
also enunciated within a prescribed ritual sequence, always in front of the
deity and always by the Brahman priest or initiated Brahman male householder. The novel ascribes chanting mantras to an act of worship. Yet the
mantra here is first heard during the aftermath of a battle between the
British-led troops of the nawab and the santans, who lead a mob of villagers
(*Bankim* 1:728–29). The hymn, then, enters the emergent cultic order of a
new form of mother worship as a chant that is unconventionally detached
from the sacred ritual sequence and also functions as a song on its own, as
congregational devotional music accessible to all in Vaishnava gatherings.
Yet, unlike those occasions, it enters into public use at a moment of war,
not of pietistic contemplation of the earthly sports of Krishna. Devotional
music, loosened from its original chant form, sacralizes a war through this
transference of indicated use; and, simultaneously, the hymn/song, which
is also a battle cry, transforms the congregation of devotees into the mono-

lithic single body of a disciplined army: "Then, in a single, resounding voice, the thousands of santan soldiers . . . sang out to the rhythms of the canon—*Bande Mataram*" (*Bankim* 1:728–29). If a Hindu community for-itself is being visualized, then, from the very moment of its inception it is a people at war, unified by violence against a shared enemy. The ascetic figure of the santan, who first pronounces the words and who initiates the act of worship, immediately merges into the figure of the military com-mander and strategist who leads the holy war.

There is, however, a crucial difference between the older figure of the priest and the new priest-cum-commander. Unlike the former, the commander raises the song but he no longer remains in custody of the sacred ritual or chant. Others—including the motley army of villagers of all castes—enter into the act of singing, and the hymn now moves into the vernacular. And, along with this, a further transformation of purpose takes place. First a chant, then successively a song and a command, the hymn now passes into a battle cry and forms the first ever political slogan in the Bengali language. The commander emerges as the political leader, the organizer par excellence. The importance of the enterprise to aggres-sive Hindutva lies in its explicitly political violence that can express itself convincingly as a religious purpose. It is underlined in the novel when, in-spired by santans, the mob begins to articulate an agenda that goes beyond simple loot. "Unless we throw these dirty bastards [that is, the Muslims] out, Hindus will be ruined. . . . When shall we raze mosques down to the ground and erect Radhamadhav's temples in their place?" (*Bankim* 1:728).

The imaginative resources of a violent political agenda are immensely enriched, however, precisely by the ability simultaneously to lay claim to gentle and peaceful images.[8] The song is held in place by a tension between contradictory impulses that constitute a delicately poised unity. The ten-sion and the tense unity are effected at the level of both sound and mean-ing. The land is beautiful and the mother is smiling, tender, and youthful. At the same time, she becomes the ruthless warrior, triumphing in battle. Her loveliness, her smiles and grace are evoked in lush, flowing, elon-gated, rich sound effects: "shubhrajyotsnapulokita yamineem phullaku-sumitadrumadalashobhineem, suhasineem, sumadhurabhashineem, sukha-

8. This was especially evident in the way the VHP ideologues simultaneously evoked the figures of the serene and the angry Ram (P. K. Datta 1993b). The other, very important point this article makes is that in bhakti philosophies, the deity's life is an object of contempla-tion for the devotee; it is not for emulation. Here, too, Bankim makes the crucial transition by insisting that Krishna's life provides the desired pattern for all Hindus: Ram is invoked as a role model by Bankim and by Hindutva.

daam baradaam mataram" [to the mother whose nights are gorgeous with silvery moonlight, who is decked out with trees that bloom happily with flowers, whose smile is beautiful, whose words are bathed in sweetness, who is the giver of pleasure, of bliss]. The sensuousness of the soft, liquid syllables is then abruptly replaced with a quicker, jagged rhythm, by an arrangement of harsh, strident, strong words: "saptakotikantha kalakala ninadakarale, dwisaptakotirbhujairdhritakharakarabale . . . bahubaladhari-neem, namaami tarineem . . ." [seven million voices boom out words of doom, fourteen million arms wield the sharp swords . . . we salute the savior mother, possessor of many kinds of strength] (*Anandamath*, in *Bankim* 1:726). Classical rhetorical conventions matched sounds with moods. But Bankim went beyond them in the dramatic art of juxtaposition, of shocking and astonishing transitions within a brief and continuous space. The rhetorical charge and power of the Hindutva project are very often trivialized by assuming a simple transition from gentle quietism to violence. The song, which remains a powerful imaginative resource for the Hindutva project, complicates and widens the notion of a binary opposition between peaceful, traditional Hinduism and violent Hindutva. Bankim's militant bhakti let go of nothing and its language was supple and inventive enough to effect many movements between opposites, which is today considered by VHP thinkers to be the essence of Rama bhakti (P. K. Datta 1993b, 69).

In the process, a great transgression takes place by inserting the profane vernacular and a political, modern purpose into a sacred order of worship that violently transforms its original nature and purpose. The seemingly democratic extension of esoteric holy words to slogans and songs to be used by all, however, has its structured limits. The leader-mob distinction is carefully underlined in the way in which each military encounter turns into chaos unless it is carefully calibrated by ascetic leaders. The leaders—here and in the later two novels—are carefully trained in leadership qualities through a pedagogical scheme that certainly is not available to or meant for the mass following, which joins up out of sheer starvation and mob instincts. It is true that the ascetic leaders give up caste codes in times of war and recruit soldiers from all social strata. But along with celibacy and asceticism, this is the last sacrifice that they must impose on themselves until the final victory is achieved. It is also described as the most difficult of sacrifices (*Anandamath*, in *Bankim* 1:751). Presumably, with victory, the restoration of the normal order would absolve them of the pledge. The point, then, is not to overturn the social hierarchy, but to qualify it in times of war. Established leaders of Hindu society may thus renew and extend their control by coming closer to the ordinary folk and by actually leading them to victory in a violent war against a common enemy. The temporary yet close intimacy that the liminal space of war offers would provide real and felt legitimacy for what had been mere custom and prescribed power. The comprehensive training with which leaders approach the work of organization ensures that the continued exercise of power has a far more secure base. (See S. Sarkar, below, on these themes in the founding of the RSS.)

## III

We have used the hymn and its function within the novel as an entry point into the rhetorical operations and structure of feelings with which Bankim proceeded to delineate the politics of the reconstructed Hindu. Since the old Hindu had suffered from the absence of a combination of physical prowess and desire for self-rule, the new Hindu will only have arrived when he proves himself in a final battle that will overwhelmingly establish his superiority over the Muslim, who had in the past always defeated the Hindu. (The agenda of the war with the Muslim occurs only in the novels.) Since the British have something to impart to the Hindu, Hindu empowerment, it seems, must unfold within an overarching colonial framework. It is the Muslim, the vanquisher of generations of past Hindus, who will be the great adversary of the new Hindu. This is the concluding note and message of *Anandamath* (*Bankim* 1:787).

The Muslim was to be the adversary for yet another reason. I would like to suggest that Bankim made a distinction between the historical experience of Muslim rule, on the one hand, and Islam as an organized religion and Muslim as a personality type, on the other. Muslim rule, he considered, brought neither material nor spiritual improvement to India, and merely emasculated defeated Hindus. Yet, Islam, and the Muslim with his supposedly violent commitment to his religion and his desire for power, had much to teach to the Hindu. "By imbibing these principles . . . the Hindu will be . . . as powerful as the Arabs in the days of Mohammad" (*Dharmatattva, Bankim* 2:647). In his polemic on world religions, Bankim seemed to grant a perfection to Hinduism only as an ideal, whereas, through a series of oblique half statements, Islam is endowed with perfection in historical times. If universal love is taken to be the highest human ideal, then, says Bankim, Hinduism has it in the largest degree. Yet, throughout history, this has led to a dangerous quietism, to an inadequate comprehension of national dangers, to subjection, and to degeneration of the community. As far as Islam and Christianity are concerned, they have both avoided that particular problem. Between the two, however, Islam went far ahead of Christianity in attaining greater unity within its own boundaries and emerged as a more successful political model. By combining the different sets of values, we can construct a single uniform scale, wherein Islam transcends the particular problems of both Christianity and Hinduism, even though Hinduism and Islam are not directly compared with each other (*Dharmatattva, Bankim* 2:648).

In a crucial and conclusive part of *Dharmatattva*, Islam is dropped from the explicit comparative scheme and there is a new triangular contest for virtues among Hinduism, Buddhism, and Christianity: "If Jesus or Sakya Singha had been householders and yet leaders of world religions, then their systems would have been more complete. Krishna as ideal man is a householder. Jesus or Sakya Singha are not ideal men" (*Dharmatattva, Bankim* 2:647). If Hinduism scores over the two other religions on this ground, then there is also a third, unmentioned presence, another leader of a world religion who, too, was a householder and who yet transcended his mundane ties—Muhammad. Islam, or rather, the figure of the Prophet, is the sunken middle term in the diagram. If he implicitly shares the honor of having founded a perfected religion with Krishna, he has the further advantage of doing so within the accepted hagiography of Islam, and in the universally acknowledged version of Islam as well. This is indeed the image of Muhammad in a very well known Western text that was much used in Bankim's time: Thomas Patrick Hughes's *Dictionary of Islam* (1885). Bankim was, however, painfully aware that his ideal type Krishna was an appropriation and construction solely of his own heroic intellectual efforts, and that here he was going against the grain of dominant Hindu interpretative schemes: *Krishnacharitra, Dharmatattva,* and *Anandamath* have to argue hard against other models of bhakti. Bankim's Krishna is a householder-king, a warrior, a politician. He is overwhelmingly a man of action, strong enough to be wily in a higher cause, to resort to seemingly amoral strategies for the higher good of his people. He is entirely unlike the morally pure or philosophically questioning Christ or Buddha. He is equally unlike the figure of total love and play that is celebrated in Vaishnava hagiography. Of all the world religions that Bankim knew about, his Krishna stands as the closest approximation to Muhammad. In fact, the silent influence on Bankim's construction is so exact in particular features

as well as in the total conception that one may even be tempted to speculate that Bankim's Krishna could, indeed, be modeled on the biography of
Muhammad. By asserting that with a correct application of bhakti, Hindus
will be transformed into Muslims of Muhammad's time, Bankim hoped
that the reinterpreted life of Krishna would play the same historic role as
the original Islamic pattern.

## IV

If the discursive prose of later years obliquely draws upon what Bankim
regarded as the enviable resources and energies of Islam, and if he did
not engage in sustained polemic against Islam in his essays on religion,
he certainly evolved a mode of extremely denunciatory speech about Muslim rule in India in his novels. While his notions of ideal Hinduism informed nineteenth-century Hindu revivalism, the particular language that
he, more than any other contemporary, developed to describe the Muslim
certainly inflected the rhetoric and the aspirations of violent Hindu communalism of the next century.

Bankim bestowed on the Muslim an unprecedented centrality in his
historical and political scheme, thereby starting a tradition. The revivalist climate of the times was shaped far more decisively by antireformist
and antimissionary propaganda and there were even a few clashes with
missionaries in the early 1890s. There are references to an attack on missionaries at Tarakeswar in 1891 (*Dainik O Samacharchandrika*, April 19,
1891) and other minor attacks that were reported from Calcutta and Ban-
kura (Bengal 1891). During the Age of Consent Bill agitation of the 1880s
and early 1890s, Muslims were written about as fellow sufferers and victims of colonialism (*Report on Native Papers*, Bengal, 1890). The nationalist
vernacular press usually took care to distinguish between the integrated,
indigenized nature of "Muslim rule" and what they described as the entirely alien nature of the colonial government. This is not to say that Bengal
was completely immune from the communal violence that was sweeping
across parts of northern India in the 1890s. Muslims had recently gained
a few educational concessions, W. W. Hunter's thesis on Muslim backwardness promised more (see M. Hasan, below), and with Muslim self-
modernization moves of the Aligarh variety, the possibility of sharpened
competition in the sphere of the new education and jobs, where Bengali
Hindus had so far enjoyed a decisive edge, seemed imminent. So far, how-

ever, that remained a rather marginal worry and Hindu revivalism had not yet targeted the Muslim as the main enemy.

Bankim bequeathed a set of historical judgments on the nature and consequences of Muslim rule in Bengal: "How does our Muslim ruler protect us? We have lost our religion, our caste, our honor and family name, and now we are about to lose our very lives. . . . How can Hinduism survive unless we drive out these dissolute swine?" (*Anandamath*, Bankim 1:727). These ideological moves do not need proper historical authentication since they are posed in a fictional space; the pseudohistorical comments, however, carry an immense weight of conviction, nonetheless, particularly since Bankim was known for a highly historicist thrust in his discursive prose. They are, therefore, insidiously authenticated, and then they justify political rallying cries of extreme virulence: "Kill the low Muslims" (*Bankim* 1:784) is the refrain that is repetitively raised in *Anandamath*. Even though Bankim never made use of the recent theories of the colonial drain of wealth, he used the same motif to describe the flight of money from Bengal to Delhi in the form of a heavy revenue burden in Mughal times ("Bangalar itihasa," *Vividha prabandha*, Bankim 2:332).

Perhaps the most significant way in which Bankim served as a bridge between nineteenth-century Hindu revivalism and the later, anti-Muslim, violent politics was by providing an immensely powerful visual image of communal violence and by giving it the status of an apocalyptic holy war. He stamped the image indelibly on the imagination of communal politics by fusing the impulse of community violence and revenge with the spectacle of a feminine body. In his last novel, *Sitaram*, Gangaram, the brother of the heroine Shree, is unjustly charged and sentenced to execution by a tyrannical Muslim faqir (holy man) and a *qazi* (judge). Unable to stop this mockery of justice, Shree goes to the place of execution, where a big crowd, including many Hindus, has gathered to watch the event. In despair, Shree tries to rally them to save a fellow Hindu, to instill a sense of brotherhood and mutual responsibility by evoking the fact that a man of their community is being killed by another community. Shree does not invoke the theme of justice, nor does she try to rally subjects against tyranny and misrule. Quite spontaneously, the words that rise to her mouth are words of community solidarity and violence.

Then Gangaram saw a goddess-like figure among the green leaves of the huge tree. Her feet resting on two branches, the right hand clutching a tender branch, the left hand swirling her sari, she was calling out: "Kill, kill . . ." Her long, unbound tresses were dancing in the wind, her proud feet were swinging the branches up and down, up and down, as if Durga herself was dancing on the lion on the battle-field. Shree had no more shame left, no consciousness, no fear, no rest. She kept calling out—"Kill, kill the enemy . . . The enemy of the country, the enemy of Hindus, my enemy . . . kill, kill the enemy . . ." That straining arm was such a lovely arm . . . such beauty in her swollen lips, her flaring nostrils, sweat drenched stray locks falling across a perspiring forehead. All the Hindus kept looking at her and then streaming towards the battlefield with "glory to Mother Chandika" on their lips. (*Sitaram, Bankim* 1:881)

In an instant, Shree had transformed a scattering of Hindus who had no previous sense of mutual connectedness into an army with a single vio-lent purpose, into a community for-itself that can be realized only through invocation of vengeance against another. It is as if, to imagine a commu-nity of Hindus, Bankim can only imagine a spectacle of violence, of war. That is the only passion that brings the community into being. But the spectacle of violence is derived from the image of a passionate feminine body that literally gives birth to the violence. If political passion is pro-duced through a feminine agency, there is little doubt about the kind of image in which this passion is cast. The woman's body moving "up and down, up and down," "that straining arm," "her swollen lips, her flaring nostrils," "sweat drenched locks," and "perspiring forehead"—all are well-remembered classical conventions for describing the woman at the moment of sexual climax. The superimposition of the icons of Durga and of Chan-dika, the goddess of war, on this body provides a sacred frame that tightly controls yet obliquely heightens the flow of sexual energy from which the visual image derives its power. The beginnings of a violently communal-ized imagination may, then, have something to do with a kind of male fan-tasizing that encompasses sexual passion and political violence in a single impulse of pleasure.

## V

Yet the consequences of such imagination do not entirely exhaust the logic of Bankim's discourse on the Muslim. We have already seen that his serious discursive prose referred to Islam with respect. In his novels, too, Bankim had been writing about Hindus and Muslims, and their relations with one another, all his life. They are ranged side by side, against one another, in dramatic and tense encounters between man and man, man and woman, woman and woman, as communities, nations, armies, as loving, fighting, making peace, arguing, negotiating. If all the novels on this theme are taken to compose a single novel, and the arrangements between people of the two religions as relations between two composite individuals, then the obvious simile is that of a conjugal or wildly emotional, dangerously fluctuating sexual relationship that may simultaneously include great intimacy along with great violence. A far cry from the way white people encounter Indians in his novels, in moments of sheer comedy (*Chandrasekhar, Bankim* 1:405; *Muchiram Gurer jibancharit, Bankim* 2:126–27), here is invariably material for high drama or for tragedy.

In his first novel, *Durgeshnandini* (1865), there is a striving for an almost mechanical symmetry of virtues and vices on both sides. The aim is to establish a shared code of conduct, be it for the heroes, the heroines, the villains or the cowards. Neither are Hindus and Muslims two monolithically integrated peoples: political alliances and expediency cut across religious boundaries (*Bankim* 1:53–138). Interestingly, Bankim—who experimented boldly with rather transgressive possibilities in sexual relationships beyond Hindu domestic and conjugal prescriptions—found in the Muslim woman, unbounded by norms of being faithful to only one man in an entire lifetime, a productive ground for playing on utterly new registers of sexual morality and commitment. The characters of Ayesha in *Durgeshnandini*, Zeb Unnisa in *Rajasingha* (1882), and Dalani in *Chandrasekhar* (1875) provide striking, diverse examples.

From the third novel, *Mrinalini*, the possibility of a shared enterprise vanishes and the Muslim becomes the great historical adversary of the Hindu. Battles between individuals are now loaded with destiny for nations. In *Rajasingha*, the Muslim adversary is not just an adversary but a hated and dreaded enemy, no less a man than the fanatical Aurangzeb. "He was born to hate the Hindus, he found Hindu offences unpardonable" (*Bankim*, 1:664). There are references to all his well-thumbed sins in the opening chapter itself—*jeziya* (tax on non-Muslims), temple wrecking, cow slaughter, forced conversion. This seems a typical case of stereotyping. Yet, let us remember the first appearance of the presumed enemy of Hindus. We meet an elderly man in white, quiet, dignified, assured, respecting strength in an enemy. All the characteristic historical associations had been revived and refamiliarized in the first chapter. Gradually, however, over the entire text, the stereotype is defamiliarized, redeemed, and humanized, especially by Aurangzeb's gentle, melancholy love for a Hindu serving maid. It is no monster but a great adversary that had been defeated in the historical battle and herein lay the true glory of Mewar (*Rajasingha*, *Bankim* 1:672–74). Unlike the anonymous, faceless English troops, Muslim adversaries, even the worst of them, wear human faces in which complex emotions are often delicately sketched.

It is in *Sitaram*, the last novel, that the Muslim combatant is largely an abstraction, an absence; yet battles with him fill up the entire novelistic space. Has Bankim, then, at the end of his life, managed to formulate and congeal an agenda at the point of blind hatred, when the enemy sheds his human features and is reduced to a simple figure of hatred?

I think that Bankim found it impossible to form and celebrate an agenda with sustained conviction even in his last, dogmatic, markedly authoritarian phase. If the agenda seems to be coherent and complete, he then proceeds to fracture it from within, to dissolve his own statement of conviction. Sitaram is defeated by his own inner flaws. The Hindu leader, whether a commander, a king, a Brahman, or a patriarch, remains weak, treacherous, greedy, and cowardly across historical and social differences. The most significant thing about the last novel, I think, is Sitaram's brutality against Hindu women, which is conventionally ascribed to the stereotypical Muslim. When Sitaram's Hindu kingdom breaks up, Hindu women celebrate the event with vindictive glee. An erstwhile tolerant Muslim faqir leaves his kingdom, vowing never to live under Hindu rule. The stereotyped notion of Muslim intolerance is turned upside down, for it is Sitaram who, by his own villainy, had forced this conclusion on him.

The novel, charged with shrill intensity, ends with uncharacteristic bathos. Bankim had never before used the device of a chorus composed of ordinary people. Here we find two common men, Ram and Shyam, having the last words.

Ram: How goes it, brother? Have you heard any news about Mohammadpur? [Sitaram's kingdom].
Shyam: Different people say different things. Some say the king [Sitaram] and the queen could not be captured. . . . The wretched Muslims executed a false king and a false queen.
Ram: . . . That sounds like a Hindu fiction, a mere novel.
Shyam: Well, who knows whose story is a fiction. Your story may well be a Muslim tale. Anyway, we are ordinary people, all this doesn't concern us. Let us enjoy a smoke in peace.

Let Ramchand and Shyamchand enjoy their pipe of tobacco. We shall end our narrative at this point. (*Sitaram, Bankim* 1:957–58)

An uncharacteristic narrative closure for Bankim who had always been intensely concerned about historicity, with problems of political bias and partisanship vitiating historical truth. All his familiar concerns are blown away with a few puffs of smoke, with rumors recounted by two ignorant and rather uninterested men who dismiss all history as ultimately unknowable, as equally uncertain versions, and, finally, as supremely irrelevant to the likes of them. What exactly is involved in this major departure?

One can only speculate at several levels. It can denote a final failure of hope in the heroic, redemptive exercise, in the possibility of nation building. It may be a criticism of the Hindu masses who have forever stayed away at decisive moments in wars, have never identified themselves with the nation. It can, on the other hand, indicate a recognition of the autonomy of the imaginative domain. The Brechtian alienation device, the underlining of the fictional nature of the work by talking about "novels and fictions" may point to the constructedness of all writings, historical and fictional. Or is it, after a long gap and after many changes, a return to the theme of *Samya*, which, in the meantime, had been overtaken by dreams of Hindu glory? Does it question the materiality of notions like political freedom and nationhood in the context of the everlasting peasant problem and ground the failure of the nation in the disjunction between the two?

Bankim thus formulates and fills out a violent Hindu agenda and immediately proceeds to deconstruct it. He powerfully projects religious militancy as a resolution to the problem of colonization. He has an equally powerful certainty about its untenable future. It is inevitable, then, that he has to simultaneously underscore the agenda in intensely heightened colors, to proclaim its message with a brutal stridency that nearly reaches a breaking point in the last novel, and immediately counterpose to it an alienation device that drags the shining vision of Hindu triumph into the realms of idle rumor and gossip.

# 8

# The Myth of Unity:
# Colonial and National Narratives

## MUSHIRUL HASAN

Of all the great religions . . . Islam alone was borne forth into
the world on a great wave of forceful conquest. . . . There was
seldom a pause in the consolidation of Mahomedan power,
seldom a break in the long-drawn tale of plunder and car-
nage, cruelty and lust, unfolded in the history of the earlier
dynasties that ruled India.

— Valentine Chirol (1852–1929)

You never ceased proclaiming that Islam spread by the sword.
You have not deigned to tell us what it is the gun has spread.

— Akbar Allahabadi (1846–1921)

Hinduism, with its love of images and symbols, and its poly-
theism, and Islam, with its strict Unitarian faith and its strong
iconoclastic principles, are at opposite poles.

— Reginald Craddock (1868–1937)

## I

A DISQUIETING FEATURE of the Hindutva wave has been not just the
demolition of the Babri Masjid at Ayodhya but the way Hindu propa-
gandists conjured up the image of a community outside the "national
mainstream." Muslims were depicted as aggressive fundamentalists and
demonized as descendants of depraved and tyrannical medieval rulers who
demolished temples and forcibly converted Hindus to Islam. They were
portrayed as "fifth columnists" tied to the world of Islam, held responsible for the country's vivisection in August 1947; they were depicted as

proceeding hand in glove with the Congress and left-wing formations in a concerted endeavor to undermine Indian/Hindu culture and civilization.

The reading of what Muslims are and the vain hope of how they ought to have been is echoed with unfailing regularity. Equally familiar are images of the Muslims and the reconstruction of their history. What is less clear is how certain images and reconstructions, having gained currency during the second half of the nineteenth century, continue to enjoy widespread appeal and acceptance. How is it that the image of the Other has not altered or modified over time? Why did alternative ideologies fail to mediate effectively and reconstruct a different paradigm? Does the explanation lie in the Muslim intelligentsia's own assertion of a unity of interest and ideal and in its conviction that all Muslims were part of an indivisible community with one way of thinking? Or that they were logical victims of their own myth-making, claiming for themselves an alien culture, if not origin, and being so regarded by others? I am inclined to believe that this was so, though the critical issue is how the colonial government fostered the growth of such ideas and helped sections of the Muslim intelligentsia to etch a certain image of themselves. I also believe that the etching of "nationalistic" images of India's Muslims was just as important as the framework adopted by the Raj to define and categorize "Indian Muslim society."

There are any number of scholarly studies, Edward Said's *Orientalism* (1978) included, replete with instances of Islam's representation as a hostile and aggressive force, of Muslim societies being caricatured as rigid, authoritarian, and uncreative (Daniel 1960, Al-Azmeh 1993). Quite a few British writers in India, some occupying government positions, perpetuated a repertoire of such images, construing Indian Islam as an emblem of repellent otherness, "the faith of a body of savage marauders and conquerors, who swept over the land . . . in a series of cruel raids, bringing rapine and destruction in their train" (Crooke [1897] 1975, 258–59). The sultans of Delhi and their Ottoman counterparts in Constantinople suffered much the same fate at the hands of leading nineteenth-century writers. Projected as the great iconoclasts, they were considered tokens of evil and scapegoats for issues with which they had no connection. Bishop Heber, who stayed in India from 1823 to 1826, wanted Hindus to be constantly reminded "that we did not conquer them, but found them conquered, that their previous rulers were as much strangers to their blood and to their religion as we are, and that they were notoriously far more oppressive masters than we have ever shown ourselves" (Laird 1971, 64). Valentine Chirol, in charge of the foreign department of the *Times* (London) from 1908 to 1912, observed that "with the monumental wreckage of those early Mohamedan dynasties, steeped in treachery and bloodshed, the plain of Delhi is still strewn" (Chirol 1921, 3).

Travelers, missionaries, administrators, and ethnographers transposed the same imagery to Victorian India.[1] According to their images, Islam was static and dogmatic. Its adherents were conservative, haughtily contemptuous of things "modern," and too much under the influence of an obsolete system of education (Low 1907, 281). The Earl of Ronaldshay (1925, 235) opined that, "a candid Muhammadan would probably admit that the most powerful factors in keeping the majority of Moslems aloof from the educational movement of the day were pride of race, a memory of bygone superiority, religious fears, and a not unnatural attachment to the learning of Islam." Major General Stockley Warren, who retired in 1885, reminisced in these terms on his reaction to a Muslim "coolie" who would not have brandy for medicinal purposes: "These men I presume we shall ultimately civilise, make them Christians and drunkards, and lead them to liberty" (IOL Warren Papers). The civil servant E. C. Bayley told the viceroy Northbrook in 1864 that the standard of "Muslim morality" was not pitched very high, and that the "corruptions" in their manners and social habits preceded their contact with the Europeans (IOL 1873a, 1873b). A "community" steeped in religious obscurantism was prone to treat the government with contempt and hostility. Recollecting the 1857 war in north India, Arthur Owen added a stereotype to those of the "wily Mahratta" and the "crafty Brahman," reporting that the "sensual Mohammadan" fanatically believed that "if one of their creed falls in battle against the infidels, Christians in particular, he is immediately translated to the garden of paradise" (IOL Warren Papers). Nearly half a century after 1857, Bampfylde Fuller, the first lieutenant governor of the new province of East Bengal and Assam, discovered among Muslims an "undertone of hostility to their Christian rulers": "Of such men it may be truly said that at heart they are disloyal, and probably await their opportunity for manifesting their feelings in hostile acts" (Fuller 1988, 41, 124; also Fuller 1913; Low 1907, 281; Steel 1905, 180).

Owen, Fuller, and others, though by no means all the British functionaries, believed that Islam in the subcontinent was indelibly stamped by

---

1. See Daniel 1960, 266–85; Greenberger 1969; Hardy 1972, 1–2, 62–91; Robinson 1974, 164–73; Pandey 1990b; Breckenridge and van der Veer 1993; M. R. Anderson 1990; Powell 1993; Carroll 1978, 223–50; Jones 1981, 83–85; and Manuel, T. Sarkar, Fox, and S. Sarkar in this volume.

its early history, particularly by its original social carriers, and that Islamic values, inherently hostile to the West, caused Muslim antipathy toward and estrangement from the government. The call to wreak a special vengeance upon Muslims in the wake of the "Wahabi movement" and the 1857 war in north India manifested how things "Islamic" were constructed, located, categorized, and connected in nineteenth-century British India (Q. Ahmad 1994; T. Metcalf 1990, 298–302).

Another common belief with serious political implications was that the British presence irked Muslims on account of the latter's close identification with the erstwhile ruling classes. They preserved in their blood the pride of a conquering race and cherished hopes of reestablishing their rule (Butler 1932, 15; Garrat 1929, 172). "Most Indian Mussulmans," commented one writer, "cherished in their hearts some memory of the days when their fathers were the masters of India, and they believe, rightly or wrongly, that if ever the English power were shaken they would regain their old dominance" (Low 1907, 281). Evidence in support of such contentions was thin and almost wholly drawn from the Mughal ruling classes and their dependents. Most Muslims had no cause to be enthused by the glory of the Mughal era or to mourn its end. The fact that a Shah Waliullah or a Mirza Ghalib bemoaned its decline should not be treated lightly, but it should also not be construed as a generalized or undifferentiated "Muslim response." Similarly, it was patently hollow for Harcourt Butler, governor of the United Provinces (1918–20) during the high noon of British imperialism, to raise the specter of a Muslim "conspiracy" to overthrow the British with the aid of their "virile" coreligionists in India and overseas (Butler 1921, 140–41, and 1931, 38).

Some Muslims at the turn of the century nursed such illusions. There were, likewise, isolated instances of elites or their interlocutors seeking an external Muslim imperium for help in reconsolidating their local or regional authority. In 1759, Shah Waliullah turned to Ahmad Shah Durrani (Abdali) to rescue India for Islam; later, Saiyid Ahman of Rae Bareli (1786–93) corresponded with Central Asian rulers to recognize his *khalifat* (Hardy 1972, 54, 58). In general, however, British officials would have known from their long experience of administering areas with sizable Muslim populations that most Muslims were prepared to make the colonial government work and to seek adjustments within and gain benefits from colonial administrative and bureaucratic structures. Yet colonial mentalities stuck to inherited frameworks and bandied about a series of generalities about Muslims. Conjuring the image of a belligerent community with extraterritorial loyalties legitimized government policies that were designed to tame and humble supposedly recalcitrant Muslims. "The world is full of groups relying on their connection with some dominant 'race' elsewhere," commented G. T. Garrat. "The claim is natural enough, but the English, in accepting this picture of the Moslems as a race apart, seem to have been misled by a writer of genius (Rudyard Kipling), who had, however, a journalist's flair for the picturesque, and who always saw the Peninsula in terms of Punjab" (Garrat 1929, 173).

The generalities extended, especially after 1857, to an appraisal of Indian Islam, the structure of the Muslim "community," and the nature of its interaction with the Hindus. Some Englishmen found it easy to get on with the Muslims at a social level—as opposed to "the Hindu, with his glib tongue, his pliant brain and back, his fantastic social rites, and his incomprehensible religion" (Low 1907, 281)—and found it easy to comprehend the essentials of their faith, "built on Jewish foundations and devoid of the crudities and subtleties of Brahminism" (IOL 1939). But most were ill-informed and crude in their exposition. The belief was common, for example, that Islam south of the Himalayas remained, to all intents and purposes, the same as in other parts of the world, and that its adherents were a well-knit religious entity, acting as a monolith and keeping the desert faith pure in the land of "idolaters" (Fuller 1910, 125; Titus 1925, 93; C. H. Hill 1911, 210). Muslims were, for this reason, endowed with "cultural coherence," a real sense of unity transcending considerations of race, class, language, and region, and "an essential community of thought and point of view that on occasion is able to speak with authority through its representative bodies" (Whitehead 1924; Garrat 1929, 172). "The solidarity of Islam was a hard fact against which it was futile to run one's head" (Lawrence 1956, 119; Holderness 1911, 127). The governor of Bengal, the province where most Muslims lived in British India, illustrated the strength of the call of Islam—"a call which rings insistently in the ears of the devout Muslims, whether of India or elsewhere, drowning the call of country and all else." He put forward the official view, unchanged for nearly a century, that

the ethnic pageant which passes across one's vision as one travels over India is made up of many tableaux. There is one such tableau which at once arrests attention because of the many points of contrast which it provides with the rest of the procession. . . . It is a tableau in which we see represented a religion, a civilization and culture, and an outlook differing profoundly in all material respects from those of Hinduism. (Ronaldshay 1924, 214)

Such a view hardly conformed to reality. Islam in its Persian-Arabic attire failed to make much sense to the masses. That is why its "cultural

mediators" were constrained to make the Islamic traditions more meaningful to the converts in syncretic and symbolic forms (A. Roy 1983, 249). In
the process, the pristine purity of dogmas and tenets, which the Faraizis in
Bengal and the *mujahidins* in the northwest tried in vain to restore, was tailored to suit the spiritual and material urges of the people. Local customs
and heterodox traditions, which were repugnant to Muslim orthodoxy,
found a place in the corpus of beliefs and religious practices. This was reflected in the diversity of religiocultural practices, and also in the variety of
political and economic experiences. The medieval sultans may have wanted
to erect a uniform religiocultural system and impose religious authority
from "great" or "middle" traditions, but geographic distances and particu-
laristic localism inhibited them. In the end, the "Islamic little tradition" developed, with its roots firmly anchored in Indian soil, autonomously from
centralized political control (Darling 1979, 21–29). The itinerant preachers
may have imposed their will sporadically in certain pockets, as indeed they
did in rural Bengal, but their impact was transient.

British civil servants—from Crooke to Malcolm Darling—knew that
this was so. Charles Alfred Elliot reported from Unnao, close to Lucknow
in UP, that there was a strong tendency among Muslims to assimilate in all
externals with their Hindu neighbors. He found them wearing dhotis and
using *Ram Ram* as the mode of salutation (Elliot 1892, 28). Fuller, likewise, wrote on Hindu influences among Muslims: in purely agricultural
districts, he commented, the people not "only understood each other's systems, but the systems often seem to overlap." Hindus and Muslims cheer-
fully attended each other's festivals and sang each other's songs (Fuller
1910, 130–31; E. J. Thompson 1930, 234). Lytton, Bengal's governor in the
1920s, commented on how the rank and file of the communities in the
province got on well with each other in all daily business of life (Lytton
1942, 172; Garrat 1929, 175–76, 181). O. M. Martin, having served in Bengal province from 1915 to 1926, emphatically stated that Hindu-Muslim
mutual dependence and friendship were an old and cherished tradition
(Martin n.d.). But such knowledge and understanding were neither reflected in concrete political decisions nor translated into constitutional
decrees. In the constitutional plans, which broadly reflected the colonial
assumptions about Indian society, the Mapilla Muslim appeared indistinguishable from Kipling's sturdy Pathan; the Urdu-speaking landed elite of
Awadh was no different from the Tamil-speaking Muslim merchant; E. M.
Forster's Cambridge buddy Syed Ross Masood was cast in the same mold
as a *karkhandar* (artisan) in Delhi's old city; Shias and Sunnis, Bohras and

Khojas, the Barelwis and the Deobandis were all part of the pan-Indian Islam; even though politically, as Bishop Heber noted from long experience in central India, the Bohras were "agreeing far better with Jains and Rajpoots than their Sunnite rivals" (Laird 1971, 282).

It is true that conventional wisdom about Muslims and established theories about their role in the 1857 revolt were questioned by the likes of George Campbell, second-in-command to James Outram after the capture of Lucknow (Outram 1893, 397ff.), W. W. Hunter, the Bengal civilian (Hunter 1871), and W. S. Blunt, an old-fashioned patriot shocked by the vulgarity of new imperialism (Kabbani 1986, 96–97). But according to the viceroy, Lord Dufferin (1884–88), the followers of Islam were still "a nation of 50 million, with their monotheism, their iconoclastic fanaticism, their animal sacrifices, their social equality and their remembrance of the days when, enthroned at Delhi, they reigned supreme from the Himalayas to Cape Cormorin" (Hardy 1972, 1). A decade after Dufferin wrote this, Anthony Macdonnell, lieutenant governor (1895–1901) of the United Provinces, treated Muslims with the same degree of suspicion and hostility. He found that theological seminaries, such as the Nadwat at-ulama, in Lucknow, promoted disaffection and sedition. Adding credence to wild notions about Pan-Islamism and its pervasive appeal the world over, he believed that Muslims were loyal to the Ottoman khalifa (M. Hasan 1991, 53–54; Robinson 1974, 133–34). What Macdonnell failed to grasp was that Pan-Islamic sensibilities were heightened not by Muslim publicists but by the colonial government to bolster its imperial concerns in the Balkans, and that there were any number of influential Muslims who denied the Turkish sultan's claim to be a khalifa. Political rights, Syed Ahmad Khan said, "were more important than religious traditions, and so long as the Muslims lived freely under British rule they would remain good subjects" (Robinson 1974, 112; Hardy 1972, 178). He agreed with Maulvi Zakaullah that the Muslims should not look to foreign countries for guidance, since "for a thousand years, our own religion of Islam had been intimately bound up with India; and in India, Islam has won some of its greatest triumphs, for its own popular form of civilization" (Schimmel 1980, 197). Syed Mehdi Ali (Nawab Mohsinul Mulk), Syed Ahmad's close friend and principal of the Aligarh college, made clear that Turkey's sultan could not exercise any of the powers and prerogatives of the khalifa over India's Muslims, who were in no way bound by their religion to obey him.

Though British functionaries continued to perpetuate the myth of the pervasive influence of Pan-Islamism, overseas writers visiting India, including the Turkish author Halide Edib, thought differently. She insisted that Muslim allegiance to England during World War I

demolished a strong historical myth—it showed that political Pan-Islamism was a mere bogey. The attachment of the Indian Muslim to the interests of his country was a greater reality than his solidarity with Muslims outside India. *It may be useful for Western powers with Muslim colonies to realize that there is a distinct sense of nationhood separate from their religious life.* The Indian Muslim would resent an Afghan-Muslim domination and fight it; the Arab-Muslim would resent a Muslim-Turkish domination and fight it as much as he would any non-Muslim domination, if he ever got his independence. (Edib 1937, 317–18; emphasis added)

The direction and flow of "Muslim politics," guided first by Syed Ahmad and later by the All-India Muslim League, went toward compromise and accommodation with the government. New generations grew up for whom foreign rule was an unchanging fact of life, whether they liked it or not. Most modern and traditionally educated Muslims, for whom the Faraizi or the Barelwi adventures were faint memories, sensed that they could no longer live in a stable and self-sufficient system of inherited culture. They recognized the need to change attitudes and generate the strength to survive in a world dominated by colonialism (M. Hasan 1993a; Hardy 1972, 94–115). The *ulema* (Islamic learned men), many of whom were harshly treated as archenemies of the British, made it clear after 1857 that adjustment with rather than repudiation of the Raj was their main plank. Abdul Hay (1848–86), a prominent *alim* (scholar) of Lucknow's theological seminary in Firangi Mahal, considered the acceptance of British presence and learning of English to be lawful as long as no harm to Islam resulted (B. D. Metcalf 1982, 279; Hardy 1972, 14). Deoband's *Dar al-ulum* (theological seminary), established in 1867, originated in a reconciliatory spirit and not in defiance of Pax Britannica. In 1870, Maulana Ahmad Raza Khan (1856–1921), founder of the Barelwi school, declared British India a *Dar al-Islam* (land of Islam) (M. Ahmad 1993, xv).

In his view on Pan-Islamism, Anthony Macdonnell was out of tune with the approved official line, which had grudgingly veered around to two sets of convictions. One was based on the bizarre belief that the Muslims had to be won over because they were so terrible and fear-inspiring (IOL 1930). The other rested on pragmatic imperial considerations. How could so many Muslims, some of whom wielded power and influence in certain areas, be alienated for so long? They had to be enlisted "as allies

and auxiliaries" (Lyall in Robinson 1974, 170), courted to thwart nationalist aspirations, and encouraged to counter rabble-rousers in the Indian
National Congress. Viceroy Lord Northbrook (1872–76) was told by the
colonial office to remove any "just cause of [Muslim] complaint, because,
in the event of any action against Russia, our allies must be the Mo-
hametans of Central Asia, Afghanistan, and of Russia" (IOL 1874). Viceroy Lord Mayo's note of June 26, 1871, on Muslim education indicated a
change in imperial policy in this direction (Hardy 1972, 90); and Mayo's
successor, Northbrook, received kudos for "doing great good in direct-
ing attention to the long and grievously neglected subject of Mussalman
education" (IOL 1874). After the 1857 difficulties with Muslim policy in
India, Mayo began to fill the cup of reconciliation, Northbrook held it out
(Hardy 1972, 91).

The Simla Deputation of October 1906—masterminded by the Aligarh college principal W. A. J. Archbold—paved the way for establishing
the Muslim League. It was seen, for this reason, as a decisive break with
the silent policy of the earlier decades. The colonial government reforms of
1909, enacted to defuse the Congress demand for a greater share in administration and decision-making, was a calculated masterstroke: it discarded
the notion and jettisoned the prospect of secular nationalism. It established
separate electorates for Muslims, along with reservations and weightages,
and thus gave birth to a religiopolitical community, sections of which
began to see themselves in the colonial image of being unified, cohesive,
and segregated from the Hindus. Separate electorates put a formal seal of
approval on the institutionalized conception of Muslim political identity
and contributed to the forging of communitarian identities that were, both
in conception and articulation, profoundly divisive and inherently conflict-
oriented. An otherwise diverse "community" was thus homogenized, like
a "caste" or a "tribe," in order to be suitably accommodated within political schemes and bureaucratic designs. The self-styled Muslim leaders could
thus stake their claims to be representatives of an "objectively" defined
community and contend with others for government patronage, employment, and political assignments. In this way, the ideological contours of
the future Pakistan were delineated by British opinion and policymakers
long before Mohammad Ali Jinnah burst upon the political scene with his
demand for a Muslim nation.

The same process extended to the formation of caste-cluster consciousness and caste politics. By viewing caste categories as units of patronage and proscription, the government forced a predictable response: those

seeking patronage or protesting proscription had to speak in the name of the bureaucratically recognized category. In such circumstances, the emergence of "caste" publicists, spokesmen, associations say more about the manner in which the foreign rulers viewed Indian society and sought to come to terms with it and the agility of the Indian response than it does about the ubiquity of "caste" sentiment (Carroll 1978, 249; Shaikh 1989, 157–59).

The Montagu-Chelmsford Reforms (1919) projected the same colonial assumptions. The Act of 1935 held out the prospect of a divided nation and implicitly endorsed the hitherto hazy notion of an incipient Muslim nation. Indeed, if the British were to incline overmuch toward the Muslim League in the early 1940s, it was in part because their own political framework left them with little choice except to depend on Muslim League leaders. They had, after all, laid the foundations of a state-support realm enabling influential Muslims to define their "community" on their own terms and to extract statutory concessions and guarantees almost at will. The structures of governance offered them much greater space for articulating and representing sectional interests.

The Muslims in the Indian National Congress were put in an awkward position. The official, colonial definition of a "community" ran contrary to secular, territorial nationalism and undermined their moral authority. They were greatly constrained and unable to operate from a position of strength, because their conception of nationhood had no place in the constitutional blueprint. The overall thrust of British policies, especially after 1909, led to their political isolation. A man of Dr. M. M. Ansari's stature was virtually prevented from attending the Round Table Conferences in London. Rank communalists, on the other hand, were feted, greeted with broad smiles, and welcomed with open arms (M. Hasan 1987). Congress Muslims like Maulana Abul Kalam Azad did not figure on the colonial agenda. They were "the wrecking horse," just because Jinnah, whose own status was far from assured, insisted on their exclusion from the Simla conference and from the interim government (Mansergh 1972, 1:629; M. Hasan 1992, 93–94). Jinnah's plea, which did not go unheeded in official quarters, was that no one but a Muslim Leaguer could represent the "Muslim interests." This moment in history must have been relished by the surviving architects of the 1909, 1991, and 1935 constitutions.

In the final analysis, the British bequeathed the Indian republic a truncated nation, a distorted perspective, a series of blurred images, and a number of vague and undifferentiated categories, most of which need to be challenged, contested, and refuted vigorously and consistently. If the history of the intercommunity relations is to be rewritten, it has to steer clear of colonial paradigms and be freed from the stranglehold of an intellectual tradition, orientalist or otherwise (Breckenridge and van der Veer 1993). Likewise, the individual and collective experiences of Muslims, which were by no means the same thing, need to be located in the subcontinent's history. They need to be viewed afresh, not in the light of abstract and arbitrary categories, but on the strength of irrefutable evidence of their complex but long-standing, day-to-day interactions with various groups and communities.

## II

A good number of educated Muslims in the last quarter of the nineteenth century longed for an "objective" assessment of their history and sociology and a rigorously argued repudiation of certain popular notions about their coreligionists. Who could they turn to? Not the theologians or the formal body of ulema, many of whom explicitly challenged the ideological tenets of the modern age. They were no doubt trained to debate and defend matters of faith but were ill-equipped, on account of their limited concerns, training, and religious orientation, to match orientalist scholarship. The intervention of scholars based in Aligarh, Delhi, Patna, and Calcutta was far more impressive and in tune with Western intellectual pursuits. The Aligarh college, for one, was a visible embodiment of the victory of forces of progress. New schools of research, interpretation, and reconstruction of "Muslim thought" developed in this sleepy town in western UP. It was here that movements of reform were consummated. A typically Aligarh version of reformed Islam, based on nineteenth-century liberalism and humanism, grew up in opposition both to the orthodox stream and to the popular syncretism of the masses. But the intellectual energy released by the pioneering endeavors of Syed Ahmad, Shibli Nomani, Altaf Husain Hali, Maulvi Zakaullah, and the "First Generation" of students lost momentum once the reformist trends became more and more intertwined with political controversies. The ambition of an average student, drawn from the landed class and the upper crust of the bourgeoisie, was government service. His pride was soothed, thanks to early Pan-Islamic stirrings, by his being reminded that he was a unit in the great democracy of Islam, and in witness of this brotherhood, he jauntily wore the Turkish fez on his head (Nehru 1936; Hardy 1972, 103–4). Aligarh produced, for the most part, cautious pedagogues instead of a few thinkers of surpassing boldness. Their appeared a cloud, to borrow Clifford Geertz's expression, of not terribly distinguished and usually rather unoriginal academicians.[2] This was also true of other centers of learning. Once the newly emergent Muslim bourgeoisie developed a vested interest in the power structures, the initial thrust given to reformist ideas was considerably diluted.

The few who stayed out of the charmed circle of government servants and addressed themselves to issues of reform and innovation were unable to correct colonial stereotypes or stir a debate comparable, in depth and vigor, to what Albert Hourani describes in *Arabic Thought in the Liberal Age, 1798–1939* (Hourani 1970). Part of the reason was their self-image of being part of a community—a monolith umma—that remained, or was normatively expected to remain, the same across spatial divisions and temporal boundaries. Time and again, this theme was powerfully expressed across a number of elite scholastic factions, especially of Sunni Islam, for which Sufi and syncretic practices and Shi'ism in general were just so many deviations from the norm (B. D. Metcalf 1982, 40–42, 57–59, 291–92, 307–8). Time and again, the theme of eternal and unmitigated Hindu-Muslim hostility was echoed. So also the view that "internal" differences among groups of Hindus and/or Muslims were secondary and irrelevant to the more fundamental religious cleavage.

Muslim intellectuals did not examine such convictions in the light of their normal way of living. Had they done so, they would have discovered ample evidence of great "internal" political, moral, and social tensions and their disruptive effects. In this way, they would have understood themselves better and made their conduct and behaviors intelligible to others (Mujeeb 1977, 68).

What about nationalist writers, historians, social reformers, and political activists? Did they conceptualize the Indian social reality differently?

2. Nehru and M. N. Roy were in substantial agreement over Aligarh's role after the death of Syed Ahmad Khan. I am fascinated by M. N. Roy's reflections even more so because he arrived at certain important conclusions without any close contact with the university or its scholars. The communist leader pointed out that Aligarh failed to produce youthful elements holding social and political ideas similar to the Hindu intellectuals who conceived of political nationalism as expressed in the Congress. While the earlier generation of the Hindu intelligentsia imbibed progressive social and political views, the Aligarh alumni belonged to the landed aristocracy with social and political tendencies predominantly feudal. M. N. Roy concluded that "the absence of a class cohesion was responsible for the political divergence between the Hindus and Muslims. . . . Elements so diverse socially could not unite in a national movement" (M. N. Roy 1971, 222).

Or question the Muslim elite's highly exaggerated and romanticized assessment of its historic role and destiny? Did they attempt to refute colonial stereotypes and set right the image of a static "community," sunk in torpid medievalism, insulated from the winds of change, influenced by the diktat of the mullahs, tied to the Islamic community, susceptible to Pan-Islamic influences, and organized, despite internal differentiations, on a pan-Indian basis?

Sections of the intelligentsia, creatively engaged in generating national consciousness across the board, had to set their own agenda within the parameters of their own framework. They were expected to redefine the terms of the debate not so much on Muslims or on Indian Islam but on intercommunity relations. They were required to harness their intellectual resources in order to demonstrate that the Muslims, both in their historical and contemporary settings, were part of and not separate from the Indian reality and that the colonial stereotypes, often reinforced by Muslim elite perceptions, were constructed on false premises. This was a necessary precondition for establishing their all-India credentials, as also to hasten the process of nation-building with Muslims as copartners. They had to contend, moreover, with a problem summed up by Gulshan and Chandra, two fictional characters in Firoz Khan Noon's novel *Scented Dust* (1942), and to bridge the gulf separating the followers of Islam and Hinduism. "Do not carry away the idea," Gulshan told Chandra,

that I think ill of you for your ignorance, because there are thousands of us Hindus, men and women, who are as ignorant of the great Muslim religion and its philosophy as you are of ours. You will meet millions amongst us, who know no more about Islam than that it introduced into India loose trousers and a spouted pot for ablutions. There are also millions amongst us who know no more about the Hindu culture than what is represented by *langoti* (jackystrap dress) and *dal-roti* (lentil and bread/vegetarian diet). It is only the irascible, fiery and short-tempered who speak evil of other people's religions. (Noon 1941, 293)

## III

There are numerous tracts and treatises on Hindu-Muslim intermingling, on social and cultural fusion, and on the commonality of intercommunity interests. There was, likewise, an enlightened conception of state and society grounded in the values of tolerance, syncretism, and fraternal living. One can also discern a wide range of liberal, eclectic, and radical ideals and movements from Raja Rammohan Roy to Jawaharlal Nehru that transcended communitarian barriers and fostered the growth of intercommunity linkages. Some of them were creatively expressed in the poetry of Rabindranath Tagore and the young Mohammad Iqbal. There were serious initiatives, such as the one taken by C. R. Das in Bengal, to resolve the communal deadlock (Ikramullah 1991, 23–24). At the same time, a tentative survey of the vast and amorphous "nationalist" literature reveals the uncritical acceptance of colonial constructions, their political legitimation through pacts, accords, "unity" conferences, and the inner religiocultural tensions within the nationalist paradigm. As a result, subcontinental themes on communal peace and understanding, shorn of their rhetorical value, ceased to be a major reference point in creating or articulating a truly national consciousness. This requires elaboration.

First and foremost, the intellectual understanding of Indian Islam and its followers was sketchy, superficial, and marred by a majoritarian perspective. The upper castes, who were convinced of their own superiority in the realm of ideas and thought, considered Islam a rather crude approach to the problems of philosophy and metaphysics (Nehru 1946, 225). There were, consequently, no serious interpreters of Islam, no counterparts of Al-Beruni, Amir Khusro, Malik Mohammad Jaisi, Abul Fazl, Raskhan, Rahim, or Dara Shikoh (Halbfass 1988). In this respect, M. N. Roy's critique, written in 1938, was illuminating. He was surprised that Hindus and Muslims who had lived together for so many centuries did not appreciate each other's culture and religion; that the Muslims, even after living in the country for many centuries, were "generally considered to be an extraneous element"; and that educated Hindus were blissfully ignorant of "the immense revolutionary significance of Islam." He concluded that a radical change in mutual attitudes "would shock the Hindus out of their arrogant self-satisfaction, and cure the narrow-mindedness of the Muslims of our day by bringing them face to face with the true spirit of the faith they profess" (M. N. Roy 1974, 59).

Nineteenth-century writers and reformers, many of whom grudgingly came to terms with the Muslim presence, accepted the "knowledge" derived from the medieval chroniclers, translated by British historians. Thus the Muslim intrusion was treated as an aberration or a break in the continuity of Brahmanic traditions; Indian culture was equated with Vedic culture; Indian philosophy was equated with Vedanta, Puranas, and the Upanishads; and Indian religion was equated with Hinduism (K. M. Panikkar 1963, 56, and 1953, 240; Lawrence 1928; Ronaldshay 1925, 2).

Most accounts, with their focus on the Muslim ruling elites, their military exploits and glittering durbars, ignored the subtle fusion of "little traditions" at the Sufi shrines particularly and in the rural hinterland generally. Islam had no Max Müller to detail how its dogmas and tenets were gradually incorporated into regional and local belief structures and rituals; how Muslims, most converted to Muhammad's religion at different points of time and for different reasons, were integrated with the rest of the population through a tangible and clearly identifiable historical process. Islam was mistakenly viewed as part of the "great tradition"—codified, rigid, unchanging, insular, and close to external influences. Its followers, whether converted or not, were cast in a specifically Muslim/Islamic mold. Regardless of economic status, caste, language, or regional affinity, their identity was understood, defined, and described in strictly textual terms.

K. M. Panikkar, otherwise identified with the liberal stream, commented that "the organization of Islam in India was . . . frankly communal, and its outlook was governed by the single fact of ensuring to the Islamic nation in India its independence and authority." Muslims constituted a society everywhere and were much more than a religious minority. Their culture and way of life was different from the Hindus and other communities around them. "Unlike the Christians who, though they profess a different religion, are not in their way of life different from the Hindus, the Muslims, whether in the South of Kerala or in Kashmir, represent a culture of their own" (K. M. Panikkar 1963, 55, 60).

The militancy of Islam and its inflexible doctrinal structure was a theme in and a major component of the Arya Samaj movement. Its founder, Swami Dayananda Saraswati, was a relentless critic of Islam and his celebrated text, *Satyarth Prakash*, was the chief source of inspiration for anti-Islamic polemics. "The Quoran, the Quoranic God and the Muslims," according to him, "are full of bigotry and ignorance" (Jordens 1978, 268). Pandit Lekh Ram, Swami Sharaddhanand, and Lala Lajput Rai carried forward the polemics of the swami. They subjected the Quran to severe criticism, depicted Muhammad as a man of dubious sexual ethics, and interpreted Islam as a religion sanctifying war and the slaughter of nonbelievers (Jones 1976, 145, 150; Llewellyn 1993, 104–5). "When I considered how devoted a Muslim is to his religion," wrote Lajput Rai, whose father turned Muslim for a while, "how he regards the propagation of Islam as a bounden duty and how he believes that the highest reward is attached to converting a man to Islam, I can well imagine what great pressure must my father's Muslim friends have brought to bear upon him . . . and how often they must have tried to induce him to become a Mussalman openly" (V. C. Joshi 1965, 14). Such views correspond to the oft-repeated colonial axiom that orthodoxy rather than heterodoxy had a more direct and profound impact on the Muslims, and that they were deeply committed to fulfilling their Islamic obligations. What distinguished them from others was their crusading zeal, their inclination to wage jihad against nonbelievers, and their abiding commitment to the spreading of their faith.

Invoking the past lent credence to such a reconstruction. Major literary writers, though by no means all, did so by contrasting the glory of pre-medieval India with the oppressive character of "Muslim dynasties." Quite a few Marathi writers were, thus, concerned with the overall degradation of Hindus and the pernicious influence of Islam on their social customs. Gopal Ganesh Agarkar (1856–95), Gopal Hari Deshmukh (1823–92) and Vishnushastri Chilunkar (1850–82) thought that Muslims were bullies and fanatics, because violence and aggression was the essence of their civilization. Bal Gangadhar Tilak, the fiery politician-writer, sought to build a Maratha identity through a conscious choice of historical figures and symbols that evoked memories of Muslim oppression and exploitation. His essentialist endeavors to define Muslims through constant references to Mahmud of Ghazna, Alauddin Khalji, Timur, Aurangzeb, and Ahmad Shah Abdali created a major religious divide in Maharashtra society and provided ideological coherence to the Hindu Mahasabha and the RSS, two of the most militant Hindu organizations in the 1930s and 1940s.

Noted Hindi writers like Bharatendu Harishchandra (1850–85), Pratap Narain Misra (1856–94), Radha Charan Goswami (1859–1923), and Kisorilal Goswami (1866–1932) portrayed medieval rule as a chronicle of rape and abduction of Hindu women, the slaughter of sacred cows, and the defilement of temples. Bharatendu referred to the "wounds in the heart" that were kept fresh by the sight of Aurangzeb's mosque that stood beside the sacred Vishwanath temple in Varanasi (S. Chandra 1987, 180–95). Two closely related themes figure in his and some of his contemporaries work: the downtrodden, long-suffering Hindu, and the dominant, oppressive Muslim. In his play *Nildevi*, Muslim characters display cruelty, cowardice, treachery, bigotry, and debauchery, while Hindus, though sometimes portrayed as meek and submissive, demonstrate courage, honor, and fidelity (King 1990, 187, 191; also Y. Malik 1990; McGregor 1991).

Kisorilal, following some notable British historians, described in his novel *Tara* (1902) the depraved conditions at the court of Shahjahan in Agra: intrigues, scenes of illicit love, murder among Muslims (Gaeffke

1978, 27). Misra and Radha Charan chastised Muslims as the "abominably impure mlechchas" and damned them as rank outsiders. They denounced the medieval rulers—"those mad elephants"—who "trampled to destruction the flourishing lotus-garden of India," and they lamented that Muslims slaughtered cows with impunity and prevented Hindu religious processions from being conducted (S. Chandra 1992).

Bankim Chandra Chattopadhyay (1838–94), who looked upon medieval India as a period of bondage, interpreted the Hindu chieftain's resistance to the Mughals as a form of national resistance. Muslim rule, he considered, brought neither material nor spiritual improvement to India. He saw in Islam a quest for power and glory, devoid of spiritual and ethical qualities, irrational, bigoted, devious, sensual, and immoral, and a complete antithesis of his "ideal" religion (T. Sarkar, above; P. Chatterjee 1986, 77; Raychaudhuri 1988, 188–89; and for a different interpretation, S. K. Das 1984). Bhudev Mukhopadhyaya (1827–94), for one, questioned this version and described it as a mischievous fabrication of British historians. In his view, the sultans of Delhi aided the process of unification and contributed significantly to the emergence of an inchoate consciousness of community among Indians. He emphasized the common ties that bound Muslims with the rest of the population. He pointed out that Islam in the subcontinent was quite different from Islam elsewhere both in doctrine and in internal social practices (Kaviraj n.d.[b]; Raychaudhuri 1988, 41–43). Romesh Chandra Dutt (1848–1909), who wrote a major denunciation of British economic policies and was the inspiration behind the rise of "economic nationalism," avoided the familiar portrayal of Muslims as innately wicked and bloodthirsty. In *The Lake of Palms*, an English translation of the Bengali text, Romesh Chandra avoided, generally, the more or less brazen confrontation of Hindus and Muslims and the attendant display of an anti-Muslim bias that provided the staple for his historical novels (S. Chandra 1990, 18); nevertheless, the picture of Muslims as alien emerges strongly in his novels and fiction. Muslims were not quite "one of us," but were enemies of "our" country and religion (S. Chandra 1990).

The Bengali intelligentsia of Nirad C. Chaudhuri's generation read and absorbed the spirit of such writings. "Nothing was more natural for us," commented Chaudhuri, "than to feel about the Muslims in the way we did." They were told, even before they could read, that the Muslims had ruled and oppressed the Hindus, spread their religion with the Quran in one hand and a sword in the other, abducted Hindu women, destroyed temples, and polluted sacred places. "As we grew older we read about the wars of the Rajputs, the Marathas, and the Sikhs against Muslims, and of the intolerance and oppression of Aurangzeb" (N. C. Chaudhuri 1987, 226).

Bengali thinkers and reformers, according to Nirad Chaudhuri, based their lifework on the formula of a synthesis of Hindu and European currents. Islamic trends and "Muslim sensitivities" did not touch the arc of their consciousness. They stood outside as an "external proletariat" (M. Mukherjee 1993, 35; P. K. Datta 1993b; T. Sarkar, above). If they wanted to enter the Bengali cultural world, they could do so "only after giving up all their Islamic values and traditions." In this way, the new Indian/Bengali culture of the nineteenth century built a perimeter of its own and put specifically Muslim influences and aspirations beyond the pale (N. C. Chaudhuri 1951, 226–27).

Nirad Chaudhuri was no different. Though a self-proclaimed liberal humanist, he nursed an arrogant contempt for and deep-seated hostility toward the Muslims in Calcutta, where he spent most of his life (N. C. Chaudhuri 1951, 228). It was just the same in Kishoreganj, now Bangladesh. "We became conscious of a new kind of hatred for the Muslims," during the Swadeshi Movement. A cold dislike for them "settled down in our heart, putting an end to all real intimacy of relationship" (1951, 232). He rejoiced at Italy's attack on Tripoli in 1911. He was pleased—"so that the Muslims would be taught a lesson"—when Turkey joined the German side at the end of 1914 (N. C. Chaudhuri 1987, 37). "Strongly anti-Muslim in 1920" owing to the khalifat upsurge, Chandhuri was uneasy with the "menacing assertiveness" of the Bengali Muslims and "repelled" by the thought of living in a province where Muslims would be a dominant social and cultural entity (N. C. Chaudhuri 1987, 466). His verdict: Muslims constituted a society of their own with a distinctive culture and could not be absorbed into a unified nation. For this reason, "no historical argument was too false or too foolish to be trotted out by the Hindus to contest the demand of the Indian Muslims to have their own way of life" (1987, 38, 330). Chaudhuri declared, "When I see the gigantic catastrophe of Hindu-Muslim discord of these days I am not surprised, because we as children held the tiny mustard in our hands and sowed it very diligently. In fact, this conflict was implicit in the very unfolding of our history, and could hardly be avoided" (1951, 225).

The following description, which must not be conveniently dismissed as an illustration of Nirad Chaudhuri's "eccentricity," sharply reflects the images of Muslims and the contempt with which they were referred to by the sections of the Bengali *bhadralok*.

One day I saw a procession of Muslim divines trooping into Sarat Babu's house. I was quite familiar with the modern Muslim dress, but had no idea that these learned Muslims wore different clothes. They did, for they had green gowns on and big turbans on their heads. . . . We, the educated and urban Bengalis . . . did not even imagine that such persons existed in Bengal. I with my knowledge of Islamic painting could only assume when I saw them that they were crude incarnations of the Muslim divines I had seen portrayed in Persian or Mughal miniatures. . . . Their faces were grave, and even stern. One face struck me very forcibly. It was pinched and peevish, but of an incredible ferocity. The eyes were large, black, and burning, and in that emaciated face they looked even blacker and larger. . . . He looked like an ill-dressed Robespierre, the sea-green Incorruptible. Sarat Babu's house was not only crowded for the occasion with these survivals of Islam, but even reeked of them. (N. C. Chaudhuri 1987, 469)

Such representations of Muslims did not augur well for the nationalist agenda of welding various communities, along with castes, regions, and linguistic units, into a unified nation. The rise of the Congress movement, in particular, imposed serious demands on its leaders to define the contours of multiculturalism and religious pluralism so as to keep intact the fragile social fabric that was being steadily undermined by British policies, as well as by the Hindu-Muslim revitalization campaigns. Otherwise, the laudable Congress agenda of creating a composite nationality on liberal and secular values was bound to run into serious difficulties. Nehru rightly emphasized that "only by thinking in terms of a different political framework—and even more so a different social framework—can we build up a stable foundation for joint action" (Nehru 1936, 137).

# IV

Nehru's perspective was influenced by his cosmopolitan family background, his education in England, his social and cultural ambiance in Allahabad, his long-standing friendship and political camaraderie with influential Congress Muslims, including M. A. Ansari, Maulana Azad, Syed Mahmud, Khaliquzzaman, Tassaduq Ahmad Khan Sherwani, and Abdul Majid Khwaja. He was a product of, and his sensibilities were influenced by, the cultural norms and intellectual ambiance of the Urdu-speaking elites of the Indo-Gangetic belt. He read history at Harrow and Trinity College, Cambridge, and was in close touch with Fabian socialists in London. Such interactions widened his intellectual horizon and enriched his appreciation of political and social transformative processes around the globe. He could thus place in perspective the rapid changes, some of a revolutionary nature, taking place in Muslim countries like Egypt, Turkey, and Iran. Discussions with Azad and other Muslim scholars helped him understand Indian Islam and medieval Indian history better. In *The Discovery of India* (1946), he analyzed late-nineteenth-century reformist currents among Muslims, appreciated Syed Ahmad Khan's bold initiatives, commented on the nationalist stir among the young Muslim intelligentsia of north India, noted the "sensation" created by Azad—"this very youthful writer and journalist"—and assessed Iqbal's impact on the younger generation of Muslims (Nehru 1946, 297–305).

More than anything else, Nehru was aware that the social, educational, and economic backwardness of most Muslims was not because of any innate failing, but because of historical and sociological factors (Nehru 1946, 340). He knew, so he said, more about their hunger and poverty than those who talked in terms of percentages and seats in councils. He was, so he claimed, in greater touch with them than most Muslim leaders. How could he then accept the Muslim League's pretentious claims? How could he recognize Jinnah as the "sole spokesman" (Jalal 1985)? The League leadership at the top deliberately sought refuge in the name of religion to avoid discussing problems of the common man.

A simple fact that eluded most of Nehru's comrades was that Indian society was at no stage structured around religious solidarities or polarized along "communal" lines. Nehru's exceptionally eclectic mind grasped this reality. He believed that intercommunity conflicts, as and when they occurred, were counterpoised to the quiet, commonplace routines in which communities intermingled. Cross-community linkages rather than religious ties influenced the direction in which patronage, authority, and economic relations flowed into everyday life. Consequently, it was both possible and desirable to reinforce traditional linkages through "mass contact" and a radical socioeconomic blueprint. It was, moreover, feasible to blunt the impact of communalism by reducing class disparities, creating opportunities for upward mobility, and making the masses aware of their mutual interdependence, their shared historical experiences, and their common concerns, interests, and destiny.

This was the impulse behind Nehru's brainchild, the Muslim Mass Contact Campaign, launched in March 1937 (M. Hasan 1988). The idea was to approach the Muslims not as a collective fraternity but as a segment of an otherwise impoverished population. The principal motivation was to convince them that they did not constitute a "nation," and that their fortunes were not tied to their Muslim brethren per se, but with fellow artisans, peasants, and workers in other communities. Nehru dialogued with Jinnah on these lines, questioned the rationale of "Muslim nationalism" in a society traditionally anchored in cultural and religious pluralism, and criticized the construct of a "Muslim identity" in religious terms. He tried in vain to delink issues of proportion and percentages of seats with the more basic and fundamental contradictions between nationalism and colonialism. He expected Jinnah to draw his constituency into this just and legitimate struggle as co-citizens and not as a preferential religiopolitical "community." The two-nation idea made no sense; it was not more than a reversion to some medieval theory.

Why only two I do not know, for if nationality was based on religion, then there were many nations in India. Of two brothers one may be a Hindu, another a Moslem; they would belong to two different nations. These two nations existed in varying proportions in most of the villages in India. They were nations which had no boundaries; they overlapped. A Bengali Moslem and a Bengali Hindu, living together, speaking the same language and having much the same traditions and customs belonged to a different nation. (Nehru 1946, 341–42)

There was much ambiguity and fuzziness in nationalist thinking about the corporate identity of the Muslims. Nehru removed some of it. He made clear: "when we enter the political plane, the solidarity is national, not communal; when we enter the economic plane the solidarity is economic" (Gopal 1972, 8:203). In what way, he asked, were the interests of the Muslim peasant different from those of the Hindu peasant? Or those of a Muslim laborer from those of his Hindu prototypes? The ties that bound people were common economic interest and, in the case of a subject country especially, a common national interest (Gopal 1972, 8:121). If the country began to think and act on these lines, the "myth" of communalism would disappear along with the pseudoreligious mentality (Gopal 1972, 8:133). Communalism was not the power it was made out to be: it was a mere creation of educated classes in search of office and employment. The "communal question" was essentially one of the protection of interests. Religion was just a useful stalking-horse for this purpose. (Gopal 1972, 2:111). "The real conflict," according to Nehru, "had nothing to do with religion, though religion often masked the issue, but was essentially between those who stood for a nationalist—democratic—socially revolutionary policy and those who were concerned with preserving the relics of a feudal regime. In a crisis, the latter inevitably depend upon foreign support which is interested in preserving the status quo" (1946, 343).

The basic premise of Nehru's argument was valid. There was nothing wrong in arguing that religious solidarity should not be the basis for political activism or that religious symbols of disunity should be shunned in Congress mobilization campaigns. The alternative strategy, worked out by Tilak and Maharashtra or the Swadeshi leaders in Bengal, had created fissures in the liberation struggle, alienated Muslims in these regions, and weakened the intellectual underpinnings of secular nationalism. Though Nehru was not the only fervent champion of secular nationalism, he can safely be credited for raising the standard of debate on the subject. He did so not on the strength of abstract principles of Western democracy, which is a commonly leveled charge against him, but in relation to his perception of and insights into wider social and political processes. There is no reason to believe that his perceptions were flawed or to find fault in his vision. There is no reason to doubt his motives or intentions.

Nehru's ideas ran contrary to Jinnah's two-nation theory, just as they were at variance with the protagonists of a Hindu nation. Some of his own colleagues in the Congress, who relied on the colonial government's intellectual resources, were equally averse to and uncomfortable with his "proMuslim" proclivities. They were haunted by the specter of Pan-Islamism, even though the rallying symbol—the khalifat—had disappeared in 1922. They insisted that the fortunes of the Islamic world counted far more with Muslims than did their country's political regeneration. They harped on Muslims' aggressive instincts and the militancy of their faith. They agreed to the Lucknow Pact (December 1916) and similar accords on the assumption that Muslims were, after all, a separate religious and political entity (M. Hasan 1991b, 102–3). In this way, they quietly legitimized what were later derided as "separatist" and "communal" demands. In so doing, they jettisoned their own moral authority to challenge the colonial assumptions outlined in the Acts of 1919 and 1935. In the long run, they created the space, sometimes unwittingly but mostly consciously, for certain strident sectional claims to be accommodated in the Congress political agenda. The political language in which such accommodation was expressed and the energy derived from recognizing the Muslims as a distinct political unit implied that the basic terms of reference precluded any lasting solution of the communal tangle.

The Congress was sensitized to this reality after the Muslim outcry over certain policies adopted by its ministries in UP, Bihar, and Bombay (M. Hasan 1993b, 16–26). But it was too late to rewrite its own history or retrace its steps. With the political currents flowing in different directions, the Congress agenda could no longer be written afresh in the postwar years without the Muslim League, the votaries of a Hindu nation, and the British who still held the scales. There were not just "two parties," as Nehru had mistakenly announced in 1937, but as many as four parties who had jumped into the fray. Nehru and his socialist comrades swallowed this bitter pill when they helplessly witnessed the collapse of the Muslim Mass Contact Campaign.

I do not intend to portray the image of an always liberal, enlightened, largely innocent Muslim community—"sinned against" but hardly ever "sinning." Nor is this essay intended to suggest that their fortunes or misfortunes could be explained solely in terms of the unremitting, overwhelming power and prejudice of the British and "Hindu" intelligentsia. I agree with Aijaz Ahmad, whose own writings have clarified several methodological issues, that sections of the Muslim intelligentsia have made their own history at least as much as others have made it for them—that they have not made it very well is a concern that should engage social scientists (see A. Ahmad 1992, and the rather uncharitable critique in *Public Culture*, September 1993).

It is therefore important to examine the depth, vigor, and variety of Muslim revivalism, to consider why the idea of a singular community appears in Muslim writings, to explore how Islamic ideas molded elite perceptions, and to analyze why Islamic symbols of disunity were sometimes preferred to Indian historical symbols of unity (Brass 1974). We need to acquaint ourselves more fully with the Muslim educational system, "the master institution," in the words of Clifford Geertz, in the perpetuation of an Islamic tradition, and in the creation of an Islamic vision (Geertz 1965, 95; B. D. Metcalf 1982). In this context, the part played by the itinerant preachers and the ulema requires detailed investigation, not just as models of "Islamic conduct" or as interpreters of the Shariat but also as leaders of a political "community" in the making. We need to delineate, just as Syed Ahmad, Hali, Iqbal, and Azad did, the implications of their social conservatism in a society that was rapidly changing under colonial rule, and also the consequences of their resistance to innovation and change and their suppression of dissent and interpretation (*ijtehad*). The issue, which sometimes escapes notice in some writings on Muslims in Western scholarship, is of considerable significance to the citizens of South Asia generally and to Muslim communities in particular.

Finally, it is necessary to deconstruct the language of minorityism and uncover the motives of those who practiced modern-day politics in the name of the *millat* they purported to represent, but whose main aim was to wield political power and to use Islam and communitarian solidarity as a shield to cover their designs. The general implication of this idea was summed up by Chandra in her conversation with her lifelong friend Gulshan. "You see, my dear," she said, "a man will use any old argument to achieve his object in all walks of life, and this communal discord is a very useful and good stick with which our men-folk can beat the old India goat—her political progress." Troubled by the communal cleavage, she remarked angrily: "This Hindu-Muslim discord only exists because it pays our men-folk to keep it going" (Noon 1941, 282).

What we ideally need is a triangular narrative in which the Muslim is not a privileged victim but as much an actor as the others. The main thrust of this discussion is to identify points of convergence between the colonial and nationalist discourses and to argue that, despite different sorts of constraints, it was still possible for fervent advocates of an Indian nationhood to undermine the ideological underpinnings of Hindu majoritarianism and Muslim nationalism. There was surely a wide range of available options. If one were to evolve, in the spirit of Ghalib's quintessential message (Russell 1982, 71), as an independent/autonomous discourse, this would have entailed discarding the communal categories created by the Raj and also ignoring the Muslim elite's own perception of its role and destiny in history. There were, objectively speaking, profound historical and sociological reasons for doing so. The fact that this was not done in a concerted and systematic manner weakened the cause of, and the case for, secular nationalism.

My creed is oneness, my belief is abandonment of rituals.
Let all communities dissolve and constitute a faith.
                    —Mirza Asadullah Khan Ghalib (1797–1869)

# PART 3

---

# COMMUNITY AND CONFLICT

# 9

## Contesting in Public:
## Colonial Legacies and
## Contemporary Communalism

SANDRIA B. FREITAG

### Civil Society and the State as an Analytical Framework

AS THE HEADLINES FROM Eastern Europe, Africa, and South Asia so aptly illustrate each morning, the tension between nation-states and competing forms of identity invoked by their citizens has become a central problematic of life in the late twentieth century. How are these contestations to be resolved? In the literature regarding citizenship and participatory institutions, the public sphere—the realm occupied by civil society—has often become the focus when analyzing the interaction between state and citizen (Habermas 1974, 1989, 1991). "Civil society in this sense exists over against the state, in partial independence from it" (Taylor 1990, 95). Its importance derives most, perhaps, from that from which it remains aloof: "it includes those dimensions of social life which cannot be confounded with, or swallowed up in the state," on the one hand, and it is "not the private sphere," on the other. At the heart of civil society lies the exercise of "public opinion"—a new notion that is an aspect of the rise of modernity, in which issues "commonly recognized as of common concern" are sharply debated (Taylor 1990, 108, 109).

I would like to argue here that, particularly in postcolonial parts of the world, the very nature and functioning of civil society, or the operation of the public sphere, is the ultimate content of the contestations that hit the headlines. That is, it is in this intermediary realm between the state and the individual citizen, in which the polity brings pressure to bear on the state, that most of the current debates are located. How citizens help shape the values of the state; the extent to which the state is seen to be obliged to protect the beliefs and values of its various citizens; and the ability of citizens to integrate or reconcile their competing national and subnational identities—all these conundrums challenge the claims to legitimate authority made by contemporary nation-states. These conundrums emerge from two developments of the nineteenth and early twentieth centuries that have interacted to form the contemporary world: (1) the processes by which people redefined how they would identify themselves and what, in this context, they deemed important; and (2) the very nature of imperialism, especially in setting the relationship of the state to its constituent communities (and, hence, the resulting nature of civil society).[1]

Let me sketch broadly conclusions I have reached from earlier research. In British India, the colonial state created institutions and political processes predicted on the assumption that "public" and "private" were easily distinguished (see also La Volpa 1992). Within this dichotomy, the state identified itself as the protector and protagonist for "general" or "public" interests; it then relegated "private" or "particular" interests to the myriad communities that constitute the realm (see Maza 1989). The problem with this neat division was that it assumed all "political" issues could be accommodated within the state's institutions. At the same time, it labeled issues related to religion, kinship, and other forms of community identity as apolitical—as private, special interest, and domestic and therefore not requiring the attention of the state and its institutions. This did not mean that the state did not intervene in the private sphere—for instance, in India, by creating civil codes for Hindus and Muslims—but that the state thought it could set in motion systems that operated essentially by virtue of a person's embeddedness in society. Yet private and domestic issues had always been highly politicized in South Asian politics. And they became more politicized when the state removed itself from that realm of interaction (Freitag 1989b). Indians discovered this removal left them much room to experiment and to contest freely the status and ideological constructs they expressed in public. As a result, what the state wished to consider "particular" or "private" issues intruded themselves relentlessly into the world of institutional politics.

This contestation around particular issues helped create an alternative

1. The Chicago Conference on Comparative Public Spheres (October 1993) considered comparatively the implications of imperialism for the creation of the public sphere within both French and British imperial systems. A key finding of the participants was the extent to which imperialism shaped the public sphere in the metropole as well as in the colonies.

realm. In this alternative cultural space, activities expressing cultural cohesion most often provided the focal point. These were often performed in public spaces and were used to integrate symbolically the discrete actions of various groups organized in the locality. It is significant that these collective activities were often connected to new developments in the institutionalization and practice of religion. They utilized kinship (including fictive kinship) structures to forge ties through the expression of shared community identities among people. And they worked from localized bases such as neighborhood, occupational organization, and voluntary associations to mobilize people. The resulting cultural expressions offered alternative ideologies to those forged in the state's political realm. As public expressions of shared values, the activities of this alternate realm included civic ceremonials—especially processions through urban streets and performances in urban open spaces—as well as local festivals that had emerged from the eighteenth century onward.

Developments important for shaping this realm began to emerge in the eighteenth century. In particular, members of the dispersed Mughal courtier class and people who exercised leadership among Hindu merchant groups took up responsibility for fostering urban integrative ceremonies; and frequently, these innovations then were capitalized upon by successor state rulers, as well (see C. A. Bayly 1983 on Ramlila and Muharram in Benares and Awadh). British withdrawal from this alternative realm created a vacuum, accelerating this process and enhancing the roles claimed by those exercising new leadership. We are beginning to have a critical mass of historical research describing the kind of cultural patronage that emerged under these circumstances. It shows how the realm continued to be important for local actors because it recognized their legitimacy as local leaders, as they laid claim to new shares of rights and honors and to new roles in regulating local society (Freitag 1989a; Lutgendorf 1991; Hansen 1990). Equally important is new work (Sanyal 1990, forthcoming; van der Veer 1993; Pinch, forthcoming) on the institutionalization of religion in the eighteenth and early nineteenth centuries, which shows that contestation and activism within and among groups of ulema and monastic sampradays carried over into public arenas. The crystallization of issues and the urge to resolve ambiguities marked the new institutionalization processes, which focused especially on the practice of religion and on forging religious vocabulary to express the important values in the relationship of community to civil society. But these activities were specific to certain communities, and they invoked the private world of religion. Therefore they were viewed by the state not as general interest activities of import to the whole society

but as particular to specific groups. They thus served no important political purpose for the state, which happily abandoned them to local leaders.
By contrast, the ways in which such activities became expressed in public
spaces was seen in the locality to be of immense general, public interest.
Indeed, in this alternative realm, a range of particular interests came to be
united within the same general ideological discursive framework, often for
purposes of contestation and competition.

It is especially in this alternative realm that people forged a new way
to argue and compete about what mattered. Indeed, at the most important level, it is only possible for people to contest each other when they
have a shared language in which to argue. This discursive space opened up
as a result of a range of important changes throughout the nineteenth century, including shifts in the exercise of cultural patronage, the infusion of
new ideological meaning into the symbolic rhetoric used on civic ceremonial occasions, and a new interaction between collective activities in open
spaces and the publicity afforded to public interest issues through print
media, with the resultant shaping and expression of public opinion.

Taken together, the activities in this discursive space certainly constituted an alternative to the political institutions created by the imperial
state. As such, they formed, to some degree, something akin to the independent realm analysts call "the public sphere." The similarity revolves
around understandings about the constitution and operation of civil society as something independent of—and often in resistance to—the imperial state. Because this discursive space continued to focus on issues and
forms of expression regarded as particular or private, however, it has often
received short shrift from analysts and activists alike. Indeed, the focus in
the nationalist movement on the development of political institutions to
meet and resist the British structures of governance followed the lead of the
state and neglected (except at certain notable moments) to integrate the
alternative realm that had emerged. In part, this reflected elite uneasiness
around mobilization of the masses. In part, it expressed a conscious desire,
pursued by Gandhi and other leaders, to play down the forms of community identity that had begun to emerge. The forms of imagined community that emerged in this alternative realm have always been perceived as
a threat to a singular, unified, national identity. Consequently, there has
been a consistent effort, from the 1920s to the present in most of the world,
to treat the discourse that has emerged from this alternative realm as illegitimate. At the same time, the vocabulary and issues inevitably have been
imported into the space occupied by political institutions and the state.

As a result of the ambiguous relationship established between the state's political institutions and the alternate realm of constructed communities, a number of unresolved issues lurked just beneath the surface in India after 1947. The moment of independence ought to have been the time when the public sphere in India could come into its own, when new understandings about the construction of civil society could have been explored. Instead, the rhetoric of a secular state (born, in fact, out of the debate about religious community), and the trauma of Gandhi's assassination (Brennan 1994, 24) by a religiopolitical party follower delayed the debate about the nature of civil society in postcolonial India. Reasons ranging from the fear of continuing partitions of the national territory to the desire to impose large-scale economic development policies enabled the supporters of secularism to triumph. It is only since 1980 that the presence of a number of competing identities with localized particular meaning has been recognized. In the intervening decades, the alternative realm continued to be an arena in which quite different bases of community identity competed with the nation-state for the primary loyalties of participants. As a consequence, the very legitimacy or authority of the state continues, now, to be challenged by demands from these competing communities that the state protect their special or particular interests. To the extent that the state cannot extend this protection, it is seen as falling short of the responsibilities that a nation-state owes its citizens.

In the remainder of this chapter, I apply this framework of analysis to the politics of communalism that has emerged over the century from the late 1890s to the present. By broadening the discursive field to include both state-encouraged political institutions and alternative cultural activities, we can look at the sources for the shared vocabulary of contestation. We may discern, as well, the genealogy of assumptions about how civil society should function in postcolonial India. Accordingly, I would like briefly to compare two key moments when agitation linked the two realms of activity: the Cow Protection Movement of the early 1890s, and the Ayodhya agitation of the early 1990s.

## Cow Protection: The Late Nineteenth Century

The Cow Protection Movement stands out among late nineteenth-century public agitations in its singular ability to unite, within one ostensible ideological movement, activities in city and countryside. Cow Protection organizations (Gaorakshini sabhas) grew up in many urban centers across British India and beyond, and in small towns and *qasbas* (market centers) as well (Freitag 1989a, 149–50). For other purposes I have found it important to distinguish between the general movement (which expanded over a large part of the subcontinent, and then contracted to rural areas of the United Provinces when government pressure succeeded in inhibiting urban leaders) and the phenomenon of riots that followed in the wake of the movement. The riots occurred in such far-flung cities as Bombay and Rangoon, and so Cow Protection should not be seen as a strictly north Indian phenomenon. But the heart of the movement lay in the Bhojpuri region overlapping eastern UP and Bihar (a linguistically coherent region; see Pandey 1983). In this area, particularly, urban and rural places were linked by organizational networks that fostered the movement of stump orators (especially sadhus) crisscrossing the region, as well as the collection of money and in-kind contributions (*chutki*, usually handfuls of rice) for the establishment of cow shelters (IOR 1894a; SVN 1888a, 250–51). Especially in the cities, the infrastructure created by existing organizations such as the Arya Samaj and the Sanatan Dharm Sabha (which, in virtually all other circumstances, competed with each other) supported the Cow Protection Movement. Although the symbol of the cow could unite a wide range of people, the meaning behind the shared symbol varied. Indeed, the very ambiguity of the symbolic language was its greatest strength: it enabled local structures to be mobilized and directed activism along local lines of schism and into local ideological pathways. This ability to link local identities and values to a broader ideology distinguished the Cow Protection Movement from otherwise similar localized collective action of the period.

The broader ideology had first taken shape in 1882, when Dayananda Saraswati, founder of the Arya Samaj, formed the first Gaorakshini Sabha in the Punjab (Farquhar 1918, 111). The book that Dayananda published soon after, along with the stump orators, spread the movement throughout the Gangetic plain and beyond. Elsewhere, I have examined in detail the process by which itinerant preachers, under the patronage of local big men, called meetings at which printed posters told stories of the need to protect Mother Cow (Freitag 1989a, 148–76). Printed rules for new sabhas were held up as a model: as people in a locality established their own sabha, they would amend these rules to reflect local mores and the particular social frictions of the area. From the printed rules we discover that in some areas sabhas targeted Muslims, while in others they targeted low-caste, untouchable, or peripatetic groups. In the cities, the target often became Christian converts (SVN 1888b; IOR 1894b). To the extent that reformists were influential in the area, the rules might reflect the goals they espoused as well, such as admonitions against "foolish expenditure on marriage" and efforts to contain the number of people in the wedding processions (IOR 1894b, 3). The heart of the rules aimed first at proper treatment of cows and the need to make small contributions in support of the movement. But an equal number of rules focused on personal religious practices and the observance of proper Hindu ritual (IOR 1894b). This emphasis on newly propagated, "proper" ritual distinguishes the Cow Protection Movement equally from both the Arya Samaj (which linked reformist Hinduism to the Westernized world of Indian administrators) and the Sanatan Dharm (which attempted to defend "traditional" practices). Indeed, it is an interesting strategy to be adopted in a movement clearly aimed at creating a middle ground where those who wanted to reform Hinduism and those who wanted to defend what they understood to be traditional Hinduism could meet. Especially significant for our purposes is that this common meeting ground brought together personal activism and the reform of personal religious practice.

But attention to texts produced for sabha meetings may mislead us. This movement to focus activism on the reform of personal religious practice, united with protection of the cow, did not expand simply by virtue of the fact that certain texts were penned (even by Dayananda) or that an infrastructure existed. Rather, it escalated dramatically in reaction to state actions: in 1888, the High Court of the North Western Provinces decreed that a cow was not a sacred object. This intervention by the colonial state meant that cows were not covered by section 295 of the Indian Penal Code, which stipulated:

Whoever destroys, damages or defiles any place of worship, or any object held sacred by a class of persons, with the intention thereby of insulting the religion of any class of persons, or with the knowledge that any class of persons is likely to consider such destruction, damage or defilement as an insult to their religion, shall be punished by imprisonment. (IOR 1894c)

With no protection from the state, several things began to happen. The movement quickened its pace, arguing that individuals had to provide the protection for cows that the state now denied. In the absence of state restrictions, more Muslims in the countryside seem to have taken the occasion to begin practicing cow sacrifice on the occasion of the festival of 'Id,

which may reflect bids by those who had recently gained status to exercise the public roles that would validate this status, because 'Id provided
the opportunity to offer hospitality and charity to extended kin and client
groups. As the tension mounted between these two sets of activists in the
following two years, it became clear that local administrators were going
to have to initiate new ways to control the competition around the cow.
They faced increasing numbers of roving bands on the roads who would
seize cows (or bullocks) from butchers and herders, to take them to safety
in cow shelters. And, on the occasion of the 'Id in 1893, crowds as large as
five and six thousand people would march for hours to gather in front of a
compound, hoping to pressure a Muslim landlord who planned to sacrifice
a cow. Indeed, the pressure of local public opinion proved very important
in the success of the movement, as attested by the trials conducted by sabhas to punish those who allowed cows to be sold to butchers (IOR 1894d).
(This desire to legitimate sabha proceedings by simulating the state's legal
apparatus is worth noting.)

What made Cow Protection succeed as a broad-based ideological
movement? In symbolic terms, the figure of the cow could unite popular
and high culture; it could serve reformist and traditionalist ends; it could
reach the hearts of townsmen and peasants alike (Yang 1980; Freitag 1989a,
148–76). Consequently, it was also useful in smoothing over social ruptures
that were beginning to upset local society. Studies of the agrarian economy of the period make it clear that many middling peasants who actually
worked the land were doing quite well at the time and had gained control
of much land that had previously been under the purview of twice-born
castes (Nevill 1905; Stokes 1978; Robb 1986). The uneasiness caused by
those economic shifts could only be mitigated by ideological appeals that
drew together these contending groups, and the cow certainly succeeded at
that. At the same time, as William Pinch's work on two movements in the
countryside in this period makes clear, local social ferment revolved around
the practice and understanding of Hindu values and around the claims for
upward mobility being launched by peasant group movements claiming
Kshatriya varna status (Pinch 1996). These movements had begun to challenge the hegemony of the twice-born castes on social grounds. Again,
emphasis on the cow could diffuse the confrontational impact of such agitation. Moreover, by reinforcing the value system of twice-born Hindus,
the movement also underscored certain traditional social schisms, setting
up all those outside this cultural system—such as Muslims, Chamars, and
Christians—as targets for protest against whom those who would other-

wise contend could unite. So Mother Cow smoothed over new schisms by setting up as targets various groups previously constructed as the Other (S. Sarkar below).

But it seems to me that the most important development in the course of the movement was the successful elision between an individual's passionate devotionalism and the new uses to which personal political activism could be put. This success cannot be attributed solely to Cow Protection, nor did it disappear when the state suppressed the movement. In fact, at least three developments external to Cow Protection should be credited with this conflation of devotionalism and activism. These included the impact of reformism, the state's need to count people within communities during census operations, and the creation of a new vocabulary to express the connections among people. As reformist movements challenged customary ways of understanding and expressing religious life, then, all participants in public religious exercises (and in the public exhortations regarding private practices) became aware that the very behavior they chose served to express support and belief (Freitag 1989a). As the state elaborated a way to work with groups (rather than individuals), it counted people by religious and other labels. The rewards went to those who invoked only certain kinds of identities (Appadurai 1993). As a discursive mode grew up around public agitations, it used the vocabulary of extended kinship and religious belief to express imagined communities. Such a form of discourse provided a way to talk about the values and collective identities that mattered the most (Freitag 1991a and 1993). The interaction of these various influences ultimately enabled a new kind of passionate devotionalism to grow up. Individuals could cast their own, personal actions in a frame that aligned them with larger, extralocal ideological movements.

## The Emergence of Civil Society

The implications of these developments for the emergence of civil society —for the emergence of a sphere of activity in which individuals aligned themselves in contradistinction to the state as well as to certain groups defined as the Other—are profound. Cow Protection is a very useful movement to examine in this context because it is so clearly not nationalism as anyone would define it. And yet it operated in the very same public spaces, utilizing the same forms of publicity and venues of communication, and made very similar kinds of demands for protection of shared values and modes of behavior and speech as did the nationalist movement. It tapped into the same emerging world of the informed individual and tried to mobilize him or her to act on behalf of a larger public interest. It was couched in a vocabulary shared with movements expressing other imagined communities, emphasizing primordial attachments and the need for moral individual behavior on behalf of a larger social good. I emphasize these points because the example speaks to what is fast becoming a truism that Indian nationalism is a "derivative discourse" (P. Chatterjee 1986). It seems to me that the forces shaping Cow Protection, as well as the language in which it was expressed, make it clear that this movement and others like it (such as the Tamil language movement that Sumathi Ramaswamy has examined so skillfully [Ramaswamy 1992]) had at least as influential an impact on the development of Indian nationalism as did the Western model from which its vocabulary was often drawn.

And that impact lies in the nature of the mental and social space carved out for the emerging civil society, for nationalism and the competing community identities that emerged in the early twentieth century helped to shape a very differently configured civil society. If we ask what the characteristics of that society were, we can begin to see how the differences — deriving equally from the impulses around constructions of community and from the constraints imposed by imperialism — have shaped postcolonial society.

Using the example of Cow Protection helps us to ask these questions. Moreover, we can put the evidence from the Cow Protection Movement next to related studies of Ramlila and Muharram in north India, as well as regional language agitations and non-Brahman and untouchable movements in the west and south. Taken together, all of these movements charted the ways in which the public expression of religious precepts evolved into larger ideological statements about imagined communities (Freitag 1991b; Lutgendorf 1991; Richman forthcoming). If we examine together the communities constructed around alternative identities rooted in religion, language, and other regional specificities that occupy this discursive space, we may identify the following shared characteristics.

1. COMMUNITY: They all rest on the evocation of an imagined community, one generally constructed in opposition not only to the imperial state, but to an indigenous Other seen to imperil their shared values. (We will return to this rhetorical use of an Other, below.)

2. STATE: In evoking a sense of community, they also draw on certain institutional preconditions established by the imperial state, particularly

the tendency of the state to deal simultaneously with individuals and with groups. Given the institutional rewards provided to groups successful in pressuring the state as groups (ranging from census enumeration to separate electorates, but also implicated in the civil and criminal laws), the tension between individual and group identity is often resolved, at moments of crisis, in terms of group identity.

3. DRAMATIC MOMENTS: Conversely, if a community perceives that the relationship between the state and itself or its imagined Other has changed, it will often seize (or manufacture) a moment of tension in order to translate that perception into a public statement. Examples of this dynamic have manifested themselves from the Benares riot of 1811 to the Bijnor riot of 1992 (Frietag 1989a, 19–51; A. Basu 1994b and 1995; also B. Roy 1994).

4. SPECIAL VOCABULARY: The evocation of community, furthermore, has created a special discursive set of idioms that elude the distinctions between the religious and the social. Religious figures stand in for larger public and social values (Rama for good rule, Husain for martyred leadership, and the like). Gendering processes identify community identity and values to be protected as "mothers" or "goddesses," and those to be resisted as "harlots." One consequence is that the conflation of religious devotionalism and community activism cries out for individuals to be "good believers" and "good citizens" simultaneously. Another consequence is the irrelevance, rhetorically and conceptually, of the Western concept of "secularism." These conditions have always imputed a significantly different understanding of the term "secularism" and the implications for state action

5. CLAIMS IN PUBLIC: At the same time, this aspect of their nature dictates the need to assert in public their claims on civil society and on the state. They rely, therefore, on very modern forms of communication and mobilization: the use of print media (newspapers, pamphlets, posters); the staging of processions through public spaces (both as demonstrations in civic centers of their claims to the public interest, and as exhortations through neighborhoods of proper behavior); the use of large public meetings to pressure politicians and other recognized "representatives" of the state; the call for volunteers to "sacrifice" themselves, usually by staging acts defined as illegal by the state. (In this last characteristic, they simultaneously challenge the state and its laws and collude with it, tacitly recognizing that the enactment of arrest ties together protester and state in the same discourse).

6. SWAYING PUBLIC OPINION: By occupying these public arenas, the movements also recognize the power of and attempt to influence public opinion. Though this has generally been treated in the scholarly literature (in an extension of the Western European model) as those literate readers of Western-style newspapers (Haynes 1991; N. Gupta 1981), we must broaden the universe to recognize the ability of such movements to influence a much broader public through visual and oral means. A quite distinct set of oratorical and visual idioms emerged in this period as a result of these kinds of appeals (Lelyveld 1993).

7. MOBILIZATION IN THE STREETS: The mobilization of volunteers and a broader public opinion leads, as well, to the general use of collective action in support of community. Particularly in the colonial context, the electoral franchise was extended to a relatively narrow band of the society. Moreover, the political structures established by the British fostered the growth of factions—shifting localized alliances—that generally worked across the larger constructed ideological communities we are discussing here. So the vote and related electoral politics, while useful, could not serve as a definitive measure of community influence. Mobilization in the streets, particularly as it carried with it the implicit threat of violence and loss of social control, provide a much more effective measure of a community's clout.

8. FEATURING VIOLENCE: The combination of mass mobilization and the tactic of pressuring one's opponent publicly through adaptation of the merchant practice of "sitting *dharna*" (a kind of sit-down strike) rather ironically created a central role for collective violence (see van der Veer, below). This tactic is not new in the twentieth century, but the advent of mass communications networks and broadly based imagined communities much enhanced the strategic value of threatened violence. We have not only the example of the crowds of thousands massed during Cow Protection to illustrate this point, but also the call to Shias all over the subcontinent to come to Lucknow to court arrest in the 1930s (Freitag 1989a, 22–47).

9. CREATION OF AN OTHER: Because a community can be much more effectively imagined in contradistinction to an Other, these movements delineated an Other as rhetorical object and actual target. For our purposes, the most important aspect of this process was that the Other was defined not only as existing outside community boundaries, but as being located outside civil society, not deserving of state protection. In many respects, the relationship between civil society and the state was perceived as one possessing limited goods: if one community benefited in new ways from

the protection of the state or through enjoyment of public recognition
from civil society, this had to mean that another community had suffered
(G. M. Foster 1965). Martyrdom thus became as effective a rhetorical device as aggressive claims to rights.

These nine characteristics of the discursive space that emerged by the
1890s became much more elaborate through the 1920s and 1930s. Our discussion of Ayodhya will measure the extraordinary extent to which they
still obtain today.

Key to the evolution in use of this new discursive space were two
unresolved tensions that still remained at independence in 1947. The first
tension revolved around the state's relationship to the individual versus its
relationship to the group. The second tension related to those activities
legitimately recognized as being of general or public interest (the political agitations that worked through state institutions) versus those activities deemed particular or private (the community agitations that worked
through cultural, kin-focused, and religious activities). This dual legacy of
unresolved tensions has shaped the continuities we can see in the agitations around Ayodhya and beyond.

## Ayodhya: The Late Twentieth Century

Just as Cow Protection brought together a number of different institutional players—the Arya Samaj, Sanatan Dharm Sabha, journalists, members of Congress and other political organizations—so Hindutva has
drawn on what is known as the Sangh Parivar, which is composed of the
BJP, now the third largest political party in India (Minault 1990) and the
first one to succeed in winning control of four regional state governments,
and its allies, the VHP, Bajrang Dal, RSS, and the Shiv Sena, which in recent years has succeeded in linking Maharashtrian regional identity with
militant defense of upper-caste Hinduism (Z. Hasan 1991; van der Veer
1993). In this coalition, a number of retired members of the Indian bureaucracy have been prominent, and interlocking directorates unite the BJP,
VHP, and RSS (van der Veer 1993). What helped elect the BJP into office in
the first place was the sustained Ram janmabhoomi campaign on behalf of
building a temple in Ayodhya. This campaign shared all of the nine characteristics listed above; perhaps the most important were the processions
that linked up public-space devotional activities in various towns across
north India with the Ayodhya site of the dispute and with New Delhi,

to bring the protest home to government figures (see Davis, above). Too, the rhetoric used was that long developed in religious defense and reform movements—discursive structures that connected individual behavior and support for community identity to the need for political solidarity, and used the mode of passionate devotionalism as the way to channel volunteer activity. The claim made on the state was made on behalf of a community and was couched (rather ironically, since it is the majoritarian culture) in terms of martyrdom at the hands of both the state and the Other.

In this volume, you have read much about the Ayodhya agitation, so here I only briefly situate some of its most prominent characteristics in the larger, on-going discourse that has emerged in independent India vis-à-vis the claims that communities can make on the state and civil society. Seen in this context, the Ayodhya chronology is punctuated not only by public mobilizations and demonstrations, but also by reference to the Shah Bano case and to the government's decision to implement the Mandal report (a process of reserving more jobs for specific groups that is usually referred to as Mandalization) (van der Veer 1993, 2–8; A. Basu 1994b and 1995; Minault 1990; G. Shah 1991; *Asian Survey* 1993). The contemporary agitation around the Babri Masjid in Ayodhya began in 1984 when the VHP asserted the demand that a lock placed on the mosque decades earlier be removed. Public processions and general agitation, overshadowed by the assassination of Indira Gandhi, gained new life when a judge of Faizabad decided on February 14, 1986, that the Babri Masjid site should be opened to the public. (That is, in a development strikingly parallel to the Cow Protection agitation, popular concern escalated dramatically in direct response to state action.) Protests across India culminated in a Muslim protest in Delhi at the end of March 1987 that was the largest since independence.

The government in any case had been searching for several years for an appropriate stance vis-à-vis "the Muslims"; much agitation in the early 1980s had revolved around the case of an elderly Muslim woman, Shah Bano, who had sought maintenance support from her former husband through the courts (Engineer 1987b). Since passage of the Hindu Succession Act in 1956, women identified legally as Hindus had been able to inherit and to seek recourse through the civil courts. The Supreme Court ruled in 1985 that Shah Bano could also use this recourse; being Muslim, that is, did not prevent her from being a citizen in a state that treated all citizens equally. Conservative Muslims agitated, arguing that this decision denied group rights, which were more important than individual rights in the kind of civil society obtaining in postcolonial India. The state, attempting to assuage what it saw as "Muslim" sensibilities, passed the (ironically named) Muslim Women's Protection of Rights on Divorce Act in 1986, amending the constitution to ensure group rights. BJP leader L. K. Advani referred to the Shah Bano case as "a watershed event" in mobilizing Hindu sentiment; and 1993 research among Hindus identified the wide perception that, in these circumstances, "secularism" to the Congress government simply "meant endless appeasement by the Hindus of never-yielding Muslim fanaticism" (*Sunday Times of India*, October 14, 1990; Thakur 1993). Acts by the state in 1986, then, should be seen as related: on the one hand, the state "placated the Muslims" through the constitutional amendment protecting group rights; on the other hand, it "placated the Hindus" by opening the Babri Masjid site. In both actions, large putative groups labeled by religious identities were recognized as having claims on rights within civil society that had to be accommodated by the state.

In 1989 and 1990, several developments escalated the Ayodhya agitations (see Basu and Davis, above). The VHP connected a broad-based ideological stance with localized issues and personal decisions through its organization of the Ram shilan puja bricks campaign. (The parallels with the networks established in other movements to collect chutki and send it forward are striking.) Such exercises of mass mobilization often led to violent confrontations, especially when clustered Muslim populations could become the targets of these mobilized activists; hundreds died as a result of this campaign. In a related move, BJP decisions in 1989 redirected that political party away from Gandhian liberalism to overt alliances with the Shiv Sena and others, while placing the Ram janmabhoomi campaign at the heart of its political platform. To counter the BJP's ownership of this issue, Rajiv Gandhi not only permitted the laying of the foundation of stone but even appeared personally at Ayodhya at the beginning of his 1989 election campaign. In 1990, renewed violence in Kashmir portrayed Hindus as the victims and brought Pakistan back into the discursive space; the threat of Pakistan always suggested that Indian Muslims occupied civil space outside the Indian imagined community. Ayodhya could now be made to stand in for other places in the subcontinent in which Hindu community rights were being denied.

And in September of 1990, the V. P. Singh government announced that it would implement the recommendations of the Mandal Commission, prompting another round of ferocious protest riots (Beteille 1992). The Mandal Commission had made two arguments critical to understanding the underlying tensions fueling the Ayodhya conflict. First, it argued that

the operative identity by which people should gain access to the resources
of the state should be their community identity, in direct disagreement with
an earlier commission that had called for economic measurements to enable
individuals to claim privileged access (Beteille 1992). Second, the Mandal
Commission wanted to expand the reservation system, previously focused
in most places on untouchable groups (scheduled tribes and castes) [2] to include the more amorphous grouping of Other Backward Classes, which
encompassed a number of low-caste groups who already exercised considerable power and control over resources in some parts of India, like
the Yadavs in UP and Bihar, and Lingayats and Okkaligas in Karnataka
(Beteille 1992, 113). The heated debates about Mandalization make clear
the extent to which much of the impetus for the Ayodhya agitation related
to issues other than religious identity. In a striking parallel to the context
surrounding the 1890s Cow Protection Movement, what we may discern
here are crucial economic changes interacting with ideological appeals.

The numbers of those who could be counted as middle class in India
had grown significantly through education as well as the expansion of
entrepreneurial possibilities. Yet these numbers had met with reduced employment opportunities, while at the same time they were increasing their
debt load by trying to live up to middle-class consumption standards.
These economic changes led to middle-class perceptions of themselves as
profoundly disadvantaged. Ghanshyam Shah's study of the BJP in Gujarat
before 1989 makes it clear that the BJP became the voice of an alienated
middle class, which had grown "significantly in the last four decades . . . disproportionate to the economic growth of the state" (G. Shah 1991, 2921).
In two very interesting surveys designed to gauge public support for destruction of the mosque in Ayodhya, a distinct subset of the Indian population can be identified as the core of support for the movement: those
who identified themselves as "Hindu," those who worked as traders, small
business people, and white-collar workers, and those who formed part of
the age cohort whose formative years occurred in the partition era (Chibber and Misra 1993, 665–72).

These very groups had been most threatened by the combination of
Mandalization and "the new economic liberalization initiatives aimed at

2. I use the term "untouchable," here and below, following Barbara Joshi's lead. Her
point is that the use of the term underscores both the fact that untouchability continues to
exist and that the terms "scheduled caste" and affiliated vocabulary place untouchables within
a Hindu framework (B. Joshi 1992, 37–54).

greater privatization and increased global competitiveness" (Parikh 1993, 684). In the last decade or so, a few agitations mounted by this portion of the middle class have aimed specifically at the groups seen to threaten them (Baxi 1990a). Most often, however, the strategies have taken a different tack. Like Cow Protection, the Ayodhya agitation attempted to displace economic competition between segments of the Hindu population onto an Other, a target more easily defined as falling outside Indian civil boundaries—the Muslim. Arguably, then, many Hindutva activities were aimed not just at asserting the rights of one group (Hindus) to control Indian civil society, but also at underscoring what (otherwise competing groups of) Hindus shared in common. Perhaps, then, we should see this protest as a measure of the extent to which shared identity falls short. In the context of Indian civil society, the vocabulary that worked presented groups as victims (of the power of an Other undeterred by the state). This vocabulary worked equally well for the purposes of drawing boundaries, where the concern was to rope members within the lines being drawn.

The Ayodhya agitation climaxed with the overnight destruction of the Babri Masjid on December 6, 1992, and the beginning of construction of a temple in its stead. Before the dust had settled, the UP and other BJP-run state governments were taken over by the center (ostensibly for failing to act to prevent the debacle, though the central government had been inactive as well), and communalist parties were banned. (Though the BJP lost badly in the 1993 elections, in early 1994 the Supreme Court declared the ban unconstitutional.) The BJP has now removed from its formal agenda the Ayodhya issue and returned to other, often more liberal stances, and in a white paper has disavowed any responsibility for the debacle. Still unresolved, of course, is the role the state should play in protecting religious susceptibilities, as well as the conundrum posed by the dual relationships the state now maintains both with constituent communities and with individuals.

In all of these developments, we can see clearly the genealogical connection to the developments previously traced for British India. It is not only that forms of organization, modes of discourse, and publicity have been tapped in ways directly reflecting these historical precedents. More profoundly, the present debates occupy a public space in large part shaped by earlier interactions. Such debates revolve, still, around ambiguous and unresolved tensions in the relationship between the state, individuals, and communities.

## Postcolonial Constraints: What Is New?

We can, then, discern the extent to which the current contestations about the nature of civil society in India have been broadly shaped by expectations emerging from the colonial experience. It is also obvious, however, that certain new conditions have emerged in the last decade or so. Minimally, we must recognize that for several decades after independence and partition in 1947 virtually no riots took place that could be traced to communal conflict, and that the scale of such conflict escalated dramatically in the 1980s (Freitag 1977; Ghurye 1968; Thakur 1993, 256).

We need a much better understanding of the process by which political leadership passed from those involved in the nationalist struggle to a younger generation rooted in regional power bases. It is clear that mass cultural consumption through ever-broader communications networks created new visions and offered competing foci for loyalty. The state played a role in this shift as well, for the initial constitutional emphasis on the relationship between individual and state began to give way before an increasing reliance on the relationship between communities and the state—a reliance that can be discerned both in terms of state policies (e.g., reservations policies for scheduled tribes and castes) and in terms of political strategizing (in the wooing of vote blocs).

Rather than challenging the concept of community identity as a basis for a relationship with the state, the debate in civil society has focused increasingly on which identities would be so legitimized. States' reorganization, for example, focused as it was primarily on linguistic divisions, legitimized the appeal of language and related regional cultural identities. Similarly, the policies adopted regarding education and job reservations for scheduled castes legitimized protoclass identities (although the related state policy to refuse access to these resources to those untouchables calling themselves Buddhists illustrated the remaining fuzziness between class and caste, and underscored the state's commitment to keeping untouchables within the Hindu fold—a very different basis for identity). At the same time, the resistance to the push for a Punjabi state, on the grounds that this demand rested on a religious identity masquerading as a linguistic one, reiterated the illegitimacy of religious identity in state political arenas.

Analysts have made much of the impact of modernity in the Indian state's desire to enumerate communities, and have laid the implications of this development at the door of the British colonial state (Pandey 1990a and b, 1994; D. Chakrabarty 1994). The reinforcement of the basic structure since 1947 has been equally important, however. Andre Beteille's point (1992; see below for more discussion) is a crucial one: the constitution laid the groundwork for a very different kind of development, and this potential has been short-circuited.

Why? Significantly, the rhetoric around community identity has never stayed within the boundaries set by state policies. One is struck especially, for instance, by the contrast between the state's economic rhetoric regarding reservations (Maheshwari 1991; Brass 1990) and the vocabulary used by untouchables when creating their own identity ideologies. The most dramatic example of this is Ambedkar's strategy of claiming Buddhism for untouchables; his speech before the mass conversion held in 1936 queried his listeners if they wanted to redress the economic and social disabilities they faced. To do so, he argued repeatedly, they had to "change their religion." It is worth noting in this context that Ambedkar served as one of the chief proponents of the constitutional provisions that underscored the relationship between the state and the individual. It was in this context of a state dealing with individuals that he urged untouchables to become Buddhists, to use their group's activism in their personal lives, and to use individual activism vis-à-vis the state (Lamb 1991; Omvedt 1993). Ambedkar's strategy points to the fact that, at the most fundamental level, state and civil society continue to debate quite explicitly the role to be played by religious concepts of the person-embedded-within-community, or religious vocabulary, and of the political viability of devotionalism. The attack on secularism within civil society indicates the extent to which this focus of the discourse, while clearly a legacy of colonialism, has taken on new meanings and significance in the postcolonial nation-state.

Bipan Chandra has argued that another important difference in the contemporary circumstances is the institutionalization of communalism.[3] By this he means, especially, the creation of political parties specifically (and solely) organized around a communal ideology: "Take away communal ideology, or make them abandon communal ideology, and nothing is left of them" (B. Chandra 1991, 131). This argument seems to view the change

---

3. Bipan Chandra's shift in the analysis of communalism can be measured by comparing his earlier argument that communal riots were unimportant because they reflected false consciousness to his more recent argument that a new institutionalization has made riots important because they are fomented and encouraged by organizational networks (B. Chandra 1984, 1991).

sideways. In the twentieth century, there have always been communal parties. Scholars like Bipan Chandra have been unwilling to see the politicized activities of social and religious reform movements as part of this institutionalized universe and so have been shocked by recent developments. (To concede the role played by such parties in institutionalized politics apparently implied a legitimation that such scholars refused to give. These impulses were, instead, dismissed as false consciousness, while popular culture was denied a legitimate place among topics to be analyzed by academics.)

This approach is sideways for another reason: to characterize the BJP as solely a communal party is to miss important nuances that Amrita Basu and others have underscored for us in this volume and elsewhere. Studies of the BJP before it adopted the Ayodhya agitation as its central focus also show that it took a variety of other liberal policy stances, including labor union organizing (G. Shah 1991). What is new, however, is the extent to which these interested parties have seized the enlarged capacity of communication networks and mass media to pursue their ideological goals, and to mobilize their followings (see Davis, Farmer, Manuel, above); and indeed, this mobilization also includes acts that foment real violence, including the provision of gasoline to start fires and sticks, bricks, and other weapons to use in riots (Freitag 1977; V. Das 1990c; K. N. Panikkar 1991). In this respect, strategists for the parties have recognized the power of popular culture even as it was denied by Indian intellectuals. This is an especially ironic development, if it signals, at last, the integration of the two spheres that the colonial regime left in tension: communal parties suggest at least one way for political and religious concerns to come together at extralocal levels.

The point about institutionalization is important, however, in a sense other than that posed by Bipan Chandra. It is not so much that communal parties have become institutionalized, as that community identity increasingly has become the basis, in general, for a range of highly institutionalized political activities. Andre Beteille makes the point most clearly, and he has focused on caste. After noting the extent to which many distinctions based on caste identity had begun to break down after independence (commensality, marriage, and so on), he notes,

However, there was one sphere of life, that of politics, in which caste not only held its ground but began to strengthen its hold. If caste has acquired a new lease on life in independent India, this is almost entirely because of the increasing use made of it in politics. . . . In the last forty years, and particularly since 1977, a tacit consensus seems to have emerged that all political bodies—zilla parishads, state cabinets, party committee—should be so constituted as to represent the major castes and communities. Representation in India has come increasingly to mean the representation of castes and communities. (Beteille 1992, 86)[4]

What makes this problematic in independent India is the lack of fit between constitutional needs and these actual practices. Beteille notes that these practices began under the British, and had at that time the goal of maintaining a balance of power. After independence, the constitution denied the need for a balance of power among communities; instead, reservations could "be justified only by the argument for greater equality," so that individuals became capable of participating in the nation. Now, however, the state has begun to move away from its connection to individuals as it elaborates a stronger relationship to communities. This does not fit well, Beteille argues, with the constitutional framework built on the relationship of individual and nation-state (Beteille 1992).

Another important difference in contemporary events relates to the extent to which a territorial base has become defined as an essential form of recognition by the nation of community rights.[5] It seems to me that what makes these territorial imperatives new and significant is the assumption that only when the state's physical boundaries coincide with community identity can group values receive sufficient recognition (a development that is not unique to South Asia, of course). While denying Kashmiri and Punjabi demands, for instance, the state has nevertheless accommodated a series of efforts to redraw state boundaries, acceding to linguistic and tribal imagined communities.

Yet the increasing emphasis on territory precludes other kinds of compromises. It shifts the modes of debate and contestation to grounds that challenge quite profoundly the premise on which civil society is based. To

4. He goes on to note that, although the constitution clearly distinguished between time-bound reservations with specific numbers of political places (in the assumption that disadvantages would disappear) and longer-term job reservations (without numerical specificity) to achieve economic equality, these distinctions have become hopelessly blurred (Beteille 1992, 86ff.). (See also Galanter 1984.)

5. Some of the earliest examples of efforts to align territorial distribution of people with community identity emerged in the 1930s: for instance, the redistribution of residents in Kanpur in the wake of the unprecedented riots of 1931 (Freitag 1989a, 220–48). This is also the period when demands for a separate territory called "Pakistan" coalesced. Van der Veer makes interesting an argument linking migration and pilgrimage to the nationalist exercise of defining a territory coexistent with national identity, and he notes that alongside these nationalist exercises grew up regionally focused movements as well (van der Veer 1994b). These exercises are, of course, linked to the fundamental effort to define one's own group against an Other.

deal with the new aspects of these debates may require a complete recon-
ceptualization of civil society in India—or at least set very different ground
rules for distinguishing how regional movements will be treated. The discursive space in which the state and civil society have been able to maneuver, however, may well have shrunk beyond the ability to set new ground
rules. For, as the very legitimacy of the state itself is denied by such activists, the demand for territorial recognition of what had been community-
based nationalism thus conflates in the real world the distinction Jaffrelot
would make analytically between territorial and community-based nationalism (Jaffrelot, forthcoming).

Finally, the increasing emphasis on territorial boundary lines around
communities also leads us to the new importance of the transnational context in which so many of these issues are now debated. Just as the Other
is important in defining one's own community, so those in the diaspora
have helped to define the boundaries of Hindustan, or the threat posed by
those embracing Islam. The presence and global influence of the "South
Asian diaspora" has significantly shaped the new ideological constructions
of community that are emerging. Funds contributed have had a great impact as sadhus raise money in Great Britain or hold summer camps in the
United States. Indeed, the overseas market for cultural productions such
as the television *Ramayana* videos or Hindi mythological films has made
the mass consumer market especially lucrative for those controlling popular cultural output. Once again, the transnational context of the discourse
renders problematic the attempts to define, at last, an appropriate civil
society for India. What happens to efforts to establish a relationship between individuals and the state if an influential number of participants has
no grounds at all for a direct relationship with the state? And is it perhaps
much easier to formulate ideological appeals of shared identity against an
Other when the fractures within the community are irrelevant in an overseas context? (See McKean 1994; van der Veer 1995.)

## Conclusion

Communalism as such, even communal riots, are thus not the problem but
simply a symptom of a much larger and more challenging process under
way: the redefinition of Indian civil social space and who will be allowed
to participate publicly inside that discursive space. The ambiguity between
the state's relationship to the individual citizen, and its increasingly in-

stitutionalized relationship to imagined communities, contributes to the conundrum now being faced in postcolonial India.

The vocabulary used in the debate remains the rhetorical idioms developed in opposition to the imperial state—particularly the language of religion, of regional/linguistic identity, and of class or ethnicity for low-caste groups. Indeed, the utility and resulting ambiguity of such language is particularly suggestive in an examination of the Bombay women's movement rhetoric, which illustrates the way the ostensibly secular use of idioms such as women's power as *shakti* (the power possessed, for instance, by Hindu goddesses) was appropriated by the BJP and Shiv Sena (Agnes 1994, 67). This language suggests the still-wide chasm between, on the one hand, the state and its institutions and, on the other hand, the public arenas shaped by communities and the identities they project publicly.[6]

That this vocabulary is frequently pursued (often, the appropriate verb would be "enacted") outside formal political and institutional structures is the most important characteristic of the contextual genealogy we have examined here. It is not coincidental that Richard Davis's study of public processions opens this volume. The use of public spaces (in a succession of urban places), the design of ritualized enactments that rest on individual activism, the harnessing of multivalent symbols, the clever manipulation of mass media—these aspects of public drama make it clear that communalism as a political act far exceeds institutional politics. Indeed, it is this expanded understanding of the political that has been most clearly inherited from the colonial past. The power of this expanded sense of the political results precisely from the ability, honed during the inadvertent blurring under imperialism of the public and the private, to fashion a civil society capable of simultaneously encompassing individual and community concerns. Indeed, the stories of Cow Protection and Ayodhya measure the ability of this civil society to link successfully local interests and extralocal ideological frameworks (Basu, above; S. Chandra 1994; Masselos 1994; Brennan 1994), to negotiate between the modern roles assigned to individuals and the protective stances assigned to communities. This ambiguity could thus be seen as a strength rather than a weakness.

Negotiating ambiguity is often the purpose of actions taken in the civil spaces examined here. Ways in which this ambiguity is dealt with mark

6. The implications of this language, in reshaping reconstructions of the past as well as narrowing options for the future, have been the subject of a number of challenging recent studies (B. D. Metcalf 1994 and Pandey 1994), although Pandey's analysis of "language" is distressingly myopic in terms of the impact of popular culture on the texts he would study.

this space out clearly from the Western public sphere: this is an analytical description of a different phenomenon, not a lament when measuring how India's civil society works against some implicit perfectly functioning alternative from the West. It is important to keep these distinctions in mind, lest activists or analysts assume that certain implications from the development of modernity or nationalism are universal. Critiquing the ostensible demise of secularism, for instance, when posing that analysis from the assumption that modernity automatically brought secularism in its wake, sets up a Western-shaped model of little relevance to colonial and postcolonial India. If we keep in mind the very specific outlines of the civil space as it emerged in postcolonial India, however, we keep the focus where it matters the most. The real outcome of the Ayodhya story that must be measured with care is the extent to which negotiating space in India's distinct civil society has disappeared. Only by understanding the extent of this change can we really understand the import of this attempt to make India Hindu.

# 10

## Communalism and Modernity

### RICHARD G. FOX

I START IN EUROPE, NOT INDIA; and with fiction, not anthropology.

Michael Ondaatje, in his Booker-Prize novel *The English Patient* (1992), tells us about Kirpal Singh, called Kip for short, a Sikh in the British Indian army, who has been seconded to sapper duty in Italy at the close of World War II. Kip reconnoiters for land mines and bombs left by the fleeing Germans. Then he defuses them. A man of the Orient, of a "race" defined as martial by its colonial masters, Kip has come to protect the West from its own modernity—to save it, that is, from a disenchanted technology so efficient it can blow people up into little bits that disappear; from a secular progress that has achieved the most advanced war yet known; from a monopoly capitalism that overproduces death.

Kip proceeds to save the West from itself until, one day, he encounters a bomb so powerful, so advanced—that is, so modern—it is beyond even his skills, and in any case, it has exploded over a Japanese city, not over any European battleground. Going AWOL, he points his motorcycle south, therefore India-bound, and rides it till he crash-sinks into the sea. The atom bomb, as Kip quickly realizes, gets dropped on the Japanese (not the Germans) because they are people of color (as we now say). Then Kip's life also explodes, as he forcefully hears the hidden message of Western modernity: that much of it is a white lie.

*I want to thank David Ludden, Victoria Farmer, Lise McKean, Sanjay Gupta, Howard Spodek, Judith Fox, and Dipesh Chakrabarty for their helpful comments.

## Western Modernity

Western modernity has in-built weaknesses and outright failures. Kip witnesses, in the Quaker sense, the explosion and fragmentation of the West. Its greatest failures and weaknesses, however, are dropped onto places like Japan and India, which serve the West as the quintessentially modern combination of scientific laboratory, prison camp, and managed-care facility. That's why, long before Kip, another Indian recognized the underside of modernity, or modern civilization, as he called it—only Gandhi in 1909 disowned it entirely, which is not my intention nor Kip's. (He survives to become a physician in India after independence.) But modernity and the West are what I am obliged to begin with, not communalism and India.

Because: communalism is not a problem of a backward and fettering Indian tradition, but of an advanced and undisciplined Western modernity. Neither is communalism a product of a powerful and manipulative colonialism in India; rather, it comes from a compromised modernity outside of the West.

Let me juxtapose the available approaches to communalism against the one I will play out:

One approach is that communalism is an excrescence of Indian tradition, an atavism or primitivism. This explanation tells us that we need only look to India's history to explain communalism: it is something culturally specific, like the caste system or the god Krishna.

A second approach is that communalism is a distortion produced by a manipulative colonial power in the interests of "divide and rule." Gyanendra Pandey (1990b) comes rather close to this position when he calls communalism a form of "colonialist knowledge." This theory also landlocks us in India, for it emphasizes the particular distortion of Indian society produced by colonialism.

This colonial conspiracy theory assumes, as does the first approach, that there are powerful forces behind communalism. That's why it's easy to combine these first two approaches into a third, hybrid argument, to the effect that there were primordial loyalties to sect and caste in India, which gained further power through their manipulation by the British, and so communalism gets produced.

Two other approaches emphasize communalism as an outcome of weakness rather than strength. Bipan Chandra (1984) and Partha Chatterjee (1986), in perhaps one of the few areas of agreement between them, represent communalism as a pathology of nationalism. They suggest that one early way of organizing a nationalist movement was to emphasize Hindu values and lifeways against British ones. This kind of nationalism established a progressive politics at the outset, but it soon came to fetter the nationalist movement and later had to be attacked by the Congress. Again, we are left with a solution that is India-specific.

I share Chandra's and Chatterjee's belief that communalism depends on weakness, but I disagree that the weakness resides in Indian nationalism or any other failure specific to India.

Ashis Nandy (1990) comes closest to my argument: for him, communalism also comes from weakness, but not a weakness in Indian nationalism. Rather, Nandy claims, communalism is a pathology or disease of modernity that attacks India under British rule. Nandy's explanation, however, conserves the problem on Indian terrain: this disease of modernity occurs in India as an outcome of the subcontinent's specific constitution. Modernity itself is not the source of infection, only the vector or carrier through which disease entered India.

Communalism, for me, is not a pathology of modernity; it is an inherent infirmity or constitutional weakness in it, bound to come out sooner or later wherever modernity has disenchanted the world. Communalism in India is only a local instance of this infirmity, which created other and different sore spots around the globe, earliest, as I said, outside the West, but now too finally in the West, as a new racism and cultural fundamentalism sickeningly erupt.

Max Weber saw the disenchantment brought into the world by bureaucratic rationality and capitalist alienation, but he did not see that in its wake would come new forms of enchanted identities, which, in the context of a disenchanted world, could only become "hyperenchanted," as I will clarify shortly. The symptoms vary: communalism in early twentieth-century India; slavery and then racism from the seventeenth century in the Americas; and cultural fundamentalism, as Verena Stolcke calls it, in a late twentieth-century Europe beset with immigrants from its former empire. The underlying infirmity, however, is the same.

Let me be a little more specific about what I mean by Western modernity. Then I'll do the same for communalism in India.

Modernity is the Enlightenment project—the Western Truths of alienated production and bureaucratic rationality and secular progress, and the associated practices of science, technology, humanism, productivity, development, and management. As it spreads over and out of Europe, modernity disenchants the world, to invoke again Weber's bittersweet notion, sweeping away the mythical and the supernatural, the familistic and the tribal, in favor of a functional, individualistic, contractual, secular, and impersonal social order. Weber's notion is of a puissant modernity exercising empire over preexisting loyalties, identities, and faiths. A bureaucratic state apparatus and a capitalist production system are the main agents that powerfully promote this disenchantment.

Just as we have gotten sick of waiting for Marx's revolution, maybe it's time to become a bit more critical about Weber's. Is it possible that modernity, as it disenchanted the old world, nevertheless created its own conditions for new enchanted identities, that is, new loyalties based on sect, tribe, or race, and came to depend on them for its own functioning? In that case, we might find that modernity creates and depends on seemingly contradictory identities and relationships, such as communalism in India—much as Greek democracy required slave labor.

## Communalism

At this point, I want to consider communalism. It clearly depends on enchanted sectarian loyalties, not on a functional, secular social order. But curiously, communalism develops in a world that has been disenchanted for some time. This situation tells us either that primordial forms of enchantment are not swept away by modernity or that modernity produces its own new forms of enchantment, ones that are more virulent and destructive because they ostensibly contradict modernity and yet function within it.

I can make my point sharper by introducing—and then modifying—Ashis Nandy's (1990) distinction between religion as an ideology, where it is used for political ends, and religion as faith, where, removed from politics, it is solely an entablature of belief. Communalism in India clearly depends on religion as an ideology, whereas religion in the West is, for the most part, a matter of faith.

I take exception to Nandy's typological treatment of this distinction and his failure to historicize it. We surely are not dealing here with cultural givens; rather there are histories behind religion as faith or religion as ideology.

What if both conditions grew out of modernity? What if religion as faith is the result of modernity at its most puissant and dominating? Disenchantment in triumph confines religion to the church and the home.

And, when religion threatens to break out again as a civil ideology, as it did with the Branch Davidians or the (Philadelphia) Move! community, the bureaucratic state has failed to co-opt and restrict it. The state then has recourse to premodern forms of repression: modernity has bombed and, in turn, the state bombs . . . others.

What if religion as ideology is the underside of modernity, and it shows up where modernity exposes its weaknesses, its white lies, earliest? That is, it surfaces in regions that received the Enlightenment project later and as a result of domination. So Gandhi and then later Kip see the underside of Western modernity long before European postmodernists and poststructuralists see the equivalent meltdown in their midst. This is not just an instance of the postcolonial guilt trip, personified in Rushdie's phrase, "the Empire writes back." In this case, the Empire telegraphs the West about its future (see Fox 1992).

## Hyperenchantment

Communalism in India is a local instance of how modernity—once it had disenchanted the premodern world—built new forms of identity.[1] Given the new means of communication and transportation that traveled along with modernity, these emergent enchanted identities were much more powerful and much more extensive (or "massive") and therefore potentially much more destructive and violent. For that reason, I like to call this a process of "hyperenchantment," much as we get hyperconsumption, otherwise known as greed, and hypermanagement, otherwise known as bureaucracy, with modernity. But unlike greed and bureaucracy, which achieved legitimacy in the capitalist market and in the welfare state, modernity depended on hyperenchantment yet it did not acknowledge it.

Communalism is the hyperenchantment of religion, racism is the hyperenchantment of biology, sexism is the hyperenchantment of gender, and ethnic prejudice is the hyperenchantment of culture. Each of these builds new forms of identity, allegiance, and loyalty that are formally inconsistent with modernity, but that are, in fact, its own creations. Each of these hyperenchantments has its particular geography and history—the Atlantic slave trade, India under colonialism, late-capitalist Europe—but

---

1. See below for the process by which a major institutional embodiment of modernity, the bureaucratic state, constitutes Sikh communal identity.

we must see their common origin and purpose: each of them creates social boundaries based on ascription rather than achievement, yet each of them sustains social orders (the family, the community) and occurs in institutional settings (the state, the workplace) ostensibly based on modernity.

Paul Gilroy (1993) has made this argument most strongly. He calls the black Atlantic "a counterculture of modernity." He criticizes Jurgen Habermas for developing a theory of the emergence of civil society, the modern state, and industrial capitalism that ignores "the histories of barbarity which appear to be such a prominent feature of the widening gap between modern experience and modern expectation" (Gilroy 1993, 49). Gilroy continues, "There is scant sense . . . that the universality and rationality of enlightened Europe and America were used to sustain and relocate rather than eradicate an order of racial difference inherited from the premodern era . . . it is hardly surprising that if it is perceived to be relevant at all, the history of slavery is somehow assigned to blacks [just as communalism refers to Hindus and Muslims—RGF]. It becomes our special property rather than a part of the ethical and intellectual heritage of the West" (Gilroy 1993, 49).

## Communalism in East and West

How will I make a similar argument in respect of communalism? First, I will show how what is called "communalism" in India and in the West are treated as wholly different. This separation permits the orientalizing of Indian communalism; it writes off the possibility that both India and the West come to it from a common cause. It also permits the West to adopt a nostalgic and celebratory view of communalism in its midst, at the same time, it condemns India for having it. I'll then go on to show, rather briefly, that current Welsh ethnic nationalism and Sikh communal militancy are susceptible to the same sort of analysis, namely, that they are responses to the weaknesses built into the Enlightenment project, and, especially, its major agency of social control. They respond to both the incompetence of the bureaucratic welfare (or postcolonial) state and its failure to disempower local governing elites. These elites then hyperenchant ethnicity or community, in resistance to that state and, initially at least, in keeping with their own rational, secular, and impersonal interests.

The first step in this inquiry into communalism is to make the case for taking up a scholarly location far beyond India itself. Scholars of India and

Indian scholars have allowed the communalism debate to remain on Indian terrain for too long (consider the many volumes, such as Das 1990c, Thapar et al. 1969, and K. N. Panikkar 1991, that restrict themselves to India). They suppose not only that India is where the phenomenon takes place, but also that India is the source of its explanation—the one exogenous factor sometimes admitted is colonialism. Some subalternists (see S. Sarkar, below) are even more remiss as they bury their heads in the soil of India in search of some presumed autonomous and authentic Indian populace. It's not surprising that their answer to the issue of communalism is too often to ignore it.

Understanding communalism must start, I think, by seeing it as a local terminus of a global web of relations spun out from Europe, and then by subjecting these relationships to a critical, historical analysis that "provincializes" (to use Dipesh Chakrabarty's 1992 phrase) them—that is, makes them appear as the parochial representations of a hegemonic Western culture rather than the grand Truths of history and all humanity.[2]

The first step in this parochialization is to show that the West has been more charitable to a recently emergent communalism in its own midst than to the form it takes in India. This communalism, coterminous with the total failure or growing incompetence of the modern bureaucratic state, is already deadly in Eastern Europe and periodically lethal in the West. Yet when modernity's weakness finally shows up in the West and we get the stirrings of hyperenchantment hereabouts, we "disappear" this condition. Only India, after all, has vicious communalism. Western scholarship and Indian nationalist scholarship have both accepted this pejorative definition of communalism in India, the only difference is where they place the blame for it. On Western terrain, however, today's blight of communalism, perhaps the initial version of what is full-blown in India, becomes the flowering of utopian spirit, and we treat as aberrant the periodic violence it produces. Burning Turks in Germany are supposedly sacrifices to a troglodyte Nazism rather than to a dead democratic secularism. Belfast gets called "the Beirut of Europe" in *In the Name of the Father* and thereby assimilated to the Orient. Branch Davidians become a "cult" not a "church," and cults, as we know, are affiliated with Eastern religion. In these cases, the bureaucratic state either completely fails at social control or it has recourse to premodern forms of repression and coercion.

2. By parochializing and historicizing modernity, we can hope to extract the worthwhile elements and discard the dross, whereas so long as it remains a received truth, it has to be taken as a package.

Let me show you just how separate and opposite the representations of Western and Eastern communalism are. I'll start with a small sampling of the excoriation of communalism of India. Most commentaries treat communalism as a negative, divisive identity (see, for example, Brass 1990). Pandey (1990b, 8) traces the term to W. C. Smith in the 1940s, who gave it this definition: "That ideology which emphasized as the social, political, and economic unit the group of adherents of each religion; and emphasizes the distinction, even the antagonism between such groups." By 1963, another Smith wrote even more negatively: communalism "is generally associated with a narrow, selfish, divisive, and aggressive attitude on the part of a religious group. The term 'communalism' as it is used in India today, refers to the functioning of religious communities, or organizations which claim to represent them, in a way which is considered detrimental to the interests of other groups or of the nation as a whole" (D. E. Smith 1963, 454). Bipan Chandra's (1984) definition emphasizes that communalism essentializes identity improperly: it associates, he says, the followers of a religion with common social, political, and economic interests. Pandey's definition (1990b, 6) is probably the most concise and nastiest: for him, communalism is "a condition of suspicion, fear and hostility between . . . different religious communities." Nothing surprising, except in all these efforts at definition, there is no attempt, no interest even, in linking communalism in India to anything anywhere else in the world.

And yet the term "communalism" or "communal" is in scholarly parlance elsewhere—otherwise why would we South Asianists have to constantly gloss our usage with the phrase, "as the term is used in India," at once an apology for boring the Western audience with India, an affirmation of India's difference from the West, and a claim to special scholarly authority over this difference (the last a false consciousness to the effect that we "control" this subject matter apart from "real world" conditions)?

The Oxford English Dictionary defines "communalism" as "the principle of the communal organization of society: a theory of government which advocates the widest extension of local autonomy." It defines "communal" as "of or pertaining to a commune" or "the Paris Commune" or "the commonality or body of citizens." There is a neutrality here, if not outright approbation, a resonance with the "commune," and with the utopian projects of the Paris Communards, the Shakers, the Oneida Perfectionists, the Owenites, the Hutterites, and the Amish, and others who thought spiritual husbandry depended on special communal living arrangements, separate from the rest of society. There is at least nostalgia, if not more, in the West for such intentional communities and loyalties. There is even social-science theory that these identities fill in the blankness of spirit, the vacuity, of modern life and supply the alienated citizens of modern states an otherwise missing sense of incorporation and "peoplehood" (that is, a group membership rather than an individual "personhood"). Pop-culture vehicles like the *Utne Reader* announce an emergent corporatism to replace the alienation of capitalism, and Professor Maybury-Lewis appears on television to advocate the wisdom of the tribal world as instructing us in a "New Tribalism." Similarly, New Age religions "crystallize" forms of spiritual communitas not really different except in longevity from sectarian communities in India.

The many programs for multiculturalism in the United States today celebrate a sanitized (and sanctified?) version of communalism, as they lock people into assumptions of cultural purity and homogeneity, sometimes based on race, other times religion, and still other times country of origin. Gilroy (1993, 7) warns us against the recent "tragic popularity of ideas about the integrity and purity of cultures." My daughter, who is adopted from India, refused to bring her "ethnic" food or "national dish" to an international day held at her middle school. My wife, mischievously resolved to be her WASP self, at least on this day, planned to send her off with lime Jell-O and Wonder Bread.

Such parody only acknowledges the nostalgia over community and the quest for reenchantment put forth in Western pop media and scholarship today. In the lead come social philosophers who have been labeled "communitarians" (Kymlicka 1989). Communitarians disown the individual freedom valued by both liberals and Marxists as illusory. They argue for a "politics of the common good," which derives from a community's standard of life and which dominates individual preferences (Kymlicka 1989, 77). Political power may be used to regulate social practices when the local community's way of life is offended, whether it be by pornography, homosexuality, or, one supposes, turbans (Kymlicka 1989, 87). Minorities, after all, must adjust their social practices to be inoffensive to community standards. Charles Taylor, Richard Rorty, and others who adopt a communitarian position try to dispose of criticism by allowing that some individual rights are basic and therefore protected from the "common good," but the question remains: who decides what is basic and what is superficial? Hindu nationalists, for example, argue that every religious community in India has a right to its own worship but must come under a uniform civil code in the interests of the common good. Muslims, however, regard the rule of religion over civil matters like divorce as a basic right. Professors Taylor, Rorty, and others who expect fair judgment to come from communities of common understanding need to recognize that the campaign for Hindutva and other communal militancies do not produce Solomonic justice.

How strange that what is evil in India is good in the West? New Agers, creationists, and neoconservatives wish to reenchant the West, but if they saw Indian communalism as proleptic rather than atavistic, they might recognize that only hyperenchantment is possible after disenchantment. They might see that nationalist chest-beating, multicultural stereotyping, sectarian soul-thumping, race-bashing, and gender-plundering are the major new forms of enchanted community—fables grimmer than Grimms'—likely after modernity proves its weakness.

## Welsh Ethnic Nationalism and Sikh Communalism

By comparing the Welsh to the Sikhs, I hope to establish that a similar pattern underlies these cases, namely, that local elites organize (hyperenchant) ethnic or sectarian communities in response to the incompetence of a bureaucratic state, which is a specific instance of the weakness of modernity. I will also employ an explanatory theory, first advanced to cover European ethnic nationalism, to explain Sikh communalism. Both substantively and theoretically, then, I make a case against seeing Indian communalism as unique, premodern, or colonial. Later, I will try to explain why the amount of violence and the role of religion differ in these two cases.

Back in the 1970s, the last time Europeanists cared about these matters, several theories of ethnicity and ethnic politics coexisted competitively. I choose to contrast two of them here. The theory of "internal colonialism," perhaps most closely associated with Michael Hechter (1975), argued that ethnic nationalist movements developed whenever there was an "ethnic division of labor." The Welsh, for example, represented an ethnic population that was excluded, by their ethnicity, from equal participation in the capitalist labor market. They were confined to certain jobs or restricted from others, and the lower overall wage they received because of ethnic prejudice constituted a form of "super-exploitation" (beyond the regular exploitation any wage worker underwent). Hechter's theory had some real drawbacks, including the fact that it took (Welsh) ethnicity as a given rather than a construction, that it assumed a mechanical relationship between economic exploitation and political consciousness, and that Welsh ethnic nationalism was proving to be strongest at the very time when the British government had launched massive development projects there to overcome existing regional disparities.

Another theory, never given an official name, could be called the "bureaucratic state" model (see Ragin 1979, n.d.; Fox, Aull, and Cimino 1978). Here, the rationality, management, secularism, and productivity associated with modernity is taken to be embodied in an institution, the bureaucratic state, and peculiar to it. The theory ignores individual state variations in the interests of analyzing the fundamentals of social control exercised or attempted by all modern states. States differ, of course, in many ways. Some are colonial, others are not; some have high levels of public legitimacy, others do not. There are also always contingencies of historical event and individual agency that make actual states "happen" in different ways. These differences represent a secondary level of variation, however. Stripped of these secondary differences, modern states share basic functions of social management, which they fulfill with more or less success.

In this theory, then, the factor underlying the creation of ethnic nationalism is the increasing intrusion of the bureaucratic or "welfare" state on local elites and their local governing institutions. Coterminously, the state intruded on family (child abuse laws, for example), working-class culture (restrictions on bars and alcohol), and the professions (licensing or certification of physicians and medical schools, as an instance).

These local elites had been left in charge of many local institutions in earlier times, when the state was less powerful. This theory supposed that ethnic nationalist movements were most likely or strongest when the state was most interventionist (including interventions through welfare transfers) and local elites most threatened. It also supposed that these movements would be more violent when the state was intrusive but not fully competent at local bureaucratic control.[3] As far as the organization of identity, it proposed that the relative strength of the state (or, said another way, the relative weakness of modernity) would dictate whether local elites worked with sectarian definitions or more secular cultural ones, like language, in defining their separation from the majority. A strong bu-

3. State intrusion, on the bureaucratic model, requires the state to take over institutional control at the local level by managing social life and executing social control bureaucratically. In my usage, "state intrusion" does not refer to the deployment of armed forces to put down or kill off local dissidence. Recourse to coercion and repression signals a failure of modern bureaucratic control.

reaucratic state would force or co-opt elites into lobbying on a secular basis. This is because bureaucratic states manage social control by creating a secular pluralistic politics, where lobbying efforts by interest groups (including ethnic or communal interest groups) lead to welfare transfers from the state. To lobby effectively with a strong state, however, requires meeting its expectations of what a legitimate basis of group organization is. The difference between Wales and the Punjab, as we shall see, is that the British state had the wherewithal to force/entice a secular, cultural ethnicity out of the Welsh, but the postcolonial Indian state, its modernity compromised by poverty and by the many conflicting interests groups that lobby it, could not.

I believe the bureaucratic-state theory makes good sense of the Welsh and Sikh situations. It shows how they share a great deal in the early stages of hyperenchantment. It also indicates how they end up at different points, in keeping with the greater competence of the British state to disreward the development of communal identity. Although I do not have space here to apply this theory to other Indian cases, the award of communal electorates to Muslims and Hindus by the British colonial state (M. Hasan, above) can be seen readily as an attempt to manage bureaucratically hyperenchantment in keeping with modernity.

Religion and religious institutions were the original locales for the formation of communal consciousness among both the Sikhs and the Welsh. In Wales, the nonconformist movement of the eighteenth and nineteenth centuries established the chapel as the central institution formulating and guaranteeing Welshness and Welsh religion against an intrusive English state and its established Anglicanism. From the chapel came the legitimacy and power behind a local elite, made up of clergy and local gentry, who controlled and staffed the educational system, the professions, and the trades at the parochial level.

The same sort of hyperenchantment begins among the Sikhs after the Akali movement and the subsequent Gurudwara Reform Act of the 1920s, only here the *gurudwara* (Sikh temple) rather than the chapel is established as a localized center of sectarian identity. The reform act "disestablished" the temple managers who had been British cronies and put gurudwaras under the control of local Sikh congregations. Gurudwaras, like chapels, then conserved Sikh identity, but they also became, again like chapels, centers of politics and consciousness-raising among the Sikh elite. Out of weakness, then, the colonial state subsidized local autonomy through community institutions it had itself produced and legitimated, the very institutions that were constructing hyperenchantment, much as the English had in Wales (and as the Canadian state used the Catholic church in French Canada).

Future Welsh political development saw the chapel left behind and a secular Welshness begin to develop around language and other cultural identities. This development began early in the twentieth century in response to the demands of an increasingly competent, modern British state. This state could require that competition for its welfare transfers be done on its own basis of determination—that is, in terms of lobbying on a secular, regional basis, and using ideologies of progress, development, and rationality. Local elites could use Welsh consciousness to support their demands for local economic and cultural development against the state, but the lobbying was on a national level and the terms of the competition were set by the national state. In the event, they won concessions—Welsh-medium schools, Welsh-language television, major capital inputs, and the like—but gave up political and sectarian community. I can end the Welsh case here, at the point where the bureaucratic state has co-opted Welsh identity and paid it off on its own terms. Variations in Welsh ethnic nationalism thereafter have to do with the decreasing fiscal capacity of the British welfare state to pay off local elites, which was the common experience of all welfare states from the 1960s. Elsewhere in Europe or the Americas, we could find instances—the Basques or the Quebecois, perhaps—where the bureaucratic state and its intrusive modernity proved weaker, where hyperenchantment is not so domesticated, and where separatism and even violence develop apace. Furthermore, if we regarded the importation of guest workers into Germany and France as an instance of state intrusion—the bureaucratic state's rational management of labor power against local supply—we could see how the new European racism or cultural fundamentalism is an even less co-opted response to modernity.

Sikh local politics similarly intertwined with sectarian identity, and at several points along the way to the present, a Sikh elite tried to safeguard its autonomy by mobilizing communal consciousness against the bureaucratic state, for example, in the Punjabi Subah agitation of the 1950s (where language thinly veiled sectarian demands). The major recent development in the Punjab was the introduction of the green revolution in the late 1960s, which rationalized agriculture and enhanced class contradictions on a massive scale. The green revolution further empowered a Sikh rural elite, who now turned to local political institutions, including sectarian identity, in support of their secular demands against the postcolonial state.

After 1974, the central government began to redefine the terms of trade between rural agriculture and urban industry in favor of the latter. That is, subsidies to agriculture, access to fertilizer, and other factors of production were controlled by the state in such a way as to force down the profits of agriculture in order to insure cheaper foodstuffs for urban labor. By the 1970s and early 1980s, Sikh landowners in Punjab began to lobby for state concessions on irrigation, fertilizer, subsidies, and other benefits to agriculture, along with a few sectarian demands. This lobbying was articulated, however, through a political party that was sectarian and local in character. The Indian state could not or did not defer to these demands; therefore, it could not domesticate the communal movement by turning it into just another interest group lobbying with the government. In fact, the state's strategy was just the opposite. It in effect recognized Sikh communalism by trying to exploit factional divisions within the sectarian movement. Hyperenchantment burgeoned under leaders like Jarnail Singh Bhindranwale, the sectarian demands soon overwhelmed the original secular ones, and the rest, unfortunately, is not yet history, but still with us at present: for the current peace in the Punjab comes from another breakdown in the Enlightenment project. The promise of personal liberty gets mistranslated into a state of pacification brought on by a premodern technology of repression and domination. (For UP parallels, see Z. Hasan, above.)

## Conclusion

What makes for our special horror at communalism in India? Is it the organization of community around a core set of values above and beyond individual preference? Charles Taylor would find that admirable; its absence, he and his fellow communitarians tell us, causes fractures in our society. Is it because social groups form on the basis of sectarian identity? If so, then why are we so nostalgic and even celebratory of Western utopian community experiments, most of which defined spirituality as a collective phenomenon? Is it because sectarian communities enter into politics? Not likely, given our familiarity with the many instances of this mixture in the U.S.: the Nation of Islam, Catholic Workers, B'nai Brith against defamation, Christians for Life. So our special horror must come from the violence and hatred that communalism in India creates. This violence and hatred, we should be mindful, comes from a very special and modern situation:

the failure of the bureaucratic state to co-opt or repress sectarian communities, its failure to make them into special interest groups lobbying for
state benefits, thus, its inability to turn them into relatively harmless crea-
tures, tamed by welfare transfers. This horror, then, is not to do with India
or with religion, but with the failure of India's bureaucratic rationality, of
its capitalist productivity, of its secular progress to overcome the hyperenchantment that they also create. Perhaps we will sorrow over the Indian
situation the more we see the growing incompetence of Western welfare
states to domesticate the cultural, racial, and gendered antagonisms within
our own midst. As Kirpal Singh came to understand and now we too,
some things the West dropped onto humanity were booby-trapped.

# II

# Writing Violence

PETER VAN DER VEER

NATIONALISM IS ABOUT THE LOVE of the nation, and this is often a self-sacrificing love, as Benedict Anderson (1983/1991, 141) insists. However, the dark underside of patriotic love is rooted in fear and hatred of the Other, and this is often also expressed in sacrificial terms. Contrary to what Anderson seems to claim, nationalism cannot be understood without these dark undercurrents, which are constantly repressed and represented as "anomalies." As we know, history is the grand narrative of the modern nation-state. Both in the colonizing and colonized regions of the world, it is a story of liberation from oppression. The dark stories of terror and bloodshed are only memorized to be interpreted as either necessary steps toward liberation or "incidents" that might as well be forgotten. The official history of Indian nationalism, as told in Indian education, is the progressive story of the liberation of the people from foreign domination, thus the narration of patriotic love. But there is also a subtext that tells the story of partition, of hatred and violence between Hindus and Muslims. The subtext is that of events, of incidents that are called "communal" in order not to let them disturb the text of the emergence of freedom, of a normal, liberated nation-state. They have to be given meaning by the narrative frame of the emergence of a liberal nation-state. It is not so much that their memory is totally obliterated, that they are repressed, but that they are memorized as fragments of a story of which the unitary, rational subject is the liberal nation-state. This narrative strategy in dealing with the past is also useful in dealing with the present. The suppression of civil riots by the state—often causing more victims than the riots themselves—is thus generally called a "return to normalcy." Civil riots are illegitimate and worrisome incidents that are "senseless" because they threaten not only the state's monopoly of physical force, but also its narration of its own legitimacy. Government, not violence, is therefore the term the state uses for its own employment of physical force.

Liberal government allows for debates in the public sphere and for the expression of the will of the people in elections, but, according to its own theory, it has to monopolize violence by suppressing violence between individuals and groups in society. In this way, the theory presupposes a distinction between the free expression of opinion and the use of violence, between speech acts and other acts. However, words can hurt and the role of insults, slander, rumors, and propaganda is quite important in the dynamics of civil violence. When slogans like *Babar ki santan: jao Pakistan ya kabristan* ("Babar's offspring [Muslims]: go to Pakistan or to the graveyard!") can be uttered freely in the streets and in writing, physical violence is just the next step and hard to prevent. More profoundly, when college and university teachers educate their students in a history of oppression by Muslims of Hindus, the discursive premises of violent acts have been laid. Finally, since words are often the main object and result of our studies—even when visual material also "tells the story"—we have to realize that the narrativization of violence in victims' accounts, police reports, media representations is what we have to interpret.

Briefly, in this chapter, I examine a limited number of narrative strategies in recent writings about "communal" violence in India. The issues I want to address are the following. First of all, I want to examine the ways some of these writings deal with the question of "religion" in Hindu-Muslim riots. Secondly, I want to examine the way social scientists write about "the state" when they interpret this kind of violence. Finally, I want to explore the role of narrativity in accounts of violence.

Let us start by looking at a fairly typical argument that derives its interpretive authority from the victims' stories, saying that what appears to be religious is not religious at all, that violence does not come from the people, but from the state. I take as a random example what the former BBC correspondent in India, Mark Tully, has recently written about the Ahmedabad riots between Hindus and Muslims in 1990. The summary of events is taken from Tully (1991). On April 3, 1990, a Muslim was stabbed to death in the old city of Ahmedabad. Within an hour of that murder, four Hindus were stabbed in separate incidents. A curfew was imposed in the immediate vicinity. Over the next three days, the trouble built up, with police opening fire to disperse groups throwing stones at each other. On the fourth day of the riots, April 6, twenty-three people were killed and seventy injured. Curfew was extended to the other areas of the city with a record of communal violence. Then, on April 7, a rumor swept through the city that the priest of the Jagannath temple had been killed. That created another round of violence, which was stopped by the army on April 14.

The violence was interpreted in the Indian press as caused by religious fundamentalism. Tully, however, spoke to poor Muslims in the city who blamed politics, not religion. In his view, most editorial writers don't speak to poor Muslims and so are easily carried away by the fashionable fear of fundamentalism. He ends his discussion of the Ahmedabad riots by writing, "the politicians and the press continue to blame the riots on religious fundamentalism. This may be convenient for the politicians and fashionable for the press, but according to the victims—who ought to know best —it's just not true. The victims of the riots don't even know the meaning of the word 'fundamentalism,' but they do know that it is not religion that divides them" (Tully 1991, 267). So, if it is not religion that divides Hindus and Muslims, what is it? In the view of the poor Muslims interviewed by Tully, it is the economy and politics that divide people into rich and poor, and the poor get killed. Tully elaborates this view by arguing that politicians make use of the underworld—heavily involved in bootlegging—to create riots between Hindus and Muslims whenever it suits them politically. Moreover, police and the underworld are hand in glove. Besides the political reasons for Hindu-Muslim riots, Tully looks at economic causes, such as large-scale unemployment due to the crisis in the textile mills.

It is a bit disingenuous of Tully to say that the political economy explanation of communal violence has escaped the Indian press, since they do not speak to the victims of riots, while he does. In fact, the political economy explanation is perhaps the most generally accepted at least in the Indian English-language press, and it cannot have escaped anyone in India. The question seems to be how that political economy is related to religion or, very simply, how Hindu-Muslim riots are related to socially structured economic inequality or class. Tully's sharp division between relevant political economy and irrelevant religion does not answer that question. Another interesting element in his account is the argument that the state—both politicians and police—is heavily involved in creating communal violence. Again, there seems to be a sharp dichotomy at work in this analysis, this time between state and society. In such accounts, the state becomes an external, autonomous agent, while, of course, the general feeling in India is that the roles of citizen and state official are highly conflated. Finally, Tully privileges the victims' narrative. The victims ought to know best, as he says. He does not attempt to confront the victim's narrative with that of the aggressor, nor with police reports. It is also important to note that the victims' account is taken after the riots had stopped. Tully does not seem to consider that this might have an effect on the narrativization of past violence.

It should be clear that it is not at all my intention to dissect and deconstruct Tully's text. It is a fine journalistic piece, which has considerable merits but cannot go very deep. I take it as an example of common-sensical writing about communal violence in India, which yields some important themes for further exploration. Let me reiterate these before I examine them one by one. The first is the role of religion. The second is the role of the state. The third is the role of narrativity in accounts of violence.

## Religion

Hindu-Muslim riots continued after partition, although on a very limited scale under the Nehru regime, until 1964. After that, there was an increase in rioting and, in the 1980s, a growing Hindu political factor in north Indian politics. A number of movements have tried to organize and strengthen radical Hinduism. Most attention has obviously gone to so-called "communalist" organizations, such as the RSS (Rasthriya Swayamsevak Sangh), but, in fact, mainstream parties, such as Mrs. Gandhi's Congress Party, also attempted to take advantage of it (A. Banerjee 1990, 46). In the 1980s, Hindu political activism became a formidable phenomenon on the Indian political scene, resulting in a revitalized Hindu-Muslim antagonism, which in its intensity resembled the pre-partition years. The developments of the eighties have been described at length elsewhere (van der Veer 1994b), but I want to draw attention to some aspects of its climax in 1992.

On December 6, 1992, two closely linked radical Hindu movements organized a rally in the north Indian pilgrimage center Ayodhya. One of these movements was the major opposition party in India, the Indian People's Party (BJP). It had won the 1991 state elections in Uttar Pradesh, a state of a hundred million people in which Ayodhya is located. The other movement, the World Hindu Council (VHP), had a leadership of Hindu monks and was Hinduism's largest transnational movement with branches in, among other countries, the United States, Britain, and Holland (McKean 1994, 1995). The publicly announced aim of the rally was to destroy a sixteenth-century mosque in Ayodhya that allegedly was built on the birthplace of Rama, one of the major gods in the Hindu pantheon. Despite this public announcement, the rally was allowed by the authorities; and under the eyes of the gathered press, and without much hindrance by the huge paramilitary police force present in Ayodhya, activists started to demolish the old structure, until, after a day of hard work, only rubble remained; and a question: Why didn't the police intervene? A high-ranking police officer told the press that the police could have easily intervened and prevented the demolition. However, they had not received orders to do so. Naturally, they did not get any orders from the state officials of Uttar Pradesh, since Uttar Pradesh was governed by the BJP, which was behind the demolition. The paramilitary forces, however, were under the direct command of what in India is called "the center," that is, the union government in Delhi. Why did the Center not act? Well, the story goes that India's prime minister, Narasimha Rao, was just taking a nap and, since he is a very old man, nobody would want to disturb him. When he woke up, the demolition had already proceeded too far.

I do not relate this story to show a certain indecisiveness on the part of the Indian government, since on the next day the Center did act very decisively by dismissing the governments of four states in which the BJP ruled. It put the leadership of the two movements (BJP and VHP) in jail for a few days and banned a few radical movements, both on the Hindu side and on the Muslim side. In that way, the union government reestablished the supremacy of the Congress Party, which had been seriously challenged by the BJP. Nevertheless, all these political actions did not prevent virtual civil war from breaking out in many parts of the country, in which thousands (mostly Muslims) were killed; nor did it do anything to prevent relations between Hindus and Muslims reaching their lowest point since partition. Very significantly, many Muslims had by now totally lost their confidence in the liberal state and its institutions, since politicians did not seem to be willing to protect the rights and lives of the Muslim minority.

This story is in many ways simple and straightforward. It shows the extent to which the so-called secular Congress Party and the institutions of the Indian secular state were complicit in the destruction of a Muslim sacred place by Hindu radicals. Clearly, the Congress Party stood to gain when the demolition of the mosque enabled it to dismantle the political power of its opponent. A story told in this way gives a narrative of demystification. It shows from the standpoint of the cynical, well-informed observer that what seems a religious conflict is in fact a political game. It is very important to tell such stories, since they show the political dynamics of conflictual situations, but it does not answer the question as to why this mosque could become an issue in the first place. To answer that more complex question, the game-theory is often replaced by a story that is perhaps even simpler or, at least, more gratifying to a Western audience. That story has it that the forces of secular modernity are up against the forces of religious obscurantism (otherwise called fundamentalism). Nehru and the successive leaders of the Congress Party up to Narasimha Rao who want to bring India into the world of modern progress are opposed by Muslim, Hindu, or Sikh extremists who dream of religious nation-states. That second story, dignified by forms of Weberian modernization-theory, is so much part of Western mythology (otherwise known as common sense) that it is constantly broadcast by the mass media when they report about world events in Egypt, Iran, Algeria, India, Sri Lanka, and other places. It is a story that is hard to question, since any alternative story is often felt to be a relativist attack on equality, liberty, and fraternity.

Nevertheless, it might be interesting to come to an alternative reading of the events in Ayodhya, as a step toward an understanding of what I would provisionally call "postcolonial modernity." The Hindu activists who destroyed the mosque, Prime Minister Narasimha Rao, and the millions who watched the events in Ayodhya on CNN, all of them are obviously fully modern, that is, they all participate fully in the material conditions and discursive practices of the modern world system of nation-states. There is no reason to say that any of them is caught in a time warp, "medieval or backward" as compared to others who are the bearers of reason and progress. However, their positions are different, because they are the product of different histories. I would argue that a singular, universal history of modernity does not exist, although I do accept that Western history since the nineteenth century has had an overriding importance in the making of the modern world. Since the nineteenth century, then, religion has been the site of difference on which the struggle for alternatives to Western modernity in many parts of the colonial world took place. In that very struggle new religious discourses and practices have emerged that, in a highly complex and unsatisfying move, have been placed in the category of fundamentalism—a term derived from U.S. Protestantism—precisely because they are different from the dominant secularized, privatized religious forms of the late-twentieth-century West. I prefer for at least some of these new discourses the term "religious nationalism," since they articulate discourse on the religious community and discourse on the nation.

The role that religion plays in nationalisms in many parts of the world is often felt to be an embarrassing anomaly for those who adhere to a Weberian modernization theory. Nationalism has to be connected to secularism to be truly modern and enlightened. "Politicized religions" threaten both reason and liberty. The post-Enlightenment urge to define religion as an autonomous sphere, separate from politics and economy, is, of course, at the same time also a liberal political demand that religion "should" be separate from politics. In that sense, Weber's theory and Nehru's political program share the same premises. However, it is precisely the effect of the normalizing and disciplining project of secular modernity that religion becomes so important as source of resistance. What is often forgotten in theories of nationalism is that the very forces of centralization and homogenization that are integral to nationalism always create centrifugal forces and resistances based on assumed difference.

Whatever the success of the political demand that religion should be apolitical in Western societies (and this is in fact an open issue), it is unwise to try to understand religious nationalism as a flawed and hybrid modernity (compare Fox, above). Rather, one should try to understand it, as one does with the nationalisms of Europe, as a product of a particular history of at least one century. That particular history is in this case one of Western colonial domination and to say this is not to blame colonialism for producing a flawed religious nationalism, since there is nothing flawed here, but to say that the postcolonial predicament can only be understood in relation to the colonial transformation of the societies I am talking about (see Freitag, above). What is regarded there as religion might be quite different from what modern Christians or modern liberals regard as religion. Surely, the question is how religious power—institutions and movements—produces religious selves and religious models for correct behavior. Part of what I refer to here is the socialization of religious identity and difference. As Talal Asad has observed, it is not mere symbols that implant true religious dispositions, but power ranging from laws and other sanctions to the disciplinary activities of social institutions. It is not the mind that moves spontaneously to religious truth, but power that creates the real and material conditions for experiencing that truth: this is what Augustine catches in one word, *disciplina*. Power does not only work positively in inculcating certain truth, but also negatively by systematically excluding, forbidding, and denouncing (Asad 1993, 34, 35).

Clearly, one of the sites in which religious selves are produced is the family, but one should not essentialize early socialization in the family (about which we know little) to the extent of forgetting, as the Freudians do, that the family is a part of a larger political economy. More in general, religious discourses and practices (symbols, rituals, disciplines) have to be looked at historically. To give a brief example: the meaning of the cow symbol for Hindus must have changed in the last decades of the nineteenth century when it became the focus of political action against both the British and the Muslims. What I want to argue is deceptively simple. Of course, a young Hindu learns that the cow is a goddess, but only a century ago he/she also learned that the cow is a symbol of a Hindu nation threatened by "outsiders." This is a very flat reading of that historical shift, but it is important to grasp that what constitutes Hindu identities has not remained the same over time, is not a transhistorical essence that can be salvaged from the sordid details of daily life.

This is not to say that the shift in the meaning of this symbol is one of the indexes that Hinduism has become "politicized" in the second half of the nineteenth century. Again, "politicization" and "depoliticization" of a separate sphere called "religion" is precisely the result of the Enlightenment discourse of modernity that assigns religious faith to the private domain as a matter of personal beliefs without political consequences in the public sphere. Religious discourse and practice in the political arena has come to be seen in the West as a transgression of what religion is supposed to be. There is a strong feeling that violent conflict between religious communities is a violation of the "original intent" of the founders of the religions involved or of God himself. "Real" religion produces harmony and tolerance and can thus be sharply distinguished from "politicized religion," politics in religious disguise. In important ways, this entire mode of thinking is the result of a specific historical development in Europe in the wake of the religious wars of the sixteenth and seventeenth centuries.

These interpretations of religion cannot account for the central role of power and violence in religious discourse as well as in religious expansion and conversion over the centuries. This is much more accepted in the analysis of Islam than in that of Hinduism. Tolerance is the prevailing trope in discourse about Hinduism and in that of the modern Hindu as well. There is a strong consensus from, say, people like Nehru to people like Advani that Hindu civilization is basically tolerant. The radical Gandhian thinker Ashis Nandy argues about Gandhi that "traditional Hinduism, or rather *sanatan dharma* was the source of his religious tolerance" (Nandy 1990, 91), and the VHP tells us that Hinduism is "a parliament of religions and the very antithesis of violence, terrorism and intolerance" (McKean 1992, 33). One of India's leading social scientists, Rajni Kothari, denies that

Hinduism is a religion. India is "a country built on the foundations of a civilisation that is fundamentally non-religious" (Kothari 1992, 2695). In the aftermath of the December events in Ayodhya, he argues that the BJP and VHP want to make pluralistic Hindu society into a "Semitic" religion, that is, an aggressive, organized, hegemonic monotheism like Islam. Kothari ends up by not only criticizing this "semitization" of Hinduism, but also by demanding from the Muslims that they give up "a religious approach to their survival in the present and prospects in the future" (Kothari 1992, 2698). In short, Hindus have a pluralistic, tolerant "civilization" and Muslims have a fanatic "religion" and the problem is that Hindus are becoming like Muslims instead of the other way around.

This consensus along the political spectrum in India is ultimately founded on a nineteenth-century construction of "Hindu spirituality" and, as such, a product of a collusion between orientalism and Hindu nationalism (S. Sarkar, below). The point here is that modern Hindus have come to interpret hierarchical relativism in Hindu discourse—there are many paths leading to God, but some are better than others—in orientalist terms, as "tolerance." This leads, in a universalist version, to an inclusion of all religions in the Vedanta, the spiritual "essence" of Hinduism in its philosophical form, as in the philosopher-president Sarvepalli Radhakrishnan's famous formula: "The Vedanta is not a religion, but religion itself in its most universal and deepest significance" (quoted in Halbfass 1988, 409). In the more narrow version of the VHP, this interpretation stresses "tolerance" within but excludes the religions that "came from outside" and are intolerantly bent on converting Hindus.

Power and violence are as crucial to Hindu discourse and practice as they are to Islam (Pinch, above). At the risk of repeating myself I want to emphasize that they express themselves not in a transhistorical way. Surely, if one wants to understand the religious imagery of Rama as it is appropriated by the BJP, one would not want to go back to the twelfth century. The emergence of the idea of "the rule of Rama" in Indian politics today does not show a continuity, but a significant rupture. The link between the Rama cult and divinization of kingship is not at all obvious in modern Hindu religiosity. It has to be inserted in the religious field through the gradual nationalization of religion, particularly in the middle class, and thus it has to be understood as a modern, ideological move. One has to realize that the BJP does not want to introduce Hindu kingship; indeed it is a "People's Party." It was Mahatma Gandhi who began to use the concept of *Rama-raj*, the rule of Rama. He used it interchangeably with the term for "self-rule" or independence (*swaraj*). In his view, "Ramaraj was not only the political Home Rule but also *dharmaraj* . . . which was something higher than ordinary political emancipation" and, distancing himself from notions of Hindu kingship: "Ramraj means rule of the people. A person like Ram would never wish to rule" (quoted in Lutgendorf 1991). Gandhi emancipated in a democratic move the notion of "the rule of Rama" from its "royal" aspects and, further, relates it to a "higher" utopian goal, namely the transformation of society by religious reform. Surely, it is not kings politicians are interested in, but a Hindu public of voters. The demand of the BJP for Rama-raj is a demand for rule by what is called "the Hindu majority." It is opposed to alleged privileges given to minorities and spe-cifically against pampering the Muslims. Rama-raj certainly also has a uto-pian aspect, a demand for clean, uncorrupted politics, jobs, and prosperity for every Hindu. This is obviously very similar to the messages of politi-cal movements in most parts of the world, while the minority complex of the majority is also not an exceptional phenomenon (Tambiah 1986). Both the secular state, as controlled by the Congress Party, and the Muslims are seen as "foreign" to Hindu India.

Power and violence in Hindu discourse express themselves most clearly in a politics of space (S. Sarkar, below). The appropriation of the Rama cult by Hindu nationalism signifies the articulation of sacred space and national territory. Communal violence in India has to be understood in the context of the politics of sacred space. Riots and rituals have come to be linked in the construction of communal identities in public arenas (Freitag 1989a). Ritual processions through sensitive areas often end in full-scale riots. Often one is confronted here with "rituals of provocation." A symbolic repertoire, derived from the ritual realm of animal sacrifice, is often used to start a riot: a slaughtered cow in a Hindu sacred space or a slaughtered pig in a Muslim sacred space. Riots often contest bound-aries between communities whose notions of public space are related to personhood and community. Irving Goffman speaks of "territories of the self," which can be invaded by specific rituals of violation. Therefore, the form of killings, the mutilation of bodies, the murder of adult men in front of their wives and children is so important not only in the creation of maximum terror, but also in violating the physical and moral integrity of the victimized community. In the anti-Muslim riots in Surat and Bom-bay after December 6, 1992, the victims were forced to utter *Jai Shri Ram* ("Hail to Lord Rama") before they were killed or raped (Engineer 1993, 263; S. Chandra 1993a, 1883). Public space itself is, to an important extent, constructed through ritual and rioting: one ends up having Muslim areas, Hindu areas, and mixed areas.

Local level politics is crucial in the dynamics of communal violence. However, one should not forget that nationalism is by definition a supra-local affair and that the spatial notion of national territory is crucial in it. This is a public space that is symbolic of the sovereignty of the Indian citizens. The Kashmir problem today, the Indo-Pakistan war of 1965, and the Bangladesh war of 1971 have kept the question of the loyalty of Muslim citizens to national sovereignty alive. This question is constantly revived by the Indo-Pakistan cricket matches and by the repeated demand by Hindu communalists that Indian Muslims better go to Pakistan. While this is of course well-known, what is less understood is the connection made between religious notions of sacred space and nationalist notions of territory. Hindu nationalists claim that there is an eternal unity of India, ritually constituted by pilgrimage networks. That motherland of all "sons of the soil" is a sacred space demarcated by Hindu shrines and sacred rivers and mountains. The ritual processions and the Ayodhya campaign of the VHP and BJP throughout India were aimed precisely at ritually constructing that notion of territory (Davis, above). Most of these processions, using an elaborate ritual repertoire, symbolically excluded Muslims from Hindu-Indian territory and were accompanied by widespread rioting, the massacre of Bhagalpur in Bihar in 1989 being the best known.

The political use of the Rama cult by the BJP and the VHP is not a "logical outcome" of a continuous, cultural narrative of Hinduism. It is the result of a series of particular, historical processes over the last century. The countryside was demilitarized in the nineteenth century with the result that militant sadhus and faqirs do not play a significant role in political violence anymore (Pinch, above). At the most general level, the great shift in the nineteenth century is the laicization of institutionalized religion. A lay Hindu and Muslim public had come to occupy a sphere that was previously the domain of sacred specialists. To put it very crudely, warfare between religious specialists was replaced by civil warfare between lay communities. To understand this shift one has to look at the creation of a public sphere in which communal representation, the politics of numbers and voting blocs, has resulted not in a "politicization" of religion but in a change in religious power and the nature of violence related to it.

## The State

In many accounts of religious nationalism, religion is merely a smoke screen, "false consciousness," "opium of the masses," and thus appropriately called "communalism." So let us go from dreams to reality. An important element in that reality is the state and, indeed, as many would argue, the state has done it. In the colonial period, it was the divide-and-rule politics of the colonial state that first created religious communities and then set them up against each other. By dividing Indian civil society along religious lines, the state had a perfect raison d'être—to ensure order. When it increasingly failed to perform that function, it was replaced by two nation-states, India and Pakistan, in which the rulers derived their legitimacy from "the people." The postcolonial state, however, inherited the divisions in civil society that had been created by the British. Politicians depend on votes, and the electoral process almost forces them to exploit the religious divisions in society. This is enhanced by the fact that the Indian state has increasingly turned to reservation policies for so-called backward classes in order to change access to education and government employment. This is part of what one might call the penetration of the modernizing state in civil society, and Ashis Nandy (1990), for example, sees this as a disruption of the social fabric of society and thus the cause of violence. In themselves, reservation policies should not affect Hindu-Muslim relations, but both in the Ahmedabad riots of 1985 and in the violence surrounding Mandal recommendations and the Babri Masjid controversy in 1990, the discomfort of the higher castes about reservation policies was rapidly transformed by Hindu politicians into anti-Muslim rioting, since it was regarded as a threat to Hindu unity.

The above summarizes part of conventional writing on both the history and the present state of communal affairs in India. One of the problems with it is its dependence on a political science boundary between state and society. The state is conceived as an autonomous entity, outside of society. It is seen as a structure of intentions, plans, policy-making that has effects on an external society. Timothy Mitchell has recently argued that this topological metaphor is misleading, since it tends to reify both state and society. He suggests that "the state should be addressed as an effect of spatial organization, temporal arrangement, functional specification, and supervision and surveillance, which create the appearance of a world fundamentally divided into state and society. The essence of modern politics is not policies formed on one side of this division being applied to or shaped

by the other, but the producing and reproducing of this line of difference"
(Mitchell 1991, 95). His argument is that the distinction between state and
society is not only an analytical tool that enables one to look at the centralizing role of powerful institutions that claim monopoly of legitimate
force. More importantly, "methods of organization and control internal to
the processes they govern create the effect of a state structure external to
those processes" (Mitchell 1991, 77). At the same time that power relations
become internal as disciplines, they appear to take the form of external
structures.

In the Indian discussion, the problems with drawing the boundary
between state and society often emerge in criticism of the role of the state.
Seemingly opposite positions about whether the state is too strong (authoritarian and centralizing) or too weak (fragile and ineffective) are often
taken by the same writer in discussions of the Indian state. For example,
Rajni Kothari has recently argued that "even the repressive character arises
out of the fragility of the modern state rather than its power, especially in
past-colonial [sic] societies. The more fragile and ineffective and powerless
a given state, the more repressive it becomes' (1991, 553). One would imagine that in order to be effectively repressive the state needs power. What
Kothari perhaps wants to say is that the state does not effect social change
in the direction he thinks desirable. One of the main reasons for its falling
short of expectation is the erosion of the autonomy of the state vis-à-vis
"dominant interests, be they the monied interests in the form of the private sector and its international purveyors trying to influence economic
decisions, be they the communal and caste interests seeking to hoodwink
the state for sectarian ends, or be they the more professional mafia interests that have spread themselves through criminalisation of the polity at
the grassroots" (Kothari 1991, 553). Again, the externality of the state becomes problematic as soon as interest groups to which the writer does not
belong become dominant.

An interesting element brought into the discussion of the state by
Kothari (and many others) is the international context. This larger context
reinforces the trope of externality, since the Indian state is part of a global
system that is often understood as even more truly external, indeed "foreign." Kothari argues that there is an "erosion of self-reliant statehood and
a growing hold over the state by transnational interests and their techno-
cratic agents" (Kothari 1991, 554). Again, there are interest groups taking
hold over the state, but now they are located mainly outside of Indian
society with, as collaborators within Indian society, the middle class. This
feeling that it is the middle class with its economic ideology of privatiza-

tion that sells a formerly self-reliant society out to world capitalism makes the Indian state seem as foreign as its predecessor, the colonial state. The connection is made with some rhetorical overkill by Jan Breman in his analysis of the causes of the anti-Muslim riots in Surat after the December 1992 events in Ayodhya: "For the flourishing condition of her informalised economy, so praised by the overseas lords of the global syndicate with its headquarters in Washington, the late-twentieth century version of the former East India and other foreign Companies, Surat has paid a high price in recent months" (Breman 1993b, 741). We seem to have come full circle: Communalism has been caused by the colonial state and independence has not liberated Indian society from this problem, imposed on it, as it were, from outside. Instead, it is perpetuated under the neocolonial conditions of late capitalism. The metaphor of "the foreign hand" is routinely used in India to summarize this and other kinds of externalizations of communal troubles. The state dissolves here to some extent in larger economic processes, although it is still the agent of privatization by giving subsidies and tax exemptions and by regulating labor and capital inputs.

In terms of modern political ideas, the state should be the instrument of the political will of the people. The modern state finds its legitimacy in the regular election of the people's representatives. One of the main difficulties here is that the modern state produces through a variety of social disciplines not only the modern individual as a disciplined social subject, but also the community as political agent. The modern state both individualizes and totalizes. This it does by means of classification, of which the census was one of the main examples in the colonial period. The modern Indian state has an elaborate system of communal representation and entitlements that produces both the modern individual and the modern community. It is a constant endeavor to try to determine where the boundary between state and society and also that between individual citizen and member of a community are, since this line is redrawn again and again in the very process of politics. The concept of the state, not as an external, essentialized agent, but as a series of often conflicting disciplines of ordering society, thus continues to be essential.

## Narration

I want to suggest that the projection of the state as external is an important trope in the narrativization of violence, to which I will turn now. The trope of externality in analyzing social processes is not only found among social scientists, but, as usual with social analysis, it is also part of common sense, of the language of ordinary people. To externalize "the state" as an outside force serves a more direct purpose here than is possible to discern in social science writings. The externality of the state shows up in everyday discourse in two different ways: first, in allegations that the state is in the hands of the rival community; and second, in suggestions that the state is outside the locality where people live their ordinary lives, as an altogether autonomous, malicious force that creates trouble.

If the modern political boundary between state and society were un-equivocally established (which it cannot be), it would not matter that someone was a policeman and, as a private citizen, a Hindu; but in reality, Muslims complain bitterly and justifiably that they are underrepresented in the police force and that the police force is an instrument in the hands of the dominant Hindu majority. They demand, therefore, to be represented as members of a group in law enforcement just as their separate commu-nity identity is recognized by law. On the other hand, Hindu nationalists argue vehemently that the Muslims are pampered by the state bureaucracy, because they are a vote bank for the politicians. The two antagonistic com-munities perceive the state as captured by the other community, without recognizing that the communities and their boundaries themselves are pro-duced by a variety of social disciplines that make up what we call the state.

The second, related, strategy in everyday discourse is to say that the state is a corrupted and corrupting force outside the community, defined as a local community, as neighborhood. Violence is created by politicians who control access to state licenses, jobs in the bureaucracy, educational opportunities. Their electoral strategies that make use of the state appara-tus are the cause of civil unrest and violence. If the people of both commu-nities would be left alone by this third force, the politicians and the police, there would be no trouble.

To call these externalizations of the state discursive strategies is not to say that they are false, since there is constantly ample evidence of the direct participation of the bureaucracy and the police (or the state) in civil vio-lence and, indeed, one of the great problems is that the police are prepon-derantly Hindu. The issue, however, is that the composition of the police reflects society; in other words, the police force is not external, but an in-tegral part of society. This explains why a Muslim in Surat who came to the police station to make a statement about the gang rape of his sister was told that his complaint could not be written down because it had happened three days ago (Breman 1993). Such an event cannot be easily explained by the fact that the police in Surat (and in many other cities in India) are heavily involved in underworld dealings, such as smuggling, bootlegging, prostitution, and illegal building activities, although it is true that they are. It bespeaks a strong anti-Muslim sentiment in the larger population shared by policemen. The cooperation of police and politicians with mafia dons of both Hindu and Muslim communities only enhances the feeling among the general public that the state is a corrupted force that cannot be trusted. In an interesting twist, it is the radical anti-Muslim Hindu movements that claim (and to some extent have the reputation) to be a scourge of the corrupted state. They, however, blame the corruption of the state on the Muslims. Police and politicians thus both partake in corrupt dealings with criminal elements in society (both Hindu and Muslim) and condone anti-Muslim violence as a method to do away with corruption. To say that this is hypocritical is probably not enough. It shows that the liberal state is not simply an abstract theory, but that its contradictions cause great moral unease, to which the anticorruption rhetoric of the Hindu radicals tries to respond.

The externality of communal violence is not only part of the narrative of that violence, but also part of the structure of narration itself. Paul Brass has recently suggested that the interpretation of virtually any act of violence between persons identified as belonging to different groups itself becomes a political act. Basically, what is recognized as violence and what is then categorized as communal violence is an interpretive act. Its acceptance depends on the power to establish truth. The interpretive process generates competing systems of knowledge about communal violence in the media, the police, the judiciary, and the social sciences. Communal violence is only communal violence when it is narrativized as such. A simple example makes the point. When a Hindu boy and a Muslim girl fall in love and decide to run off against the wishes of their respective families, this can easily be narrativized as communal violence: a case of abduction, which can set off a communal riot when that story is spread via rumor or the media. Of course, the opposite may also happen. Social scientists or activists may say that what seems a communal riot is in fact a dispute between two families.

Often these opposite interpretations feed upon each other in significant ways. They are textualizations of violent events that are open to a variety of interpretations, but, as Gyan Pandey (1990b) has argued in his book on the colonial construction of communalism, there are many versions of what happened, but only one version gets an official status and that version is often plotted along the lines of a master narrative. The official version is often established not so much by marginalizing other accounts, but by the systematic destruction of evidence, as witnessed by Gyan Pandey on a fact-finding mission in the aftermath of the Bhagalpur massacre of 1989 (Pandey 1990b, 563). Not only do the police records (historian's favorite source for studies of violence) ignore the massacre as much as they can, but one of the elements of violence itself is the destruction of evidence. Fire is a favorite instrument in communal riots to destroy the bodies of the victims and the houses in which they lived, so that the story of the victimized community can be more easily disputed. The fetishization of numbers in these disputes is often striking. It is impossible to deny totally that anything happened, but numbers play an important role in the calculus of how "serious" events were. Ironically, it is the politics of numbers in modern democracies that is a motivating force in these events in the first place.

One of the strategies to go beyond the official version is, of course, to listen to the victim's story, as Tully has done in his account and what Jan Breman has also done when he worked in Ahmedabad in the beginning of 1993. In the victims' stories, both in Tully's and in Breman's narration, one often finds the trope of "externality": the aggressors came from outside. Breman (1993a) interprets this as a sign that the victims want to stay on in the neighborhood and try to recreate the imaginary community of the neighborhood (see also Pandey 1991, 563). Only those who have been forced out without any hope of return sometimes allow themselves the story of the closeness of the aggressors: the neighbors did it. In the case of the Surat riots of December 1992, the story is a bit more complicated: the neighbors were from outside. According to Jan Breman (1993b, 739):

the victims, the next of kin of those who did not survive, and other eyewitnesses are unanimous in naming the "kathiawadi" diamond cutters, the UP "bhaiyas" and the Oriya "malis" operating the powerlooms as the main culprits. As if to confess their guilty implication in the pillage and massacre an exodus took place in the days immediately after the pogrom. On a single day 85,000 tickets were sold at the counters of the Surat railway station, an absolute record, and extra trains had to be brought in to ease the pressure on the overflowing platforms to a somewhat manageable level. Reliable estimates are difficult to come by, but altogether more than two lakh labour migrants are reported to have fled to their home towns and villages far away in order to distance themselves from the scene of pillage and massacre.

Breman points out that this massive exodus could not have been simply one of aggressors fearing retaliation. It is much more likely that these migrant workers themselves had become very afraid of the violent chaos in which they found themselves. There can be, however, no doubt that migrant workers were predominant among the mobs that attacked Muslims. Rather, the question is how "migrant" were they. Surat is a huge industrial agglomeration in which most of the workers come "from outside." In this kind of industrial city the distinction between "inside" and "outside" does not make too much sense anymore. Moreover, there is considerable evidence that middle-class inhabitants of Surat participated in the rioting and even more in the looting of Muslim-owned luxury stores. Sudhir Chandra has argued persuasively that in Surat the Hindu middle classes massively supported the need for violence to teach the Muslims a lesson they would not forget (Chandra 1993a, 1883). Nevertheless, the attempt to single out the migrant workers, those without a firm footing in the city's middle class, is perfectly understandable as an attempt to maintain the myth of Surat civic solidarity.

What is unfortunately lacking from most accounts we have is the narration by the aggressor. Breman (1993a) reports that the residents of Ahmedabad neighborhoods from which Muslims had been violently expelled resented his inquiries and did not want to say what had happened. Similarly, Hindus in Bhagalpur met Gyan Pandey's team "with studied silence, if not hostility" (Pandey 1991, 563). One could, of course, interpret this as a sign of shame, but I do not think that would be correct. In fact, there are often clear signs of pride that express themselves in the taunting of the victimized community. Provocations and humiliations continue after riots. When I visited Surat in May 1993, Muslims told me that after the riots they were constantly humiliated in the streets as "cowards" who could not protect their families. This had only stopped after the bombing of several buildings in Bombay in April and May 1993. One could say that the aggressors have less need to bring their story to the outside world, while the story is one of the few resources that victims have left. This is nicely captured by the title of Veena Das's essay on the victims of the Delhi riots of 1984: "Our Work to Cry, Your Work to Listen" (1990b).

Obviously, the aggressors would also be careful about openly telling their story to outsiders for fear of retaliation. There is a self-perpetuating element in this violence: the need for revenge on the part of the victimized community, which is only too well understood by the aggressors. According to the logic of communal violence, only revenge can salvage the honor (izzat) of the victimized community, which becomes truly inferior if it is unable to avenge itself. Veena Das (1990b, 387) reports that the male victims of the anti-Sikh riots in Delhi in 1984 constantly talked about their loss of face and their fear of their own desire for vengeance. They actually wanted to move away from the area because of the pressure to regain self-esteem by revenge.

The story of the aggressors thus has to be inferred from public statements about the other community. Recurrent themes here are that Muslims are not loyal to India, since they do not fully belong; their loyalty is to powers outside of India, primarily Pakistan, but also the oil-producing countries of the Middle East; furthermore, they are a threat to the Hindu community, since their religion prevents them from observing family planning and allows them to marry four wives, so that their number grows much faster than that of the Hindus. A related theme is that Muslims try to induce Hindus with money to convert to Islam, a "dirty" religion in which the cow is sacrificed and eaten. Muslims are also pampered by the state, because they are united as a voting bloc for the Congress Party, while Hindus are divided and thus discriminated against in their own country. Muslims have to realize that they are second-rate citizens as long as they are Muslims, but they can redeem themselves by returning to the national creed, Hinduism. These stories are often related to a precolonial past of Muslim hegemony in which Muslims oppressed Hindus.

These stereotypes can be found in all kinds of combinations, but they do not give direct motivations for violence besides the general one that Muslims have to be taught a lesson, so that they will know their place. They form a general narrative for condoning violence or even incitement of violence, as in the speeches of radical leaders like Sadhvi Ritambara. The direct causes of violence are extremely variable. The riots in Bhagalpur and Surat, to which I have been referring in this chapter, were immediately connected to the Ayodhya affair and thus directly caused by the campaigns orchestrated by the VHP and BJP. While these movements can be said to be directly responsible for the widespread kilings, their more fundamental impact is that the general narrative of Hindu-Muslim relations in India is perhaps not drastically changed, but has become more and more acceptable for public expression in wide sections of the Hindu population. Again, words do matter as does the way they are expressed.

## Conclusion

Violence is in my view a "total" social phenomenon. As Marcel Mauss explains in *The Gift* (1974, 76), "these phenomena are at once legal, economic, religious, aesthetic, morphological and so on." It is interesting to note, however, that in modern society, this total fact is discursively cut up in different pieces. The economic and political pieces constitute the real elements, while the religious is relegated to the unreal. As I have argued, this depends, to a significant degree, on a discursive construction of Western modernity, in which a modern construction of public and private makes religion a private matter of the individual. Something similar is also true for the way modern power results in the drawing of a boundary between state and society. Unlike religion, however, the state comes to be seen as a very real, but external agent whose actions impinge on society.

It is important to see how closely social science discourse follows common discourse in the narration of violence. The trope of externality is also used by victims of violence, but in a very functional manner, namely to pacify communal relations on the local level. To say that it is the changing economy or the changing maneuvers of politicians or the changing tactics of the police functions as an externalization of violence that is endemic among the common people themselves. It seems to be difficult to regard religion as an external, historical force like the state. Religion makes itself appear as a habit of the heart, the hard core of a community's identity, as a thing that cannot change and is nonnegotiable. To say that the violence is religiously motivated makes it seem inescapable, although, definitely, we know that religion does change, that religious institutions lose functions over time and, sometimes, disappear. But religious discourse tries to deny historical change and derives its power to an important degree from its success at doing so. Indeed, in that sense, religion is ideology, but it does not hide class dominance; it hides its own history, its own dependence on social movements, institutions, and political economy.

There is no true story of violence. Violence is a total phenomenon, but it comes to us as a total fragment (Pandey 1991). Something terrible has happened and there is no plot, no narrative, only traces that lead nowhere.

# 12

# Indian Nationalism and the
# Politics of Hindutva

## SUMIT SARKAR

## I

MY CHOICE OF TITLE has not been entirely innocent, for its evident conventionality seems to indicate a simple and all-embracing dichotomy that my argument will seek to undermine. Though it is true that, in South Asian politics, a polar contrast between national and communal politics has been assumed often enough since the 1920s, more complicated patterns of affinities and distinctions emerge when we consider majoritarian communalisms. Claiming to represent both a communal population and a nation—Hindus in India, and Muslims in Pakistan and Bangladesh—majoritarian movements have appropriated the mantle of authentic nationalism. In the aftermath of December 1992, however, we need to look at the relationship between nationalism and communalism more closely.

Problematization has to go further, however, into a more basic questioning of the assumption that Indian nationalism and Hindu and Muslim communalism have comprised the entire meaningful world of political action and discourse. Such an assumption involves an uncritical acceptance of ideological claims by nationalism and communalism, which have tried to homogenize a variety of differences—of region, class, caste, and gender—through elision of conflicts and power relations conceived as internal to the community being constructed thereby. Even radical historiography has seldom questioned the absolute priority of the anticolonial struggle, while emphasizing the role within it of organized class struggle or autonomous subaltern initiatives. Elision has been most powerful in respect of caste, which has figured remarkably little in general historical reconstructions of modern India. Yet it is precisely this dimension that has shot into unexpected prominence in recent days, with Mandal confronting mandir and a backward-dalit electoral combination halting the advance of the BJP in Uttar Pradesh state politics.

This chapter attempts a preliminary exploration of the ways that questions of caste—more precisely, lower-caste aspirations—have been handled in the constructions of Hindutva and Indian nationalism. Even a brief glance reveals major difficulties of incorporation and points to the presence of other histories not neatly encapsulable within narratives of anticolonial nationalism or religious communities, which dominate historiography. Only very recently have a few efforts been made to explore the interrelations between such partially autonomous histories without postulating an a priori normative primacy of the nationalist, or anticolonial, "mainstream" (Omvedt 1993, 1994). The current Mandal-mandir dichotomy suggests that the construction of homogenized Hindutva should be considered in part as an effort to respond to and counter pressures from below in the form of lower-caste aspirations. One needs, perhaps, to recuperate and extend some aspects of the logic of the early *Subaltern Studies* scholarship (Guha 1982–89), which has been largely abandoned by many of its present stalwarts (S. Sarkar 1994, and forthcoming). A few concluding remarks would be warranted, then, about the intellectual assumptions that have sustained the relative silence I am trying to disrupt—a silence that still gives a title like mine a deceptive aura of naturalness.

## II

The enormous overlap in personnel, assumptions, and symbols between mainstream Indian nationalism and Hindu communalism is too obvious to need much elaboration. One can think of the "Bande Mataram" hymn-cum-slogan, central to much anti-British patriotism and at the same time a Hindu rallying cry, at least in Bengal, during confrontations with Muslims. (I recall hearing it used in that way during a Calcutta riot in the winter of 1964–65.) A more dramatic example would be the murder of the Mahatma by Nathuram Godse: both these protagonists in that total confrontation of January 30, 1948, could in some senses be called nationalists and pious Hindus, and for both Rama was a central icon. Nationalism and communalism, again, far from being definite and stable signifiers, can quickly change and even reverse their signifieds as one crosses the Indo-

Pakistan border: Muslim separatism or communalism, pejorative terms in
India, become, in Pakistan, laudable nationalism, with a reverse process
operative with respect to Indian and Hindu.

Nationalisms grounded in religious identity have been hardly uncommon in history: one thinks of Iran today, Ireland, or even the concept of
"God's Englishmen" in the making of patriotism in Protestant England. It
is possible, therefore, to speak of Hindu or Muslim nationalism in place of
the obviously pejorative communalism, provided one does not go on from
there to make the historically absurd assumption that nationalism itself is
somehow laudable (or always harmful to the same extent) and that distinctions cannot be drawn between various types of nationalisms in terms
of objectives and consequences. One way in which the ground for such
distinctions is being undercut today is through the argument that communalism has been a mere labeling exercise that secular nationalists took
over from colonial knowledge and used pejoratively to brand community
identities, which perhaps need rather to be valorized as counterpoints to
the tyranny of the modern, post-Enlightenment nation-state (which is one
way of understanding Pandey 1990b). I am afraid I find such an application
of Edward Said both politically and academically disabling, particularly in
today's context.

Distinction is necessary, above all, in the context of the Hindutva
logic that identifies the RSS-VHP-BJP combine uniquely with the Hindu
community, and then, through a specious majoritarian argument, transforms it into the authentic voice of the nation. What this majoritarian
argument deliberately ignores is the contradiction between the notion of a
permanent majority, based solely on the census definition of a Hindu, and
the democratic determination of changing electoral majorities and their
governments. Making appropriate distinctions becomes logically possible,
once, in the specific conditions of a multireligious subcontinent, communalism is not taken to mean (as it often loosely and inconsistently has
been) the construction, assumption, or deployment of more-or-less homogenized community identities claiming a religious basis. Developed
communal ideology needs to be distinguished even from the politicization
of such identities through demands for quotas in jobs or seats, or the use
of religious appeals in election campaigns. These have often contributed
massively to communal developments but should be considered necessary,
rather than sufficient, conditions. For a full-fledged communal ideology —
as distinct from occasional, usually localized clashes between groups of
Hindus and Muslims, which could have an enormous variety of causes and

did not generate conceptions of countrywide, mutually opposed blocs before the late nineteenth and early twentieth century—two further assumptions seem indispensable. Conflict with a similarly conceived community Other has to be assumed to be both inevitable and overriding in the sense of being more crucial than other tensions or projects (such as ending British rule, before 1947, or alternative programs of national economic development and social transformations, after 1947).

A genealogy of Hindu communalism, in other words, would have to think in terms of two historical transitions. The first is a transition from a relatively inchoate Hindu world, without firmly defined boundaries, to the late-nineteenth-century construction of ideologies of unified Hinduism, in the context of integrative colonial communication, administrative, and economic structures. The second transition, roughly datable to the mid-1920s, is a move in some quarters toward an aggressive Hindutva postulated usually upon an enemy image of a similarly conceived Islam.

Distinguishing among Indian, Hindu, and Muslim nationalisms—rather than simply between nationalism and communalism—is helpful also because, in the specific conditions of subcontinental religious, linguistic, and cultural diversity, Indian nationalism did have to develop thrusts or tendencies (not more than that, and often reversed) that can be seen to be contradicted by the ideology and practice of Hindutva. Indian nationalism had to seek a fundamentally territorial focus, attempting to unite everyone living in the territory of British-dominated India, irrespective of religious or other differences. Ways of building or maintaining that unity included efforts to create public spaces where religious difference would not be allowed entrance, and also included conceptions of composite or federal nationalism with religious communities as its building blocks. Thus the early, moderate Congress forbade the raising of any issue to which delegates from any religious community strongly objected, while in Bepinchandra Pal's ideal of composite patriotism, "Hindus, Muslims, Christians and tribals would each preserve distinctive features and by cultivating them contribute to the common national life" (Pal 1903). By contrast, thoroughgoing projects of agnostic secularization remained a relatively minor strand. "Secular" in India, in other words, has meant, principally, "anticommunal," and this makes the argument that "hard secularists" are somehow responsible for the growth of communalism seem both curious and tendentious (Madan 1993; Pandey 1990a).

Territoriality remains the starting point in developed Hindutva ideology, as epitomized above all in V. D. Savarkar's *Hindutva—Who Is a*

*Hindu?* (published in 1923), in which *pitribhumi* (fatherland) is immediately equated with *punyabhumi* (holy land), and the latter is unambiguously
identified with "the cradle-land of . . . religion" (Savarkar 1923, iii, 95).
Only Hindus, therefore, can be true patriots, not Indian Muslims or Christians, with their holy lands in Arabia or Palestine. The edge of the entire
argument is clearly directed against Indian Muslims and Christians, and
not against British rulers, who never claimed India to be either fatherland
or holy land. The logic proceeds here, as in the entire subsequent discourse
of Hindutva, by using "culture" as an apparently innocent middle term in-
vested with Hindu religious meanings and associations. A generation later,
M. S. Golwalkar expounded the distinction with enviable clarity:

The theories of territorial nationalism and of common danger, which formed the
basis for our concept of nation, had deprived us of the real and positive content
of our real Hindu nationhood and made of the freedom movements virtually anti-
British movements. Being anti-British was equated with patriotism and nationalism. This reactionary view has had disastrous effects upon the entire course of the independence struggle, its leaders and the common people. (Golwalkar 1966, 142–43)

Two important corollaries, in significant contrast, that could follow
from Indian nationalism's unificatory project were an orientation toward
the future (the concept of a nation that had to be built, that was still in
the making, as implied for instance by the title of Surendranath Banerji's
autobiography; and a rejection or softening of hard, closed, impenetrable
identities. Gandhi's philosophy of change of heart through *ahimsa* (nonviolence) for instance, involved not just nonviolence but an assumption that
human communication was possible across even the sharpest of divides,
and so efforts should be made to combine change with avoidance of total,
violent ruptures. Gandhi tried to apply this philosophy to a whole range
of contradictions: British and Indian, Hindu and Muslim, propertied and
propertyless (in the concept of zamindars and capitalists as "trustees"),
high and low castes, men and women. There are manifold problems here
for anyone who is not a Gandhian, yet perhaps a point can be made even by
an unbeliever about the greatly varied degree of relevance of the strategy
with respect to specific kinds of tensions. The Hindu-Muslim relationship,
it seems to me, stands on a significantly different level from the others, in
that it alone does not point toward any generalized structure of domination, as contrasted to colonial rule, caste hierarchy, class exploitation, and
gender inequality. It is not, therefore, accidental that leftist commentators—otherwise often sharp critics of Gandhian nonviolence and change of

heart as ultimately fitting in with the interests of dominant groups—have generally been warm admirers of Gandhi's ideal (if not necessarily always of his specific methods) of achieving a "unity of hearts" among Hindus and Muslims even at moments of maximum communal strife—an ideal for which Gandhi sacrificed his life. And the court statement of his murderer, Nathuram Godse, a self-acknowledged disciple of Savarkar who had had his early training in the RSS, indicates with equal clarity the nature of the divide. Godse rejected Gandhi's philosophy of ahimsa, not on the ground of its possible inefficacy and utopianism (the traditional leftist critique), but because it "would ultimately result in the emasculation of the Hindu Community" (Godse 1977, 7). Emasculation—a word with significant resonances.

Yet the logical distinctions I have been emphasizing have been blurred repeatedly. It has often seemed important for even the most secular nationalists to derive sustenance and authenticity from an image of subcontinental unity (or what is called "unity-in-diversity") extending back into a glorious past. Because, except for brief periods of imperial unity (often excessively valorized), this image is difficult to substantiate at the political level, the tendency has remained strong to assume some kind of cultural or civilizational integration as the ultimate foundation of nationalism. And then it becomes difficult—even for a Nehru, writing his *Discovery of India*—to resist the further slide toward assuming that that unity, after all, has been primarily Hindu (and upper-caste, often north Indian Hindu at that). The slide was made easier by the undeniable fact that the bulk of the leading cadres of the nationalist and even leftist movements have come from Hindu upper-caste backgrounds. The harsh words of a contemporary dalit writer thus indicate an important dimension, exaggerated and unfair though they might sound to many:

The national movement was turned into a form of historical mythological movement and ancestor worship. . . . Those who . . . did not want society to be democratic started eulogising history, mythology and ages gone by, because in those mythological and historical ages, they were the supreme victors and leaders. . . . People such as Phule, Agarkar, Gokhale and Ranade who talked about misery and servitude of Shudras and Ati-Shudras . . . were declared enemies. . . . The intelligentsia won, they succeeded in turning the Indian liberation struggle into a lop-sided fight, and in reducing the other movements to a secondary status. (Baburao Bagul, quoted in Omvedt 1994, 15)

The blurring of distinctions became qualitatively more powerful after 1947, and most blatant of all after the withering of Nehruvian hopes of sustained

independent economic growth, socialistic change, and populistic allevia-
tion of poverty. Transformed from inspiration for mass awakening into the
official ideology of an increasingly bureaucratized and centralized nation-
state, Indian nationalism has become more and more of an icon, with predominantly, though not invariably, Hindu lineaments. The dividing line
between national and Hindu communal assumptions and values became
increasingly porous, to the great advantage of Hindutva political forces.

## III

The differential ways in which caste has entered the discourses of nationalism and Hindutva have certain paradoxical features. Mass anticolonial
struggle obviously required the mobilization of large numbers of lower
castes and dalits, and it was hardly accidental that the emergence of Gandhian nationalism roughly coincided with the incorporation of issues of
caste discrimination, in however partial and tokenistic a manner, in the
Congress agenda. Gandhi made ending untouchability one of the preconditions for the realization of his "Swaraj within one year" promise of 1921,
and after the confrontation with Ambedkar in 1932, harijan welfare became
for some years his principal activity. Nor was there any logical difficulty in
incorporating anticaste principles within programs of anticolonial nationalism in both its liberal and leftist forms. Hereditary caste inequality clearly
contradicted both bourgeois-liberal principles of citizenship and socialist ideals of thorough egalitarianism. The characteristic left programmatic
combination of anticolonial with antifeudal revolution could incorporate
caste among its targets as a presumably feudal relic. Yet caste, along with
gender oppression, all too often became issues of social reform less immediately relevant than basic questions of political independence or class
struggle. They could be postponed, would be more or less automatically
resolved with changes in political and economic structures, and might be
divisive from the point of view of anti-British struggle. The limitations
of orthodox Marxism, on the whole dogmatic and economistic, evidently
played a critical role here, blocking theorization from the realities of left-
led mass action in which lower castes and dalits were often very prominent.
R. P. Dutt's pioneering and still valuable Marxist study of modern Indian
history and society did not include caste among its index entries, and contained only three references to "depressed classes" (R. P. Dutt 1940).
    Caste, in significant contrast, was both vital and embarrassing for

projects of Hindu unity and Hindutva, and so, to some extent, has been gender. For some two thousand years, for instance, the characteristic high Hindu dystopia of *Kali Yuga*—the last and most degenerate of eras that is always imagined as the present—has firmly located the sources of evil in the insubordination of Shudras to upper castes and of women to men. It has been next to impossible to think of Hinduism without some form of varna and jati. The votaries of Hindutva have tended to come in the main from high castes quite self-conscious about their status privileges, and yet the conflicts that tended to emerge from hierarchical rigidities needed to be resolved or kept in check if unity was to be achieved. Evasion through postponement, as an admitted evil that would be remedied in the future, was thus more difficult. There were, rather, uneasy oscillations between volubility and deliberate silencing through diversion, between projects of limited, integrative, Sanskritizing reform and aggressive assertions of hierarchy. The ebb and flow of lower-caste pressures seem to have played a critical role in these variations.

A convenient entry point and focus is provided here by the prominence of the concept of *adhikari-bheda* in mid- and late-nineteenth-century discourses leading up to the construction of unified notions of Hinduism, particularly in Bengal, which I take up here as a brief case study. Adhikari-bheda (literally, "differential rights, claims, or powers") conveyed the notion that each jati (caste) and sampraday (sect) has its own rituals and beliefs, in a unified, but hierarchically differentiated structure within which each knows its appropriate place. Catholicity could thus be combined with conservative maintenance of norms appropriate to a group's location within the overall hierarchy. Louis Dumont's structuralist analysis comes very close to this basic Hindu-conservative principle through the much-quoted statement that "Hinduism hierarchizes and includes." What needs to be emphasized, however, is that classificatory devices like adhikari-bheda are not just innocent objective descriptions, but projects of specific groups for acting on social reality: having some relationship with it if they are at all effective, but never of a one-to-one, purely reflexive kind (Duby 1980, 8–9). The historian needs to explore their undersides, as E. P. Thompson for instance did with concepts like paternalism and deference in eighteenth-century England (Thompson 1991).

Thus adhikari-bheda, looked at from below, may point toward a relative openness to the emergence and survival of a multitude of practices and beliefs. Such catholicity may have been more or less inevitable under premodern conditions of undeveloped communication integration within a set of traditions—a "Hindu" world without firm boundaries, not yet "Hinduism"—which did not have an unitary textual base, centralized priesthood, inquisition, or consistent state backing on a subcontinental scale. Diversities, in other words, were not necessarily perceived as building blocks in a Hinduism unified through a single, hierarchically differentiated order as is indicated by the difficulties modern observers have faced in classifying the Kabirpanthis or the Bauls, say, as Hindu or Muslim.

Adhikari-bheda, as a formal doctrine, seems to have emerged in the seventeenth and eighteenth centuries as a Brahmanic way of accommodating and keeping within proper limits differences in ritual, belief, and philosophy (V. Bhattacharji 1948, 287–88). By the late-nineteenth, adhikari-bheda tended to signify not fluidity and openness, but neat compartmentalization, the drawing-up of definite boundaries, and the arrangement of differences in a fixed hierarchy, to the obvious advantage of established power relations of caste and gender. Symptomatic here, perhaps, was a definite efflorescence in many late-nineteenth-century high-caste Bengali tracts, plays, and farces of the Kali Yuga dystopia of breakdown of proper boundaries, with Shudras and women on top (S. Sarkar 1989, 1992). Education and jobs had now become theoretically accessible to all, and there was much talk and a few concrete measures in the direction of what was called *stri-swadhinata* (emancipation of women). And so the Kali Yuga myth flourished in some quarters for at least a couple of generations after the entry, under colonial auspices, of clocks and modern notions of linear time, which could have been expected to erode a construction grounded in assumptions of cycle time.

The social contexts of the emergence of precolonial notions of adhikari-bheda and Hindu unity (like for instance the high Hindu conception of *smarta-panchapasana* (the equal validity of devotion to Ganesh, Vishnu, Shiva, Shakti, and Surya) remain unexplored (Bandopadhyay 1960, chap. 4). But we might speculate that the communicational linkages relevant and necessary for such conceptions would tend to be predominantly Brahmanic: learned contacts during pilgrimages, the wanderings of ascetics, centers of religious and philosophical discussion like Vrindaban, Nabadwip, or some south Indian temples, the courts of princes and zamindars dispensing patronage to Brahman pandits and offering sites for debates on such theological matters. Biographical data about nineteenth-century leaders like Dayananda Saraswati or Ramakrishna Paramhansa occasionally provide glimpses of this older world. Dayananda Saraswati's early years were full of acrimonious debates with orthodox Brahmans about the meaning of sacred texts (*shastrartha*), carried on in Sanskrit and organized by zamindars, merchants, and bankers of western United Provinces. The virtually unlettered Ramakrishna's religious training came from a succession of holy men who had passed through Dakshineswar on their way to the pilgrimage of Gangasagar (Jordens 1978; S. Sarkar 1992). Colonial rule both stimulated such unificatory tendencies and provoked them into existence through its exploitative and aggressive presence. Communications were qualitatively transformed through print, modern education, and new transport facilities. Orientalist scholarly constructions of Hinduism as being grounded essentially in ancient sacred texts like the Vedas and the Upanishads (Breckenridge and van der Veer 1993), missionary polemics denigrating Hindus for the absence of indispensable elements of true religion, and incipient patriotic sentiments, all contributed in diverse ways to unificatory projects. And, crucially, the operations of the census from the 1870s onward insisted on firm definitions and boundaries for purposes of enumeration and control through classification. For instance, in 1911, Census Commissioner E. A. Gait rebuked the Bombay census superintendent for using the hybrid term "Hindu-Muhammadans" for some groups whose responses and customs refused clear identification: he should have relegated "the persons concerned to the one religion or the other as best he could" (Gait 1912, 1:i, 118).

It is important, however, to avoid bland, mechanistic depictions of the impact of late-colonial integration or of colonial discourse. Such depictions had been the pitfalls of much modernization theory, and one feels at times that the Saidian counterorthodoxy of today has run into similar problems through an inversion of values that retains implicit assumptions of passivity among the colonized. There is need for greater specificity about the precise location, ethos, and strategies of the groups directly involved in the transitions from "Hindu" toward "Hinduism." That they were, overwhelmingly, upper caste and male would occasion no surprise, for already-existing hierarchies of caste and gender played a critical role in determining early access to the new integrative networks. The predominantly high-caste slant of projects of Hindu unity, in other words, continued on an enhanced scale in the late-colonial era and beyond.

Schematically, it is helpful to make a further distinction between three groups participating in and/or responding favorably to constructions of Hinduism that were built up in the late nineteenth century around notions of adhikari-bheda. Many of the tracts relevant for our argument were written by fairly obscure men, high-caste and predominantly Brahman, with little or no connection with Western education. Colonial transformations within this world of traditional literati and religious specialists seem to have gone in several directions at the same time (Frykenburg 1991). The initial British dependence on pandits and *maulvis* (Muslim learned men) in revenue and judicial administration as well as in the early accumulation of orientalist knowledge must have strengthened the traditional literati considerably. Confining ourselves (for reasons of manageability, as throughout this essay) to the "Hindu" world, it is important to note in the first place that the influence of Brahmanic sacred texts and of notions of varna hierarchy was being simultaneously extended and deepened. These texts were now disseminated on a vastly enhanced scale through print and translation, and colonial administration of Hindu law in many domains of everyday life as interpreted by Brahman experts heightened the importance of high Hindu texts where notions of hierarchy had always been most clearcut (Derrett 1981; Carroll 1978). There are many indications—particularly in Bengal where Western education came earliest and had established fairly deep roots by the late nineteenth century among gentlefolk—of a considerable decline in the prestige of traditional literati sticking to older ways, and also of a drying up of their sources of patronage. Both their continued or enhanced influence and a decline in their prestige and income could in different ways stimulate an emphasis upon conservative, hierarchized Hindu unity, where Brahman males would once again be firmly on top. This was all the more likely under conditions of an alien rule often suspected of encouraging Christian conversions and Hindu reform.

The crucial ideological and organizational initiatives in the formation of both Hinduism and, later, Hindutva, however, have come primarily from a new middle class produced by colonial education. It is widely recognized that this middle-class social phenomenon—like its contemporary counterparts in Indian Islam and communalism in general—is basically modern, colonial, and postcolonial. There is little need to rehearse once more the familiar narratives of both reform and revival that contributed in different ways to a new emphasis on Hindu unity among the middle class (which are delved into from new perspectives by T. Sarkar above; see also S. Joshi 1995). The linkages between the late-nineteenth-century strengthening of such tendencies and growing middle-class disenchantment about British tutelage is also a much-explored theme.

Two aspects relevant for our argument, however, have been relatively neglected. That the Western-educated were for long almost invariably of high-caste origin is well known, but possible implications of this fact have not been sufficiently highlighted. Yet, focusing on Bengal once again, it is surely symptomatic that the terms *jat*, *jati*, and *jatiya* were used in Bengali from around the third quarter of the nineteenth century to indicate, indiscriminately, "caste," "the Hindu people" (*Hindujati*), "nation," and "national." Theoretical Brahmo Samaj criticism of caste, to take another example, goes back to Rammohan Roy, yet even the radical social reformers among Brahmos did little in practice about it, barring the encouragement of intercaste marriages within their own community and symbolic steps like insisting that Brahmo preachers give up their sacred thread. The first substantial Brahmo tract systematically attacking caste, Sibnath Shastri's *Jatibheda*, came out only in 1884, and a Depressed Classes Mission for philanthropic work among Bengal's low castes and untouchables had to wait for its inauguration till 1909 (Shastri 1963). The Arya Samaj perspective on caste reform was much more limited, and here, too, the integrative, Sanskritizing device of *shuddhi*—through which lower castes were given the sacred thread, emblematic of the three high varnas, and purification was sought for their rituals and ways of life—became widely adopted as a strategy only from around the turn of this century. These dates are rather significant in terms of the relevance of partially autonomous lower-caste pressures.

The colonial middle class, in the second place, has been generally studied in terms of its prominent or successful men (and a few women) alone: well-known writers, lawyers, journalists, doctors, scholars, officials, politicians. But it also included an increasing number of humbler, though still overwhelmingly upper-caste folk, remnants of the traditional literati who had lost patronage in the new era, obscure hack writers, humble teachers, clerks in government offices or predominantly British-owned mercantile firms, unemployed educated youth, high-school or college dropouts with highly uncertain job prospects. This lower middle class, neglected in historiography (Mayer 1975; Crossick 1977 are notable exceptions) had certain specific features: the lack of an artisan element due to caste distinctions and, in Bengal (though not in northern India), the weakness initially of a small-trader-shopkeeper component due to British, followed to some extent by Marwari, predominance. *Chakri* (the clerical office job) thus became in Bengal the dominant signifier of this social group, in actuality and even more in imagery.

Despite great differences in living standards and ways of life, education (at least in the vernacular) and print culture helped to constitute a community of readers (and viewers, after the development of the public stage in Calcutta from the 1870s) that extended over both the successful and the obscure high-caste bhadralok (the gentlefolk or respectable classes, in Bengal); and increasingly, it also included a small but growing number of women. As actual or target readers and audiences of cheap tracts, prints, plays, and farces, the world of genteel upper-caste poverty was able to set its distinctive mark on many of the vernacular texts that constitute our primary evidence. Bhadralok aspirations, lacking the wherewithal for their fulfillment, possibly made caste status even more vital and enhanced the attraction of ideologies grounded in adhikari-bheda. Kali Yuga, significantly, took on new modulations, with a reordering of its package of evils around clerical work (chakri). This was often combined with a neatly gendered shifting of guilt. In many plays and farces, the insubordinate wife with her modern, Westernized, extravagant ways forces the husband to take up a clerical job that is depicted as peculiarly demeaning, a kind of *dasatya* (bondage), due to its association with a new discipline of clock time being imposed by alien bosses. The conversations of Ramakrishna—the saint of poor rustic Brahman origin whose first intimate disciples in the Calcutta of the early 1880s came mostly from a clerical milieu—regularly conjoined lust (always given a feminine form), money, and chakri as the triple evils of Kali Yuga. Ramakrishna and many late nineteenth-century religious tracts argued that clerical work—governed by the rigors of clock time—left no time for complicated ritual worship or deep philosophical contemplation. The simpler ways of bhakti (devotional piety, which might consist of no more than recitation of the name of the deity) was therefore preferable. Ultimately, perhaps, what remained was little more than a sense of belonging or identity: this was becoming more indispensable than ever before, particularly for obscure newcomers to city life. In twentieth-century Hindutva, one may note, the denudation of Hindu traditions of theological or scholastic argument has kept pace with increasingly aggressive assertions of Hindu unity, while despite many transformations, the social lineaments of the movement appear not unfamiliar. An urban or small-town, predominantly high-caste, lower middle class of professionals, clerks, and traders has been the principal and stable base of the Sangh Parivar. There has been a marked influx also, particularly in recent years, of the more successful and upwardly mobile urbanites; while simultaneously links have been established through the VHP with what remains of, or can be claimed to be, a traditional religious literati of holy men, heads of ascetic orders, sants and mahants (Pinch, above).

There are discursive and contextual shifts here, however, that demand emphasis. Early printed tracts centering around adhikari-bheda, as well as the conversations of Ramakrishna, were primarily concerned with the justification of ritual and behavioral norms against Christian polemic and reformist attacks. There are no developed enemy images—not even of Christians, while Muslims are hardly mentioned—and adhikari-bheda is repeatedly combined with apparently wide notions of catholicity. "All [forms of worship] are acceptable, to each according to his taste," says an 1845 tract, while Lokenath Basu's *Hindu-dharma-marma* (1858) similarly argues that "what is bad is to lose one's *dharma* [religious duty]; the possibility of salvation remains so long as any *dharma* is devoutly followed" (B. Mukherji 1845; L. Basu 1858). One is reminded of Ramakrishna's well-known parables of the mother cooking many dishes to suit the diverse tastes of her children, and the man getting to a roof by staircase, ladder, or rope, but falling if he did not stick firmly to any one way.

A second striking feature of these and similar nineteenth-century texts is the remarkable openness of assertions of inequality and hierarchy. "Remember that distinctions of *varna* (*varna-vivedha*) are indispensable to *mukti* [salvation]. Parameswar has given different kinds of *shakti* [power] to different *jatis*—if one takes up the *dharma* of another, only harm can follow" (L. Basu 1858, 60). And even the supremely catholic and gentle Ramakrishna became very angry when Vidyasagar asked him why God should have given varying shakti to different people (M. Gupta 1908, 3:10).

Defense of caste hierarchy possibly figured in the early adhikari-bheda texts of Bengal largely as a routine matter, for it was not yet perceived as under serious attack, unlike, say, in Maharashtra. Women's rights, in contrast, had become the central divisive issue in nineteenth-century bhadralok life, and it is significant that the explications of the Kali Yuga during these decades focused obsessively on the insubordination of wives and was much less concerned with any Shudra threat. It was primarily in this gender context, too, that the aggressive assertions of Hindu hierarchy and discipline reached a point of climax during the 1880s and early 1890s, particularly in relation to the virulent campaign against the Age of Consent Bill of 1891. Discipline was glorified, in an almost sadomasochistic manner, precisely because of the suffering and pain it often admittedly caused. Thus a pamphlet by the leading conservative writer Chandranath Basu in 1892 categorically located the ultimate virtues and superiority of Hindutva in the "woman who cooks in her kitchen, all but burnt by the flames, suffocated by the thick smoke" (C. Basu 1892, 105; see A. Sen 1993; T. Sarkar 1993b and c).

Such a note of near hysteria, however, could not be sustained or be effective for long, and men like Chandranath Basu were soon almost forgotten. Hindu unity, after all, needed the willing consent of substantial numbers of women and lower castes, and for that, it seems, adhikari-bheda had to be softened through devotion (bhakti). A servant can never normally expect to sit next to his master, Ramakrishna once explained in another of his homely parables, but moved by the servant's devoted service, the master might one day elevate the servant to a seat next to him (M. Gupta 1908, 2:63). Medieval bhakti texts had already introduced significant modulations in the high-caste myth of Kali Yuga, through which that worst of times became in some ways the best, for simple devotion was now declared sufficient for salvation. Textual learning and complicated rituals, from which women and Shudras were excluded, were no longer necessary, and sometimes, paradoxically, the social categories otherwise held responsible for degeneration were even privileged. The humble, it was announced, constitute the ideal devotee (*bhakta*) and women and Shudras "can attain good simply through performing their duties" to husbands and high-caste men (*Vishnupurana*, in Sangari 1990). One notices a similar dualism in the portrayal of Kali Yuga in many late-nineteenth-century Bengali plays and farces. If evil is located in the insubordinate Anglicized wife who dominates her worthless husband, counterpoints are often found in figures of pure women (and, occasionally, good plebeians—devoted domestic servants, even one or two peasants), who act decisively, while always maintaining proper deference, to set right the disturbed moral order. A literary trope of what I have elsewhere called "deferential assertion" thus emerges, in which women are given an active role, going considerably beyond the traditional Sita model in the *Ramayana* of patient, entirely passive suffering that ennobles but does not modify the course of events. The limits remain clear, however, as does, above all, the fact that such initiative invariably culminates in the restoration of proper patriarchal and Brahmanic order (S. Sarkar 1989). And once again, it is tempting to find affinities: twentieth-century Hindutva has also oscillated between frank assertions of hierarchical structures and projections, principally through bhakti, of a softer, more populist, hegemonic face. The greatest success of Hindutva to date has been through the appropriation and development of the image of Rama, a central bhakti hero, in whom benign paternalism (*udarata*) and martial prowess (*krodhita mudra*) have been classically combined (P. K. Datta 1993b).

But there were major discursive shifts, too, between the 1890s and the mid-1920s, when—with Savarkar's text and the foundation of the RSS, in 1925—Hindutva became crystallized as an ideological-political formation. Fundamental here were certain well-known contextual changes, which for our purpose may be summed up as a transition toward qualitatively new kinds of mass politics, interrelated with institutional changes like extension of the franchise and safeguards for minority or backward groups, accompanied by spells of communal violence and the organization and proliferation, from around the turn of the century, of lower-caste movements and caste associations. Bengal is not generally associated with the kind of caste politics that is most relevant for our present argument: it is all the more significant, therefore, to recall that a fairly large number of lower-caste movements developed even in Bengal around this time, particularly among the Mahishyas, the Namashudras, and the Rajbansis (Bose 1993). A rough indicator of the extent of transformation is provided by the India Office Library classified catalogs of printed Bengali tracts. Only 24 entries appear under the heading "Castes and Tribes," before 1905; by contrast, 140 titles appear for the period 1905–20. The role here of British divide-and-rule and classificatory (specifically, census) strategies has been explored often enough: one might mention in particular the efforts of Risley and Gait as census commissioners to fix jati hierarchies and even determine whether or not the lower castes could be considered Hindus at all. The more important question, however, concerns the widely divergent ways in which incipient subordinate-caste movements and high-caste advocates of Hindu unity responded to such colonial moves and discourses. What was frankly accepted as a great opportunity by low-caste movements was a threat to high castes, almost on a par at times in some regions with threats posed by what was termed "Muslim separatism."

One consequence of the increasing presence of lower-caste groups in political life and as members of the vernacular reading public was that frank assertions of adhikari-bheda started becoming less common in the Bengali texts. The Kali Yuga theme, too, seems to have declined, and it is interesting that in one of the last farces that I have come across built around that motif, published in the early 1920s, caste mobility had become the major theme (P. Chattopadhyay 1926). The adhikari-bheda argument for Hindu unity, if used at all, is now increasingly given an abstract, philosophical color, detached from blunt avowals of caste (and gender) inequality. One notices this rarification already in Vivekananda, and again, some thirty years later, in Radhakrishnan: both were engaged in projecting attractive and impressive images of Hindu unity before external audi-

ences. In an argument, which to Vivekananda's disciple Nivedita marked
the transition from the "religious ideas of the Hindus" to "Hinduism"
(Nivedita 1970, 1:10), Vivekananda—at Chicago, in 1893—located fundamental Hindu unity in a hierarchy apexed by Vedanta that pertained to
philosophy rather than to ritual, belief, or social difference (Vivekananda
[1940] 1970b, 227). In his Oxford lectures, *The Hindu View of Life*, in 1926,
Radhakrishnan similarly assumed Hinduism to be unified by an "absolute . . . Vedanta standard" that has been able to incorporate differences as
"expressions of one and the same force at different levels" (Radhakrishnan
1926, 24).

Adhikari-bheda, alternatively, could be displaced by a new image of
upper-caste leadership, formulated in terms of paternalist philanthropy and
Sanskritizing reform that would uplift or purify the lower castes, an agenda
that was now coming to be recognized as indispensable for building Hindu
or national unity. Already in Vivekananda, passionate denunciations of
caste oppression were combined with fear of Christian and Muslim prose-
lytization, and emerging anti-Brahman movements of the south were criticized for being in too much of a hurry and encouraging "fighting among
the castes" (Vivekananda 1970a, 3: 294–98). The recent research of Pradip Kumar Datta has established the centrality in the development of this
paternalist "reform for Hindu unity" argument of U. N. Mukherji, "the influence of whose *Hindus: A Dying Race* (1909) provides a convenient case-
study of the importance of such hegemonizing strategies . . . as well as of
their crucial limits" (P. K. Datta 1993a). Mukherji interpreted some Bengal
census data as indicating an inexorable decline in Hindu numbers relative
to Muslims, attributed it to the wretched conditions of the lower castes as
contrasted to the supposedly more virile, energetic, united, and prosperous Muslim peasants, and urged paternalistic upliftment at Brahmanic initiative as means to the end of Hindu survival, unity, and rejuvenation. In a
slightly later pamphlet, Mukherji posed as the key problem the question of
"authority" in Hindu society: the upper castes could legitimize their ebb-
ing authority only through initiating or helping processes of orderly social
readjustment. Mukherji's pamphlet, which praised a movement of Malis
in East Bengal to obtain with some support from upper-caste gentry the
services of the slightly superior barber caste, contained a revealing extract
from the Calcutta vernacular newspaper *Hitavadi*. The Malis were praised
for being devoted servants of high-caste gentlefolk (bhadralok), and the
newspaper urged the latter to reciprocate such devotion on the interesting

analogy of Yudhishthira in the *Mahabharata*, who refused to enter heaven without his faithful dog (U. N. Mukherji 1911).

Mukherji's influence is eminently visible in the pamphlets and activities of Digindranarayan Bhattacharji, who wrote copiously against the evils of caste, composed many histories of subordinate jatis, tried to spread high-caste customs among upwardly mobile Shudras, and was hailed in his lifetime by a lower-caste activist (Manindranath Mandal) as comparable to Chaitanya, the Buddha, and Muhammad (Mandal 1927). Bhattacharji's *Jatibheda* (Faridpur, 1912) carried an introduction by U. N. Mukherji and quoted extensively from his *Hindus: A Dying Race*. Yet it also borrowed anticaste arguments from the identically titled 1884 Brahmo Samaj tract of Sibnath Shastri, and in some passages went very much further than Mukherji in attacking caste oppression and its justifications in ancient texts like the *Manusmriti*. Interestingly, Bhattacharji's *Jatibheda* contains also a direct repudiation of adhikari-bheda: God has given "the same powers [*saman shakti*] to all human beings, just as he has made the same sun for Brahman and Chandal [untouchable]" (Bhattacharji 1912, 4–5). The theme of Hindu unity against external, primarily Muslim threat, central for Mukherji's *Dying Race*, is occasionally mentioned but has become a subsidiary motif in Bhattacharji. Its further marginalization and, indeed, implicit rejection become clearer in tracts connected directly with the Namashudra movement, which from 1905 to 1912 distanced itself from the bhadralok-dominated Swadeshi agitation against the partition of Bengal. We may take as examples two pamphlets, published within a month of each other, in 1911, but somewhat different in aims and style of argument. *Namashudra-dwijatattva* deploys historical arguments to establish claims to high-caste status, while at the same time making more radical attacks on caste oppression: untouchability, for instance, is contrasted to the care lavished by the bhadralok on their dogs (Bareibiswas 1911). *Namshudra-Gyana bhandar* adopts a milder tone and urges self-improvement efforts in education and agriculture (B. Sarkar 1911). What the two tracts have in common, however, is a firm distancing from all forms of bhadralok politics, expressed at times through loyalist effusions to British rule.

If such were the travails of unificatory projects in Bengal, the problems must have been far more acute in regions like Maharashtra and many parts of the south, where many lower-caste and dalit movements explicitly rejected Sanskritizing claims to higher status in the varna hierarchy and developed alternative versions of subcontinental history in which upper-caste Aryans figured as alien conquerors, neatly inverting both nationalist and Hindutva arguments of territoriality or pitribhumi. Maharashtra appears particularly relevant in this context, as the land of low-caste political leaders Jyotirao Phule and B. R. Ambedkar—as well as RSS founding fathers V. D. Savarkar, K. B. Hedgewar, and M. S. Golwalkar. The crystallization of the ideology and organization of Hindutva in the mid-1920s in Maharashtra, despite the relatively weak presence in that region of the supposed Muslim threat, which was its overt justification, may become easier to explain through such a juxtaposition. Nagpur, the birthplace of the RSS in 1925, had also been the site of the All India Depressed Classes Conference, in May 1920, when Ambedkar began wresting the leadership of dalits from more moderate groups associated with Vithal Ramji Shinde's efforts at reform from above under high-caste initiative (Omvedt 1994, 142–47). And the RSS image of its own origins as embodied, for instance, in the official biography of its founder, K. B. Hedgewar, locates lower-caste assertion on par with the Muslim threat as the twin dangers that lay behind Hedgewar's initiative: "Conflicts between various communities had started. Brahman-Non-Brahman conflict was nakedly on view" (C. P. Bhishikar, quoted in T. Basu et al. 1993, 14).

U. N. Mukherji's emphasis on the need for lower-caste upliftment had played a significant role in the turn toward aggressive Hindutva in the early 1920s. Shraddhanand, who from 1923 had made removal of untouchability and Sanskritization through shuddhi the major planks in his drive for Hindu organization (*sangathan*) with an openly anti-Muslim thrust, acknowledged his debt to Mukherji through the title of his last tract: *Hindu Sangathan: Saviour of the Dying Race* (1925) (Jordens 1981). Savarkar, too, acquired something of a reputation as a social reformer by his support for moves to bestow the sacred thread and open temples to low castes. But the limits of such reformism were once again revealed when Savarkar advised Mahars to stick to their traditional occupations as village menials, against which they had started agitating under Ambedkar's leadership (Keer 1966, 177–97).

Much more significant, however, is the silence about both lower-caste movements and reform efforts in Savarkar's crucial *Hindutva* text. This, as well as the whole the subsequent organizational practice of the RSS, developed yet another strategy for dealing with caste difference, distinct from both aggressive assertions of hierarchy and efforts at controlled paternalistic reform. Savarkar's definition of the Hindu solely in terms of the *pitribhumi = punyabhumi* equation made caste differences and differences of ritual and belief among Hindus irrelevant: what mattered was not content or status, but authentic indigenous origin in *Bharatvarsha* (classical India). Caste (and gender) inequality became implicitly unimportant and could be more or less left alone, except when they specifically hindered Hindu unity and mobilization. Difference, in fact, could be celebrated as so many flowers making up the single garland of Hinduism, which was how K. S. Sudarshan, senior official of the RSS, eloquently described it in a recent interview (see T. Basu et al. 1993). A space remained even for reassertions of adhikari-bheda, since that, presumably, would be as indigenous and authentic as anything else. "Diversities in the path of devotion did not mean division in society," argued Golwalkar, in an essay that went on to justify varna hierarchy. "Special concessions to scheduled castes and tribes [i.e., affirmative action], on the other hand inculcated a separatist consciousness" (Golwalkar 1966, 135, 144). The central unificatory thrust of Hindutva ideology made autonomous lower-caste assertions appear inevitably divisive. This is made fairly obvious, for instance, by the notes kept by an RSS member attending an officer's training camp, which have been reprinted in a generally sympathetic history of the organization: "In the last thousand years, the bonds that linked society were broken. This led to selfish caste mentality that divided society. . . . The RSS was organised to prevent the further disintegration of Hindu society" (Anderson and Damle 1987, 95–97).

Another passage in these lecture notes predictably asserted that "Non-Hindus must be assimilated to the Hindu way of life." A construction of Hindu unity that evaded rather than sought to reform or even significantly ameliorate hierarchy needs for its sustenance the notion of the Muslim as an ever-present, existential threat, actualized and renewed, furthermore, in recurrent communal riots. (An identical logic has operated in the production and reproduction of Muslim communalism, with similar consequences in terms of subordinated groups, particularly women; the only difference, in postindependence India, has been its relative weakness and incapacity for influencing state policies and administration). The theme of medieval Muslim tyranny—elaborated in numerous late-nineteenth-century literary texts, like the historical novels of Bankim Chandra Chattopadhyay—was given new immediacy in the 1920s, and linked up, through the trope of the "dying Hindu," with interrelated counterimages of the Muslim as ever proliferating, sexually prolific, and lusting after Hindu women (P. K. Datta 1993a). Such assumptions have entered deep into middle-class Hindu common sense in many parts of the country, helping to constitute attitudes of approval or compliance about communal violence among many who would never actively participate in riots themselves. Communalism here veers close to everyday racism, with the Muslim—like the black or colored immigrant—felt to be a biological danger, a threat simply by being born, giving birth—even dying. A highly respectable gentleman of South Delhi told a group of us investigating the Nizamuddin riot of 1990 that every time a Muslim died, a bit of Mother India's soil was lost through his grave, while the self-effacing Hindu is cremated and does not waste space (P. K. Datta et al. 1990).

But how different, it will be asked, was Indian nationalism in its handling of difference, and specifically of lower-caste assertions? Surely all nationalisms, with their projects of constructing modern nation-states, inevitably homogenize and repress internal differences. So is Hindutva in this respect no more than a particularly aggressive and crude variant of a far more general trend? The sincerity of Gandhi's indictment of untouchability is unquestionable, but his defense of a supposedly original and pure *varnasrama* (duties appropriate for every status in society) against later distortions was unacceptable to E. V. Ramaswamy Naicker, Ambedkar, and many other lower-caste and dalit activists (Ambedkar 1989, 1:81–96). The specific programs of harijan welfare and upliftment—the opening of wells and temples to them, and village-level constructive work—as well as the term *harijan* (god's children) itself, can be rejected as mere paternalism. They were perhaps not all that different from the projects of high-caste reform from above that we have already considered in brief, and that at times encountered similar difficulties. And the record of the non-Gandhian left is at first sight even more dismal, whether Nehruvian, Communist, or Socialist—with the exception of R. M. Lohia's movement (Omvedt 1994, 37, 63). The treatment of caste oppression as epiphenomenal to more basic questions of class struggle might even appear to a really harsh critic as not all that different from Hindutva subordination of the same issue to the higher requirements of Hindu unity.

A closer look, however, would indicate some significant differences and make assessments of the kind I have just outlined unfair. Crystallized Hindutva, since the mid-1920s, has on the whole kept away from even paternalistic caste reform, preferring the Savarkar argument of irrelevance; and it has worked, as the general RSS practice indicates, overwhelmingly in urban or small-town upper-caste milieus. This did change significantly, through VHP activity in the main, during the height of the Ram janmabhoomi campaign—but then there can be little doubt that it was the hysteria sparked off by V. P. Singh's decision to implement, after years of delay, the Mandal Commission recommendations that enhanced greatly the appeal of Hindutva among high-caste groups. The recent provincial elections indicate the instability, at best, of gains among lower-castes by utilizing in vastly modified form the appeal of Rama bhakti. Signs of internal tensions and oscillations still beset Hindutva's relationships with lower castes. The electoral reverses of late-1993 immediately produced a flurry of gestures directed toward regaining the support of subordinate groups, balanced soon after by an aggressive speech by the new RSS chief Rajendra Singh at a Delhi rally hailing the special role of the Brahman, warrior, and trader castes in safeguarding the entire country (*Times of India*, April 11, 1994). The Sangh Parivar nowadays makes occasional efforts at appropriating the memory of Ambedkar through stray quotations, but Ambedkar's call for the "annihilation of caste" through a direct onslaught on Hindu sacred texts and eventually mass conversion of dalits to Buddhism remain logically irreconcilable with Hindutva ideology. Ambedkar, way back in 1936, pinpointed this contradiction through his polemical assertion that Hindu society is "really a myth," because "a caste has no feeling that it is affiliated to other castes except when there is a Hindu-Muslim riot" (Ambedkar 1936, 42–43).

Mainstream nationalism, in (partial) contrast and mainly at Gandhi's insistence, refused to consider caste oppression and particularly untouchability to be unimportant or irrelevant, thus moving away to some extent from the earlier Congress separation of political from social matters, which Tilak had crystallized by expelling the Social Conference from the venue of the Congress session in 1895. Despite many bitter conflicts, a basis for dialogue and compromise with lower-caste and dalit movements therefore remained. In the 1930s, the Maharashtra Congress was able to absorb the bulk of the Non-Brahman Satyashodhak activists, and it is surely significant that the murder of Gandhi by a Maharashtrian Brahman was followed by widespread anti-Brahman riots in that region. Gandhi and Ambedkar could, after all, agree in the end to the 1932 Poona Pact, which was bitterly denounced by the more aggressive orthodox Hindu elements inside and outside the Congress. Ambedkar had a seminal role in drawing up the Indian constitution, as well as in preparing the earlier drafts of the Hindu Code bill, and the postindependence Congress enjoyed a substantial harijan electoral base that has been eroded only in recent years. As for the left, it undoubtedly paid a high price in many regions for its long underestimation of caste as a possible form of subordinate assertion. But it would be quite unhistorical to deny the substantial gains achieved, in terms of human dignity and not just economic advantages, by lower-caste and dalit groups in other areas and times under leftist leadership and through exploring the mobilizing capacities of class. Caste identity, after all, is not a natural, given, unchanging, or hermetically sealed entity, any more than class.

It may be appropriate to end, as I began, with a consideration of historiographical silencing. Ambedkar's *Annihilation of Caste* includes a powerful section giving specific examples of caste oppression between 1928 and 1935, which he had taken from contemporary newspapers (Ambedkar 1936, 22–25). Such incidents keep recurring even after nearly five decades of independence and, along with violence against women, probably on an ascending scale. Yet they find little or no place in most standard works on modern Indian history. At a different, but not unrelated level, a large number of leading Indian intellectuals and social scientists denounced the extension of reservations to backward castes attempted by V. P. Singh in 1990 as "pandering to casteism." They included several scholars who had spent a lifetime writing in fairly sympathetic terms about Sanskritization: surely the kind of caste movement that is the most casteist, in the sense of encouraging narrow sectional loyalties through the quest for mere positional mobility on behalf of a caste group (jati), while maintaining and even strengthening the basic hierarchical order. Movements claiming to represent Other Backward Castes (OBCs) or dalits, in contrast, have to try to build new, wider, horizontal solidarities, overcoming narrow caste boundaries. Fairly often, as notably under Phule, Ramaswamy Naicker, or Ambedkar, they have directly attacked caste.

There are very obvious links between such silencing and the priorities of mainstream nationalist (or Hindu communalist) history writing that center around the building and maintenance of the nation-state. Less obvious, and therefore more worrying, are some recent tendencies that seem to be reproducing that silence precisely through what is accepted by many as the most radical and chic critique of all such nation-state projects. The burden of this critique is no longer class or even elite domination, but the alleged root of the modern or postcolonial nation-state in Western, Enlightenment rationalism, successfully imposed on the Third World by colonial cultural domination. The logical corollary of this total concentration on the critique of colonial discourse is that only movements or aspects of life demonstrably free of such Western or rationalist taint can be given the status of authentic, properly indigenous, protest, resistance, and culture. It then becomes difficult to study with any marked sympathy not only the history of the traditional Marxist left, but also figures like Phule or Ambedkar or the many movements that have tried to extend the rights of lower castes and women by selectively appropriating elements from Western discourses and even on occasion using colonial state policies as resources. The fairly deafening silence of the bulk of *Subaltern Studies* historiography (R. Guha 1982–89; R. Guha and G. C. Spivak 1988; P. Chatterjee and G. Pandey 1993; D. Arnold and D. Hardiman 1994) in these areas may be taken as symptomatic. Within such a framework, again, a critique of Hindutva can only take the form of presenting it as a Western or modern distortion of a basically pure and problem-free precolonial Hindu world. The first part of this proposition may be acceptable; the second is not.

The most lucid statement of these positions was made a decade ago by Ashis Nandy, in his admirably clear declaration of intent at the beginning of *Intimate Enemy* (Nandy 1983): "to justify and defend the innocence which confronted modern Western colonialism." The "innocence" here involves a deeply disturbing elision of centuries of caste, gender, and class oppression. Arguments like these threaten to leave us today with no language adequate for analyzing many of the most basic issues of contemporary Indian society and history.

# Glossary

Many words have several transliterations representing different language forms and usages. Variations appear in parentheses. (See also Embree 1988; Hay 1988; Netton 1992; and glossaries in Brown 1985; Freitag 1989a; King 1994; Lapidus 1988; Pandey 1990b; Stokes 1978.)

| | |
|---|---|
| *acharya* | Religious leader, e.g., of the Ramanuji Ramanandi sect. |
| *adhikari-bheda* | Differential rights, claims, or powers for *jati* and *sampraday*, each with its own rituals and beliefs, in a system of *varnashramadharma* (q.v.). |
| *ahimsa* | Nonviolence. |
| Akali Dal | Political party in Punjab. |
| *akhara* | Tight-knit organization of performers and other groups in north India, under strong personal leadership. |
| *alap* | In Hindustani music, the opening, free-rhythmic exposition of a *rag*. |
| *alim* | An individual Islamic learned man. |
| *amavasaya* | Moonless night and subsequent phase of the moon. |
| *antyodhya* | A program of economic assistance for the poorest rural families that the BJP implemented while in office in Himachal Pradesh. |
| *anushilandharma* | In Bankim Chandra Chattopadhyay's work, "internalized and reinterpreted concepts of Hindu knowledge." |
| *ardh-kumbh* | Half *kumbh* festival (see *kumbh*). |
| Arya Samaj | Hindu reformist organization. |
| *Aryavarta* | The traditional land of the Vedic Aryans in northern India. |
| avatar | (*avatara*). Incarnation, embodiment of God on earth. |
| *bahujan* | "Majority people." Term used in movements of Shudra castes. |
| Bahujan Samaj | Political party in UP based on scheduled caste support. |
| *bairagi* | Hindu ascetic warrior. |
| *bajra* | A millet. |
| Bajrang Dal | The youth organization of the VHP. |
| *balmiki* | Term of caste self-definition by scheduled castes in Ghaziabad and Khurja. |

| | |
|---|---|
| *bande mataram* | Hail to the mother(land). |
| Barelwi | Muslim sect that defended customary practices. |
| Baul | A tribal group in Bengal. Also a class of folk mystics. |
| *bhadralok* | (Bengali) "Respectable people." A multi-caste elite in Bengal. |
| *bhagwan* | God. |
| *bhai-bhai* | Brotherhood. |
| Bhaiya | A caste group in UP. |
| *bhajan* | Generic term for Hindu devotional song. |
| *bhakta* | A devotee. |
| *bhakti* | Devotion; specifically, Bhakti refers to an approach to Hinduism stressing personal devotion rather than orthodox ritual and caste. |
| *Bharat* | Sanskrit term for "India." |
| *Bharatiya* | Pertaining to Bharat. |
| *Bharatmata* | Mother Bharat. |
| *Bharatvarsha* | The land of Bharat. |
| *bhasha* | Language. |
| Bhojpuri | Pertaining to the Bhojpur linguistic region that covers eastern UP and northwestern Bihar. |
| *bhoomi* | (*bhumi*). Land, earth. |
| *bindi* | Mark of adornment worn by women on the forehead. |
| *birha* | Bhojpuri folk music genre. |
| Bohra | A merchant group. |
| Brahman | (Brahmin). The highest *varna*, Hindu priests, the religious elite. |
| Brahmanic | That which follows the ways of Brahmans. |
| Brahmo | Pertaining to the Brahmo Samaj; a follower of the Brahmo Samaj. |
| Brahmo Samaj | A reformist Hindu group in Bengal. |
| *Braj-bhasha* | An old literary form of Hindi; also its cultural region in southwestern UP. |
| *chakra* | Wheel, discus (see *sudarshana chakra*). |
| *chakri* | In Bengal, a clerical office job. |
| Chamar | A scheduled caste of laborers in northern India. |
| *chimta* | A weapon: large, iron pincers with sharpened ends. |
| Chishti | A major Sufi order founded in India. |
| *chutki* | Contributions to Cow Protection Movement, usually in units of a handful or "pinch" of rice. |
| *crore* | Ten million. |
| *dacoit* | Highway robber. |
| *dadra* | Hindustani light-classical music genre, often combining *Braj-bhasha* and Urdu lyrics. |
| Dadupanthis | A Hindu monastic sect. |
| *dal* | lentils. |
| *dalit* | "Downtrodden." Militant term for scheduled castes. |

| | |
|---|---|
| *dandi* | A Dasnami *sannyasi* order associated with high-caste orthodoxy. |
| *Dar al-ulum* | "Abode of learning." An Islamic theological seminary. |
| *Dar al-Islam* | "Abode of Islam." The land of Islam. |
| *darshan* | Auspicious viewing, usually of god. |
| *dasatya* | Bondage, in Bengal associated with a new discipline of clock time being imposed by alien bosses. |
| Dasnami | A sect of Shaiva monks associated with the origins of soldier monasticism. |
| *debbhasha* | (Bengali) Bhasha of the devas, language of the gods: i.e., Sanskrit. |
| *Debothan Ekadashi* | A Hindu holy day. |
| Deobandi | Reformist Muslim sect. |
| *desam* | (*desham*). Country. |
| *deva* | A generic term for a god. |
| *devadasi* | Courtesan-performer, often associated with Hindu temple. |
| Devanagari | (also Nagari). The script of Sanskrit, Hindi, and Marathi; relatives of Devanagari are also used for several other north Indian languages. |
| *dharma* | Cosmic and social order; code of proper conduct, righteousness; religion. |
| *dharmaraj* | Righteous rule according to dharma. |
| dharmic | Following dharma. |
| *dharna* | A sit-down strike. |
| *dhol* | (*dholak*). A common barrel drum used throughout India. |
| dhoti | Wrap-around cloth worn by men. |
| *dhrupad* | Archaic Hindustani music genre. |
| *duhul* | Persian for dhol. |
| *durbar* | A royal audience. |
| Dravidian languages | Tamil, Malayalam, Telugu, and Kannada, in south India, are the largest members of the Dravidian language family. |
| Durga | Hindu goddess. |
| *ekatamata yajna* | "Sacrifice for unanimity" staged by VHP. |
| *faqir* | Muslim holy man. |
| Faraizi | A nineteenth-century Muslim peasant movement in Bengal. |
| *faujdar* | Guard, officer. |
| *filmi geet* | Film music. |
| *funun-e-latifah* | (Urdu) The fine arts. |
| *Gandiv* | In *Mahabharata*, Arjuna's bow. |
| Ganesh | Hindu god. |
| Gaorakshini Sabha | Cow Protection Society. |

| | |
|---|---|
| *garibi hatao* | "End poverty!" Indira Gandhi's election slogan in 1971. |
| *gharana* | In Hindustani music, a musical family lineage. |
| *ghat* | A riverbank. |
| *ghazal* | Urdu, Persian, and Arabic poetic form; a light-classical music genre using that form. |
| Giri | A Dasnami group. |
| *goonda* | Thug. |
| *gosain* | Mendicant soldier/trader. |
| *grihasta* | Householder. |
| *guru* | Teacher. |
| *gurudwara* | Sikh temple. |
| Hanafi | A school of Islamic jurisprudence. |
| Hanuman | Monkey-warrior in epic *Ramayana*. |
| *Hari* | A name for Vishnu; an epithet also for Rama. |
| *harijan* | "People of God"; Mohandas Gandhi's term for scheduled castes. |
| *Hindujati* | Hindu people. |
| *Hindurashtra* | Hindu nation or state. |
| Hindustan | A term for India, applied particularly to northern India. |
| Hindustani | Pertaining to northern Indian culture, language, music; in linguistics, also refers to Urdu. |
| *Hindutva* | "Hindu-ness." Hindu nationalism. |
| Hindu Mahasabha | Conservative Hindu reformist organization, predecessor of the Jan Sangh and RSS. |
| Hindvi | An old form of Hindi. |
| *Hir-Ranjha* | Punjabi folk ballad. |
| *holi* | Hindu springtime festival. |
| Id | A semi-annual Muslim festival. |
| *ijtehad* | The exercise of independent judgment in Islamic jurisprudence. |
| *ishvar* | God. |
| *izzat* | Honor. |
| *jagadguru* | Supreme pontiff, as in *Jagadguru Ramanandacharya* (of the Ramanandi *sampraday*). |
| *jamaat* | Short form for Jamaat-e-Islami. |
| Jamaat-e-Islami | (Jama'at-i Islami). Muslim revivalist and fundamentalist movement and party, founded in 1941. |
| *Jana gana mana* | The opening words of the Indian national anthem, written by Rabindranath Tagore. |
| Janata Dal | A political party formed in opposition to the Congress. |
| *janma* | (Re)birth. |
| *janmabhoomi* | (*janambhumi, janmabhumi*). Place of birth. |
| *janmasthan* | Birthplace. |

| | |
|---|---|
| Jat | A north Indian agrarian caste group. |
| *jati* | An endogamous caste group. |
| *jatibheda* | Distinctions among castes. |
| *jeziya* | (*jizya*). A tax on non-Muslims under the Mughal empire. |
| *jihad* | Striving (in the way of Allah), whether to expand the world of Islam externally (through holy war) or to bring inner religious perfection. |
| *jowar* | A millet. |
| Kabirpanthi | Followers of Kabir, fifteenth-century Hindi poet. |
| Kaikeyi | In *Ramayana*, Ram's stepmother who brings about Ram's exile. |
| Kali | Hindu goddess. |
| *kaliyuga* | The last and most degenerate of all ages in Hindu cosmology. |
| *karkhandar* | Artisan. |
| *karma* | Fateful action. |
| Karnatak | Refers to south Indian musical traditions (contrasted to Hindustani). |
| *kar sevak* | Volunteer worker; a Sangh Parivar term for activists in the *Ram janmabhoomi* movement. |
| *karsewa* | The work of kar sevaks. |
| Kathiawadi | Pertaining to Kathiawad, a region of Gujarat. |
| *Khalifa* | Caliph, a successor to Muhammad as temporal and spiritual head of the *umma*, an elected office among Sunnis, terminated by Ataturk after World War I. |
| Khalifat | (*khilafat*). The office of the caliph, the caliphate; specifically, the chief spiritual authority vested in the Ottoman sultans and terminated by Ataturk after World War I. |
| Khilafat Movement | Indian protest movement of the 1920s seeking the restoration of the Khalifat. |
| *Khalsa* | "Army of the pure." Sikh brotherhood. |
| Khoja | A group found primarily in western India and East Africa, many of whom adhere to the Nizari Isma'ili form of Shi'ism. |
| *khyal* | Thought, idea; the main genre of Hindustani music. |
| *kirtan* | Krishnaite devotional song. |
| Krishna | Hindu god, who plays a significant role in the *Mahabharata*. |
| Krishnaite | Pertaining to the worship of Krishna. |
| *krodhita mudra* | Martial prowess, e.g., as an attribute of Rama. |
| Kshatriya | The warrior *varna*, second in status to Brahmans. |
| *kumbh mela* | (or simply, *kumbh*). India's preeminent pilgrimage festival, which every three years alternates between Hardwar. Allahabad (Prayag), Nasik, and Ujjain. |

| | |
|---|---|
| Kurmi | An agrarian caste. |
| *kurta* | A loose, knee-length upper-body dress. |
| *lakh* | One hundred thousand. |
| Lakshmana | In the epic *Ramayana*, Rama's brother. |
| *langoti* | Loincloth. |
| Lingayat | A caste and sectarian group in Karnataka. |
| *lok* | People, world. |
| Lok Sabha | The lower house of the Indian parliament. |
| *madrassah* | Islamic school. |
| *Mahabharata* | (*Mahabharat*) Sanskrit epic. |
| *mahant* | Leader or head of religious establishment. |
| Mahar | An untouchable caste group in northern India. |
| Mahishya | An agrarian group in Bengal. |
| Mali | An agrarian caste group. |
| *mandir* | Hindu temple. |
| Manganhar | A caste of Muslim musicians in western Rajasthan. |
| *Manusmriti* | Sanskrit text on dharma (usually referred in English to as "the laws of Manu") which focuses on cosmic, moral, and social order and duty. |
| Mapilla | A Muslim community in Kerala. |
| *maqam* | A melodic mode in Persian music. |
| Maratha | A dominant caste group in Maharashtra; also an empire in western India, circa 1660–1818. |
| Marathi | The language of Maharashtra. |
| *marsiya* | A genre of Shiʻite devotional song. |
| Marwari | A caste group from Rajasthan, which became prominent as a Calcutta business group. |
| *masala* | Spicy mixture. |
| *masjid* | Mosque. |
| *math* | (*matha*). A monastery, sectarian center of learning. |
| *maulvi* | A Muslim learned man. |
| *mauni amavasaya* | The most important bathing day of the kumbh mela. |
| Maurya | An empire spanning northern India, circa 322–185 B.C.E. |
| *mazdoor* | Worker. |
| *mela* | Fair, festival. |
| *millat* | Millet, religious community. |
| Mirasi | A caste of Muslim hereditary professional musicians. |
| *mlechcha* | In classical Sanskrit, unclean people, foreigners. |
| Mughal | Empire in northern India, 1556 to circa 1730. |
| Mughlai | Pertaining to Mughal cultural forms. |
| Muharram | Month during which mourning is observed, particularly by Shiʻas, for the death of Husain and his followers. |
| *mujahidin* | Warriors in jihad. |
| *mukti* | Salvation. |

| | |
|---|---|
| *naga* | Literally "snake." Warrior ascetic (*sadhu*). |
| *nagara* | (*naqqara*). Kettle-drum pair. |
| Nagari | See Devanagari. |
| *nagaswaram* | Large double-reed instrument used in Karnatak music. |
| *nam* | Name. |
| Namashudra | An agrarian group in Bengal. |
| Nanakpanthi | Followers of Guru Nanak, better known as Sikh. |
| *naqqara* | See *nagara*. |
| *na't* | A genre of Muslim devotional song and poetry. |
| *Navaratri* | "Nine Nights" festival, a pan-Indian religious holiday. |
| *nawab* | Governor, regional ruler, e.g., in Awadh. |
| *nidhi* | Justice. |
| Nimbarki | A Vaishnava sectarian order. |
| *Nom-tom* | Nonlexical syllables used in dhrupad alap. |
| Okkaliga | A caste group in Karnataka. |
| *Om* | Hindu sacred syllable. |
| *Panch Koshi Parikrama* | Ritual circumambulation of Ayodhya. |
| *pandal* | A covered stage. |
| *parikrama* | Ritual circumambulation. |
| Pathan | Ethnic group in Afghanistan and Pakistan. |
| Peshwa | Title of rulers of Maratha empire in Poona (Pune). |
| pith | Administrative center. |
| *pitribhumi* | Fatherland. |
| *pradesh* | Region, territory. |
| *puja* | Hindu ceremony to worship a deity. |
| Punjabi | (Panjabi). The language of Punjab; pertaining to the Panjab. |
| *punyabhumi* | Holy land. |
| *Purana* | A form of historical/genealogical legend text derived from Sanskrit classics collectively called *Puranas*. |
| Puranic | Appropriate to Puranas. |
| *purdah* | Isolation of women. |
| Puri | A Dasnami subgrouping. |
| *qabristan* | Graveyard. |
| *qasba* | Market town. |
| *qawwali* | North Indian Muslim devotional song. |
| *qazi* | An Islamic judge. |
| *rag* | (*raga*). In Hindustani music, a melodic mode. |
| *raj* | Rule, government; as the Raj, British rule in India. |
| Rajasthani | Pertaining to, or from Rajasthan. |
| Rajbansi | An agrarian group in Bengal. |
| Rajput | A Kshatriya caste group in northern India, dominant in Rajasthan. |
| *rajya* | Government, nation, state. |
| Rajya Sabha | The upper house of the Indian Parliament. |
| Rama | (Ram). One of the high Hindu gods. |

| | |
|---|---|
| *Rama bhakti* | *(Rambhakti).* Devotion to Rama. |
| Ramanandi | A Vaishnava *sampraday.* |
| Ramanuji | A member of a sectarian group within the Ramanandi *sampraday;* pertaining to the Ramanujis. |
| *Rama-rajya* | *(Ramraj, Ram-rajya).* The regime of Rama; utopia. |
| *Ramayana* | Sanskrit epic about the life of Rama. |
| *Ramcharitmanas* | Hindi version of the *Ramayana* by Tulsidas (sixteenth century). |
| *Ram janmabhoomi* | *(ramjanambhoomi, ramajanambhoomi).* The birthplace of Rama. |
| Ramlila | Festival during which the life of Rama is dramatized. |
| *Ram shilan puja* | Ceremonial consecration of bricks intended for the Ram janmabhoomi temple, Ayodhya. |
| *rashtra* | Nation, state. |
| *rasiya* | Sybarite; a genre of Braj folk music. |
| *rath* | *(ratha).* Chariot, vehicle (on which divine images ride during Hindu festivals). |
| *Rath Yatra* | The 1990 chariot procession from Somnath to Ayodhya organized by the BJP and VHP. |
| Ravana | In *Ramayana,* demon ruler of the kingdom of Lanka, and Ram's primary adversary in the epic. |
| *roti* | Round, flat bread. |
| *sabha* | Organization. |
| *sadhu* | Ascetic. |
| *sadhvi* | Female ascetic. |
| Samajwadi Party | Political party in UP based on scheduled caste support. |
| *sampraday* | Sectarian group. |
| *samsara* | In Hinduism, the round of births and deaths. |
| Sanatan Dharm Sabha | A traditionalist Hindu organization. |
| *sanatana dharma* | Eternal religion. |
| *sangathan* | Hindu movement for self-defense. |
| *sangh* | Organization; specifically, Sangh refers to the Sangh Parivar. |
| Sangh Parivar | The RSS "family," as it terms itself. |
| Sankhya | "Reasoning," one of the oldest Hindu philosophical schools. |
| *sannyasi* | Ascetic. |
| *sannyasini* | Female ascetic. |
| Sanskritize | Render into Sanskrit or forms grounded in the rules and norms stipulated in classical Sanskrit texts; hence, purify (as in social practices) and reform along classical lines. |
| *santan* | (Hindi) "Offspring." In *Anandamath,* by Bankim Chandra Chattopadhyay, (in Bengali) the *santan* is the ascetic warrior figure who first pronounces the words *bande mataram.* |

| | |
|---|---|
| *sant* | Saint. |
| sarod | A Hindustani string instrument. |
| *sati* | The state and title attained by a widow immolated on her husband's cremation pyre. |
| Satnami | A sectarian group. |
| *satya* | Truth. |
| *satyagraha* | Gandhi's strategy of nonviolent social protest. |
| scheduled castes | Castes on a list of the lowest, poorest, and most disadvantaged castes scheduled in the Indian constitution for special remedial efforts by the state. (See also *balmiki, dalit, harijan,* and untouchable.) |
| *sena* | Army. |
| *sevak* | Worker. |
| *shahnai* | A north Indian double-reed instrument. |
| Shaiva | Pertaining to the worship of Shiva; a worshiper of Shiva. |
| *shakha* | RSS training meeting. |
| *shakti* | Power, energy; mother goddess. |
| *Sharia* | (*Shari'a, Shariat*). Islamic law. |
| Shastras | General term for Hindu sacred scriptures. |
| *shastrartha* | The meaning of sacred texts. |
| Shastric | According to the shastras. |
| *sherwani* | A Muslim north Indian garment. |
| Shia | (Shi'a). Follower of or pertaining to Shi'ism. |
| Shiism | Minority Islamic tradition based on the schism concerning the successor to the Prophet, which holds that Ali should have followed Muhammad as khalifa. |
| *Shila* | Brick. |
| *shilan puja* | (*shilan pujan*). The VHP "worship of the bricks" ceremony of collecting bricks and money to send to Ayodhya for the construction of a Rama temple. |
| Shiva | One of the high Hindu gods. |
| Shiv Sena | Militant Hindu party in Maharashtra. |
| *shuddhi* | Purification; a Hindu reconversion ceremony; a movement to reconvert Hindus, started in the late nineteenth century. |
| Shudra | (*Sudra*) The last and ritually lowest of the four *varnas*. |
| Sita | In *Ramayana*, Ram's wife, abducted by Ravana. |
| sitar | Hindustani stringed instrument. |
| *smarta-panchapasana* | The equal validity of devotion to the gods Ganesh, Vishnu, Shiva, Shakti and Surya. |
| *sringar* | Ritual decoration of a temple deity; the erotic sentiment. |
| *sthan* | Place. |
| *stri-swadhinata* | Emancipation of women. |
| *sudarshana chakra* | In mythology, Vishnu's irresistible discus weapon. |

| | |
|---|---|
| Sufi | Islamic mystic. |
| Sufism | Islamic mysticism. |
| Surya | Vedic sun god. |
| *swadeshi* | "Of one's own country," particularly used as a term to denote items made in one's country, hence native products. The Swadeshi Movement sought to replace foreign with native products in British India. |
| *swaraj* | Self-rule, independence. |
| *tabla* | A drum used in Hindustani music. |
| *tahsil* | A county-sized administrative unit, subdivision of district. |
| Tamil | One of the four Dravidian languages of South India; a native Tamil language speaker. |
| Tantra | A mystical form of Hindu philosophy and worship. |
| Tantric | Pertaining to Tantra. |
| *tarana* | A genre of Hindustani music using nonlexical syllables. |
| Telugu | One of the four Dravidian languages of south India. |
| Thakur | A dominant agrarian caste in UP and Bihar. |
| *thumri* | A light-classical genre of Hindustani music, using Braj-bhasha text. |
| tilak | (*tilaka*). Auspicious mark on the forehead. |
| *tirtha* | Local sources of sacred water, such as temple tanks and river bathing places. |
| *triveni* | Sacred confluence of three rivers at Allahabad. |
| *udarata* | Benign paternalism, e.g., as an attribute of Rama. |
| *ulema* | Islamic learned men. |
| *umma* | The community of believers in Islam. |
| untouchable | Term used for schedule castes as bearers of ritual pollution. |
| Urdu | Hindustani language derived from Persian and Hindi, now the official language of Pakistan. |
| *vahini* | Army. |
| Vaishnava | (Vaishnavite) Pertaining to the worship of Vishnu; also a worshiper of Vishnu. |
| Vaishya | The third-ranked, merchant *varna*. |
| Vallabhachari | A Vaishnava sampraday. |
| *varna* | Hindu ritual status rank. The first three, highest *varnas* (Brahman, Kshatriya, and Vaishya) are called "twice born." Untouchable (harijan, dalit) castes are below even the lowest varna (Shudras). |
| *varnasrama* | Stages of life for each varna. |
| *varnashramadharma* | The dharma that is appropriate for each stage of life for everyone in Hindu society. |
| *varna-vivedha* | Distinctions among *varna*s. |
| Veda | The most ancient Sanskrit texts, which concern ritual. |

| Vedanta | Literally "the end of the Vedas," referring to the Upanishads, a body of texts that is the basis for this school of Hindu philosophy. |
| Vedic | Pertaining to or as prescribed by the Vedas. |
| Vishnu | One of the high Hindu gods. |
| Vishnuswami | A Vaishnava sampraday. |
| Vishwanath | Deity of the Kashi Vishwanath temple in Benares. |
| Yadav | A low-status but powerful caste group in UP and Bihar. |
| *yajna* | (*yagna*). Sacrifice. |
| *yatra* | Procession, pilgrimage. |
| *yuga* | Cyclical era in Hindu cosmology, see Kaliyuga. |
| zamindar | Landlord. |
| zillah | A local administrative unit. |

# Bibliography

Abbasi, M. Yusuf. 1988. *The Genesis of Muslim Fundamentalism in British India*. New Delhi.

Abu al-Fazl. 1939. *The Akbar Nama of Abu-l-Fazl*, trans. H. Beveridge. 3 vols. Delhi. 1902–39, repr. 1972–73, 1989.

Adas, Michael. 1989. *Machines as the Measure of Men: Science, Technology, and Ideologies of Western Dominance*. Ithaca.

———, ed. 1993. *Islamic and European Expansion: The Forming of a Global Order*. Philadelphia.

Advani, L.K. 1979. *The People Betrayed*. Delhi.

———. 1978. *A Prisoner's Scrapbook*. Delhi.

Agnes, Flavia. 1994. "Redefining the Agenda of the Women's Movement Within a Secular Framework." *South Asia* 17 (Special Issue), I: 63–78.

Ahluwalia, Montek. 1987. "Rural Poverty and Agricultural Performance in India." *Journal of Development Studies* 8 (April): 289–324.

Ahmad, Aijaz. 2002. *On Communalism and Globalization: Offensives of the Far Right*. New Delhi: Three Essays Press.

———. 1994. "Nation, Community Violence." *South Asia Bulletin: Comparative studies in South Asia, Africa and the Middle East* 14 (1994): 24–32.

———. 1992. *In Theory: Classes, Nations, Literatures*. London.

Ahmad, Mujeeb. 1993. *Jamiyrat Ulama-i Pakistan, 1949–1979*. Islamabad.

Ahmad, Nizamuddin. 1975. *Tabakat-i akbari of Nizam-ud-din Ahmad Bakshi*. Lahore.

Ahmad, Qeyamuddin. 1994. *The wahabi Movement in India*. New Delhi.

Ahmad, Syed Nesar. 1991. *Origins of Muslim Consciousness in India: A World-System Perspective*. New York.

Ahmed, Akbar S. 1988. *Discovering Islam: Making Sense of Muslim History and Society*. Lahore and London.

———. 1986. *Pakistan Society: Islam, Ethnicity and Leadership in South Asia*. Karchi.

Ahmed, Sufia. 1974. *Muslim Community in Bengal 1884–1912*. Dacca.

Akbar, M.J. 1988. *Riot after Riot: Reports on Caste and Communal Violence in India*. New Delhi.

———. 1985. *India: The Siege Within. Challenges to a Nation's Unity*. Middlesex.

Alavi, Hamza. 1989. "Nationhood and Nationalism in Pakistan." *Economic and Political Weekly*, July 8, 1527–34.

Al-Azmeh, Aziz. 1993. *Islams and Modernities*. London.

Allen, Douglas, ed. 1992. *Religion and Political Conflict in South Asia*. Westport.

Alter, Joseph. 1992. *The Wrestler's Body: Identity and Ideology in North India.* Berkeley.

Ambedkar, B. R. 1989. *Dr. Babasaheb Ambedkar: Writings and Speeches.* Bombay.

———. [1936.] 1968. *Annihilation of Caste, with a Reply to Mahatma Gandhi, and Castes in India: Their Mechanism, Genesis, and Development.* Jullundur.

Anand, V. K. 1980. *Conflict in Nagaland: A Study of Insurgency and Counter-Insurgency.* Delhi.

Anandhi. S.1995. *Contending Identities: Dalits and Secular Politics in Madras Slums.* New Delhi: Indian Social Institute.

Anderson, Benedict. 1983. *Imagined Communities: Reflections on the Origin and Spread of Nationalism.* London (later editions).

Anderson, Michael R. 1990. "Islamic Law and the Colonial Encounter in British India." In *Islamic Family Law*, ed. Chibli Mallat and Jane Connors. London.

Anderson, Walter K., and Sridhar D. Damle. 1987. *The Brotherhood in Saffron: The Rashtriya Swayamsevak Sangh and Hindu Revivalism.* Boulder.

Ansari, Iqbal A. Editor. 1997. *Communal Riots: The State and Law in India.* New Delhi: Institute of Objective Studies.

Appadurai, Arjun. 1993. "Number in the Colonial Imagination". In *Orientalism and the Postcolonial Predicament: Perspectives on South Asia*, ed. Carol Breckenridge and Peter van der Veer. Philadelphia.

———. 1990. "Disjuncture and Difference in the Global Culture Economy." *Public Culture* 2: 1–24.

Apte, Babasaheb. 1973. *Apani Prarthana.* Lucknow.

Arnold, David, and Hardimann, David. 1994. *Subaltern Studies VIII: Writings on South Asian History and Society.* Delhi.

Arora, Balveer and Douglas V. Verney. Editors. 1995. *Multiple Identities in a Single State: Indian Federalism in Comparative Perspective.* New Delhi: Konark.

Arthur, Paul. 1991. "Our Greater Ireland beyond the Seas." *Diaspora* 1: 365–72.

Asad, Talal, 1993. *Genealogies of Religion: Discipline and Reasons of Power in Christianity and Islam.* Baltimore.

Asher, Catherine. Forthcoming. "Negotiating Local and National Identities: Reconstruction of the Jaipur Jami Mosque." In *Visions of Community: The South Asian Muslim Imaginaire.* Edited by David Gilmartin, Bruce Lawrence, & Tony Stewart.

Ashraf, Mujeeb. 1987. *Muslim Attitudes towards British Rule and Western Culture in India.* Delhi.

Asia Society. 1976. *Asia in American Textbooks.* New York.

*Asian Survey.* 1993. Issue on "South Asia: Responses to the Ayodhya Crisis." Vol. 33 (July): 645–737.

Aswathanarayana, Vani. 1999. "After the Demolition: Constructing the Communal Riots of 1992–93 in the Indian Media." PhD dissertation, University of Illinois at Urbana-Champaign: University Microfilms International, Ann Arbor.

Aziz, K. K. 1967. *The Making of Pakistan: A Study in Nationalism.* London.

Babb, Lawrence A., and Susan Wadley, ed. 1994. *Media and the Transformation of Religion in South Asia.* Philadelphia.

Babu, Hemant. 2002. "The Social Engineering of Gujarat." *HIMAL* 15, 5, May: 16–32.

Badauni. 1898. *Tarikh-i Badauni. Muntakhah ut-Tawarikh.* Trans. W. H. Lowe, 3 vols.

Bagal, J. C. 1965. Introduction to *Bankim Rachanabali,* vol. 1, by Bankim Chandra Chattopadhyay. Calcutta.

———. 1969. Introduction to *Bankim Rachanabali,* vol. 2, by Bankim Chandra Chattopadhyay. Calcutta.

Bagchi, Amiya Kumar. 1991. "Predatory Commercialization and Communalism in India." In *Anatomy of a Confrontation: the Babri Masjid-Ram Janmabhumi Issue,* ed. S. Gopal. New Delhi.

Baird, Robert D., ed. 1993. *Religion and Law in Independent India.* New Delhi.

Bakker, Hans. 1986. *Ayodhya.* Gronigen.

Bandopadhyay, Jitendranath. 1960. *Pancha-Upasana.* Calcutta.

Bandopadhyay, Sekhara. 1990. *Caste, Politics and the Raj: Bengal, 1872–1937.* Calcutta.

———. 1985. "Social Mobility in the Late 19th and 20th Centuries." Unpublished thesis, Calcutta University.

Banerjee, Ashish. 1990. "'Comparative Curfew': Changing Dimensions of Communal Politics in India." In *Mirrors of Violence: Communities, Riots and Survivors in South Asia,* ed. Veena Das. Delhi.

Banerjee, Sumanta. 1980. *In the Wake of Naxalbari: A History of the Naxalite Movement in India.* Calcutta.

Banerjee, Sumanta. 2003. "Bengali Left: From Pink to Saffron," *Economic and Political Weekly,* March 1: 864–5.

———. 2002. "When the 'Silent Majority' Backs a Violent Minority," *Economic and Political Weekly.* March 30: 1183–5.

———. 1989. *The Parlour and the Streets: Elite and Popular Culture in Nineteenth Century Calcutta.* Calcutta: Seagull Books, 1989.

*Bankim* (see Chattopadhyay, Bankim Chandra).

Banu, Zenab, 1989. *Politics of Communalism; A Politico-Historical Analysis of Communal Riots in Post-Independence India with Special Reference to the Gujarat and Rajasthan Riots.* Bombay.

Baral, Lok Raj. 1990. *Regional Migrations, Ethnicity and Security: The South Asian Case.* New Delhi.

Barbora, Sanjay. 2003. "Ethnic Politics and Land Use: Genesis of Conflicts in India's North-East". *Economic and Political Weekly.* March 30: 1285–92.

Bareibiswas, Kaviraj Sashikumar. 1911. *Namashudra-dwijatattva.* Barisal.

Barnett, Marguerite Ross. 1976. *The Politics of Cultural Nationalism in South India.* Princeton.

———. 1974. "Creating Political Identity: The Emergent South Indian Tamils." *Ethnicity* 1 (1974): 237–60.

Barnett, Richard B. 1980. *North India between Empires: Awadh, the Mughuls, and the British 1720–1801.* Berkeley:

Barrier, Gerald N. 1976a. "The Cawnpore Riots." In Roots of Communal Politics: The Congress Report That Was Banned in 1933, ed. Gerald N. Barier. New Delhi and Columbus.

———. 1976b. *Roots of Communal Politics: The Congress Report That Was Banned in 1933.* New Delhi and Columbus.

————. 1968. "The Punjab Government and Communal Politics, 1870–1908." *Journal of Asian Studies* 27 (1968): 523–40.

Baruah, Apurba K. 2003. "Meghalaya Elections 2003: Decline of Regionalism." *Economic and Political Weekly.* April 19: 1538–41.

Baruah, Sanjib. 1986. "Immigration, Ethnic Conflict and Political Turmoil—Assam, 1979–1985." *Asian Survey* 26 (November).

Baruah, Sanjib. 2002. "Gulliver's Troubles: State and Militants in North-East India." *Economic and Political Weekly.* October 12: 4178–82.

————. 1999. *India Against Itself: Assam and the Politics of Nationality.* Philadelphia: University of Pennsylvania Press.

Bastian, Sunil. 1990. "Political Economy of Ethnic Violence in Sri Lanka: The July 1983 Riots." In *Mirrors of Violence: Communities, Riots and Survivors in South Asia,* ed. Veena Das. Delhi.

Basu Amrita. 1995. "Why Local Riots Are Not Merely Local: Collective Violence and the State in Bijnor, India, 1988–1993." *Theory and Society* 24: 35–78.

————. 1994a. "Bhopal Revisited: The View from Below." *Bulletin of Concerned Asian Scholars* 26 (January): 3–14.

————. 1994b. "When Local Riots Are Not Merely Local: Bringing the State Back In, Bijnor, 1988–1992." *Economic and Political Weekly,* October 1, 2605–21.

Basu, Amrita and Atul Kohli. Editors. 1998. *Community Conflicts and the State in India.* Oxford: Oxford University Press.

Basu, Amrita, 2002. "Parliamentary Democracy as a Historical Phenomenon: The CPM in West Bengal." In *Parties and Party Politics in India.* Edited by Zoya Hasan. Delhi: Oxford University Press. pp.317–50.

————. 2001. "The Dialectics of Hindu Nationalism." In *The Success of India's Democracy.* Edited by Atul Kohli. Cambridge: Cambridge University Press. pp.163–190.

————. 1999. "Rethinking Communalism and Fundamentalism: Women's Activism and Religious Politics in India," *Journal of Women's History,* 10, 4, 104–124.

————. 1997 "Reflections on Community Conflicts and the State In India," *Journal of Asian Studies,* 56, 2, 1997, 391–7.

Basu, Amrita. 1993. "Feminism Inverted: The Real Women and Gendered Imagery of Hindu Nationalism." *Bulletin of Concerned Asian Scholars* 25, no. 4 (October–December). (Special Issue on women and religion and nationalism in India.)

Basu, Aparna. 1980. "Growth of Education and Muslim Separation, 1919–1939." In *Essays in Modern Indian History,* ed. B. R. Nanda. Delhi.

Basu, Chandranath. 1892. *Hindutva.* Calcutta.

Basu, Kaushik, and Sanjay Subrahmanyam, eds. 1995. *Unravelling the Nation: Sectarian Conflict and India's Secular Identity.* Delhi.

Basu, Lokenath. 1858. *Hindu-dharma-marma.* Calcutta.

Basu, Sajal. 1992. *Regional Movements: Politics of Language, Ethnicity-Identity.* Shimla.

Basu, Taan, Pradip Datta, Sumit Sarkar, Tanika Sarkar, and Sambudda Sen. 1993. *Khaki Shorts and Saffron Flags.* New Delhi.

Baxi, Upendra, Alice Jacob and Tarlok Singh. Editors. 1999. *Reconstructing the Republic.* New Delhi: Har-Anand Publications.

Baxi, Upendra. 1990a. "Reflections on the Reservation Crisis in Gujarat." In *Mirrors of Violence: Communities, Riots and Survivors in South Asia*, ed. Veena Das. Delhi.

———. 1990b. "Social Change, Criminality and Social Control in India: Trends, Achievements, and Perspectives." In *Essays on Crime and Development*, ed. Uglesa Zvekic. Rome.

Bayly, C.A. 1988. *Indian Society and the Making of the British Empire*. Cambridge.

———. 1985. "The Pre-History of 'Communalism'? Religious Conflict in India, 1700–1860." *Modern Asian Studies* 19:177–203.

———. 1983. *Rulers, Townsmen and Bazaars: North Indian Society in the Age of British Expansion, 1770–1870*. Cambridge.

Bayly, Susan. 1990. *Saints, goddesses and Kings: Muslims and Christians in South Asian Society, 1700–1900*. New York, 1990.

———. 1984. "Hindu Kingship and the Origins of Community: Religion, State and Society in Kerala, 1750–1850." *Modern Asian Studies* 18 (April): 177–214.

Bedi, Rahul. 1990. "5,000 Who Volunteered for Arrest." *India abroad*. December 14.

Bengal. 1891. Government of Bengal. *Report on native Papers*. January-March. Calcutta.

———. 1890. Government of Bengal. *Report on Native Papers*. Calcutta.

Beteille, Andre. 1992. *The backward Classes in Contemporary India*. Delhi.

———. 1990. "Caste and Politics: The Subversion of Public Institutions." *Times of India* (September), repr. in Beteille 1992.

———. 1982. "The Indian Road to Equality: More Jobs for More castes." *Times of India* (August), repr. in Beteille 1992.

———. 1961. "The Politics of Caste: Competition in backwardness." *Indian Express* (August 22 and 23), repr. in Beteille 1992.

Bhabha, Homi. 1986. "The Other Question: Difference, Discrimination and the Discourse of Colonialism." In *Literature, Politics, and Theory*, ed. Francis Barker et al. London.

Bhadra, G. 1976. "Social Groups and Relations in the Town of Murshidabad, 1765–1793." *Indian Historical Review* 2:312–38.

Bhalla, P.N. 1944. "The Gosain Brothers." *Journal of Indian History* 23:128–36.

Bhandari, Vivek. 1994. "Historicizing Language: The Urdu-Hindi Controversy in Late Nineteenth Century Punjab." Master's thesis, University of Pennsylvania.

Bharatiya Janata Party (BJP). 1993. *White Paper on Ayodhya and the Rama Temple Movement*. New Delhi.

Bharatiya Janata Party. 1995. *BJP Economic Resolutions*. New Delhi: Bharatiya Janata Party.

Bhatt, Chetan. 2001. *Hindu Nationalism: Origins, Ideologies and Modern Myths*. Oxford: Berg.

Bhattacharji, Digindranarayan. 1912. *Jatibheda*. Calcutta.

Bhattacharya, Neeladri. 1991. "Myth, History and the Politics of Ramajanmbhumi." In *Anatomy of a Confrontation: The Babri Masjid-Ram Janmabhumi Issue*, ed. S. Gopal. Delhi.

Bhattacharya, Sabyaschi. 1991. "Traders and Trade in Old Calcutta." In *Calcutta the Living City*, ed. S. Chaudhuri. Calcutta.

Bhishikar, C.P. 1979. *Keshav Sanghnirmata*. Pune. (Hindi translation, Delhi, 1980).

Bhushan, Shashi. 1986. *Fundamentalism: A Weapon Against Human Aspirations*. New Delhi.

Bidwai, Praful, Harbans Mukhia, and Achin Vanaik. Editors. 1996. *Religion, Religiosity, and Communalism*. New Delhi: Manohar.

Bidwai, Praful. 2002. "Dalits and Adivasis: Canon Fodder for Hindutva?" HIMAL 15,5, May: 30–2.

Bihar and Orissa. 1921. Government of Bihar and Orissa, Political Department. Special section. *Report of Sadhus Taking Part in Non-Cooperation*. File no. 80 1921.

Bilgrami, Akeel. 1993. "What Is a Muslim? Fundamental Commitment and Cultural Identity." In *Hindus and Others: The Question of Identity in India Today*, ed. Gyanendra Pandey. Delhi.

Bjorkman, James Warner, ed. 1988. *Fundamentalists, Revivalists, and Violence in South Asia*. New Delhi.

Blunt, Wilfred S. 1975. [1882]. *The Future of Islam*. Lahore.

Bookman, L.M. 1978. "Hindus and Muslims: Communal Relations." In *Cohesion and Conflict in Modern India*, ed. Giri Raja Gupta. Durham.

Boreham, Noel. 1993. "Decolonisation and Provincial Muslim Politics: Sind, 1937–47." *South Asia* 16 (June): 53–72.

Bose, Sugata. 1993. *Peasant Labour and Colonial Capital: Rural Bengal since 1770*. Cambridge.

Brass, Paul R. 1992. *Ethnicity and Nationalism: Theory and Comparison*. Newbury Park, CA.

———. 1990. *The Politics of India since Independence*. Cambridge.

———. 1985. *Caste, Faction, and Party in Indian Politics*. Delhi.

———. 1984. *Ethnic Groups and the State*. Totowa.

———. 1979. "Elite Groups, Symbol Manipulation, and Ethnic Identity among the Muslims of South Asia." In *Political Identity in South Asia*, ed. David Taylor and Malcolm Yapp. London.

———. 1974. *Language, Religion and Politics in North India*. Cambridge.

Brass, Paul R. 2003. *The Production of Hindu-Muslim Violence in Contemporary India*. Seattle: University of Washington Press

———. 1999. *The Politics of India Since Independence*. Cambridge: Cambridge University Press.

———. 1997. *Theft of an Idol: Text and Context in the Representation of Collective Violence* Princeton: Princeton University Press

———. 1997. "National Power and Local Politics in India: A Twenty-Year Perspective." In *State and Politics in India*. Editor Partha Chatterjee, 303–35. Delhi: Oxford University Press.

———. 1996. *Riots and Pogroms*. New York: New York University Press.

Brass, Paul R. and Achin Vinayak. Editors. 2002. *Competing Nationalisms in South Asia: Essays for Asghar Ali Engineer*. Hyderabad: Orient Longman.

Breckenridge, Carol, and Peter van der Veer, eds. 1993. *Orientalism and the Postcolonial Predicament: Perspectives on South Asia*. Philadelphia.

Breman, Jan, Arvind N. Das, Ravi Agarwal, and Brinda Datta. 2000. *Down and Out: Labouring under Global Capitalism*. New Delhi: Oxford University Press.

Breman, Jan, Ghanshyam Shah, Mario Rutten and Hein Streefkert. 2002. *Development and Deprivation in Gujarat*. New Delhi: Sage Publications.

Breman, Jan, Peter Kloos, Ashwani Saith. Editors. 1997. *The Village in Asia Revisited*. Delhi: Oxford University Press.

Breman, Jan. 1993a. "Anti-Muslim Pogrom in Surat." *Economic and Political Weekly*, April 17, 737–41.

———. 1993b. "Op weg narr hat Ghetto. De transformative van een moslimsloppenwijk in Ahmedabad, India." *De Gids* 156:456–72.

Breman, Jan. 2002. "Communal Upheaval as Resurgence of Social Darwinism," *Economic and Political Weekly*, 37, 16, April 20–26, 1485–88.

———. 1996. *Footloose Labour: Working in India's Informal Economy*. Cambridge: Cambridge University Press.

Brennan, Lance. 1994. "The State and Communal Violence in UP: 1947–1992." *South Asia* 17:19–34.

———. 1984. "The Illusion of Security: The Background of Muslim Separatism in the United Provinces." *Modern Asian Studies* 18:237–72.

Brosius, Christiane. 2003. "Hindutva Intervisuality: Videos and the Politics of Representation" in *Beyond Appearances? Visual Practices and Ideologies in Modern India*. Edited by Sumathi Ramaswami, New Delhi: Sage, pp. 265–296.

Broughton, Thomas. 1977. *Letters from a Mahratta Camp during the Year 1809: Description of the Character, Manners, Domestic Habits, and Religious Ceremonies of the Mahrattas*. Calcutta (first published in London, 1813).

Brown, Judith M. 1985. *Modern India: The Origins of an Asian Democracy*. Oxford.

Brown, Percy. 1956. *Indian Architecture (Islamic Period)*. Bombay.

Burghart. Richard. 1978. "The Founding of the Ramanandi Sect." *Ethnohistory*, 225:121–39.

Butalia, Urvashi, 2002. "Gender and Nation: Some Reflections from India." In *From Gender to Nation*. Edited by Radha Ivekovic and Julie Mostov. Ravenna: Longo Editore Ivekovic, pp. 99–112.

———. 2000. *The Other Side of Silence*. Duke: Duke University Press.

Butalia, Urvashi. Forthcoming. "Community, State and Gender—Women's Experiences During Partition." *Economic and Political Weekly*.

Butani. D.H. 1986. *The Third Sikh War? Towards or Away from Khalistan*. New Delhi.

Butler, David. 1997. "India Decides: Elections, 1952–1995." In *State and Politics in India*. Edited by Partha Chatterjee, pp. 125–76. Delhi: Oxford University Press.

Butler, Harcourt. 1932. "The Country Peoples: Language and Creeds." In *Modern India: A Co-operative Survey*, ed. John Cumming. London.

———. 1931. *India Insistent*. London.

———. 1921. *Speeches*. Allahabad. (Deliveed at the M.A.O. College, Aligarh, on November 25, 1919).

Carroll, Lucy. 1978. "Colonial Perceptions of Indian Society and the Emergence of Caste(s) Associations." *Journal of Asian Studies* 37:233–50.

———. 1977. "Caste, Community, and Caste(s) Association: A Note on the Organization of the Kayashta Conference and the definitions of a Kayastha Community." *Contributions to Asian Studies* 10:3–23.

Cecil, Wes, Pranav Jani, and Stacy Takacs. 1994. "India Is(n't): (Mis) Representations of India in the U.S. Media." *Samar* (June): 4–10.

Chakrabarty, Bidyut. 1990. *Subhas Chandra Bose and Middle Class Radicalism: A Study in Indian Nationalism, 1928–1940*. London.

———. 1989. "The Communal Award of 1932 and Its Implications in Bengal." *Modern Asian Studies* 23:493–524.

Chakrabarty, Dipesh. 1994. "Modernity and Ethnicity in India." *South Asia* 17:143–55.

———. 1993. "The Difference/Deferral of (a) Colonial Modernity—Public Debate on Domesticity in British Bengal." *History Workshop Journal* 36 (September): 1–34. Special issue.

———. 1992. "Postcoloniality and the Artifice of History: Who Speaks for 'India's' Pasts?" *Representations* 37:1–26.

———. 1990. "Communal riots and Labour: Bengal's Jute Mill-hands in the 1890s." In *Mirrors of Violence: Communities, Riots and survivors in South Asia*, ed. Veena Das. Delhi.

Chakraborty, Sujit. 1989. "Communal Contagion at the Kumbh." *Link*, February 19, 4–7.

Chakravarti, Gargi. 1987. *Gandhi—A Challenge to Communalism*. New Delhi.

Chakravarti, Uma, and Nandita Haksar. 1987. *The Delhi Riots: Three Days in the Life of a Nation*. New Delhi.

Chakravarti, Uma, Prem Chaudhury, Pradip Datta, Zoya Hasan, Kumkum Sagari, and Tanika Sarkar. 1992. "Khurja Riots, 1990–91: Understanding the Conjuncture." *Economic and Political Weekly*, May 2, 951–65.

Chakravarty, Subhash. 2002. *Afghanistan and the Great Game*. Delhi: New Century Publications.

Chand, Kailash. 1986. *Jinnah and the Communal Problem in India*. New Delhi.

Chander, Sunil. 1987. "Congress-Raj Conflict and the Rise of the Muslim League in the Ministry Period, 1937–39." *Modern Asian Studies* 21 (April): 303–28.

Chandoke, Neera. 2003. "Governance and the Pluralisation of the State: Implications for Democratic Citizenship." *Economic and Political Weekly*. July 12: 2957–67.

Chandra, Bipan. 1991. "Communalism and the State." In *Communalism in India: History, Politics, and Culture*, ed. K.N. Panikkar. New Delhi.

———. 1984. *Communalism in Modern India*. New Delhi.

———. 1979. *Nationalism and Colonialism in Modern India*. New Delhi.

———. 1966. *The Rise and Growth of Economic Nationalism in India: Economic Policies of Indian National Leadership*. New Delhi.

Chandra, Sudhir. 1994. "Of Communal Consciousness and Communal Violence: Impressions from Post-Riot Surat." *South Asia* 17:49–61.

———. 1993a. "Of Communal Consciousness and Communal Violence: Impressions from Post-Riot Surat." *Economic and Political Weekly*, September 4, 1883–87.

———. 1993b. "Towards an Integrated Understanding of Early Indian Nationalism: Notes on *The Lake of Palms*." In *Indian Responses to Colonialism in the Nineteenth Century*, ed. Alok Bhalla and Sudhir Chandra. New Delhi.

———. 1992. *The Oppressive Present: Literature and Social Consciousness in Colonial India.* Delhi.

———. 1990. "The Lengthening Shadow: Secular and Communal Consciousness." In *Secularism and Indian Polity,* ed. Bidyut Chakrabarty. New Delhi.

———. 1987. "Communal Consciousness in Late Nineteenth Century Hindi Literature." In *Communal and Pan-Islamic Trends in Colonial India,* ed. Mushirul Hasan. New Delhi.

———. 1986. "Maithilisharan Gupta and the Idea of India Nationalism." *Economic and Political Weekly,* March 20.

———. 1985. "The Cultural Complement of Economic Nationalism: R.C. Dutt's *The Lake of Palms.*" *Indian Historical Review* 12:106–20.

———. 1983. "Towards Secularization: Nationalism in Nineteenth Century India." In *Problems of Secularization in Multi-Religious Societies,* ed. S. C. Dube and V. N. Basilov. New Delhi.

Charu and Mukul. 1990. *Print Media and Communalism.* New Delhi.

Chatterjee, Abhas. 1995. *The Concept of Hindu Nation.* New Delhi: Voice of India.

Chatterjee, Partha, and Gyanendra Pandey, eds. 1993. *Subaltern Studies VII: Writings on South Asian History and Society.* Delhi.

Chatterjee, Partha. 1993. *The Nation and Its Fragments: Colonial and Post-Colonial Histories.* Princeton.

———. 1986. *Nationalist Thought and the Colonial World: A Derivative Discourse?* Delhi.

———. 1984. "Gandhi and the Critique of Civil Society." In *Subaltern Studies III: Writings on South Asian History and Society,* ed. Ranajit Guha. Delhi.

———. 1982. "Agrarian Relations and Communalism in Bengal, 1926–1935." In *Subaltern Studies I: Writings on South Asian History and Society,* ed. Ranajit Guha. Delhi.

Chatterji, Joya. 1995. *Bengal Divided: Hindu Communalism and Partition, 1932–47.* Cambridge: Cambridge University Press.

Chatterji, M. 1994. "The BJP: Political Mobilization for Hindutva." *South Asia Bulletin: Comparative Studies of South Asia, Africa and the Middle East* 14:14–23.

Chattopadhyay, Bankim Chandra. 1992. *Anandamath,* trans. Basanta Koomar Roy. New Delhi.

———. 1969. *Bankim Rachanabali,* vol. 2, ed. J.C. Bagal. Calcutta.

*Lokrahasya.* 1–48.

*Muchiram Gurer Jibancharit.* 126–27.

*Vividha prabandha* [Selected essays]. 159–380.

"Bahuvivaha."

Bangadesher Krishak.

"Bangalir Bahubul Prabandha Pustak."

"Bangalar Itihasa."

"Bharatbaishe swadinata Ebong Paradhinata."

"Gaurdas Babajir Bhikshar Jhuli."

"Sankhyadarshan."

*Samya* [Equality]. (381–406?)

*Krishmacharitra.* 407–583.

*Dharmatattva*. 584–679.
"Srimadbhagavat Gita." 680–775.
"Devatattva o Hindudharma." 776–872.
———. 1965. *Bankim Rachanabali*, vol. I, ed. J.C. Bagal. Calcutta.
*Durgeshnandini*. 53–138.
*Mrinalini*. 189–260.
*Chandrasekhar*. 399–432.
*Rajasingha*. 609–714.
*Anandamath*. 715–88.
*Debi Choudhurani*. 789–872.
*Sitaram*. 873–958.

Chattopadhyay, Basudeb, Ashis Ranjan Guha and Ramkrishna Chatterjee. 2002. *Communalism Condemned, Gujarat Genocide 2002*. Kolkata: Progressive Publishers.

Chattopadhyay, Dilip Kumar. 1990. *History of the Assamese Movement since 1947*. Calcutta.

Chattopadhyay, Pasupati. 1926. *Kalir Bamun*. Calcutta.

Chaudhuri, B.B. 1967. "Agrarian Economy and Agrarian Relations in Bengal, 1859–1885." In *History of Bengal, 1757–1905*, ed. N. K. Sinha. Calcutta.

Chaudhuri, Nirad C. 1987. *The Hand Great Anarch! India, 1921–1952*. London.

———. 1951. *The Autobiography of an Unknown Indian*. New York.

Chibber, Pradeep, and Subhash Misra. 1993. "Hindus and the Bari Masjid: The Sectional basis of Communal Attitudes." *Asian Survey* 33 (July): 665–72.

Chirol, Sir Valentine. [1921] 1975. *India, Old and New*. New Delhi.

Chitkara, M. G. 1997. *Hindutva*. New Delhi: APH Publications.

Chopra, Pran. 1993. "The Fate of the BJP." *The Hindu*, December 3.

Chopra, V.D. 1990. *Genesis of Indo-Pakistan Conflict on Kashmir*. New Delhi.

Chowgule, Ashok. 1999. *Christianity in India: The Hindutva Perspective*. Mumbai: Hindu Vivek Kendra.

Cohn, Bernard S. 1964. "The Role of the Gosains in the Economy of Eighteenth and Nineteenth-Century Upper India." *Indian Economic and Social History Review* I:185–82.

Cole, Juan Ricardo. 1989. *Roots of North Indian Shi'ism in Iran and Iraq: Religion and State in Awadh, c. 1722–1859*. Delhi.

Coll, Steve. 1994. *On the Grand Trunk Road: A Journey to South Asia*. New York.

Connor, Walker. 1994. *Ethnonationalism: The Quest for Understanding*. Princeton.

Crooke, W. [1897] 1975. *The North-Western Provinces of India: Their History, Ethnology, and Administration*. Reprint, Delhi.

Crossick, Geoffrey. 1977. *The Lower Middle Class of Britain, 1870–1914*. New York.

Daniel, Norman. 1960. *Islam and the West: The Making of an Image*. Edinburgh.

Dar, Bishan Narain. 1921. *Collected Speeches and Writings of Pt. Bishan Narain Dar, Volume I*, ed. H. L. Chatterjee. Lucknow.

———. 1893. *An Appeal to the English Public on Behalf of the Hindus of North-Western Provinces and Oudh*. Lucknow.

Darling, Frank C. 1979. *The Westernization of Asia: A Comparative Political Analysis*. Boston.

Das Gupta, Chidananda. 1991. *The Painted Face: Studies in India's Popular Cinema*. New Delhi.

Das Gupta, Uma. 1978. "Rabindranath Tagore on Rural Reconstruction: The Sriniketan Program." *Indian Historical Review* 4:354–78.

Das, Gurcharan. 2002. *India Unbound: The Social and Economic Revolution from Independence to the Global Information Age*. New York: Anchor Books.

Das, Sisir Kumar. 1984. *The Artist in Chains: The Life of Bankimchandra Chatterjee*. Appendix C, "A Muslim Baiter?" Delhi.

Das, Suranjan. 1991. *Communal Riots in Bengal, 1905–1947*. Delhi.

Das, Veena. 1990a. "Introduction: Communities, Riots, Survivors—the South Asian Experience." In *Mirrors of Violence: Communities, Riots, and Survivors in South Asia*, ed. Veena Das. Delhi.

———. 1990b. "Our Work to Cry: Your Work to Listen." In *Mirrors of Violence: Communities, Riots, and Survivors in South Asia*, ed. Veena Das. Delhi.

——— ed. 1990c. *Mirrors of Violence: Communities, Riots, and Survivors in South Asia*. Delhi.

Das. N.K. 1989. *Ethnic Identity, Ethnicity and Social Stratification in North East India*. Delhi.

Dasgupta, Anindita. 2000. "Emergence of a Community: The Muslims of East Bengal Origin in Assam in Colonial and Post-Colonial Period." Unpublished PhD dissertation, University of Guwahati.

Dasgupta, Swapan. 2003. "BJP's Finest Hour." *India Today*, 10 February 2003: 26–34.

Datta, Pradip K., Biswamoy Pati, Sumit Sarkar, Tanika Sarkar, Sambuddha Sen. 1990. "Understanding Communal Violence: The Nizamuddin Riots." *Economic and Political Weekly*, November 10, 2487–95.

Datta, Pradip Kumar. 1993a. "Dying Hindus: Production of Hindu Communal Common Sense in Early-20th Century Bengal." *Economic and Political Weekly* (June): 1305–25.

———. 1993b. "VHP's Ram: The Hindutva movement in Ayodhya." In *Hindus and Others: The Question of Identity in India Today*, ed. Gyanendra Pandey. Delhi.

———. 1991. "VHP's Ram." *Economic and Political Weekly* (November 2): 2517–26.

Datta, V.N. 1988. *Sati: A Historical, Social, and Philosophical Enquiry into the Hindu Rite of Widow Burning*. Westwood, MA.

Davis, Richard H. 1997. *Lives of Indian Images*, Princeton: Princeton University Press and Delhi: Motilal Banarsidass.

Davis, Richard H. Editor. Forthcoming. *Iconographies and the Nation in India*. New Delhi, Orient Longman.

De, Barun. 1985. "Towards Freedom: No Focus on the Role of Masses." *Indian Historical Review* 12 (June): 373–77. (Review of P.N. Chopra, ed., *Towards Freedom*).

*Delhi Gazette*. 1850. (June 12 and 15, 1850) "The Great Fair at Oojein."

Derrett, J.D.M. 1961. "The Administration of Hindu law by the British." *Comparative Studies in Society and History* 4: 10–52.

———. 1968. *Religion, Law, and the State in India*. London.

Desai, A.R. 1985. *Caste and Communal Violence in Independent India*. Bombay.

Dhawan, Rajiv. 1987. *Only the Good news: On the law of the Press in India*. New Delhi.

Dixit, Prabha. 1974. *Communalism: A Struggle for Power*. New Delhi.

Dubey, S.K. 1989. "Building of Ayodhya Temple from November 9." *Times of India*, February 13.

Duby, Georges. 1980. *The Three Orders: Feudal Society Imagined*. Chicago.

Dusenbery, Vene. 1995. "A Sikh Diaspora?: Contested Identities and Constructed Realities." In *Nation and Migration: The Politics of Space in the South Asian Diaspora*, ed. Peter van der Veer. Philadelphia.

Dutt, R.C., ed. 1989. *Challenges to the Polity: Communalism, Casteism and Economic Challenges*. New Delhi.

Dutt, R.P. [1940] 1947. *Indian Today*. Bombay.

Dutta, P.K. 1991. "War over Music: The Riots of 1926 in Bengal." In *Communalism in India: History, Politics and Culture*, ed. K.N. Panikkar. New Delhi.

Eaton, Richard M. 1994. *The Rise of Islam and the Bengal Frontier, 1204–1760*. Berkeley.

————. 1993. "Islamic History as Global History." In *Islamic and European Expansion: The Forming of a Global Order*, ed. Michael Adas. Philadelphia.

————. 1985. "Approaches to the Study of Conversion to Islam in India." In *Approaches to Islam in Religious Studies*, ed. Richard C. Martin. Tucson.

Eco, Umberto. 1995. "Ur-Fascism." *New York Review of Books*, June 22, 12–15.

Edib, Halide. 1937. *Inside India*. London.

Ehrenreich, Barbara. 1990. *Fear of Falling: The Inner Life of the Middle Class*. New York.

Elliot, C.A. 1892. *Laborious Days*. Calcutta.

Elliott, H.M., and John Dowson, eds. 1867–77. *The History of India as told by its Own Historians*. 8 vols. London.

Elst, Koenraaad. 1991. *Ayodhya and After: Issues Before Hindu Society*. New Delhi.

————. 1990. *Ram Janmabhoomi vs. Babri Masjid: A Case Study in Hindu-Muslim Conflict*. New Delhi.

Elst, Koenraad. 2002a. *Ayodhya: The Case Against the Temple*. New Delhi: Voice of India.

————. 2002b. *Who is a Hindu? Hindu Revivalist Views of Animism, Buddhism, Sikhism, and Other Offshoots of Hinduism*. New Delhi: Voice of India.

Embree, Ainslee. 1988. *Sources of Indian Tradition. Volume One: From the Beginning to 1800*. Second edition. New York.

EMI CLP 1308. N.d. "Classical Music from Pakistan," by Nazakat and Salamat Ali. (LP record).

Engineer, Asghar Ali. 1994. "Communal Violence and the Role of Law Enforcement Agencies." *South Asia Bulletin: Comparative Studies of South Asia, Africa, and the Middle East* 14:16–23.

————. 1993. "Bastion of Communal Amity Crumbles." *Economic and Political Weekly* February 13, 262–64.

————. 1992. "Indian Muslims in a Contemporary Multi-Religious Society." In *Religion and Political Conflict in South Asia*, ed. Douglas Allen. Westprt.

————. 1989. *Communalism and Communal Violence in India: An Analytical Approach to Hindu-Muslim Conflict*. Delhi.

———— 1988. *Delhi Meerut Riots: Compilation, Documentation and Analysis*. Delhi.

————. 1987a. *Ethnic Conflict in South Asia*. Delhi.

———. 1987b. *The Shah Bano Controversy*. Delhi.

———. 1984. *Communal riots in Post Independence India*. Delhi.

———, ed. 1990. *Babri Masjid-Ramjanmabhoomi Controversy*. New Delhi.

Engineer, Asghar Ali. 2003a. "Lessons of Best Bakery Case." *Economic and Political Weekly*. July 19: 3046–7.

———. 2003b. "Communal Riots in 2002." *Economic and Political Weekly* . January 25: 280–2.

———. 2002a. "Gujarat Riots in the Light of the History of Communal Violence." *Economic and Political Weekly* . December 14: 5047–54.

———. 2002b. "Communal Riots: Review of 2001." *Economic and Political Weekly*. January 12: 100–4.

———. 1995. *Communalism in India: A Historical and Empirical Study*. New Delhi: Vikas.

Engineer, Asghar Ali and Moin Shakir, eds. 1985. *Communalism in India*. Delhi.

Enzensberger, Hans Magnus. 1970. "Constituents of a Theory of the Media." *New Left Review* 64:13–36.

Farmer, Victoria L., 1996. "The Limits of Image-Making: Doordarshan and the 1989 Lok Sabha Election: In *Media, Elections and Democracy in Asia*, ed. Anura Goonasekera and Duncan Holaday. Singapore.

Farmer, Victoria. 2003. "Television, Governance and Social Change: Media Policy Through India's First Half-Century of Independence," PhD Dissertation in Political Science, University of Pennsylvania.

———. 2000. "Depicting the Nation: Media Politics in Independent India." In *Transforming India: Social and Political Dynamics of a Democracy*. Edited by Francine R. Frankel et al. New Delhi: Oxford University Press, pp.254–287.

Farquhar. J.N. 1925a. "The Fighting Ascetics of India." *Bulletin of the John Rylands Library* 9:431–52.

———. 1925b. "The Organization of the Sannyasis of the Vedanta." *Journal of the Royal Asiatic Society* (July): 479–86.

———. 1920. "The Historical Position of Ramananda." *Journal of the Royal Asiatic Society* (April): 185–92.

———. [1914] 1977. *Modern Religious Movement in India*. (Based on a series of lectures given in 1913 at Hartford Seminary, Connecticut.) New Delhi.

Flavia, Agnes. 1994. "Redefining the Agenda of the Women's Movement within a Secular Framework." *South Asia* 18:63–78.

Foster, George M. 1965. "Peasant Society and the Image of Limited Good." *American Anthropologist* 67 (April): 293–315.

Foster, Robert J. 1991. "Making National Cultures in the Global Ecumene." *Annual Review of Anthropology* 20:235–60.

Fox, Richard G. 1992. "Twice-Told Tales from India." *Anthropology Today* 8, I.

———. 1990. "Gandhian Socialism and Hindu Nationalism: Cultural Domination in the World System." In *South Asia and World Capitalism*, ed. Sugata Bose. Delhi.

———. 1984. "Urban Class and Communal Consciousness in Colonial Punjab: The Genesis of India's Intermediate Regime." *Modern Asian Studies* 18:459–89.

Fox, Richard G., Charlotte Aull, and Louis Cimino. 1978. "Ethnic Nationalism and Political Mobilization in Complex Socieities." In *Interethnic Communication*, ed. E. Lamar Ross. Athens.

Frankel, Francine R. 1991. "Middle Classes and Castes in India's Politics: prospects for Political Accommodation." In *India's Democracy: An Analysis of Changing State-Society Relations*, ed. Atul Kohli. Princeton and Delhi.

————. 1990. "Decline of a Social Order." In *Dominance and State Power in India*, vol. 2, ed. Francine R. Frankel and M.S.A. Rao. New York and Delhi.

————. 1989. "Caste, Land and Dominance in Bihar: breakdown of the Brahmanical Social Order." In *Dominance and State Power in Modern India*, vol. I, ed. Francine R. Frankel and M.S.A. Rao. New York and Delhi.

Frankel, Francine R., and M.S.A. Rao, eds. 1990. *Dominance and State Power in Modern India*, vol. 2. New York and Delhi.

————. 1989. *Dominance and State Power in Modern India*, vol. I. New York and Delhi.

Frawley, David (Vamadeva Shastri). 2001. *Hinduism and the Clash of Civilizations*, Santa Fe: American Institute of Vedic Studies. http://www.bharatvani.org/

————. 1998. *Awaken Bharata: A Call for India's Rebirth*. New Delhi: Voice of India.

Freitag, Sandria B. 1994. "Sansiaha and the State." Paper presented to the SOAS/Nehru Library Conference, "Changing Concepts of Justice," March.

————. 1993. "Shaping a Visual Discourse: Cultural Production, Mass Consumption, and the Nation." Paper Presented to the Chicago Conference on Comparative Publics Spheres, October.

————. 1991a. "Enactments of Ram's Story and the Changing Nature of 'The Public' in British India." *South Asia* 14:65–90.

————. 1991b. Introduction. Special Issue, *South Asia* 14 (June): 1–13.

————. 1991c. "Two Discursive Spaces for Hindu-Muslim Riots in India." Paper presented to the Committee for Comparative studies in Ethnicity and Nationality, Washington, May.

————. 1989a. *Collective Action and Community: Public Arenas and the Emergency of Communalism in North India*. Berkeley.

————. 1989b. "State and Community: Symbolic Popular Protest in Banaras' Public Arenas." In *Culture and Power in Banaras: Community, performance and Environment, 1800–1980*, ed. Sandria B. Freitag. Berkeley.

————. 1988. "Muslim Separatism in South Asia: Bombay and Kanpur Compared." In *Islamic Movements of the Twentieth Century*, ed. Ira Lapidus and Edmund Burke III. Berkeley.

————. 1984. "Sunnis and Shi'a: From Community Identity to Communal Sectarianism in North Indian Islam." In *Proceedings of the South Asia Seminar, 1980–1981*, ed. Peter Gaeffke. Philadelphia.

————. 1980. "Sacred Symbol as Mobilizing Ideology: The North Indian Search for a Hindu Community." *Comparative Studies in Society and History* 22:597–625.

————. 1977. "Hindu-Muslim Riots in India: A preliminary Overview." *Berkeley Working Papers on South and Southeast Asia*. vol. I. Berkeley.

————, ed. Forthcoming (a). *Contesting in Public: Colonial Legacies and Contemporary Communalism*.

————, ed. Forthcoming (b). *Culture as Contested Site*.

Freitag, Sandria. Forthcoming. "More than Meets the (Hindu) Eye: The Public Sphere as a Space for Alternative Visions" in *Iconographies and the Nation in India* Edited by Richard Davis, Delhi: Orient Longman.

Frykenberg, Robert E. 1991. "The Emergence of Modern Hinduism as a Concept and as an Institution: A Reappraisal with Special Reference to South India." In *Hinduism Reconsidered*, ed. Gunther D. Sontheimer and Hermann Kulke. New Delhi.

Fuller, Bamyfylde. [1910] 1988. *India: The Land and Its People*. Repr., New Delhi.

————. 1913. *The Empire of India*. London.

————. 1910. *Studies of Indian Life and Sentiments*. London.

Fusefled, Warren. Forthcoming. "The Kumbh Mela in Allahabad: Networks of Communication in Nineteenth-Century North India." In *Contesting in Public: Colonial Legacies and Contemporary Communalism*, ed. Sandria B. Freitag.

Gaeffke, Peter. 1978. *Hindi Literature in the Twentieth Century*. Wiesbaden.

Gait, E.A. 1912. Introduction to *Census of India 1911*. Calcutta.

Galanter, Marc. 1984. *Competing Equalities: Law and the Backward Classes in India*. Delhi.

Ganesh, S. and Mrudul Mody. 2002. "Ahmedabadi Youth: What Causes Moral Amnesia?" *Economic and Political Weekly*. May 25: 1969–73.

Ganguly, Sumit. 1993. "Ethno-Religious Conflict in South Asia." *Survival* 35 (June): 88–109.

Ganti, Tejaswini. 1933. "Police, Kanoon aur Insaaf: The State in Hindi Cinema." Paper presented at the 22nd Annual Conference on South Asia, Madison, WI, November 5.

Garrat, G.T. 1929. *An Indian Commentary*. London.

Gavaskar, Mahesh, "Fractured Mandates and Their Concoctions," *Economic and Political Weekly*, June 12, 2004, online edition http://www.epw.org

Geertz, Clifford. 1965. "Modernization in a Muslim Society: The Indonesian Case." In *Religion and Progress in Modern Asia*, ed. Robert N. Bellah. New York.

Gellner, Ernest. 1983. *Nations and Nationalism*. Ithaca and London.

Ghosh, Jamini Mohan. 1930. *Sannyasi and Fakir Raiders in Bengal*. Calcutta.

Ghosh, S.K. 1987. *Communal Riots in India: Meet the Challenge Unitedly*. New Delhi.

Ghurye, G.S. 1968. *Social Tensions in India*. Bombay.

————. 1964. *Indian Sadhus*. Bombay.

Gilmartin, David and Bruce B. Lawrence. Editors. 2000. *Beyond Turk and Hindu: Rethinking Religious Identities in Islamicate South Asia*. Gainesville: University Press of Florida.

Gilmartin, David. 1989. *Empire and Islam: Punjab and the Making of Pakistan*. Delhi.

Gilroy, Paul. 1993. *The Black Atlantic*. Cambridge.

Godse, Gopal, ed. 1977. *May It Please Your Honour: Statement of Nathuram Godse, 8 November 1948*. Pune.

Goel, Sita Ram. 1997. *Time for Stock-taking, Whither Sangh Parivar*. New Delhi: Voice of India.

Goel, Sita Ram. Editor. 1998a. *Freedom of Expression: Secular Theocracy Versus Liberal Democracy*. New Delhi: Voice of India.

———. 1998b. *Hindu Temples, What Happened to Them?* New Delhi: Voice of India.

Gold, Daniel 1991. "Organized Hinduisms: From Vedic Truth to Hindu Nation." In *Fundamentalisms Observed*, ed. Martin E. Marty and R. Scott Appleby. Chicago.

Golwalkar, Madhav Sadashiv. 1980. *Vicaradhana*. Pune.

———. 1966a. *Bunch of Thoughts*. Bangalore.

———. 1966b. "The Nation and Its Problems." In Golwalkar 1966a.

——— 1939. *We, or Our Nation Defined*. Nagpur.

Gooptu, Nandini, *The Politics of the Urban Poor in Early Twentieth-century India*, Cambridge: Cambridge University, Press, 2001, pp.185–243, "Militant Hinduism."

Gopal, S. 1991. *Anatomy of a Confrontation: The Babri Masjid-Ram Janmabhumi Issue*. New Delhi.

———. 1966. *British Policy in India, 1858–1905*. Cambridge.

———. 1953. *The Viceroyality of Lord Ripon, 1880–1884*. London.

———, ed. 1972–1995. *Selected Works of Jawaharlal Nehru*. 17 volumes. Delhi.

Gordon, Leonard A., and Philip Oldenburg. 1992. *Indian Briefing, 1992*. New York.

Gosh, Papiya. 1991. "Articulating Community Rights: The Muslim League and Hindu Mahasabha in Congress Bihar, 1937–39." *South Asia* 14.

Goswami, Manu. 2004. *Producing India: From Colonial Economy to National Space*. Chicago: University of Chicago Press.

———. 1998. "From Swadeshi to Swaraj: Colonialism, Nationalism and Territorial Nativism, 1870–1948," *Comparative Studies in Society and History*, 40, 4, 609–636.

Gottschalk, Peter. 2001. *Beyond Hindu and Muslim: Multiple Identity in Narratives from Village India*. New Delhi: Oxford University Press.

Graham, Bruce. 1993. *Representation and Party Politics: A Comparative Perspecitve*. Cambridge.

———. 1990. *Hindu Nationalism and Indian Politics: The Origins and Development of the Bharatiya Jana Sangh*. Cambridge.

Graves, Nelsa. 1995. "Hindu Nationalist Groups in India Target Foreign Goods." Reuters News Service, August 9.

Greenberger, Allen J. 1969. *The British Image of India: A Study on the Literature of Imperialism, 1880–1960*. London.

Greenfield, Liah. 1992. *Nationalism: Five Roads to Modernity*. Cambridge, MA.

Greig, J. Alexander. 1987. "Tarikh-i-Sangita: The Foundations of North Indian Music in the Sixteenth Century." Ph.D. dissertation, University of California, Los Angeles.

Guha, Ranajit, ed. 1982–89. *Subaltern Studies: Writings on South Asian History and Society*, 6 vols. Delhi.

Guja, Ranajit, and Spivak, Gayatri, eds. 1988. *Selected Subaltern Studies*. New York.

Gupta, Charu. 2002. *Sexuality, Obscenity, Community: Women, Muslims, and the Hindu Public in Colonial India*. New York: Palgrave.

Gupta, Dipankar. 1982. *Nativism in a Metropolis: Shiv Sena in Bombay*. New Delhi.

Gupta, Narayani. 1981. *Delhi between Two Empires, 1803–1931*. Delhi.

Gupta, Raghuraja. 1976. *Hindu-Muslim Relations*. Lucknow.

Gupta, Surendra K., and Indira B. Gupta. 1990. *Conflict and Communications: Mass Upsurge in Assam*. New Delhi.

Gurr, Ted Robert. 1994. *Ethnic Conflict in World Politics*. Boulder.

————. 1993. *Minorities at Risk: A Global View of Ethnopolitical Conflict*. Washington.

————. 1986. "Persisting Patterns of repression and Rebellion: Foundations for a General Theory of Political Coercion." In *Persistent Patterns and Emergent Structures in a Waning Century*, ed. Margaret P. Karns. New York.

Guta, Mahendranath. 1908. *Sriramakrishna-kathamrita*. Calcutta.

Habermas, Jürgen. 1991. "The Public Sphere." In *Rethinking Popular Culture*, ed. Chandra Mukherji and Michael Schudson. Berkeley.

————. 1989. *The Structural Transformation of the Public Sphere: An Inquiry into a Category of Bourgeois Society*, trans. Thomas Burger, with the assistance of Frederick Lawrence. Cambridge, MA.

————. 1974. "The Public Sphere: An Encyclopedia Article." *The New German Critique* 3 (September): 49–55.

Habib, Irfan. 1988. *Interpreting Indian History*. Shillong.

Halbfass, Wilhelm. 1988. *India and Europe: An Essay in Understanding*. Albany.

Hansen, Kathryn. 1992. *Grounds for Play: The Nautanki Theater of North India*. Berkeley.

Hansen, Thomas Blom. 1999. *The Saffron Wave: Democracy and Hindu Nationalism in Modern India*. Princeton: Princeton University Press.

Hardiman, David. 2002. "Passing Blame on Godhra Muslims." *Economic and Political Weekly*. May 11: 1785.

Hardwicke, Thomas. 1801. "Narrative of a Journey to Sirinagur." *Asiatic Researches* 6:309–347.

Hardy, Peter. 1972. *The Muslims of British India*. Cambridge.

————. 1971. *Partners in Freedom—and True Muslims: The Political Thought of Some Muslim Scholars in British India*. Lund.

Hariharan, K. 1994. "Trends in Indian Cinema." Keynote presentation at South Asia Graduate Student Association forum on "Indian Cinema Today," University of Pennsylvania, April 4.

Harinarayanand, Swami. 1986. *Bharat Sadhu Samaj*. Delhi.

Harriss, John. 2001. *Depoliticising Development: The World Bank and Social Capital*, London: Anthem; New Delhi: Manohar.

————.1999. "Comparing Political Regimes Across Indian States." *Economic and Political Weekly*. November 27: 3367–77.

Hasan, Mushirul and Mohammad Asaduddin. Editors. 2000. *Image and Representation: Stories of Muslim Lives in India*. New Delhi: Oxford University Press

Hasan, Mushirul. 1994. "Minority Identity and its Discontents: Ayodhya and Its Aftermath." *South Asia Bulletin: Comparative Studies of South Asia, Africa, and the Middle East* 14:24–40.

————. 1993a. "Resistance and Acquiescence in North India." In *India's Colonial Encounter: Essays in Memory of Eric Stokes*, ed. Mushirul Hasan and Narayani Gupta. New Delhi.

————. 1992. *Islam and Indian Nationalism: Reflections on Abul Kalam Azad*. New Delhi.

———. 1991a. "Adjustment and Accommodation: Indian Muslims after Partition." In *Communalism in India: History, Politics and Culture*, ed. K.N. Panikkar. New Delhi.

———. 1991b. *Nationalism and Communal Politics in India, 1885–1930*. New Delhi.

———. 1988. "The Muslim Mass Contact Campaign: Analysis of a Strategy of Political Mobilization." In *Congress and Indian Nationalism: The Pre-Independence Phase*, ed. Richard Sisson and Stanley Wolpert. Berkeley.

———. 1987a. *Communal and Pan-Islamic Trends in Colonial India*. New Delhi.

———. 1987b. *A Nationalist Conscience: M. A. Ansari, the Congress, and the Raj*. New Delhi.

———. 1979. *Nationalism and Communal Politics in India: 1916–1928*. Delhi.

———. 1978. "Communalism in Indian Politics: A Study of the Nehru Report". *Indian Historical Review* 4 (January): 379–404.

———, ed. 1993b. *India's Partition: Process, Strategy and Mobilization*. Delhi.

Hasan, Mushirul. 2004. *From Pluralism to Separatism: Qasbas in Colonial Awadh*. Delhi: Oxford University Press.

———. 2002. *Islam in the Subcontinent: Muslims in a Plural Society*. New Delhi: Manohar.

———.1997. *Legacy of a Divided Nation: India's Muslims since Independence*. London: Hurst & Company.

Hasan, Mushirul. Editor. 2002. *Inventing Boundaries: Gender, Politics, and the Partition of India*. New Delhi: Oxford University Press.

———.Editor. 1998. *Islam, Communities and the Nation: Muslim Identities in South Asia and Beyond*. New Delhi: Manohar.

———.Editor. 1995. *India Partitioned: The Other Face of Freedom*. New Delhi: Lotus Collection.

Hasan, Zoya. 1994a. "Party Politics and Communal Mobilization in Uttar Pradesh." *South Asia Bulletin: Comparative Studies in South Asia, Africa, and the Middle East* 14:42–52.

———. 1994b. "Shifting Ground: Hindutva Politics and Farmers' Movement in Uttar Pradesh." *Journal of Peasant Studies* 21 (April): 165–94.

———. 1991. "Changing Orientation of the State and the Emergence of Majoritarianism in the 1980s." In *Communalism in India: History, Politics and Culture*, ed. K.N. Panikkar. New Delhi.

———. 1989. "Power and Mobilization: Patterns of Resilience and Change in Uttar Pradesh Politics." In *Dominance and State Power in Modern India: Decline of a Social Order*, ed. Francine R. Frankel and M.S.A. Rao. New Delhi.

Hay, Steven, ed. 1988. *Sources of Indian Tradition. Volume Two: Modern India and Pakistan*. Second edition. New York.

Haynes, Douglas. 1991. *Rhetoric and Ritual in Colonial India: The Shaping of a Public Culture in Surat City, 1852–1928*. Berkeley.

Hazarika, Sanjoy, 2000. *Rites of Passage: Border Crossings, Imagined Homelands, India's East and Bangladesh*. Delhi: Penguin.

Heath, Anthony and Yogendra Yadav. 1999. "Social Profile of Congress Voters, 1996 and 1999." *Economic and Political Weekly* . September 27: 2518–28.

Heath, Oliver. 1999a. "Anatomy of BJP's Rise to Power." *Economic and Political Weekly*. September 27: 2511–17.

———. 1999b. "The Fractionalisation of Indian States." *Seminar*, no. 480: 66–71.

Heber, Reginald. 1971. *Bishop Heber in Northern India: Selections from Heber's Journal*, ed. M.A. Laird. London.

Hechter, Michael. 1975. *Internal Colonialism: The Celtic Fringe in British National Development, 1536–1966*. Berkeley.

Heimsath, Charles. 1964. *Indian Nationalism and Hindu Social Reform*. Princeton.

Hess, Linda. 1994. "Martialing Religious Texts in the Battle over Ram's Birthplace: Or, Does God Want His devotees to Kill Enemies, Destroy shrines, Gain Territories, and Rule Nations?" Unpublished essay. University of California, Berkeley.

Hettne, Bjorn. 1993. "Ethnicity and Development—an Elusive Relationship." *Contemporary South Asia* 2:123–50.

Hill, Claude, H. 1911. "Religion and Caste in India." In *India and the Durbar*. London.

Hill, W. Douglas P., trans. 1952. *The Holy Lake of the Acts of Rama*, by Tulsidas. Bombay.

Hobsbawm, E.J. 1990. *Nations and Nationalism since 1780: Programme, Myth, Reality*. Cambridge.

Holderness, T.W. 1911. *Peoples and Problems of India*. London.

Hourani, Albert. 1970. *Arabic Thought in the Liberal Age, 1798–1939*. London.

Hughes, Thomas Patrick. 1885. *Dictionary of Islam*. Calcutta.

Human Rights Watch. 2002. " 'We Have No Orders To Save You': State Participation and Complicity in Communal Violence in Gujarat." http://www.hrw.org/reports/2002/india/ and http://www.hrw.org/press/2002/04/gujarat.htm

———. 2003. "Compounding Injustice: The Government's Failure to Redress Massacres at Gujarat." Volume 15, No.3, July. http://www.hrw.org

Hunter William W. 2002. *Indian Mussalmans: Are They Bound in Conscience to Rebel against the Queen?* (original edition, London, 1871) Delhi: Rupa and Company.

Hunter, W.W. [1871] 1945 (Calcutta edition). *Indian Mussalmans: Are They Bound in Conscience to Rebel against the Queen?* Lahore.

Huntington, Samuel P. 1993. "The Clash of Civilizations?" *Foreign Affairs* 72 (June): 22–49.

Huntington, Samuel. 1996. *The Clash of Civilizations and the Remaking of the World Order*. New York: Simon and Schuster.

Ikram, Sheikh Mohammed. 1964. *Muslim Civilization in India*. New York.

Ikramullah, Begum Shaista. 1991. *Huseyn Shahbeed Subrawardy: A Biography*. Karachi.

Ilaiah, Kancha. 1996. *Why I am not a Hindu: A Sudra Critique of Hindutva*. Kolkata: Samya.

India Office Library (IOL). N.d. Warren Papers. European Manuscripts. C-607. London.

———. *Reminiscences* [typescript]. London. Mss. Eur. C-607.

———. 1873a. Mss. Eur. C-144/21. E.C. Bayley to Northbrook. London, July 19.

———. 1873b. Mss. Eur. C-144/21. E.C. Bayley to Northbrook. February 21.

———. 1874. India Office Library. Mss. Eur. C-144/177. Northbrook Papers, July 10.

———. 1939. India Office Library. L/P&J/8/645. George Lumley to Linlithgow, December 14.

———. 1930. India Office Library. L/PO/6/74 (ii). Edward Thompson to Wedgewood Benn, December 31.

India Office Records (IOR). 1894a. H.E.L.P. Dupernex. "Report on Azamgarh." L.P&J/ 6, vol. 365 file 55.

———. 1894b. Mr. Hoey. "Note on the Cow Protection Campaign in the Gorakhpur District." L/P&J/365, file 84.

———. 1894c. "Note on the Agitation against Cow Killing." L/P&J/376, p. 4, footnote.

———. 1894d. D.J. Lyall, Secretary of State Government of India. "Report on Azamgarh," Letter to Advocate General. L/P&J/376, file 298.

India. 1895. Government of India, National Archives. Home (Municipal) 3 (7–13). July.

India. Supreme Court. 1996. *Supreme Court Judgment on "Hindutva": A Major Landmark*. New Delhi: Suruchi Prakashan.

———. 1995. *The Ayodhya Reference: Supreme Court Judgment and Commentaries*. New Delhi: Voice of India.

Isaacs, Harold R. 1972. *Images of Asia: American Views of China and India* (originally titled *Scratches on Our Minds*). New York.

———. 1965. *India's Ex-Untouchables*. New York.

Islam, Mustafa Nurul. 1973. *Bengali Muslim Public Opinion as Reflected in the Bengali Press, 1901–1930*. Dacca.

Iyengar, Shanto. 1991. *Is Anyone Responsible? How Television Frames Political Issues*. Chicago.

Jaffrelot, Christophe. 1996. *The Hindu Nationalist Movement and Indian Politics, 1925 to the 1990s*. New Delhi: Viking.

———. 1995. *The Hindu Nationalist Movement in India*. New York: Columbia University Press.

Jaffrelot, Christophe. Forthcoming. *The Hindu Nationalist Movement and Politics in India, c. 1925–1993*. New York.

———. 1993. "The BJP in Madhya Pradesh: Networks, Strategies, and Power." In *Hindus and Others: The Question of Identity in India Today*, ed. Gyanendra Pandey. Delhi.

Jain Madhu. 1994. "Reeling from the Impact." *India Today*, September 15, 106–9.

Jain, Kajri. 2004. "The Efficacious Image: Pictures and Power in Indian Mass Culture" in *Iconographies and the Nation in India*. Edited by Richard Davis. New Delhi: Orient Longman.

Jairazbhoy, Nazir. 1977. "Music in Western Rajasthan: Stability and Change." *Yearbook of the International Folk Music Council* 9:50–66.

Jaiswal, Suvira. 1991. "Semitising Hinduism: Changing Paradigms of Brahmanical Integration." *Social Scientist* 19:20–32.

Jalal, Ayesha, and Anil Seal. 1981. "Alternative to Partition: Muslim Politics between the Wars." *Modern Asian Studies* 15: 415–54.

Jalal, Ayesha. 1985. *The Sole Spokesman: Jinnah, the Muslim League and the Demand for Pakistan*. Cambridge.

Jalal, Ayesha. 2000. *Self and Sovereignty: Individual and Community in South Asian Islam since 1850*. London: Routlege.

Jana, Arun K. and Bhupen Sarmah. Editors. 2002. *Class, Ideology, and Political Parties in India*. New Delhi: South Asian Publishers.

Jayal, Niraja Gopal. Editor. 2001. *Democracy in India*. Delhi: Oxford University Press.

Jeffery, Patricia and Amrita Basu. Editors. 1999. *Resisting the Sacred and the Secular.* Columbia MO: South Asia Books.

————. 1998. *Appropriating Gender: Women's Activism and Politicized Religion in South Asia.* New York: Routledge and New Delhi: Kali for Women.

Jones, Kenneth W. 1981. "Religious Identity and the Census." In *The Census in British India*, ed. N. Gerald Barrier. New Delhi.

————. 1976. *Arya Dharm: Hindu Consciousness in Nineteenth-Century Punjab.* Berkeley.

Jordens, J.T.F. 1981. *Swami Shraddhanand: His Life and Causes.* Delhi.

————. 1978. *Dayananda Saraswati: His Life and Ideas.* Delhi.

Joshi, Barbara. 1992. "Untouchables, Religion, and Politics: The Changing Face of Struggle." In *Religion and Political Conflict in south Asia: India, Pakistan, and Sri Lanka*, ed. Douglas Allen. Westport.

Joshi, P. C. 1995. *Secularism and Development: The Indian Experiment.* New Delhi: Vikas.

Joshi, Sanjay. 1995. "Empowerment and Identity: Hindu Communalism in Colonial Lucknow, 1830–1930." Ph.D. diss., University of Pennsylvania.

Joshi, V. C. 1965. *Lajpat Rai: Autobiographical Writings.* Delhi.

Joshi, Sanjay. 2001. *Fractured Modernity: Making of a Middle Class in Colonial North India.* New Delhi: Oxford University Press.

JPRS Report. 1993. *India: Secularism Reconsidered.* February 18.

Juergensmeyer, Mark. 1993. *The New Cold War? Religious Nationalism Confronts the Secular State.* Berkeley.

Justice, Glen. 1995. "Extremist Groups Using Modern Media to Spread Views." *Philadelphia Inquirer*, July 2.

Kabbani, Rana. 1986. *Europe's Myths of Orient.* Bloomington.

Kakar, Sudhir. 1996. *The Colors of Violence: Cultural Identities, Religion, and Conflict.* Chicago: University of Chicago Press.

Kamra, A. J. 2000. *The Prolonged Partition and its Pogroms: Testimonies on Violence against Hindus in East Bengal, 1946–1964.* New Delhi: Voice of India.

Kanjamala, Augustine and Arun Shourie. 1995. *Arun Shourie and his Christian Critic.* New Delhi: Voice of India.

Kanungo, Pralay. 2003. "Hindutva's Entry into a 'Hindu Province': Early Years of RSS in Orissa. *Economic and Political Weekly* . August 2, 3293–303.

————. 2002. *RSS's Tryst with Politics: From Hedgewar to Sudarshan.* Delhi: Manohar.

Kaplan, Robert D. 1994. "The Coming Anarchy: How Scarcity, Crime, Overpopulation, Tribalism, and Disease Are Rapidly Destroying the Social Fabric of Our Planet." *Atlantic Monthly*, February, 44–76.

Kapur, Anuradha. 1991. "Militant Images of a Tranquil God." *Times of India*, October 1.

Kapur, Rajiv. 198. *Sikh Separatism: The Politics of Faith.* London.

Kaviraj, Sudipta. N.d. (a). "The Myth of Praxis: The Construction of the Figure of Krishna in Krishnacharitra." Occasional paper, Nehru Memorial Museum and Library.

————. N.d. (b). "The Reversal of Orientalism: Bhudev Mukhopadhyaya and the Project of Indigenist Social Theory." Unpublished paper.

Keene, H.G. 1891. *Madhava Rao Sindia and the Hindu Reconquest of India.* Oxford.

Keer, Dhananjay. 1966. *Veer Savarkar*. Bombay.

Khan, Afaque. 1986. *Gandhian Approach to Communal Harmony (a Critical Study)*. Delhi.

Khan, Nadir Ali. 1991. *A History of Urdu Journalism, 1822–1857*. Delhi.

Khare, Ravindra. 1976. *Hindu Hearth and Home*. Delhi.

Khetarpal, S. P. 1968. "Codification of Hindu Law." In *Family Law and Customary Law in Asia: A Contemporary Legal perspective*, ed. David C. Buxbaum. The Hague.

Khosla, G. D. 1992. *Stern Reckoning: A Survey of the Events Leading Up to and Following the Partition of India*. Delhi.

King, Christopher R. 1994. *One Language, Two Scripts: The Hindi Movement in Nineteenth Century North India*. Bombay.

———. 1990. "Hindu Nationalism in the Nineteenth Century U.P." In *Boeings and Bullock-Carts: Essays in Honour of K. Ishwaran*, ed. Yogendra Malik. Delhi.

Kippen, James. 1988. *The Table of Lucknow: A Cultural Analysis of a Musical Tradition*. Cambridge.

Kishwar, Madhu. 1990. "In Defense of Our Dharma." In *Manushi* 60:2–15.

Kohli, Atul. 1990. *Democracy and Discontent: India's Growing Crisis of Governability*. Cambridge.

———. 1987. *The State and Poverty in India: The Politics of Reform*. Cambridge.

———, ed. 1988. *India's Democracy: An Analysis of Changing State-Society Relations*. Princeton.

Kolff, D. H. A. 1971. "Sanyasi Trader-Soldiers." *Indian Economic and Social History Review* 8:213–20.

Koonz, Claudia. 1977. "Mothers in the Fatherland: Women in Nazi Germany." In *Becoming Visible: Women in European History*, ed. R. Briedenthal and Claudia Koonz. Boston.

Kopf, David. 1968. *British Orientalism and the Bengal Renaissance*. Berkeley.

Kothari, Rajni. 1994. "Caste, Communalism and the Democratic Process." *South Asia Bulletin: Comparative Studies of South Asia, Africa and the Middle East* 14:7–13.

———. 1992. "Pluralism and Secularism: Lessons of Ayodhya." *Economic and Political Weekly*, December 19–26, 2695–98.

———. 1991. "State and statelessness in Our Time." *Economic and Political Weekly*, Annual number vol. xxvi, nos. 11–12 (March): 533–58.

———. 1989a. *State against Democracy: In Search of Humane Governance*. Delhi.

———. 1989b. *Transformation and Survival: In Search of Humane Work Order*. Delhi.

———. 1970. *Politics in India*. Boston.

Kothari, Rajni. 1998. *Communalism in Indian Politics*. Ahmedabad: Rainbow Publishers.

Kozlowski, Gregory. 1993. "Muslim Personal law and Political identity in Independent India." In *Religion and Law in Independent India*, ed. Robert D. Baird. New Delhi.

———. 1990. "Shah Banu's Case, Britain's Legal Legacy and Muslim Politics in Modern India." In *Boeings and Bullock-Carts: Essays in Honour of K. Ishwaram*, ed. Yogendra Malik. Delhi.

———. 1985. *Muslim Endowments and Society in British India*. Cambridge.

Krishnan, Sankaran. 1996. "Cartographic Anxiety: Mapping the Body Politic in India." In *Challenging Boundaries: Global Flows, Territorial Identities*. Edited by Michael J. Shapiro and Wayward R. Alker. Minneapolis: University of Minnesota Press. pp.193–214.

Kshem Chandra, Suman. 1981. *Divangat Hindi-Sevi*. 2 vols. Delhi.

Kudaisyu, Gyanesh. 2002. "Constructing the 'Heartland': Uttar Pradesh in India's Body-Politic," *South Asia*, NS 25, 2, Aug 2002, 53–181.

Kulke, Hermann, and Dietmar Rothemund. 1990. *A History of India*. London.

Kumar, Dharma. 1994. "Left Secularists and Communalism." *Economic and Political Weekly*, July 28, 1803–9.

Kumar, Krishna. 1991. *Political Agenda of Education*. New Delhi.

Kumar, Ravindra. 1990. *Problem of Communalism in India*. New Delhi.

Kumar, Sanjay. 2003. "Gujarat Assembly Elections 2002: Analysing the Verdict." *Economic and Political Weekly*, January 25: 270–5.

Kumar, Sunil. 2001. *Communalism and Secularism in Indian Politics: Study of the BJP*. Jaipur: Rawat Publications.

Kumar, Vijendra. 2001. *Rise of Dalit Power in India*. Jaipur: ABD Publishers.

Kymlicka, Will. 1989. *Liberalism, Community and Culture*. Oxford.

La Volpa, Anthony J. 1992. "Conceiving a Public: ideas and Society in Eighteenth-Century Europe." *Journal of Modern History* 64 (march): 79–116.

Laird, M.A., ed. 1971. *Bishop Heber in Northern India: Selections from Heber's Journal*. London.

Lamb, Ramdas. 1991. "Personalizing the Ramayan: Ramnamis and Their Use of the Ramcaritmanas." In *Many Ramayanas: The Diversity of a Narrative Tradition in South Asia*, ed. Paula Richman. Berkeley.

Lapidus, Ira M. 1988. *A History of Islamic Societies*. Cambridge.

Lariviere, Richard. 1989. "Justices and Pandita: Some Ironies in Contemporary Readings of the Hindu Legal Past." *Journal of Asian Studies* 48:757–69.

Lateef, Shahida. 1990. *Muslim Women in India; Political and Private Realities, 1890s–1980s*. New Delhi.

Lavan, Spencer. 1974. *The Ahmadiya Movement*. Delhi.

Lawrence, Bruce. 1991. "Tracking Fundamentalists and Those Who Study Them: A Sequel to Sadik Al-Azm, "Islamic Fundamentalism Reconsidered." *South Asia Bulletin: Comparative Studies of South Asia, Africa and the Middle East* 14:41–50.

Lawrence, Second Marquess of Zetland. 1956. *Essayez*. London.

Lawrence, Sir Walter Roper. 1928. *The India We Served*. London.

Lee, Raymond L.M., and R. Rajoo. 1987. "Sanskritization and Indian Ethnicity in Malaysia." *Modern Asian Studies* 21: 389–416.

Lele, Jayant. 1995. *Hindutva, the Emergence of the Right*. Chennai: Earthwork Books.

Lelyveld, David. Forthcoming. "Upon the Subdominant: Administering Music on all India Radio." In *Consuming Modernity*, ed. Carol Breckenridge. Minneapolis.

———. 1993. "The Fate of Hindustani." In *Orientalism and the Postcolonial predicament: perspectives on South Asia*, ed. Carol Breckenridge and Peter van der Veer. Philadelphia.

———. 1990. "Transmitters and Culture: The Colonial Roots of Indian broadcasting." *South Asia Research* 10:41–52.

———. 1978. *Aligarh's First Generation: Muslim Solidarity in British India*. Princeton.

Leslie, I. Julia. 1989. *The Perfect Wife: The Orthodox Hindu Woman According to the Stridharmaphaddhati of Tryambakayajvan*. New Delhi.

Leslie, Julia. Editor, 2000. *Gender, Religion and Social Definition in South Asia*. Delhi: Oxford University Press.

Lieten, G.K. 1994. "On Casteism and Communalism in Uttar Pradesh." *Economic and Political Weekly*, April 2, 777–81.

Llewellyn, J.S. 1993. *The Arya Samaj as a Fundamentalist movement: A Study in Comparative Fundamentalism*. New Delhi.

Lobo, Lancy. 2002. *Globalisation, Hindu Nationalism, and Christians in India*. Rawat Publications:

Lochtefeld, James G. 1994. "New Wine, Old Skins: The Sangh Parivar and the Transformation of Hinduism." Unpublished essay, Carthage College.

Lochtefeld, James G. 1994. "The Vishva Hindu Parishad and the Roots of Hindu Militancy," *Journal of the American Academy of Religion*, 62, 2, 587–602.

Lorenzen, David. 1978. "Warrior Ascetics in Indian History." *Journal of the American Oriental Society* 98 (January): 61–75.

Low, Sidney. 1907. *A Vision of India*. London.

Ludden, David. 19994. "History Outside Civilisation and the Mobility of South Asia." *South Asia* 17:1–23.

———. 1993. "Orientalist Empiricism: Transformations of Colonial Knowledge." In *Orientalism and the Postcolonial Predicament: perspectives from South Asia*, ed. Carol Breckenridge and Peter van der Veer. Philadelphia.

———. 1992. "India's Development Regime." In *Colonialism and Culture*, ed. Nicholas B. Dirks, Ann Arbor.

Ludden, David. 2003. "Maps in the Mind and the Mobility of Asia," *Journal of Asian Studies*, 62, 4, 1057–78.

———. 2002. *India and South Asia: A Short History*. Oxford: OneWorld Publications.

———. 1999. *An Agrarian History of South Asia*. Cambridge: Cambridge University Press.

Lutgendorf, Philip. 1991. *The Life of a Text: Performing the Ramcaritmanas of Tulsidas*. Berkeley.

———. 1990. "The Video-Ramayana." *Drama Review* 34 (June): 127–76.

———. 1989. "The View from the Ghats: Traditional Exegesis of a Hindu Epic." *Journal of Asian Studies* 48:272–288.

Lytton, Second Earl of. 1942. *Pundits and Elephants: Being the Experiences of Five Years as Governor of an Indian Province*. London.

Madan, T.N. 1993. "Whither Indian Secularism." *Modern Asian studies* 27, no. 3 (July): 667–97.

———. 1987. "Secularism in Its Place." *Journal of Asian Studies* 46:747–60. Madhok, Balraj. 1986. *RSS and Politics*. New Delhi.

Maheshwari, Shriram. 1991. *The Mandal Commission and Mandalisation: A Critique*. New Delhi.

Mahmood, Cynthia Keppley. 1993. "Rethinking Indian Communalism: Culture and Counter-Culture." *Asian Survey* 33:722–37.

———. 1989. "Sikh Rebellion and the Hindu Concept of Order." *Asian Survey* 29: 326–40.

Malik, Dipak. 1994. "Three Riots in Varansi, 1989–90 to 1992." *South Asian Bulletin: Comparative Studies in South Asia, Africa and the Middle east* 14:53–56.

Malik, Hafeez. 1970. "Sir Sayyid Ahmad Khan's Contribution to the Development of Muslim Nationalism in India." *Modern Asian Studies* 4:129–48.

———. 1968. "Sir Sayyid Ahmad Khan's Doctrines of Muslim nationalism and National progress." *Modern Asian Studies* 2:221–44.

Malik, Yogendra. 1990. "Reflections of Inter-Communal relations through Hindi Fiction." In *Boeings and Bullock-Carts: Essays in Honour of K. Ishwaran*, ed. Yogednra malik. Delhi.

Mandal, Manindranath. 1927. *Bange Digindranarayan*. Calcutta.

Mangalwadi, Vishal. 1996. *Missionary Conspiracy: Letters to a Postmodern Hindu*. Mussoorie: Nivedit Good Books.

Mansergh, Nicholas, ed. 1970–83. *The Transfer of Power, 1942–47* 12 vols. 12. London.

Manuel, Peter. 1993. *Cassette Culture: Popular Music and Technology in North India*. Chicago.

———. 1990. *Thumri in Historical and Stylistic Perspectives*. Delhi.

Mar Gregorios, Paulos. 1998. *The Secular Ideology: An Impotent Remedy for India's Communal Problem*. Delhi: Indian Society for Promoting Christian Knowledge.

Marchall, S.E. 1984. "Paradoxes of Cultural Change: Culture Crisis, Islamic Revival and Reactivation of Patriarchy." *Journal of Asian and African Studies* 19:1–17.

Martin, O. M. N.d. *Memoirs of O. M. Martin*. South Asia Center, Cambridge. (Manuscript)

Marty, Martin E., and R. Scott Appleby. 1991. "Conclusion: An Interim Report on a Hypothetical Family." In *Fundamentalism Observed*, ed. Martin E. Marty and R. Scott Appleby. Chicago.

Masland, Tom, with Tony Clifton and Sudip Mazumdar. 1992. "Holy War in India," *Newsweek*, December 21, 46–47.

Masselos, Jim. 1994. "The Bombay Riots of January 1993: The Politics of Urban Conflagration." *South Asia* 17:79–95.

———. 1972. *Nationalism on the Indian Subcontinent: An Introductory History*. Melbourne.

Mathur, Shubh, 2003. "Mapping the Enemy: Images of Islam," *Economic and Political Weekly*, September 13: 3875–78

Mauss, Marcel. 1974. *The Gift: Forms and Functions of Exchange in Archaic Societies*. London.

Mayaram, Shail. 1993. "Communal Violence in Jaipur." *Economic and Political Weekly*, November 13.

Mayer, Arno. 1975. "The Lower Middle Class as a Historical problem." *Journal of Modern History* 47 (September): 409–36.

Maza, Sarah. 1989. "Domestic Melodrama as Political Ideology: The Case of the Comte de Sanois." *American Historical Review* 94 (December): 1249–64.

Mazumdar, Sucheta. 1992. "Women, Culture and Politics: Engendering the Hindu Nation." *South Asia Bulletin* 12:1–24.

McCully, Bruce T. 1940. *English Education and the Origin of Indian Nationalism*. New York.

McGregor, R.S. 1991. "A Hindu Writer's Views of Social Political and Language Issues of His Time: Attitude of Harischandra of Banaras (1850–1885)." *Modern Asian Studies* 25:91–100.

McGuire, John, Peter Reeves and Howard Brasted. Editors. 1996. *Politics of Violence: from Ayodhya to Behrampada* . New Delhi: Sage.

McKean, Lise. 1994. "The Transnational Context of Communalism: The 1993 Parliament of the World's Religions and Hindu Nationalism." Unpublished paper presented at the South Asia Seminar, University of Pennsylvania, Philadelphia.

————. 1992. "Towards a Politics of Spirituality: Hindu Religious Organizations and Nationalism." Ph.D. thesis, University of Sydney.

McKean, Lise. 1995. *Divine Enterprise: Gurus and the Hindu Nationalist Movement.* Chicago.

McKean, Lise. 1996. *Divine Enterprise : Gurus and the Hindu Nationalist Movement.* Chicago: University of Chicago Press.

McLane, John R. 1977. *Indian Nationalism and the Early Congress.* Princeton.

Mediawatch. N.d. *Mediawatch on Communalism.* New Delhi.

Meer, Wim van der. 1980. *Hindustani Music in the Twentieth Century.* New Delhi.

Menon, Ritu and Kamla Bhasin. 2000. *Borders and Boundaries.* New Brunswick: Rutgers University Press.

Menon, Ritu. 2002. "Do Women Have a Country?" In *From Gender to Nation.* Edited by Rada Ivekovic and Julie Mostov. Ravenna: Longo Editore. pp.43–62.

Metcalf, Barbara Daly. 1994. "Presidential Address to the Association for Asian Studies." *Journal of Asian Studies.*

————. 1982. *Islamic Revival in British India: Deoband, 1860–1900.* Princeton.

Metcalf, Thomas R. 1990. *The Aftermath of Revolt: India, 1857–1870.* Repr., New Delhi.

————. 1979. *Land, landlords, and the British Raj: Northern India in the Nineteenth Century.* Delhi.

Midlarsky, Manus I., ed. 1992. *The Internationalization of Communal Strife.* London.

Miller, Barbara Stoler. 1991. "Contending Narratives: The Political Life of the Indian Epis." *Journal of Asian studies* 50:783–92.

Minault, Gail. 1990. "Hinduism and Politics." *Economic and Political Weekly* 25 (April 7): 723–29.

Mirsepassi, Ali, Amrita Basu and Frederick Weaver. Editors. 2002. *Localizing Knowledge In a Globalizing World.* Syracuse: Syracuse University Press.

Mitchell, Timothy. 1991. "The Limits of the State: Beyond Statist Approaches and Their Critics." *American Political Science Review* 85:77–96.

Mitra, Subrata K. and V. B. Singh. 1999. *Democracy and Social Change in India: A Cross-Sectional Analysis of the Indian Electorate.* New Delhi: Sage.

Mookerjee, Firoze. 1992. *Lucknow and the World of Sarshar.* Karachi.

Mookherji, P.C. N.d. *The Pictorial Lucknow.* Unpublished galley proofs of MS, Lucknow.

Mujeeb, Mohammad. 1977. *Islamic Influence on Indian Society.* Meerut.

Mukherjee, Meenakshi. 1993. "Rhetoric Identity: History and Fiction in Nineteenth Century India." In *Indian Responses to Colonialism in the Nineteenth Century,* ed. Alok Bhall and Sudhir Chandra. Delhi.

Mukherji, Baidyanath. 1845. *Achar-Darpan.* Calcutta.

Mukherji, U.N. 1911. *The Malis of East Bengal.* Calcutta.

————. 1909. *Hindus: A Dying Race.* Calcutta.

Nahar, Sultana. 1998. *Communalism in Bangladesh and India: A Comparative Study*. Dhaka: M.I. Farooqui & Associates.

Naim, C.M. 1994. "The Second Tyranny of Religious Majorities." *South Asia Bulletin: Comparative Studies of South Asia, Africa and the Middle East* 14:104–7.

Nair, Savita. 2001. "Moving Life Histories: Gujarat, East Africa and the Indian Diaspora, 1880–2000." Unpublished Dissertation, History, University of Pennsylvania.

Nandy, Ashis, Shikha Trivedi, Shail Mayaram, and Achut Yagnik. 1995. *Creating a Nationality: Ramjanmabhumi Movement and the Fear of the Self*. Delhi.

Nandy, Ashis. 1990. "The Politics of Secularism and the Recovery of Religious Tolerance." In *Mirrors of Violence: Communities, Riots and Survivors in South Asia*, ed. Veena Das. Delhi.

———. 1983. *The Intimate Enemy: Loss and Recovery of the Self under Colonialism*. Delhi.

Nandy, Ashish, Shikha Trivedi, Shail Mayaram, and Achyut Yagnik. 1995. *Creating a Nationality: The Ramjanambhoomi Movement and the Fear of Self*. Delhi: Oxford University Press.

Naples, Nancy A, and Manishi Desai. 2002. *Women's Activism and Globalization: Linking Local Struggles and Transnational Politics*. New York: Routledge.

Nehru, jawaharlal. 1946. *The Discovery of India*. Calcutta.

———. 1936. *An Autobiography*. London.

Netton, Ian Richard. 1992. *A Popular Dictionary of Islam*. London.

Neuman, Daniel. 1985. "Indian Music as a Cultural System." *Asian Music* 17:98–113.

Nevill, H.R. 1905. *Fyzabad: A Gazetteer*. vol. 43 of *District Gazetteers of the United Provinces of Agra and Oudh*. Allahabad.

Newfeldt, Ronald W. 1981. "Islam and India: the Views of Muhammad Iqbal." *Muslim World* 71:178–91.

Nivedita, ed. 1970. *The Complete Works of Swami Vivekananda*. Mayavati/Calcutta. vols. 8 (See also Vivekananda, Swami).

Noon, Firoz Khan. 1942. *Scented Dust*. Lahore.

Noorani, Abdul Gafoor Abdul Majeed. 2000. *The RSS and the BJP: A Division of Labour*. New Delhi: LeftWord Books.

Northwest Provinces (NWP). 1893. Government of Northwest Provinces and Oudh. *Reports on Publications Registered under Act XXV of 1867 during 1884–93*.

———. 1892. Government of Northwest Provinces and Oudh, *Proceedings of the Educational Department*. July. File no. 344.

Nugent, David. Editor. 2002. *Locating Capitalism in Time and Space: Global Restructuring, Politics, and Identity*. Stanford: Stanford University Press.

O'Hanlon, Rosalind. 1993. "Historical Approaches to communalism: Perspectives from Western India." In *Society and Ideology: Essays in South Asian History*, ed. Peter Robb. Delhi.

———. 1989. *The Making of Colonial Lucknow, 1856–1877*. Delhi.

Olsen, Keri. 1994. "Discursive Formation of Communal Riots in *Economic and Political Weekly*, 1988–1993". Master's thesis, University of Pennsylvania.

Omvedt, Gail. 1994. *Dalits and the Democratic Revolution: Dr Ambedkar and the Dalit Movement in Colonial India.* New Delhi.

———. 1993. *Reinventing Revolution: New Social Movements and the Socialist Tradition in India.* Armonk, NY.

———. 1992. "Hinduism, Social Inequality, and the State." In *Religion and Political Conflict in South Asia,* ed. Douglas Allen. Westport.

———. 1990. "Hinduism and Politics." *Economic and Political Weekly,* April 7, 723–29.

Ondaatje, Michael. 1992. *The English Patient.* New York.

Orr, W.G. 1940. "Armed Religious Ascetics in Northern India." *Bulletin of the John Rylands Library* 25:81–100.

Outram, James. 1893. *Memoirs of My Indian Career.* London.

Owen, Arthur. 1915. *Recollections of a Veteran of the Days of the Great Indian Mutiny of 1857.* Lahore.

Padgaonkar, Dilip. 1993. *When Bombay Burned: Reportage and Comments on the Riots and Blasts from the Times of India.* New Delhi.

Padmanabhan, Mukund, and Shiraz Sidhva. 1990. "Chalo, Ayodhya!' *Sunday,* October 21–27, pp. 60–61.

Page, David. 1982. *Prelude to Partition: All Indian Muslim Politics, 1918–1932.* Delhi.

Pal, Bepinchandra. 1906. *Shivaji Utsava.* Calcutta.

———. [1903]. 1954. "Shivaji Festival." In *Swadeshi and Swaraj,* ed. B.C. Pal. Calcutta.

Pandey, Gyanendra. 1994. "The New Hindu History." *South Asia* 17:97–112.

———. 1993a. "The Civilized and the Barbarian: The 'New' Politics of Late Twentieth Century India and the World." In *Hindus and Others: The Question of Identity in India Today,* ed. G. Pandey. New Delhi.

———. 1992. "In Defence of the Fragment: Writing about Hindu-Muslim Riots in India Today." *Representations* 37 (December): 27–55.

———. 1991. "In Defence of the Fragment: Writing about Hindu-Muslim Riots in India Today." *Economic and Political Weekly,* XXVI, nos. 11 and 12 (March): 559–72.

———. 1990a. "The Colonial Construction of 'Communalism': British Writings on Benares in the Nineteenth Century." In *Mirrors of Violence: Communities, Riots and Survivors in South Asia,* ed. Veena Das. Delhi.

———. 1990b. *The Construction of Communalism in Colonial North India.* Delhi.

———. 1988. "Peasant Revolt and Indian Nationalism: The Peasant Movement in Awadh, 1919–199". In *Selected Subaltern Studies,* ed. Ranajit Guha and Gayatri Chakravorty Spivak. Delhi.

———. 1983. "Rallying Round the Cow: Sectarian Strife in the Bhojpuri Region." *Subaltern Studies II,* ed. Ranajit Guha. Delhi.

———, ed. 1993b. *Hindus and Others: The Question of Identity in India Today.* Delhi.

Pandey, Gyanendra. 2001. *Remembering Partition.* Cambridge: Cambridge University Press.

Panikkar, K. N. Editor. 1999. *The Concerned Indian's Guide to Communalism.* New Delhi: Penguin Books.

Panikkar, K. N. 1991a. "Historical Overview." In *anatomy of a Confrontation: The Babri Masjid-Ramjanmabhumi Issue,* ed. S. Gopal. New Delhi/New York.

———., ed. 1991b. *Communalism in India: History, Politics and Culture.* New Delhi.

Panikkar. K.M. 1963. *The Foundations of New India*. London.

———— 1953. *Asia and Western Dominance: A Survey of the Vasco da Gama Epoch of Asian History, 1498–1945*. London.

Panofsky, Erwin. 1955. *Meaning in the Visual Arts*. Chicago.

Parikh, Manju. 1993. "The Debacle at Ayodhya: Why Militant Hinduism Met with a Weak Response." *Asian Survey* 33:673–84.

Parry, Jonathan P. Jan Breman, and Karin Kapadia. Editors. 1999. *The Worlds of Indian Industrial Labour*. New Delhi: Sage Publications.

Parthasarathy, D. 2002. "Riot Cheerleaders: The Anomaly of Hindu Women in Violence." HIMAL 15, 5, May: 28–29.

Patel, Alaknanda. 2002. "Gujarat Violence: A Personal Diary." *Economic and Political Weekly*, December 14: 4985–7.

People's Union for Democratic Rights (PUDR). 1990a. "Bhagalpur Riots" (April). Delhi.

————. 1990b. "Disputed Passages: A Report on law, Reservations, and Agitations' (December). Delhi.

Phadnis, Urmila. 1990. *Ethnicity and Nation-Building in South Asia*. New Delhi.

————, ed. 1986. *Domestic Conflict in South Asia*. vols. 2 vol. I: *Political Dimensions;* vol. 2: *Economic and Ethnic Dimensions*. New Delhi.

Pinch, William. 1996. *Peasants and Monks in British India*. Berkeley.

Pollock, Sheldon. Forthcoming. "Popular Participation and Dispute Resolution; The Barelwis in 1914." In *Culture as Contested Site*, ed. Sandria B. Freitag.

————. 1993. "Ramayana and Political Imagination in India." *Journal of Asian Studies* 52:261–97.

Powell, Avril. 1993. *Muslims and Missionaries in pre-Mutiny India*. Surrey.

Powers, David S. 1989. "Orientalism, Colonialism, and Legal History: The Attack on Muslim Family Endowments in Algeria and India." *Comparative Studies in Society and History* 31:535–71.

Powers, Harold S. 1986. "Classical Music, Cultural Roots, and Colonial Rule: An Indic Musicologist Looks at the Muslim World." *Asian Music* 12 (January): 5–39.

Prabhakara, M.S. 1994. "BJP and the North-East." *South Asia Bulletin: Comparative Studies of South Asia, Africa and the Middle East* 14:66–72.

Prakash, Aseem. 2003. "Re-imagination of the State and Gujarat's Electoral Verdict." *Economic and Political Weekly*, April 19: 1601–10.

Prakash, Gyan. 1990. "Writing Post-Orientalist Histories of the Third World: Perspectives from Indian Historiography." *Comparative Studies in Society and History* 32:383–408.

Prakashana, Jagarana. 1979. *Why Hindu Rashtra?* Bangalore.

Prapann, Vijay Raghav. 1992. "Ramanand Sampraday Men Ujjain Kumbh: Ek Adhyayan' [The Ramanandi sampraday at the Ujjain kumbh: An investigation]. In *Amrit kalash* [The nectar jar]. Varanasi.

Premchand. 1987. *Asad Katha*. Delhi.

Press Council of India. 1991. *Crisis and Credibility: Report of the Press Council of India, January and July 1991*. New Delhi.

Price, Pamela. 1993. "Democracy and Ethnic Conflict in India: Precolonial Legacies in Tamil Nadu." *Asian Survey* 33:493–506.

————. 1988. "Ideology and Ethnicity under British Imperial Rule: 'Brahmans,' Lawyers and Kin-Caste Rules in Madras Presidency." *Modern Asian Studies* 22:151–78.

Prior, Katharine. 1993. "Angry Pandas: Hindu Priests and the Colonial Government in the Dispersal of the Hardwar Mela in 1892." *South Asia* 16 (June): 25–52.

*Public Culture.* 1993. Issue on Aijaz Ahmad's book, *In Theory: Classes, Nations, Literatures,* 6 (September).

Puniyani, Ram. 2001. *Communal Politics: An Illustrated Primer.* New Delhi: Safdar Hashmi Memorial Trust.

Purohit, Vinayak. 1988. *Arts of Transitional India: Twentieth Century, Volume II.* Bombay.

Qureshi, Ishtiaq Hussain. 1971. *The Muslim Community of the Indian Subcontinent.* Karachi.

Qureshi, Regula. 1991. "Whose Music? Sources and Contexts in Indic Musicology." In *Comparative Musicology and the Anthropology of Music: Essays in the History of Ethnomusicology,* ed. Bruno Nettl and Philip Bohlman. Chicago.

Radhakrishnan, S. 1940. *Eastern Religions and Western Thought.* London.

————. [1926] 1961. *The Hindu View of Life.* London.

Ragin, Charles, 1979. "Ethnic Political Mobilization: The Welsh Case." *American Sociological Review* 44:619–35.

————. 1977. "Class, Status, and 'Reactive Ethnic Cleavages': The Social Bases of Political Regionalism." *American Sociological Review* 42, no. 3:438–50.

————. N.d. "Comparative Ethnic Mobilization: Conceptual and Methodological Issues."

Rais, Qamar. 1991. *Ratan Nath Sarshar.* New Delhi.

Rajagopal, Arvind. 2001. *Politics after Television: Hindu Nationalism and the Reshaping of the Public in India,* Cambridge: Cambridge University Press.

Rajesh, R. 2002. "National Curriculum Framework and its Values: A Parent's Perspective." *Economic and Political Weekly,* October 19: 4273–77.

Rajgopal, P.R. 1987a. *Communal Violence in India.* New Delhi.

————. 1987b. *Social Change and Violence: The Indian Experience.* New Delhi.

Ram, N. 1992. "Communalism and the Press." *Sunday Observer,* December 15.

Ram, P. R. Editor. 1998. *Secular Challenge to Communal Politics: A Reader.* Mumbai: Vikas Adhyayan Kendra.

Ramachandran, Hari. 1995. "Hindu Group Targets Foreign Consumer Giants." Reuters News Service, August 7.

Ramachandran, Sujata. 1999. "Of Boundaries and Border Crossings: Undocumented Bangladeshi 'Infiltrators' and the Hegemony of Hindu Nationalism in India." *Interventions,* 1, 2: 235–53.

Ramakrishnan, Venkitesh. 1995. "Saffron Offensive." "Changing the Rules." *Frontline,* September 8, 4–16.

Ramaseshan, Radhika. 1990. "The Press on Ayodhya." *Economic and Political Weekly,* December 15, 2701–4.

Ramaswamy, Sumathi. 1992. "En/gendering Language: The Poetics and Politics of Tamil Identity, 1891–1970." Ph.D. dissertation, University of California, Berkeley.

Ramlakhansharan, Baba. 1976. *Shri Ram Janambhumi Ka Romanchakari Itihas* [The shocking history of the birthplace of Shri Ram]. Ayodhya.

Ram-Prasad, C. 1993. "Hindutva Ideology: Extracting the Fundamentals." *Contemporary South Asia* 2:285–309.

Rao, Ramesh N. and Koenraad Elst. Editors. 2003. *Gujarat after Godhra: Real Violence, Selective Outrage.* New Delhi: Har Anand.

Raychaudhuri. Tapan. 1988. *Europe Reconsidered: Perceptions of the West in Nineteenth Century Bengal.* Delhi.

Richman, Paula. Forthcoming. "Epic and State: E.V. Ramasami and C. Rajagopalachari Contest the Meaning of the Ramayana." In *Culture as Contested Site,* ed. Sandria B. Freitag.

Robb, Peter. 1993. "The Impact of British Rule on Religious Community: Reflections on the Trial of Maulvi Ahmadullah of Patna in 1865." In *Society and ideology: Essays in South Asian History,* ed. Peter Robb (in collaboration with K.N. Chaudhuri and Avril Powell). Delhi.

———. 1986. "The Challenge of Gau Mata: British Policy and Religious Change in India, 1880–1916." *Modern Asian Studies* 20:289–319.

Roberts, Michael. 1990. "Noise as Cultural Struggle: Tom-tom Beating, the British, and Communal Disturbances in Sri Lanka, 1880s–1930s." In *Mirrors of Violence: Communities, Riots and Survivors in South Asia,* ed. Veena Das. Delhi.

Robinson, Francis. 1974. *Separatism among Indian Muslims: The Politics of the United Provinces, Muslims, 1860–1923.* Cambridge.

Ronaldshay, Earl of 1925. *The Heart of Aryavarta: A Study of the Psychology of Indian Unrest.* London.

———. 1924. *India: A Bird's-Eye View.* Boston.

Roy, A.K. 1978. *History of Jaipur City.* New Delhi.

Roy, Asim. 1987. "The Bengal Muslim 'Cultural Mediators" and the Bengal Muslim Identity in the Nineteenth and Early Twentieth Centuries." *South Asia* 10:11–34.

———. 1983. *The Islamic Syncretistic Tradition in Bengal.* Princeton.

Roy, Beth. 1994. *Some Trouble with Cows: Making Sense of Social Conflict.* Berkeley.

Roy, M.N. [1922] 1971. *India in Transition.* repr. Bombay.

———. 1974. *The Historical Role of Islam.* Delhi.

Roy, P.K. 1990. "Coming Storm." *Frontline,* October 13–26, pp. 26–29.

Roy, Ramashray and Paul Wallace. Editors. 1999. *Indian Politics and the 1998 Elections: Regionalism, Hindutva, and State Politics.* New Delhi: Sage.

Rudolph, Susanne Hoeber, and Lloyd Rudolph. 1993. "Modern Hate." *New Republic* (March 22).

———, eds. 1972. *Education and Politics in India: Studies in Organization, Society and Policy.* Cambridge.

Russell, Ralph, 1982. *The Pursuit of Urdu Literature: A Select History.* Delhi.

———. 1970. "The urdu Ghazal in Muslim Society." *South Asian Review* 3 (January): 141–49.

Ruswa, Mirza Mohammad Hadi. 1982. *Umrao Jan Ada.* Hyderabad.

Saberwal, Satish. 1996. *Roots of Crisis: Interpreting Contemporary Indian Society.* New Delhi: Sage.

Sabrang.com. 2001. *Against Communalisation of Education*. Mumbai: Safdar Hashmi Memorial Trust. (http://www.sabrang.com)

Said, Edward W. 1978. *Orientalism*. London.

Saikia, Sayeeda Yasmin. 2004. *Fragmented Memories: Struggling to be Tai–Ahom in India*. Durham: Duke University Press.

———. 1997. *In the Meadows of Gold: Telling Tales of the Swargadeos at the Crossroads of Assam*. Guwahati: Spectrum.

Saksena, Ram Babu. [1927] 1990. *A History of Urdu Literature*. Allahabad. Repr., Delhi.

Samaddar, Ranabir. 1999. *The Marginal Nation: Transborder Migration from Bangladesh*. Dhaka: University Press Limited.

———. 1997. "Reflexive Nationalism and the Indian North-East." In *Insurgency in North-East India*. Edited by Barrister Pakem, New Delhi: Omsoms. pp.128–37.

Sangari, Kumkum. 1990. "Mirabai and the Spiritual Economy of Bhakti." *Economic and Political Weekly*, July 7.

Sanghvi, Vir, and Mukund Padmanabhan. 1990. "Crunch." *Sunday*, October 28–November 3, pp. 30–37.

Sanyal, Usha. Forthcoming. "Popular Participation and Dispute Resolution: The Barelwis in 1914." *Culture as Contested Site*, ed. Sandria B. Freitag.

———. 1990. "In the Path of the Prophet: Maulana Ahmad Riza Khan Barelwi and the Ahl-e Sunnat wa Jama'at Movement in British India, c. 1870–1921." Ph.D. dissertation, Columbia University.

Sarabhai, Vikram. 1974. *Management for Development*. Ed. Kamla Chowdhry. Delhi.

Saraswati, Baidyanath, and Surajit Sinha. 1978. *Ascetics of Kashi: An Anthropological Exploration*. Varanasi.

Sarkar, Balaram. 1911. *Namashudra-Gyanabhandar*. Faridpur.

Sarkar, Jadunath, and Nirad Bhushan Roy. 1958. *A History of Sadnami Naga Sanyasis*. Allahabad.

Sarkar, Sumit. Forthcoming. "The Decline of the Subaltern in Subaltern Studies." *Economic and Political Weekly*.

———. 1993. "Fascism of the Sangh Parivar." *Economic and Political Weekly* January 30.

———. 1992. "Kaliyuga, Chakri and Bhakti: Ramakrishna and His Times." *Economic and Political Weekly*, July 18, pp. 1543–66.

———. 1989. "The Kalki-avatar of Bikrampur: A Village Scandal in Early Twentieth Century Bengal." In *Subaltern Studies, VI: Writings on South Asian History and Society*, ed. Ranajit Guha. Delhi.

———. 1983. *Modern India, 1885–1947*. Delhi.

———. 1976. "The Logic of Gandhian Nationalism: Civil Disobedience and the Gandhi-Irwin Act (1930–1931)." *Indian Historical Review* 3:114–46.

———. 1973. *Swadeshi Movement in Bengal, 1903–08*. Delhi.

———. 1972. "Hindu-Moslem Relations in Swadeshi Bengal." *Indian Economic and Social History Review* 9:163–216.

Sarkar, Tanika and Urvashi Butalia. Editors. 1998. *Women and the Hindu Right*. New Delhi: Kali for Women.

Sarkar, Tanika. 1994a. "Bankimchandra and the Impossibility of a Political Agenda: A Predicament of Nineteenth-Century Bengal." *Oxford Literary Review* 16:177–204.

————. 1994b. "Educating the Children of the Hindu Rashtra, Notes on RSS Schools." *South Asia Bulletin: Comparative Studies of South Asia, Africa and the Middle East* 14:10–15.

————. 1994c. "Imagining a Hindu Nation: Hindu and Muslim In Bankimchandra's Later Writings." *Economic and Political Weekly*, September 24, 2553–61.

————. 1993a. "Rhetoric against Age of Consent: Resisting Colonial Reason and the Death of a Child Wife." *Economic and Political Weekly*, September 4.

————. 1993b. "The Women of the Hindutva brigade." *Bulletin of Concerned Asian Scholars* 25:16–24.

————. 1993c. "Women's Agency within Authoritarian Communalism: The Rashtrasevika Samiti and Ramjanmabhoomi." In *Hindus and Others: The Question of Identity in India today*, ed. Gyanendra Pandey. Delhi.

————. 1992. "The Hindu Wife and the Hindu Nation: Domesticity and Nationalism in Late Nineteenth Century Bengal." *Studies in History* 8:213–36.

————. 1991. "Woman as Communal Subject: Rashtrasevika Samiti and Ramjanambhoomi Movement." *Economic and Political Weekly*, August 31.

Sarkar, Tanika. 2001. *Hindu Wife, Hindu Nation: Community, Religion and Cultural Nationalism,* New Delhi: Permanent Black, 2001.

————. 1998. "Polarised Communities." *Seminar,* no. 470: 30–6.

Savarkar, V.D. 1971. *Hindu-pad-padashahi; or, A Review of the Hindu Empire of Maharashtra.* 4th edition. New Delhi.

————. [1923] 1949. *Hindutva-Who Is a Hindu?* Nagpur/Pune.

Saxena, Kiran. 1993. "The Hindu Trade Union Movement in India. The Bharatiya Mazdoor Sangh." *Asian Survey* 33 (July): 685–96.

Schimmel Annemarie. 1980. *Islam in the Indian Subcontinent.* Leiden.

Seal, Anil. 1968. *The Emergence of Indian Nationalism: Competition and Collaboration in the Latter Nineteenth Century.* Cambridge.

Searle-Chatterjee, Mary. 1994. "'Wahabi's Sectarianism among Muslims of Banaras." *Contemporary South Asia* 3:83–93.

Selections from Vernacular Newspapers (SVN). 1888a. India Office Library. *Alam-i Taswir,* April 6, 250–51.

————. 1888b. India Office Library. *Dinkar Prakash* (June 1888): 419–20.

*Seminar.* 1992. vol. 100. Special issue on "Education and Ideology: A Symposium on Using Education as a Political Tool."

Sen, Amiya. 1993. *Hindu Revivalism in Bengal, 1872–1905: Some Essays in Interpretation.* Delhi.

————. 1980. "Hindu Revivalism in Action—The Age of Consent Bill Agitation in Bengal." *Indian Historical Review* 7 (July): 160–84.

Sen, S.P., ed. 1972. *Dictionary of National Biography.* Calcutta.

Seshadri, H.V., ed. 1988. *RSS: A Vision in Action.* Bangalore.

Shah, Ghanshyam. 1994. "The BJP and Backward Castes in Gujarat." *South Asia Bulletin: Comparative Studies of South Asia, Africa, and the Middle East* 14:57–65.

————. 1991. "Tenth Lok Sabha Elections: BJP's Victory in Gujarat." *Economic and Political Weekly*, December 21, 2921–24.

Shaikh, Farzana. 1989. *Community and Consensus in Islam: Muslim Representation in Colonial India, 1860–1947.* Cambridge.

Shakir, Moin, ed. 1989. *Religion, State and Politics in India.* Delhi.

Sharma, Shalendra D. 1991. "India's Precarious Democracy: between Crisis and Resilience." *Contemporary South Asia* 3:145–63. Review article.

Shastri, Sibnath. [1884] 1963. *Jatibheda.* Reprint, ed. Dilipkumar Biswas. Calcutta.

Sheth, D. L. 1999. "Secularisation of Caste and Making of New Middle Class." *Economic and Political Weekly*, August 27-September 3: 2502–10.

Sheth, Prain, and Ramesh Menon. 1986. *Caste and Communal Time-Bomb.* Ahmedabad.

Shimray, U. A. 2001. "Ethnicity and Socio-Political Assertion." *Economic and Political Weekly*, September 29: 3674–77.

Shourie, Arun et al. 1989. *Religion in Politics.* New Delhi.

Shourie, Arun. 2002. *Eminent Historians: Their Technology, Their Life, Their Fraud.* New Delhi: ASA Publications.

————. 2001. *Courts and Their Judgments: Premises, Prerequisites, Consequences.* New Delhi: Rupa and Company.

————. 2000. *Harvesting our Souls: Missionaries, Their Design, Their Claims.* New Delhi: ASA Publications.

————. 1997. *Worshipping False Gods: Ambedkar, and the Facts Which Have Been Erased.* New Delhi: ASA Publications.

————. 1995. *The World of Fatwas, or, The Shariah in Action.* New Delhi: ASA Publications.

Shyamali. 1988. *Bankimchandra o Bhatparvar Panditsamaj.* Baromash.

Siefert, Ruth. 2002. "Rape: The Female Body as a Symbol and a Sign. Gender-specific Violence and the Cultural Construction of War." In *War or Health? A Reader*, edited by Ilkka Taipole. London: Zed Press, pp. 280–94.

Singh, Khuswant, and Bipan Chandra. 1985. *Many Faces of Communalism.* Chandigarh.

Singh, N.K. 1990. "Rumbustious Ride." *India Today*, October 31, pp. 57–59.

Singh, R.P. 1985. "The Complexities of Communalism, 1922–27." *Indian Historical Review* 12:251–65.

Sinha, B.P. 1957. *Ram-bhakti Men Rasik Sampraday.* Balrampur.

Sivaramakrishnan, K. and Arun Agrawal. Editors. 2003. *Regional Modernities: The Cultural Politics of Development in India.* New Delhi: Oxford University Press.

Smith, Donald Dugene. 1963. *India as a Secular state.* Princeton.

Smith, Vincent A. 1917. *Akbar: The Great Mogul, 1542–1605.* Oxford.

Sondhi, M. L. and Apratim Mukarji. 2002. *The Black Book of Gujarat.* New Delhi: Manak Publications.

Srinivasan, Amrit. 1990. "The Survivor in the Study of Violence." In *Mirrors of Violence: Communities, Riots and Survivors in South Asia*, ed. Veena Das. Delhi.

Srivastava, Sushil. 1991. *The Disputed Mosque: A Historical Inquiry.* New Delhi.

Srivastava, Ashirbadi Lal. 1933. *The First Two Nawabs of Oudh.* Lucknow.

Steel, Flora Annie. 1905. *India*. London.

Stokes, Eric. 1978. *The Peasant and the Raj: Studies in Agrarian Society and Peasant Rebellion in Colonial India*. Cambridge.

Stonehill, Brian. 1995. "Looking for Peace in the Culture War." *Philadelphia Inquirer*, July 6.

Tagore, Rabindranath. 1917. *Nationalism*. London,

Talbot, Ian. 1993. "Muslim Political Mobilization in Rural Punjab, 1937–46." In *Rural India: Land, Power and Society under British Rule*, ed. Peter Robb. London.

———. 1988. *Provincial Politics and the Pakistan Movement: The Growth of the Muslim League in North-West and North-East India, 1937–1947*. Karachi.

———. 1982a. "Deserted Collaborators: The Political Background to the Rise and Fall of the Punjab Unionist Party, 1923–1947." *Journal of Imperial and Commonwealth History* I (October).

———. 1982b. "The Growth of the Muslim League in the Punjab, 1937–1946." *Journal of Commonwealth and Comp. Politics* 20 (March): 5–24.

Tambiah, S.J. 1990. "Presidential Address: Reflections on Communal Violence in South Asia." *Journal of Asian Studies* 49:741–60.

———. 1986. *Sri Lanka: Ethnic Fratricide and the Dismantling of Democracy*. Chicago.

Taylor, Charles. 1990. "Modes of Civil Society." *Public Culture* 3 (September): 95–117.

Thakur, Ramesh. 1993. "Ayodhya and the Politics of India's Secularism: A Double-Standards Discourse." *Asian Survey* 33 (July): 245–64.

Thapar, Romila, Harbans Mukhia, and Bipan Chandra. 1969. *Communalism and the Writing of Indian History*. Delhi.

Thapar, Romila. 1993. "Communalism and the Interpretation of Early Indian History." Paper presented at the South Asia Seminar, University of Pennsylvania, September 22.

———. 1991. "Communalism and the Historical Legacy, Some Facets." In *Communalism in India: History, Politics and Culture*, ed. K.N. Panikkar. New Delhi.

———. 1989a. "Imagined Religious Communities? Ancient History and the Modern Search for a Hindu Identity.". *Modern Asian Studies* 23:209–32.

———. 1989b. "The Ramayana Syndrome." *Seminar* 353 (January): 71–75.

———. 1996. *A History of India: volume One*. Harmondsworth.

Thiel-Horstmann, Monika. N.d. "Warrior Ascetics in Eighteenth-Century Rajasthan and the Religious Policy of Jai Singh II." Unpublished essay.

Thompson, E.P. 1991. "The Patricians and the Plebs." In *Customs in Common*, ed. E.P. Thompson. London.

Thompson, Edward John. 1930. *The Reconstruction of India*. London.

Titus, W.W. 1925. "The Reaction of Muslim India to Western Islam." In *The Muslim World of Today*, ed. John R. Mott. London.

Tripathi, A. 1967. *The Extremist Challenges, India between 1890–1910*. Calcutta.

Tully, Mark. 1991. *No Full Stops in India*. London.

Turner, Bryan S. 1994. *Orientalism. Postmodernism and Globalism*. London and New York.

Uberoi, Patricia. 2003. " 'Unity in diversity?' Dilemmas of Nationhood in Indian Calendar art" in *Beyond Appearances? Visual Practices and Ideologies in Modern India.* Edited by Sumathi Ramaswami, New Delhi: Sage, pp. 91–232.

Udai Pratap Singh, Raja of Bhinga Raj. 1984. *Democracy Not Suited to India* (originally published 1888). Calcutta.

Upadhyay, Shashi Bhushan. 1989. "Communalism and the Working Class: Riots of 1893 in Bombay." *Economic and Political Weekly,* July 29, PE69–80.

Upadhyaya, D. 1965. *Integral Humanism.* New Delhi.

Vajpeyi, Ananya. 2002. "Teaching Against Communalism: Role of Social Science Pedagogy." *Economic and Political Weekly,* December 21: 5093–7.

Vajpeyi, Dhirendra. 1989. "Muslim Fundamentalism in India: A Crisis of Identity in a Secular State." In *Religious and Ethnic Minority Politics in South Asia,* ed. Dhirendra Vajpeyi and Yogendra K. Malik. New Delhi.

van der Veer, Peter. 1994a. "The Politics of the Rama Cult: Gender, State, and Nation." Paper presented to the Delhi Conference on Gender and State.

————. 1994b. *Religious Nationalism: Hindus and Muslims in India.* Berkeley.

————. 1993. "The Laicization of Hinduism: Creating Hindu Public." Paper presented to the Chicago Conference on Comparative Public Sphere.

————. 1988. *Gods on Earth: The Management of Religious Experience and Identity in a North Indian Pilgrimage Center.* London.

————. 1987. "'God Must be Liberated!' A Hindu Liberation Movement in Ayodhya." *Modern Asian Studies* 21:283–302.

————, ed. 1995. *National and Migration: The Politics of Space in the South Asian Diaspora.* Philadelphia.

Vanaik, Achin. 1997. *The Furies of Indian Communalism: Religion, Modernity, and Secularization.* London: Verso.

Varshney, Ashutosh. 1993. "Contested Meanings: India's national Identity, Hindu Nationalism, and the Politics of Anxiety." *Daedalus* 122 (June): 227–61.

Varshney, Ashutosh. 2002. *Ethnic Conflict and Civic Life: Hindus and Muslims in India.* New Haven: Yale University Press.

Vidyalankar, Satyaketu, and Haridutt Vedalankar. 1984. *Arya Samaj ka Ithihas.* vols. 2. Delhi.

Vijapurkar, Mahes. 1990. "To ayodhya." *Frontline,* October 13–26, pp. 20–26.

Vishva Hindu Parishad (VHP). N.d. *The Hindu Awakening: Retrospect and Promise.* New Delhi.

————. 1991a. *The Great Evidence of Shri Ram Janmbhoomi Mandir.* New Delhi.

————. 1991b. *History Versus Casuistry; Evidence of the Ramajanmabhoomi Mandir Presented by the Vishva Hindu Parishad to the Government of India in December–January 1990–91.* New Delhi.

Vivekananda, Swami. 1970a. "The Future of India." In *The Complete works of Swami Vivekananda, Volume III,* ed. Nivedita. Calcutta.

————. [1940] 1970b. *Letters of Swami Vivekananda.* Reprint of Mayavati edition, Calcutta.

Wadley, Susan. 1977. "Power in Hindu Ideology and Practice." In *The New Wind: Changing Identities and South Asia,* ed. Kenneth David. The Hague.

Wallbank, T. Walter. 1965. *A Short History of India and Pakistan*. New York.

Washbrook, David A. 1981. "Law, State and Agrarian Society in Colonial India." *Modern Asian Studies* 3:649–721.

Weber Max. 1964. *Sociology of Religion*. Boston.

Weiner, Myron, 1978. *Sons of the Soil: Migration and Ethnic Conflict in India*. Princeton: Princeton University Press.

Weiner, Myron. 1967. *Party Building in a New Nation: The Indian National Congress*. Chicago.

Whitehead, Henry. 1924. *Indian Problems in Religion, Education, Politics*. London.

Widdess, Richard. 1994. "Dhrupad as a Musical Tradition." *Journal of Vaisnava Studies* 3:61–81.

Wilkinson, Steven I. 2002. "Putting Gujarat in Perspective." *Economic and Political Weekly*. April 27: 1579–83.

Yadav, K.C. 1983. "The Partition of India: A Study of The Muslim Politics in Panjab, 1849–1947." *Punjab Past and Present* 17:105–44.

———. 1981. *Elections in Punjab, 1920–1947*. Tokyo.

Yadav, Yogendra. 1999. "India's Third Electoral System, 1989–99." *Economic and Political Weekly*. August 21–September 3: 2393–99.

———. 1996. "Reconfiguration in Indian Politics: State Assembly Elections, 1993–1995." *Economic and Political Weekly*. January 20: 95–105.

Yang, Anand. 1980. "Sacred Symbol and sacred Place in Rural India: Community Mobilization in the 'Anti-Cow Killing' Riot of 1893." *Modern Asian Studies* 22:576–96.

Yeager, Patricia. Editor. 1995. *The Geography of Identity*. Ann Arbor: University of Michigan Press.

Zeff, Adam. 1994. "Report on Media Coverage of Ayodhya." Unpublished seminar paper. University of Pennsylvania.

# Contributors

AMRITA BASU is Professor of Political Science and Women's and Gender Studies at Amherst College.

RICHARD H. DAVIS is Associate Professor of Religion and Asian Studies at the Bard College.

VICTORIA L. FARMER was South Asia Associate, The Asia Society (New York) and Assistant Director, the Center for the Advanced Study of India (Philadelphia). She has taught American foreign policy and international and comparative politics at the University of Pennsylvania and Drexel and Widener Universities. She is currently a independent scholar and editor.

RICHARD G. FOX is President of the Wenner-Gren Foundation for Anthropological Research.

SANDRIA B. FREITAG is Director of the Monterey Bay History and Cultures Project, University of California at Santa Cruz.

MUSHIRUL HASAN is Vice Chancellor, Jamia Millia Islamia, New Delhi.

ZOYA HASAN is Professor at the Center of Political Studies at the Jawaharlal Nehru University, New Delhi

DAVID LUDDEN is Professor of History at the University of Pennsylvania.

PETER MANUEL is Associate Professor at John Jay College and the CUNY Graduate Center.

WILLIAM R. PINCH is Associate Professor of History at Wesleyan University.

SUMIT SARKAR is Professor of History at the University of Delhi.

TANIKA SARKAR is Professor of History, Centre for Historical Studies, Jawaharlal Nehru University.

PETER VAN DER VEER is University Professor at Utrecht University.

# Index